W9-AVW-208

Democracy and Deep-Rooted
Conflict: Options for Negotiators

Democracy and Deep-Rooted Conflict: Options for Negotiators

Editors:

Peter Harris and Ben Reilly

With a Foreword by
Kofi A. Annan

Contributors:

*Mark Anstey, Christopher Bennett, David Bloomfield,
K. M. de Silva, Nomboniso Gasa, Yash Ghai, Peter Harris,
Luc Huyse, Rasma Karklins, Michael Lund, Charles Nupen,
David M. Olson, Anthony J. Regan, Ben Reilly,
Andrew Reynolds, Carlos Santiso and Timothy D. Sisk*

Handbook Series

INTERNATIONAL

INSTITUTE FOR
DEMOCRACY AND
ELECTORAL
ASSISTANCE

1 9 9 8

Handbook Series 3. The International IDEA Handbook Series aims to present information on a range of democratic institutions, procedures and issues in an easy-to-use handbook format. Handbooks are primarily aimed at policy-makers and practitioners in the field.

This is an International IDEA publication. International IDEA's publications are not a reflection of any specific national or political interest. Views expressed in this publication do not necessarily represent the views of International IDEA, its Board or its Council Members. Countries are referred to by the names that were in official use at the time the relevant data were collected. Maps represented in this publication do not imply on the part of International IDEA any judgement on the legal status of any territory or the endorsement of such boundaries, nor does the placement or size of any country or territory reflect a political view of the Institute. Maps have been created for this publication in order to add clarity to the text.

Copyright © International Institute for Democracy and Electoral Assistance, (International IDEA) 1998. All rights reserved.

Application for permission to reproduce or translate all or any part of this publication should be made to:

Information Services
International IDEA
S – 103 34 Stockholm
Sweden

International IDEA encourages dissemination of its work and will promptly respond to requests.

Publication Editor: Salma Hasan Ali
AD & Design: Eduard Čehovin, Ljubljana; Pre-press: Studio Signum, Ljubljana
Publication Manager: Lee Woodyear
Publication Assistant: Jaklina Strand
Printed by Korotan Ljubljana d.o.o., Ljubljana 1998.
ISSN: 1402-6759
ISBN: 91-89098-22-6

Preface

Most of today's violent conflicts are not the wars between contending states of former years, but take place within existing states. Many are inextricably bound up with concepts of identity, nation and nationalism, and many stem from the competition for resources, recognition and power. While these conflicts may appear very differently from place to place, they often have, at their base, similar issues of unmet needs, and of the necessity to accommodate the interests of majorities and minorities alike.

Despite the many excellent studies on how to build peace in divided societies, there remains a dearth of practical advice for policy-makers on how to design and implement democratic levers that can make peace endure. Conflict is a normal part of any healthy society, but a great deal of attention has been focused in recent years on how to prevent conflict, and less on finding peaceful methods of conflict management. In particular, there needs to be more attention given to the type of political choices that those negotiating an end to a period of violent conflict have to make to rebuild their country, and how they can build an enduring *democracy* – the only sustainable form of government – from the ashes of conflict.

This handbook attempts to meet this need by providing negotiators and policy-makers with detailed information on options for building democracy in post-conflict societies. We have brought together international experts, both academics and practitioners, in many fields – from negotiation techniques to power-sharing formulas, from questions of federalism and autonomy to electoral systems and parliaments – to provide practical, policy-relevant advice. The handbook draws on the experience of peace settlements and democracy building from places such as Bosnia, Fiji, Northern Ireland and South Africa to illustrate the many, often unrecognized, options that negotiators can draw upon when attempting to build a nascent democracy.

International IDEA was created in 1995 with precisely this objective – to make available practical instruments for building sustainable democracy so as to enhance the prospects for democracy's growth world-wide. We strongly believe that the way democratic procedures and institutions are developed and implemented can play a much more important role in post-conflict peace building than has been the case to date. This handbook has therefore been written and presented so as to ensure maximum accessibility for busy policy-makers.

Many good people have contributed to this handbook. We are grateful to all of them, but particularly to David Storey for his early conceptual input, to David Bloomfield, who was the lead writer on a number of chapters, to Tim Sisk for his many excellent suggestions for improving the text, and to Salma Hasan Ali and the publication team at IDEA, who turned the raw material into a usable publication.

My greatest thanks, however, must go to the two IDEA staff members, Mr Peter Harris and Dr Ben Reilly, who developed, and edited the handbook from its inception. Between them, they have produced a publication which we hope will be of great utility in the coming years, when the challenge of building sustainable democracy has never been more pressing.

We are very much aware of the huge scope of a subject like democracy and deep-rooted conflict, and would welcome your comments, ideas and suggestions on any aspects of the handbook.

Bengt Säve-Söderbergh

Secretary-General
International IDEA

Foreword

The United Nations exists, among other reasons, for the fundamental purpose of maintaining peace and security in the world. One of its main activities, therefore, is the resolution of conflicts – a task which has become more complex in recent times when many conflicts take the form of internal factional and civil strife, though often with very serious external repercussions.

This has obliged the international community to develop new instruments of conflict resolution, many of which relate to the electoral process and, more generally, to the entrenchment of a democratic culture in war-torn societies, with a view to making peace sustainable. This handbook lists an impressive range of such instruments, based on lessons learned from recent experience in the field.

The United Nations system as a whole is focusing on avoiding relapse into violence, especially in intra-state conflicts, by establishing the foundations of a lasting peace. That focus is admirably reflected in this handbook. It shows that building stable and solid internal political structures is not a separate task from crisis management, but needs to be part of it; and it proposes an array of practical resources for those of us engaged in the search for comprehensive and lasting settlements in specific conflicts. Competing forces have to be brought to discuss their differences within a legal and administrative framework, and to seek solutions based on systems of rules which derive their legitimacy from the will of the people, and from universal principles of human dignity. That in turn requires the creation of institutions built to last.

Happily, there is a growing trend throughout the world towards democratization and respect of human rights. Some 120 countries now hold generally free and fair elections, and a large number of internal conflicts end with a negotiated peace which includes an electoral process aimed at building political structures acceptable to all. The parties themselves agree to deliver a sustainable peaceful settlement through a democratic transition.

Democratic principles provide the essential starting point for implementation of such settlements, which usually involve not only democratizing the state but also giving more power to civil society. Once political actors accept the need for peaceful management of deep-rooted conflicts, democratic systems of government can help them develop habits of compromise, co-operation and consensus building. These are not abstract statements, but practical conclusions drawn from UN experiences of conflict resolution in the field. This handbook, which presents systematically the lessons learned by the UN and other organizations, constitutes an invaluable addition to the literature on conflict prevention, management and resolution.

Kofi A. Annan

Secretary-General
United Nations

Table of Contents

Table of Contents

Menus, Factsheets, Boxes, Graphs and Maps

Overview

The nature of violent conflict in the world has changed in recent decades, both in its actual subject-matter and in the form of its expression. One of the most dramatic changes has been the trend away from traditional *inter-state* conflict (that is, a war between sovereign states) and towards *intra-state* conflict (that is, one which takes place between factions within an existing state). Whereas most violent conflicts over the course of the twentieth century have been *between* states, in the 1990s almost all major conflicts around the world have taken place *within* states. Between 1989 and 1996, for example, 95 of the 101 armed conflicts identified around the world were such internal disputes. Most of these conflicts were propelled, at least in part, by quests for self-determination or adequate recognition of communal identity rather than by ideology or the conquest of territory. This represents a major shift in the manifestation of human conflict, especially compared to the world wars and major inter-state conflicts fought over the course of this century.

By comparison, our methods of managing such intra-state conflicts have evolved much more slowly. Peaceful management of domestic conflicts needs approaches which recognize the importance of building sustainable *internal* political structures, rather than those designed and implemented primarily by external actors. This means that issues about the internal political organization of a state are of much greater importance in managing conflicts today than in the past, and accordingly there is now a greater focus than ever on the role of domestic political actors engaged in a deep-rooted conflict. Traditional approaches all too often fail to address the needs and interests which fuel such conflicts, resulting in attempts to impose unsuitable solutions in ad hoc and inappropriate ways. There is a tremendous need for new and better tools that will more effectively address the new context of intra-state conflict.

This handbook contains practical resources for those involved in bringing intra-state conflict out of a prolonged phase of violence and designing a feasible and sustainable model for its peaceful management. Unlike many works on the subject, it is

The question that concerns us in this handbook is: how do we get an agreement at the negotiating table that will deliver a sustainable and peaceful outcome to a violent conflict? Our answer is: by structuring both the process of the negotiations and the agreed outcomes in such a way as to maximize the prospects of democracy taking root in the post-conflict period.

1

not primarily concerned with the role of the international community. Rather, its focus is on what happens at the negotiating table between the parties to the conflict themselves. It offers politicians, negotiators, mediators and other political actors a range of tools and materials needed for the construction of a settlement. These can assist both in the negotiation process itself – *how* one works towards an agreement; and in the building of a settlement – *what* one reaches agreement about. It is not concerned with preventive diplomacy, conflict early warning systems, conflict prevention in the narrow sense, and so on, important though those topics are. The question that concerns us in this handbook is: how do we get an agreement at the negotiating table that will deliver a sustainable and peaceful outcome to a violent conflict? Our answer is: by structuring both the *process* of the negotiations and the agreed *outcomes* in such a way as to maximize the prospects of democracy taking root in the post-conflict period.

The Need for this Handbook

The end-game of violent conflict is perhaps the most difficult phase of transformation in a hugely difficult process. In that phase, parties need two overall aids. They need to be able to avail themselves of the most effective and appropriate dialogue process to facilitate their negotiations; and they then need to successfully negotiate a sustainable settlement by putting in place effective and appropriate democratic structures and political institutions. Our aim is to assist the users of this handbook in the difficult task of creating comprehensive and durable solutions to long-term violent conflicts. In so doing, we draw on the experience of a number of recent peace settlements in Northern Ireland, South Africa, Bougainville, Guatemala and elsewhere.

Negotiators need practical, accessible options for building a sustainable democracy.

However, this handbook does not provide any panacea. It would be ludicrous to prescribe one overall single design for use across a variety of situations, each in many ways unique. Rather than offer some universal recipe for success, or reinvent the wheel for every new situation, the handbook offers options for the construction of solutions, helping to focus attention on the core issues, providing many examples and lessons from other contexts, and in very practical ways assisting creativity in solution building. This is not an academic thesis. It is presented in readable, straightforward language, and is grounded in wide experience of real negotiation situations, the better to be of interest and practical use to the practitioner and the policy-maker.

Anyone can suggest *ideal* solutions; but only those involved can, through negotiation, discover and create the shape of a *practical* solution.

Negotiation and mediation skills and processes have been the subject of a great deal of academic study in recent years. The practicalities of these processes have also been studied in depth at inter-group, institutional and international levels. In addition, the study of democratization and democracy building, both as a concept and in its varied applications in the world, has become a major field of academic interest. This project aims uniquely to bring together all three areas, adapting the best work from each, and constantly using each related area of knowledge to shed light on the other areas. Our aim here is to synthesize them into a unified approach in the form of a practical handbook. Above all, we want to bridge the gap between the worlds of theory and of policy, using the best of the former to strengthen the latter in a practical, policy-oriented approach.

The Aims of the Handbook

The handbook will be of primary use to negotiators and politicians representing conflicting parties, but also relevant to third-party intervenors, to civil servants and policy analysts, to scholars and specialists of deeply divided societies, to journalists and advisers, and so on. It is designed specifically for use with conflicts which are, in the terminology, in the *pre-negotiation* or *negotiation* phase: that is, situations which have reached a stage where negotiation has become at least a serious possibility, if not an imminent eventuality. Put simply, the handbook aims:

- To assist parties who are in, or about to enter, the process of negotiating a political settlement following a period of violent conflict, by helping them to generate creative scenarios for progress towards an acceptable outcome.

- To provide them with a wide range of practical options, both for designing the most appropriate negotiation process for them, and for choosing the democratic structures most suited to their situation and their future. Using the resources offered in the handbook in this construction process, they can thus engineer an appropriate sequence of events, a path to progress, which will co-ordinate the difficult but vital process of peace building through democracy building.

- To assist them in developing solutions which are not only feasible, acceptable and appropriate during the conflict

Among the aims of this handbook is to provide negotiators with a wide range of practical options, both for designing the most appropriate negotiation process for them, and for choosing the democratic structures most suited to their situation and their future.

3

management phase, but which are also viable and sustainable in the long term, via appropriately designed democratic institutions which protect and strengthen human rights within the new post-conflict society.

– More generally, to provide information on the range of varied approaches to building sustainable democracy that have been used in post-conflict situations around the world, for the benefit of domestic actors and the international community alike.

How to Use the Handbook

Building peace is an immense challenge. Our aim is simply to offer support and guidance, options and examples along the way to those involved in the task.

The layout of the handbook is practically orientated. It is accepted that building peace is an immense challenge, and our aim is simply to offer support and guidance, options and examples along the way to those involved in the task. In Chapter 1, we examine the changing nature of conflict in recent decades and discuss how democratic values and institutions provide the framework for building effective and lasting settlements. The handbook then consists of four consecutive stages: analysis, process design, outcome design, and sustainability. Each stage is given a chapter.

Analysis

First, we analyse the conflict in question and reach a descriptive understanding of its issues and elements. Chapter 2 initially provides some insights on the nature of deep-rooted conflict, on various typologies of conflict, and on the process of analysing conflict. It then offers a range of analytic tools, so that readers can be assisted in making a diagnosis of their specific conflict. This involves reaching a detailed understanding of its issues, themes, actors, dynamics, history, resources, phases, and so on. The result should provide a rich and informative "snapshot" of the conflict.

Process

Once diagnosis is complete, Chapter 3 guides readers through the design of the most appropriate negotiation process to suit their situation. It offers important general considerations about designing good process, and then some specific factors to be considered in building the process most suitable to the particular conflict. It assists readers to identify and design the basic building blocks of their process, such as choice of venue, participants, agenda design, the structure and ground-rules for talks, and so on. It offers specific tools for breaking deadlock, and a menu of negotiation/facilitation techniques from which readers can choose the most appropriate options according to their previous diagnosis, the better to construct a solid talks process best suited to their specific needs.

Outcome

Once *process* has been agreed, the next phase is to address *outcome*. Here we consider, in particular, the forms and functions of the wide range of practical democratic institutions and structures which can make up the ingredients of a high-quality outcome negotiated by means of the process designed in Chapter 3. Chapter 4 reviews the value of such structures, and the issues involved in their design. Then it offers a detailed and wide-ranging menu of the possible democratic "levers" which those engineering an outcome can consider, use and adapt. The list of options ranges from key questions about the structure of the state such as the distribution of power, forms of executives and legislatures, federalism and autonomy, electoral systems, judiciaries, etc.; to mechanisms which address specific issues or interests such as truth and reconciliation commissions, language boards, gender commissions and so on.

Sustainability

Finally, Chapter 5 looks at how to sustain the outcome in the long term, and identifies the obstacles and pitfalls that may affect the implementation of the agreement as well as the specific mechanisms that will sustain and nourish the negotiated settlement. It also offers some underlying principles for supporting the implementation phase. The role of the international community in promoting and assisting democratic settlements in post-conflict situations is also discussed and analysed from a policy perspective.

Case Studies

The handbook includes a wide range of case studies from deep-rooted conflicts around the world. These case studies offer insights into both successes and failures in peace building and democracy. All of them, both successes and failures, contain important lessons for those attempting to build an enduring settlement to their own crisis. Most of these case studies – from places ranging from Bougainville to Bosnia, and from South Africa to Northern Ireland – are classic examples of "intra-state" conflicts discussed earlier, in which a focus on negotiated outcomes based on democratic principles were key to building a lasting peace. As the case studies illustrate, building democracy in such circumstances is extremely difficult, but the alternatives to it almost inevitably mean a return to bloodshed.

Tools

Our goal is to make this handbook as accessible and easy-to-read as possible – to make it a handy instrument that negotiators and policy-makers can turn to in order to understand the range of options available to them in negotiating deep-rooted conflicts. Therefore, we include throughout the book what we refer to as "A Menu of Options", and factsheets. These are one- or two-page overviews that present the main options, issues, or lessons discussed in each section in a clear and concise manner. Also, we include at the top of each page the number and title of each main section heading so readers can situate themselves anywhere in the the book easily and quickly.

Sources and Acknowledgements

The handbook illustrates its procedures by extensive use of examples and case studies drawn from real events. This allows the reader to learn from past and present successes and failures, and to compare other diagnoses and designs with their own situations.

The two main sources of material for this handbook are practical examples of contemporary conflict and its management from around the world, and academic scholarship. At every point along the way, the handbook illustrates its procedures by extensive use of examples and case studies drawn from real events and situations. One reason for this is obviously to help illustrate the points the handbook is making. Perhaps more importantly, the examples offer readers the opportunity to learn from instances of past and present successes and failures, and to compare other diagnoses and designs with their own situations.

With the academic material, the handbook aims to synthesize the best in contemporary scholarship and offer it in an accessible and practical form to policy-makers. It bridges the gap between theory and policy by offering a composite of the best and most practically oriented work of theorists. The best theories are always those that inform, and are informed by, reality and practice. First and foremost, readers will bring their own expert knowledge of their conflict to the handbook; this is then complemented both by expert knowledge and analysis of other real situations, and by the best of the relevant theoretical work.

To make the handbook as immediately practical as possible to its readership we have listed all reference material at the end of each chapter. Readers can pursue their particular interests further through these many authors on whose work we have drawn. We are deeply indebted to all of them.

1

C H A P T E R

Increasingly, internal conflict, rooted in ideas of human identity and often expressed with frightening intensity, is the major threat to stability and peace, at the individual, local and international levels.

In this first chapter we examine the changing nature of conflict – conflict that is increasingly taking place within states (intra-state) rather than between states (inter-state) and that is posing a severe challenge to traditional conflict management techniques.

David Bloomfield
and Ben Reilly

The Changing Nature of Conflict
and Conflict Management

1.1 Characteristics of Deep-Rooted Conflict

I n recent years a new type of conflict has come increasingly to the fore: conflict that takes place within and across states, or *intra-state* conflict, in the form of civil wars, armed insurrections, violent secessionist movements and other domestic warfare. The change has been dramatic: in the last three years, for example, every major armed conflict originated at the domestic level within a state, rather than between states. Two powerful elements often combine in such conflicts. One is *identity*: the mobilization of people in communal identity groups based on race, religion, culture, language, and so on. The other is *distribution*: the means of sharing the economic, social and political resources within a society. Where perceived imbalance in distribution coincides with identity differences (where, for example, one religious group is deprived of certain resources available to others) we have the potential for conflict. It is this combination of potent identity-based factors with wider perceptions of economic and social injustice that often fuels what we call "deep-rooted conflict".

The combination of potent identity-based factors with wider perceptions of economic and social injustice often fuels what we call "deep-rooted conflict".

A striking characteristic of such internal conflict is its sheer persistence. And this arises, above all, because its origins often lie in deep-seated issues of identity. In this respect, the term *ethnic conflict* is often invoked. Ethnicity is a broad concept, covering a multiplicity of elements: race, culture, religion, heritage, history, language, and so on. But at bottom, these are all *identity* issues. What they fuel is termed identity-related conflict – in short, conflict over any concept around which a community of people focuses its fundamental identity and sense of itself as a group, and over which it chooses, or feels compelled, to resort to violent means to protect that identity under threat. Often, such identity-related factors combine with conflicts over the distribution of *resources* – such as territory, economic power, employment prospects, and so on. Cases where the identity and distributive issues are combined provide the opportunity for exploitation and manipulation by opportunistic leaders, and the highest potential for conflict.

9

Increasingly this kind of conflict, rooted in ideas of human identity and often expressed with frightening intensity, is the major threat to stability and peace, whether at the individual, local and communal levels, or in the collective terms of international security. Of the 27 conflicts in 1996 classified as "major armed conflicts" (essentially, over 1000 deaths per year), for example, fully 22 had a clear identity component to them. These included conflicts in Russia (Chechnya), Northern Ireland, Iran and Iraq (with the Kurds), Israel, Afghanistan, Bangladesh (Chittagong Hill Tribes), Indonesia (East Timor), Sri Lanka, Burma, Algeria and elsewhere. Only guerrilla-based struggles in Peru, Cambodia, Guatemala, Colombia and Sierra Leone appeared to be straightforward contests for power. Even amongst these cases, there is no shortage of identity-based conflicts. In sum, the vast majority of contemporary examples of violent intra-state hostilities exhibit such characteristics.

A conflict in which one's community is deprived of certain resources is bad enough; but one may hope to negotiate a better deal over those resources. A conflict that also threatens our very sense of who we are is much more difficult to manage.

Such conflicts are clearly very different from the more straightforward wars between states – over land, resources, political power, ideology, etc. – of earlier times. (Such wars included identity elements as well, of course, but usually not in the same centrally motivating way.) Identity-related conflict is far more complex, persistent and intractable, instantly much less amenable to compromise, negotiation or trade-off. These conflicts involve claims of group rights: national groups, gender groups, racial groups, religious groups, cultural groups, and so on. A conflict in which one's community is deprived of certain resources is bad enough; but one may hope to negotiate a better deal over those resources. A conflict that also threatens our very sense of who we are is much more difficult to manage.

Such complex and fundamental issues, then, fuel wars that are smaller in scale than the ideological or geopolitical struggles of the past, but which flourish with much greater intensity. That is due not only to the depth of meaning invested in them by combatants, but also to the proliferation and easy availability of lethal weapons. Since World War Two, cheap, mass-produced, small-calibre weapons have killed far more people than the heavier, more traditional battlefield weaponry. With arms markets flourishing, the Armalite, the Kalashnikov and the land mine have brought war within the reach of any community with the will and the means to organize an armed force. This proliferation of small arms has exponentially increased the intensity of identity-related conflicts.

Intra-state conflict over identity tends to be persistent over the long term, alternating between latent phases and outbursts of

1.1 Characteristics of Deep-Rooted Conflict

sustained violence for periods of years or decades. The scale of human suffering is breathtaking in this new context. During World War One, just five per cent of casualties were civilians; by World War Two the figure had risen to around 50 per cent. But in the 1990s, the proportion of civilian war casualties has soared to around 80 per cent. By 1992 there were around 17 million refugees pushed by war across borders into foreign countries, and a staggering estimate of a further 20 million displaced persons rendered homeless by internal war but remaining within national boundaries (Bosnian victims of ethnic cleansing, for example). The long-term effect is to militarize the entire society: violence becomes accepted and institutionalized. Society becomes brutalized: civilian casualties multiply, rape and starvation become organized weapons of war, and non-combatants – traditionally children and women – bear the brunt of the dehumanizing processes involved in this type of conflict. Such communal trauma breeds deep and festering wounds and establishes heroes and martyrs on all sides whose memories and sacrifices serve to deepen the real and perceived divide between the conflicting identities.

1.1.1 Identity-driven, emotionally charged

What makes this kind of conflict so prevalent, so pervasive, so durable and so insoluble, is the way in which the issues of the dispute are so emotionally charged. They go right to the heart of what gives people their sense of themselves, defining a person's bond with her or his community and defining the source of satisfaction for her or his need for identity. Since such conflict is by no means restricted to the so-called developing world, an example will serve from the heart of the Western establishment. In the United Kingdom, people in Scotland debate widely among themselves about the ideal degree of autonomy from England. The argument ranges from complete independence from, to complete integration with, Britain. The political debate over these important issues is spirited; but it does not mobilize into violence.

Meanwhile, in another part of the UK, people have been dying violently for centuries over just such a question. Irish nationalists in Northern Ireland fear that under British rule they can never achieve full self-expression of their communal identity as Irish people. Their counterparts, the pro-British Unionists, fear their disappearance as an identity group if they lose the union with Britain and join an Irish republic. So while Scots argue over political control, economic resources and so on, they do not violently struggle over matters of communal identity and

What makes deep-rooted conflict so prevalent, so pervasive, so durable and so insoluble, is the way in which the issues of the dispute are so emotionaly charged.

self-expression, since the UK has apparently satisfied these needs. In Northern Ireland, the same question goes so deep – to the heart of people's fears of who they are and where they belong in the world – that they leave political debate behind and resort to violence.

1.1.2 Beyond borders

Internal as its origins may be, however, such conflict has ramifications far beyond its own geographical borders. Because of the increasingly complex interdependence among states, such conflict tends not to be confined within the boundaries of the particular state for long, if at all, but rapidly diffuses. It spills over across frontiers and enmeshes other states, or parts of states, in its grip. This process of diffusion and contagion means that low-level intra-state conflicts can potentially escalate into more intense inter-state ones.

In the interconnectedness of the modern world and the instantaneous transmission of news (the so-called "CNN effect", conflict respects few boundaries, borders or jurisdictions.

Several factors contribute to this spillover effect. Neighbouring governments will have a strong self-interest in supporting one side or another of an adjacent civil war, and their own reasons for seeing the stabilization or destabilization of the state in conflict. Quite apart from governments, population groups do not necessarily neatly reside within state borders. There may be large diaspora populations outside the state – refugee or emigrant communities, or a section of a community cut off by partition – who engage with the conflict through close identification with one side or another. Hutus and Tutsis outside Rwanda, Tamils outside Sri Lanka and Basques outside Spain are only a few among many examples. Beyond the immediate context, of course, there exist more distant states, powers or regional blocs, whose interests are directly concerned with the outcome of the conflict: for instance, the European Union's security concerns over Bosnia, US interests in Central America, Russian involvement in Georgia, and so on. Such factors immediately extend the geography of the conflict, adding to its complexity as well as its scale. In the interconnectedness of the modern world and the instantaneous transmission of news (the so-called "CNN effect"), conflict respects few boundaries, borders or jurisdictions.

When it comes to managing such conflict, its complexities cause immense difficulties. There can even be a difficulty in correctly identifying the parties to the conflict. The picture is even more confused when we factor in the external sponsors of the conflict. Sponsors, regional allies, kin states or whatever, will usually be operating in general support of one side's agenda, while also bringing their own specific agenda and interests to the conflict. The result can be a degree of interference, which actually reduces the disputing parties' chances of resolving the conflict. With so many factions involved, both internal and external, the task of satisfying the key interests of the various actors makes a solution far more difficult to achieve. It also makes the conflict management process more prone to abuse and disruption.

1.2 New Tools for Conflict Management

Many existing conflict management tools were constructed during, and in response to, world wars and the Cold War. The narrow, containment-oriented strategies of coercion and crisis-management that prevailed during the era of superpower rivalry have been exposed as arthritic, inflexible and increasingly impotent against a wave of reinvigorated intra-state, identity-driven, deep-rooted conflicts. The Cold War froze many such deep-rooted conflicts, so that they simply went into a latent phase, invisible on the surface but with their roots as deep as ever. Cold War strategists focused on short-term stability rather than longer-term sustainability. What is needed now is a new range of flexible and adaptable instruments that can take into account the more subjective, complex and deep-rooted needs and interests that underpin identity-related conflict.

It is the aim of this handbook not to engage too deeply in the somewhat philosophical, if important, argument about overall approaches to conflict management, but to concentrate on developing the resources and the materials for doing the job by assisting the construction of settlements that properly address all the aspects of a conflict. To this end, the following chapters offer tools for designing good conflict management processes, and the basic building blocks for putting in place sustainable, durable and flexible solutions to conflict. There is a premium placed on democratic outcomes, but democracy itself is not a panacea. Democratic states suffer from conflicts just as others do, and the presence of democracy is no guarantee of a society without political violence. But – and this is a major theme of this handbook – democratic societies tend to develop the institutions, resources and flexibility, in the long term, to peacefully manage these kinds of conflict.

Today's predominant pattern of conflict is proving resistant to the available and accepted tools of conflict management.

13

THE NEW STATE OF CONFLICT: SOME FACTS

Deep-Rooted Conflict: *Conflict, originating largely within states, which combines two powerful elements: potent identity-based factors, based on differences in race, religion, culture, language and so on, with perceived imbalance in the distribution of economic, political and social resources.*

Characteristics: complex, persistent, and intractable; much less amenable to compromise, negotiation or trade-off; rapidly diffuses beyond the boundaries of the particular state.

Intra-state, not inter-state. In the last three years, every major armed conflict originated at the domestic level within a state (intra-state), rather than between states (inter-state).

Of the 101 armed conflicts during 1989-1996, only six were inter-state. The remaining 95 took place within existing states.

Identity-based. Of the 27 conflicts in 1996 classified as "major armed conflicts" (more than 1,000 dead per year), 22 had a clear identity component to them.

New weapons of war. Since World War Two, cheap, mass-produced, small-calibre weapons have killed far more people than the heavier more traditional battlefield weaponry.

Civilian casualties. During World War One, five per cent of casualties were civilian; by World War Two the figure had risen to 50 per cent. In the 1990s, the proportion of civilian casualties has soared to 80 per cent.

Refugees. By 1992, there were about 17 million refugees, and a further 20 million people who were internally displaced.

Examples. Deep-rooted conflicts include Russia (Chechnya), Northern Ireland, Iran and Iraq (with the Kurds), Israel, Afghanistan, Bangladesh (Chittagong Hill Tribes), Indonesia (East Timor), Sri Lanka, Burma, Algeria and elsewhere.

Source: SIPRI Yearbook 1997: Armaments, Disarmament and International Security. Oxford: Oxford University Press for SIPRI.

FACTSHEET 1 [P. 14]

THE NEW STATE OF CONFLICT: SOME FACTS

Rising Rate of Civilian Casualties

The percentage of civilian casualties soared from five per cent during WWI to 80 per cent during the 1990s.

Source: Ramsbotham, Oliver, and Tom Woodhouse. 1996.

Cost of United Nations Peace-keeping Operations 1986–1997

The cost of peace-keeping has risen from less than $US 200 million to over $US 1 billion in the last ten years.

Source: Peace-keeping Financing Division /DPKO/UNHQ.

Global Refugee Population 1978–1997

The number of refugees has nearly quadrupled in the last two decades.

Source: UNHCR

Statistic at January each year. Totals do not include other groups of concern to UNHCR and Palestinians assisted by the UN Relief and Works Agency for Palestine Refugees in the Near East.

Internally Displaced Persons During the 1990s

The number of internally displaced persons (IDPs) reached 26 million in 1994.

Source: U.S. Committee for Refugees. (Figures taken from: World Refugee Statistics.)

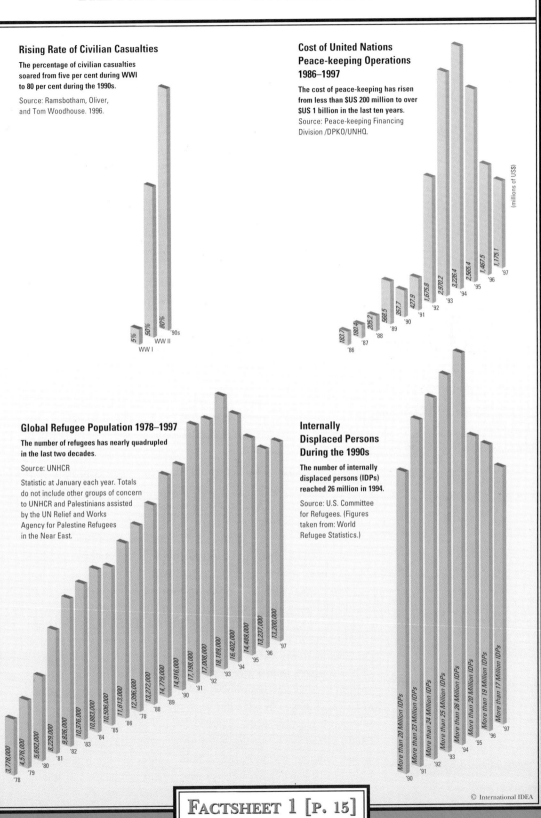

Rising Rate of Civilian Casualties:
- 5% — WW I
- 50% — WW II
- 80% — '90s

Cost of United Nations Peace-keeping Operations (millions of US$):
- 183.7 — '86
- 180.4 — '87
- 205.2 — '88
- 568.5 — '89
- 357.7 — '90
- 427.9 — '91
- 1,675.8 — '92
- 2,970.2 — '93
- 3,226.4 — '94
- 2,565.4 — '95
- 1,467.5 — '96
- 1,175.1 — '97

Global Refugee Population 1978–1997:
- 3,778,000 — '78
- 4,576,000 — '79
- 5,692,000 — '80
- 8,229,000 — '81
- 9,826,000 — '82
- 10,376,000 — '83
- 10,883,000 — '84
- 10,506,000 — '85
- 11,613,000 — '86
- 12,396,000 — '87
- 13,272,000 — '88
- 14,779,000 — '89
- 14,916,000 — '90
- 17,198,000 — '91
- 17,008,000 — '92
- 18,189,000 — '93
- 16,402,000 — '94
- 14,489,000 — '95
- 13,237,000 — '96
- 13,200,000 — '97

Internally Displaced Persons During the 1990s:
- More than 20 Million IDPs — '90
- More than 23 Million IDPs — '91
- More than 24 Million IDPs — '92
- More than 25 Million IDPs — '93
- More than 26 Million IDPs — '94
- More than 20 Million IDPs — '95
- More than 19 Million IDPs — '96
- More than 17 Million IDPs — '97

© International IDEA

FACTSHEET 1 [P. 15]

1.3 The Importance of Democratic Institutions

Three central themes dominate this handbook. The first is the crucial role that appropriate democratic political structures play in forging an enduring settlement to an internal conflict. It is important to understand that there is no single or simple model of democracy. Those wishing to build a sustainable settlement to a conflict have often overlooked the importance of making appropriate institutional choices about systems of governance. Seldom do they have access to all the information necessary to make informed decisions about *which* institutions might best suit their particular needs. This handbook attempts to fill this gap. The choice of appropriate democratic institutions – forms of devolution or autonomy, electoral system design, legislative bodies, judicial structures, and so on – designed and developed through fair and honest negotiation processes, are vital ingredients in building an enduring and peaceful settlement to even the most intractable conflict. Conversely, the international scene is littered with post-conflict settlements that broke down in part because of inappropriate and unsustainable institutional choices for deeply divided societies. Selecting unsuitable institutions can increase the possibility of a conflict persisting or even escalating.

Democratic structures can offer an effective means for the peaceful handling of deep-rooted conflict through inclusive, just and accountable frameworks.

At Bicesse in 1991, for example, parties to the Angolan conflict built an agreement by focusing on the goal of holding democratic elections which, it was presumed, would lead to a subsequent power sharing among the parties in a coalition government. However, the Angolan constitution was unsuited to support the power-sharing government which the Bicesse process aimed to bring about, since it concentrated political power not in a broad-based and inclusive parliament but in the hands of one person – the president. With both the incumbent government of President dos Santos and guerrilla leader Jonas Savimbi competing for the office of president – the only prize worth having in the context of the Angolan Constitution – the loser had a greater incentive to opt out of the political transition and resume fighting than to stay inside the process in a powerless position. And this was precisely what happened: Savimbi expected to lose the second round of the 1992 election and the fighting immediately resumed. One of the reasons why this settlement did not last may have been the lack of a system that realistically enabled both parties to share power (although as we are seeing at the time this publication goes to press, August 1998, it may not have been the only reason).

Democracy, like any other political system, is not without its flaws in this imperfect world. But in the absence of a better alternative, experience from around the world convinces us that democratic structures, in their myriad permutations, can offer an effective means for the peaceful handling of deep-rooted difference through inclusive, just and accountable social frameworks. Democratic systems of government have a degree of legitimacy, inclusiveness, flexibility and capacity for constant adaptation that enables deep-rooted conflicts to be managed peacefully. Moreover, by building norms of behaviour of negotiation, compromise, and co-operation amongst political actors, democracy itself has a pacifying effect on the nature of political relations between people and between governments.

Despite the importance of democracy and democratic solutions, however, poorly designed democratic institutions can also inflame communal conflicts rather than ameliorate them. And the introduction of "democratic" politics can easily be used to mobilize ethnicity, turning elections into "us" versus "them" conflicts. In deeply divided societies, a combination of majoritarian political institutions and elections can often make things worse. Other democratic institutions that lend themselves towards divisive, yes or no political campaigns, such as referendums, can also have negative effects in divided societies. That is why basic democratic values such as pluralism, tolerance, inclusiveness, negotiation, and compromise are keys to building lasting settlements to conflicts. Often, the institutional embodiment of these values requires institutions that emphasize different features than simple winner-take-all majority rule: features such as power sharing, autonomy, proportionality, forms of group recognition, and so on. These themes will reappear throughout this handbook.

1.4 Democracy and Conflict Management

The second theme of this handbook concerns moving away from thinking about the *resolution* of conflict, towards a more pragmatic interest in conflict *management*. This is an important distinction. *Conflict resolution* suggests the ending or removal of a conflict. The implication is that conflict is a negative phenomenon, which should be resolved, ended, and eradicated. On the contrary, conflict can be positive as well as negative. Conflict is the interaction of different and opposing aspirations and goals

17

in which disputes are processed, but not definitively resolved. It is a necessary part of healthy democratic debate and dialogue, provided it remains within the boundaries of the commonly accepted "rules of the democratic game". The violent expression of conflict is its destructive side. But conflict can be the starting point for energizing social change and improvement. *Conflict management*, then, is the positive and constructive handling of difference and divergence. Rather than advocating methods for removing conflict, this handbook addresses the more realistic question of managing conflict: how to deal with it in a constructive way, how to bring opposing sides together in a co-operative process, how to design a practical, achievable, co-operative system for the constructive management of difference.

Democracy operates as a conflict management system without recourse to violence.

This handbook is relatively unusual in putting a premium upon the need for negotiated settlements that are based on democratic outcomes. But there are good historical reasons for skepticism about the track record of negotiated settlements to deep-rooted conflicts. Scholars point to 20th century experience that reflects the fact that only 15 per cent of internal conflicts end in negotiated settlements. Most have ended in military victories. Moreover, many (roughly half) of those that have ended in negotiations fail within five years (disputants return to the battlefield, as they did in Sudan in 1984 following a peace accord that had been reached in 1972). For this reason, some scholars point to partition as the only answer to identity-based conflict. However, in the post-Cold War period, there have clearly been many more settlements to violent internal conflicts than in the past, and almost half of the internal conflicts that have ceased in the last eight years ended through negotiation. We know intuitively that negotiated settlements are much more likely in the post-Cold War era than before. Moreover, even when military victory occurs (as in Zaire/Democratic Republic of Congo), issues of democracy continue to be raised making a resumption of conflict far more likely. Although it is important to keep the historical record in mind, recent experience shows a clear swing towards negotiated settlements in which issues of democracy building are paramount.

Our emphasis on democracy is not an ideological conviction. On the contrary, it is a pragmatic argument based on wide experience and study. Democracy is presented in this handbook not only as a guiding principle, but as a workable system for the positive management of conflict. Our definition of democracy is a

1.4 Democracy and Conflict Management

practical one. For a system of government to be considered democratic, it must combine three essential conditions: meaningful *competition* for political power amongst individuals and organized groups; inclusive *participation* in the selection of leaders and policies, at least through free and fair elections; and a level of *civil and political liberties* sufficient to ensure the integrity of political competition and participation. Participation and contestation are crucial: while democracy can take many forms, no system can be called democratic without a meaningful level of both.

A 1993 study of 233 internal conflicts around the world found that democracies had a far better record of peacefully managing such conflicts than alternative systems. The evidence for the "democratic peace" proposition – the empirical fact that democracies are far less likely to go to war with each other than other regime types – lends further support to this relationship between conflict and democracy. Authoritarian or totalitarian systems simply do not have the institutions by which such conflicts can be peacefully expressed and resolved. They generally try to deal with such conflicts by ignoring or denying them, by suppressing them or by attempting to eliminate them. While some conflicts can indeed be controlled in this way, albeit usually at severe cost, deep-rooted conflicts generally cannot. The type of fundamental issues of identity and cultural integrity inherent in such conflicts mean that almost nothing, short of mass expulsions or genocide, will make them disappear. The ethnic conflict that erupted in the former Yugoslavia in 1990, for example, had been suppressed and held in check for almost 50 years during the years of the Eastern Bloc, but it was always present and unresolved. Authoritarian systems can present an illusion of short-term stability, but are unlikely to be sustainable over the long term.

Under a democracy, by contrast, disputes arise, are processed, debated and reacted to, rather than being resolved definitively and permanently. All outcomes are temporary, as the loser today may be the winner tomorrow. Unlike other systems, democratic government permits grievances to be expressed openly and responded to. In short, democracy operates as a conflict management system without recourse to violence. It is this ability to handle conflicts without having to suppress them or be engulfed by them which distinguishes democratic government from its major alternatives. This does not mean that democracy is perfect, or that democratic governance will itself lead to peaceful outcomes. There are a number of cases of democratic institutions being hastily "transplanted" to post-conflict societies without taking root, or with a subsequent resumption of hostilities – the case of Burundi, for example, or Cambodia. But it is equally true that these cases have many lessons in terms of how deals are struck and which choices are made that are of crucial importance to building a sustainable outcome. Democracy is often messy, incremental, and difficult, but it is also by far the best hope of building sustainable settlements to most of the conflicts being fought around the world today.

Box 1

THEMES OF THIS HANDBOOK

Three central themes dominate this handbook:

1. **Importance of Democratic Institutions**

   Democracy provides the foundation for building an effective and lasting settlement to internal conflicts. Therefore making appropriate choices about *democratic institutions* – forms of devolution or autonomy, electoral system design, legislative bodies, judicial structures, and so on – is crucial in building an enduring and peaceful settlement.

2. **Conflict Management, not Resolution**

   There needs to be move away from thinking about the *resolution* of conflict towards a more pragmatic interest in conflict *management*. This handbook addresses the more realistic question of managing conflict: how to deal with it in a constructive way, how to bring opposing sides together in a co-operative process, how to design a practical, achievable, co-operative system for the constructive management of difference.

3. **The Importance of Process**

   The *process* by which parties reach an outcome impacts significantly on the quality of the outcome. Attention must be paid to every aspect of the process of negotiations in order to reach a durable outcome.

1.5 Addressing the Real Causes of Conflict

Conflict management is one of the most difficult and complex tasks that can face human beings, both individually and col-

1.5 Addressing the Real Causes
of Conflict

lectively. Even without time-pressures and political tensions, it is a supreme challenge. But in the real world, such factors are always present. Their effect is manifest as intense pressure to produce results, irrespective of the difficulty of the task. The near-irresistible temptation is to respond by simplifying the task, and focusing on surfaces and symptoms, searching for the fastest way to some result. But speed does not equate with quality. A simplistic approach cannot wholly succeed in addressing a complex problem. The kind of conflict we are addressing here – that which results in prolonged violence, that which comes about over deep-seated and profound differences – is caused at a much deeper level. Hence the term *deep-rooted* conflict. If conflict were simply a surface phenomenon, it would be easily dealt with at the surface level. But deep-rooted conflict demands deep-rooted conflict management. A doctor who treats a patient's symptoms may bring short-term relief of suffering. But a doctor who treats and cures the underlying illness that caused the symptoms brings a long-term solution to the patient's problem. In conflict management there needs to be a shift of focus, beyond the surface approach of treating *symptoms,* to a deeper level where underlying *illnesses* are directly addressed.

However, any doctor will rightly argue that treating symptoms is a vital humanitarian act, bringing short-term relief of suffering. A negotiation process that fails abysmally in its attempt to design a long-term settlement, but achieves a six-month cease-fire, has saved many lives. We must therefore not decry the genuine value of short-term measures, especially in situations of desperation and suffering. But the point is simply that short-term pain relief should not be confused with long-term cure. This is not to blame politicians and negotiators for yielding to pressures that are part and parcel of political life but simply to acknowledge that, within the pressures of the situation, a shift in focus beyond the immediate to the longer term, a reorientation from the surface symptoms to their underlying cause, is vital for both the short-term process and the long-term future. Failure to make this shift will inevitably harm the entire process as well as the future result. Ultimately, it may even make the situation worse than before. The challenge then, for domestic and international actors, is to seriously consider the temptation of short-term stability (and quick rewards and success) and move towards the long-term objective of a sustainable settlement.

A shift in focus beyond the immediate to the longer term, a reorientation from the surface symptoms to their underlying cause, is vital for both the short-term process and the long-term future.

1.6 Process and Outcome

The third theme of this handbook is that the *process* of designing negotiations is critical to the success and durability of the outcome. In thinking about the search for a settlement, a useful distinction can be made between *process* and *outcome*. *Process* is the business of negotiation and dialogue. If conflicting parties now need to discuss the elements of a solution, how exactly should that discussion be structured? For example, would the intervention of a third party be useful or distracting? What types of third-party intervention might be used, and how have they worked, or failed, in the past? Who exactly should participate in the talks process? Leaders only? Political parties? Non-governmental agencies? Outside observers? Would a time-limit on talks help or hinder the process? Should the talks be secret or public? What are the issues involved in choosing a venue for negotiations? These and many other pertinent questions need to be addressed in order to design the optimum process, the one that offers the best hope of a successful outcome.

Process asks: how do we get to a solution? Outcome asks: what do we include in that solution?

The answers depend on the specific situation under discussion. From an analysis of the conflict – identifying its history, its core issues, its participants, and so on – one identifies the factors which need to go into the design of a suitable process. From an overview of many conflicts and peace processes around the world, this handbook directs readers to the most critical factors that they will need to consider, and then helps them to find the answers pertinent to their specific context.

Process involves every aspect of the way parties get to an outcome. The type of process used, of course, impacts significantly on the quality of the outcome. In particular, a sound process helps to contribute to the legitimacy of the outcome. For example, if the process employed is an inclusive one, where all parties who claim an interest in the conflict feel involvement in it, feel they have been heard and their views respected, and feel that the process has permitted them to make a contribution to the ultimate settlement, they are far more motivated to put subsequent effort into making that settlement work. In contrast, a group who feel excluded from the process will be far more likely to question the legitimacy of the settlement and to obstruct efforts to implement it. So good process not only makes for efficient working practice, it also strengthens the outcome. It is an essential ingredient for a durable, long-term solution.

Outcome focuses not on the way to reach a solution, but on the substance of that solution itself. Democratic structures and insti-

1.6 Process and Outcome

tutions offer practical components for a successful outcome, because their democratic nature implies a degree of consensus and accountability in their implementation. As with good process, the design of a sound outcome again lessens the chance of any party subsequently feeling the solution has been imposed upon them and thus questioning its legitimacy. What sort of political structures will be the components of the solution over which the parties negotiate during the process? What are the various kinds of democratic institutions that have been negotiated as settlements in the past? What were their strengths, and their weaknesses? What roles can outside agents usefully play in implementing or supporting these institutions? The business of mutually thinking these questions through to agreement will contribute to a better method of building sustainable and just systems of democratic government. In sum, the sustainability of a solution depends both on its outcome – its character and its content – and on the process by which it was agreed.

It is an analytic exercise to separate process and outcome completely. The distinction is offered as a useful method of concentrating on different but equally important aspects of conflict management. But in reality they are tightly intertwined and interdependent. Bad process will greatly impede agreement. It can even contribute to ultimate failure, no matter how well designed the outcome, simply because the way in which the talks were structured may cause friction and distrust and leave at least some parties questioning the legitimacy of the whole venture. Likewise the best process cannot guarantee success or sustainability if the outcome is poorly designed, is imposed on some of the parties or does not satisfy their real interests, no matter how fairly the process of dialogue was constructed. In practice, some parties will want assurances on what the broad parameters of the outcome will be before they agree to talks.

It is worth noting here that many of the conflict situations which readers will bring to the handbook have attracted the attention and involvement of the international community, increasingly in the form of third-party intervention or mediation. Third-party intervention can be of significant assistance in a conflict situation and is dealt with in more detail in Chapter 3. But parties need to be aware that there may also be dangers. Third parties may bring their own agendas, benign or otherwise: their own substantive interests in the issues of the conflict, perhaps their own desire for international acclamation as directors of the peace process, and so on. Mediators may focus too much on process at the expense of outcome and often lack the necessary expertise in relation to institutional options. In addition, powerful intervenors may be tempted to force parties into a superficial agreement that fails to address underlying interests and needs, thus simply storing up trouble for the future.

1.7 Maximizing Women's Participation

In all conflicts, particularly those in which deep-seated identity issues are prominent, it is the most vulnerable members of society who often pay the highest cost. One of the characteristics of contemporary, intra-state conflicts is that the most marginalized social groups – small ethnic minorities, indigenous peoples and so on – are the most affected. Indeed, in some conflicts it is these very groups, such as the Kurdish peoples who are often described as the world's largest stateless ethnic group, who are directly targeted as victims.

Women should be included around the negotiating table because their experiences, values and priorities, as women, can bring a perspective that can help find a solution to the conflict.

Similarly, in almost all contemporary within-state conflicts, civilians in general, and women and children in particular, feature disproportionately amongst the casualty list. This makes the issue of gender a particularly salient feature of peace building. While the aggressors in today's conflicts, and the armies that fight them, continue to be predominantly male, the high casualty rates of civilians means that it is often women who bear the brunt of the consequences of the conflicts, a factor only emphasized by the effect of such conflicts on children.

It is therefore vital that any attempt at rebuilding democracy in the wake of a violent ethnic conflict builds women into the process as much as possible. In fact, in many cases this does not happen – the same people who started the conflict are also those who negotiate its end. This has detrimental effects on the long-term sustainability of a settlement, because vital voices and interests are not heard. This can be addressed by building gender considerations into every aspect of the peace process.

In the pre-negotiation phase, for instance, it is important to identify all constituencies, and to structure the process so as to maximize their participation. During the negotiations itself, it is essential that efforts are made to include considerations of gender, both thematically and via the representation of women as parties to the negotiations – rather than as being observers locked out of a process driven and dominated by men. During the implementation phase, each and every political institution needs to be structured such that it incorporates issues of gender and addresses wider issues of equality. This can take place both at a macro-level – through, for example, consideration of issues of gender and equality when designing political institutions – and at a more micro-level, via the establishment of specific mechanisms for gender equality (see the specific section on this issue in Chapter 4).

Beyond such structuring of mechanisms, however, there needs to be a recognition of the importance of involving women in the negotiation process because of what they, as women, can bring to the process of finding peace. Women should be included around the negotiating table because their experiences, values and priorities, as women, brings a perspective that is important and valuable to both process and outcome.

1.8 Short- and Long-Term Planning

The management of post-conflict democratic peace building is first and foremost the management of political *time* in a complex and highly volatile context. From the moment peace negotiations start, the pressure is intense on those involved to reach agreement as quickly as possible. That pressure often becomes irresistible. Time may be very limited. Political demands for fast results may be overwhelming. In a context of ongoing violence, many lives may be at stake. The temptation is to push for superficial success at the expense of concentration on the *outcome*. The need to reach an agreement – *any* agreement – becomes more important than the quality of the agreement, especially its all-important elements of sustainability and durability. Long-term stability is sacrificed for short-term expediency. This pressure can build from many sources: a limited window of opportunity for talks; a tenuous cease-fire agreement that may collapse without quick results; the influence of outside actors who need their own results; the limited patience of a constituency who demand immediate improvements or guarantees; military issues, economic needs and contingencies, and so on.

These pressures are genuine and difficult to resist. Nonetheless, time spent in the dialogue phase pays off afterwards. There is always a trade-off between the urgent pressure for a result in response to the immediate circumstances, and the time needed to build a sustainable outcome with long-term stability. A *slow-fast* approach to conflict management is one where the initial stage of reaching agreement is done as slowly as necessary, to ensure that the agreement, when reached, is as comprehensive and detailed as possible. This permits more speed subsequently in implementing the agreement. By contrast, many agreements

There is a need to balance the necessity of achieving results from negotiation against the stability and longevity of the outcome – a need, in other words, to balance short- and long-term goals.

are reached in a *fast-slow* mode: pressure for results encourages the parties to rush through the negotiation phase and reach a less than optimum agreement, so that problems remain which slow down, or altogether obstruct, the implementation phase.

The *fast-slow* approach was exemplified when, in November 1995, Bosnian leaders endured intensive pressure from their US hosts during negotiations in Dayton, Ohio. The US agenda – which included, in significant part, a strong White House desire for demonstrable negotiating successes in Bosnia, the Middle East and Northern Ireland – as well as the domestic constituencies of the Bosnian parties, placed a premium on an agreement being reached. This agenda, coupled with the extreme urgency of ending a vicious and devastating war, meant that intense pressure was applied on the three Bosnian leaders and their delegates at Dayton not to leave the site without a signed result on paper. The resulting Dayton Peace Accords were acclaimed as the framework for a comprehensive settlement of the conflict in Bosnia. But in the rush to reach an agreement, many details had to be overlooked. The effect was to sacrifice long-term planning for short-term results: the insistence on a fast result at the negotiation stage simply piled up problems which remained to obstruct and delay the implementation of the Accords (see Bosnia Case Study). On the other hand, it stopped the war and the killing, which was a great achievement. It is not suggested that these two approaches are necessarily exclusive, rather that they need to be balanced as much as possible.

In some important ways, the South African constitutional negotiations of the early 1990s stand as a successful example of the reverse, a *slow-fast* approach. The negotiation process was at times painstakingly slow, not least because of the wide range of participating groups and factions as well as the complexity of the issues. Undoubtedly, an outcome could have been designed much more rapidly between just the major participants, the government and the African National Congress (ANC), and by leaving certain aspects for later resolution. But the apparently interminable talking between so many parties and the variety of issues addressed, which made the negotiation stage so slow, paid considerable rewards in the implementation phase, when the multilateral nature of the talks made the subsequent "sell" much faster and avoided breakdowns as a result of "constituency lag" between leaders and their supporters. When eventually signed,

1.8 Short- and Long-Term Planning

the legitimacy of the outcome was far stronger than a more exclusive version would have been.

Perhaps in an ideal world, conflicting parties would have the luxury of a *slow-slow* approach – one where every stage of the settlement process is given sufficient time to attend to every detail. But such luxury is rarely available. Indeed, the most frequent pressure is for a *fast-fast* approach, the worst possible scenario, where there is no time to do justice to any aspect of the conflict management process. Avoiding both of these unlikely or unproductive extremes, we simply highlight the tension between fast-slow and slow-fast, and emphasize the long-term value of the latter.

There is a need, then, to balance the necessity of achieving results from negotiation against the stability and longevity of the outcome, a need, in other words, to balance short- and long-term goals. So a compromise that may appear to be the best achievable result in the urgent present tense of the negotiating process can often prove too weak to be sustainable in the future. The effect is simply to postpone, rather than solve, problems. While recognizing the difficulty of the advice, experience from around the world repeatedly teaches the value of retaining a strong sense of future ramifications during the design stage. Attention paid to detail in that earlier negotiation phase will save much time, and possibly the whole settlement, during the subsequent phase of implementation.

REFERENCES AND FURTHER READING

Diamond, Larry, Juan Linz and Seymour Martin Lipset. 1995. *Politics in Developing Countries: Comparing Experiences with Democracy.* Boulder and London: Lynne Reiner Publishers.

Gurr, Ted Robert. 1993. *Minorities at Risk: A Global View of Ethnopolitical Conflicts.* Washington, DC: United States Institute of Peace Press.

Huntington, Samuel P. 1991. *The Third Wave: Democratization in the Late Twentieth Century.* Norman and London: University of Oklahoma Press.

Przeworski, Adam. 1991. *Democracy and the Market: Political and Economic Reforms in Eastern Europe and Latin America.* Cambridge: Cambridge University Press.

Ramsbotham, Oliver and Tom Woodhouse. 1996. *Humanitarian Intervention in Contemporary Conflict: A Reconceptualisation.* Cambridge: Polity Press.

Ray, James Lee. April 1997. "The Democratic Path to Peace",
Journal of Democracy, vol. 8, no. 2, pp. 49–64.

Reid, Ann. 1993. "Conflict Resolution in Africa: Lessons
from Angola", INR Foreign Affairs Brief. Washington DC:
Bureau of Intelligence and Research, U.S. Department of
State, April 6.

Sollenberg, Margareta and Peter Wallensteen. 1997. "Major
Armed Conflicts", in *SIPRI Yearbook 1997: Armaments,
Disarmament and International Security*. Oxford: Oxford
University Press for SIPRI.

Sollenberg, Margareta. ed. 1997. *States in Armed Conflict 1996.*
Report no. 46. Uppsala, Sweden: Uppsala University,
Department of Peace and Conflict Research.

CHAPTER 2

Most conflicts feature complex interactions of different forces. Each requires the crafting of well-designed structures that are purposely oriented to the needs of the specific situation.

Analysis is a necessary prelude to problem-solving. This chapter focuses on the process of analysing a conflict in all its aspects – from looking at how conflicts in general are expressed (macro-level) to examining how a particular conflict can be understood by examining its component parts (micro-level).

Box 2   Analysing a Conflict: Three Approaches (p. 40)

David Bloomfield,
Yash Ghai and
Ben Reilly

Analysing Deep-Rooted Conflict

2.1 Introduction

T hroughout this handbook, our approach is based on an assumption that democratic governance is key to developing sustainable settlements. But the relationship of many deep-rooted conflicts to democracy is complex, and indeed democracy can encourage or even aggravate civil conflicts. The political mobilization of people for electoral or other purposes is frequently achieved by narrow identity appeals (as demonstrated, again and again, in Sri Lanka, India, Fiji, the former Yugoslavia and elsewhere). In that sense mass politics, associated with the rise of modern democratic states, has given a particularly sharp edge to identity. Ethnic animosities can often lie dormant until groups perceive themselves to be competing in a "zero-sum" game for resources, rights or territory. Issues of identity often provide a convenient cloak for other issues that concern the distribution of these resources.

A "one size fits all" conflict management package cannot be prescribed for all conflicts.

Most conflicts feature complex interactions of different forces. Some are sustained by the separation of hostile groups, so that antagonisms are reinforced by ignorance and suspicion fueled by a lack of contact between contending parties. The traditional approach of the international community in such situations has been the imposition of "peace-keeping forces" between the groups – such as those stationed in Cyprus, Bosnia or Lebanon – a useful but blunt and surface-oriented instrument which often does not address the underlying needs of the groups in question. In other cases, the problem is not separation but proximity and day-to-day interaction that breeds mutual antagonisms – such as in relations between Malays, Chinese and Indians in Malaysia or between indigenous and Indo-Fijians in Fiji. All of these cases represent relatively familiar types of deep-rooted internal conflicts, and all of them require different approaches and different types of political institutions to manage disputes and build a sustainable peace. Further, each requires the crafting of well-designed structures that are purposely oriented to the needs of the specific situation. It is therefore surprising that sometimes a "one size fits all" conflict management package is still prescribed by even the most informed of practitioners.

2.2 Conflict as Both Positive and Negative

Cultural or ethnic claims and identities are not always nega-tive. Identity itself can act as both a constructive force and a de-stabilizing one. Nationalist movements involved in the construc-tion of new states during the struggle for independence, for example, are often based on dynamic combinations of both identity and nationalism. The emotional and cultural bonds thus forged have proved to be a major factor in ensuring the legitimacy and support of many potentially fragile new states.

Similarly, basic identity-related factors such as religious and ethnic affiliations, for example, are often of fundamental impor-tance to the psychic and moral well-being of communities. Cul-tural identity is a vital and enriching part of human life; and cul-tural diversity can be as energizing as it can be threatening. Many of today's functioning multicultural societies – such as Canada, Australia and the United States – have built their success on being a melting pot of many different cultures and religions. Elsewhere, divided communities with distinct religious or cultu-ral traditions, as in Belgium, Mauritius, Trinidad and Tobago, and so on, have nonetheless been able to maintain competitive but cordial relations between different groups.

While such differences can lend themselves to political ma-nipulation by *ethnic entrepreneurs*, who seek to mobilize and capi-talize on ethnic differences for their personal or political gain, this exploitation is likely to be successful only in specific circum-stances – such as where a community perceives reasons to fear the policies or activities of other communities, or experiences its economic or social position as clearly inferior to that of other groups with little prospect of amelioration, or where its abiding experience is one of disempowerment and vulnerability. Some-times such manipulation results in a genuine galvanization of the community into an energizing force for positive and neces-sary social change; sometimes it fails to move beyond a surface reaction to intimidation and violence. Just as denial of identity-related claims can be a way to harass other groups, assertions of them – such as civil rights campaigns – can be a useful device to secure more justice and equity. Ethnic mobilization is a doubled-edged sword.

In the same way, conflict itself is not necessarily a negative process. Indeed, conflict is one of the most powerfully positive factors for change in a society. Conflict tells us that something is wrong; conflict is the generator of change and improvement.

Conflict is one of the most powerfully positive factors for change in a society. Without conflict, we would have stagnation.

Without conflict, we would have stagnation. The nature of competitive representative democracy, for example, involves a certain degree of conflict between opposing forces, ideologies and parties. This is healthy because this conflict takes place within a forum of bounded behaviour – there are "rules of the game" that need to be observed. This handbook is based on the assumption that even very intense conflicts are capable of being managed, given the right combination of procedures and institutions, in a way that is both peaceful and sustainable. But we do not pretend that it is easy, or even likely. We simply argue that it is possible. This is especially the case in the immediate post-conflict period, where negotiations between conflicting groups are beginning to take place. It is precisely in this interim period, where new patterns of interaction are possible, when parties are most amenable to the consideration of novel alternatives and different solutions, that the best hope for making sustainable settlements lies.

2.3 Patterns of Deep-Rooted Conflict

Three main areas of dispute often appear to dovetail with identity-related issues. The first are broadly *economic factors*. Economic slumps are often accompanied by an upsurge in inter-ethnic conflict. The post-communist movement from a controlled economy to a free market in Eastern Europe and parts of Asia and Africa in recent years has created a host of social problems that provide fertile breeding ground for sectarian sentiment. Similarly, the racist anti-immigration movements which have arisen in a number of western countries over the past decade have their root causes in increasing economic insecurity for many of the established population, particularly those at the lower end of the socio-economic ladder. In other areas, there are deliberate policies that discriminate economically for or against certain groups. These include the "affirmative action" policies for certain castes in India, or for *bumiputra* (literally "sons of the soil", i.e., Malays) in Malaysia, which have created resentment among those who feel such policies threaten their place in the economic system. Elsewhere, deliberate economic discrimination against what are seen as a privileged group, such as the Tamils in Sri Lanka, has been evident.

A second group of conflicts revolve around questions of *culture*. A classic issue is the question of minority language rights or religious freedoms. The conflict over language rights in the Baltic states between the local and Russian-speaking populations

Three main areas of dispute often appear to dovetail with identity-related issues: economic insecurity, cultural conflicts and territorial disputes.

described in Chapter 4 is a good example of this. Often, such conflicts are manifested via a demand for some form of group autonomy, such as culturally specific schooling for minorities, freedom to establish communal places of worship, or application of traditional or religious law. Many multi-ethnic countries have faced this issue in recent times, as demands for cultural autonomy increase and "assimilationist" policies are increasingly regarded with suspicion. More unusual variants of this issue have occurred in demands for culturally specific forms of law by threatened indigenous groups trying to maintain their own cultural integrity (e.g., punishments of criminal offences by traditional forms such as "banishment" or even spearing in some aboriginal cultures).

The third broad area of conflicts concerns disputes over *territory*. Territorial disputes are likely to mesh with ethnic ones when ethnic groups are territorially concentrated. In such cases, the manifestation of self-determination is often secession from the existing state altogether. Secession requires the dismemberment of the existing state, and for this reason has often been strongly opposed both by dominant members of an existing state and by the international community. If a state is to stay together under such circumstances, it requires the use of innovative institutional arrangements that deliver forms of devolution of power, federalism or autonomy. In Spain and Canada, for example, "asymmetric" federal arrangements for the Basque and Quebecois regions respectively have been used to try and dampen calls for secession, while federalism has been promoted as an institution of conflict management in countries as diverse as India, Malaysia, Germany, Nigeria, South Africa, and Switzerland.

2.4 National and International Factors in Deep-Rooted Conflict

Many of the world's most bitter deep-rooted internal conflicts have a significant international dimension. The fact that the boundaries of a state, particularly in post-colonial societies, rarely match the boundaries of a "nation" – an identity group – means that it is rare for domestic conflicts to stay entirely within the boundaries of the state. The Sri Lankan conflict has been fueled by the proximity and involvement of India; the Northern Ireland conflict by the competing claims of Britain and the Irish Republic and the involvement of Irish Americans; the Cyprus conflict is intertwined with the dispute between Turkey and

2.4 National and International Factors in Deep-Rooted Conflict

Greece, and so on. Understanding these international dimensions is key to any analysis of the conflict itself.

Tension between "settler" and "indigenous" groups is present in almost all states in which such terms are meaningful. Indian settlers in Fiji; Chinese and Indians in Malaysia; Russians in the Baltics and Central Asian Republics: all are examples of groups who are seen as being less than fully legitimate members of a multi-ethnic state by their indigenous counterparts. The legacy of colonialism thus plays a role in many of the current eruptions of identity-related conflict.

2.4.1 Decolonization

The process of decolonization after World War Two left a vast range of disputed territories and arbitrary boundaries in the developing world, leading inevitably to conflict over the adjustment of boundaries and over the legitimacy of states formed during colonization. Post-colonial polities suddenly found themselves in the position of sovereign states, but often with too diverse an ethnic mix to build easily the shared values and identities that might make a functioning nation. More often, their populations consisted of more than one nation, or parts of several. Given the potent impact of the decolonization process upon ethnic antagonisms, it is no surprise to find that "ethno-political" conflicts have been steadily increasing since the "winds of change" in the early 1960s led to independence for former colonial states in Africa, Asia and the Pacific.

One example among many is the legacy left in Western Sahara by the departing Spanish in 1975: an artificial frontier between Morocco and "Spanish Sahara" which became the subject of a long dispute between the Moroccan state and the Polisario Front, the army of the Saharawi people. Put simply, their sense of themselves as a community – their ethnic identity – contradicted the arbitrary maplines drawn by the colonizer, and they set about correcting the map as soon as they were free to do so. A difference of identity, combined with a dispute over territory, resulted in violent conflict, which remains unresolved today. Similarly, as Britain left the Indian subcontinent in 1947, bitter fighting erupted between identity groups organized along religious lines. The result was the partitioning of the area between India and Pakistan. But, as so often, simple partition has failed to satisfy the underlying root-causes of the conflict: in Kashmir and elsewhere, fighting continues as peoples contest their identity and disagree over self-determination *versus* territorial integrity.

It is rare for domestic conflicts to stay entirely within the boundaries of the state since the boundaries of a state rarely match the boundaries of a "nation", an identity group.

2.4.2 End of the Cold War

The end of the Cold War further intensified these conflicts over boundaries. The Soviet Union disintegrated into multiple states. Its influence, which had served to glue together imperfect nation-states within its realm, dissipated and permitted the rise of ethnic frustrations and tensions which expressed themselves in bitter conflicts over Yugoslavia, Georgia, Chechnya and elsewhere. The dissolution of the Soviet Union also left large populations of Russian speakers in a number of new republics in the Baltics, Eastern Europe and Central Asia, many of whom became a focus for the long-standing grievances of the indigenous populations. Discrimination and conflict between Russians and local populations became a potent issue in a number of these states, with language and citizenship rights an area of particular concern.

2.4.3 The state in crisis

Additionally, the state itself has been facing a crisis for some time. The deep contradictions or anachronisms of the nation-state have led it now to face a crisis of legitimization. To retain its legitimate position of power, a state must inspire some sense of shared identity among all its diverse population, as some have argued is the case in India. It must also ensure the participation of all groups in the affairs of the state as well as equity in the sharing of its resources. Identity groups tend to demand self-determination, or assert their rights to be treated equally with all citizens, precisely when a state is not fulfilling these objectives. Democratic states suffer these problems just as others do: democracy is no guarantee of a conflict-free existence. But democratic societies tend to have built-in institutional mechanisms and the requisite flexibility to manage this kind of conflict by non-violent means.

But what turns such ethnically based dissatisfaction into actual violent conflict? Unscrupulous leaders have realized the value of mobilizing dissent along the powerful fault-lines of race, religion, language and so on. The ideas of human and civil rights, of self-expression and self-determination, have flourished in the hearts of many people, permeating societies and making oppression more difficult and its resistance more energized. Indeed, self-determination can often be used by dissidents to express their case and mobilize their resources along ethnic divisions. Certainly, increased international media attention can raise the temperature of dispute, as it can help to sustain rigid positions within a conflict.

With intra-state conflict, most often the state itself is a disputing party, even a major source of violence. This makes internal processes for conflict regulation difficult, since state organs may be delegitimized by their involvement in the conflict. Often governments will be much more powerful than the rebels they face: such asymmetry of power can mitigate the chances of bringing the sides together, and can encourage both sides to strengthen themselves as far as possible by violence or its threat, prior to entering negotiations. A referee is difficult to find within the state who will hold the respect of both sides. The type of inclusive, power sharing and devolutionary mechanisms examined in detail in Chapter 4 are thus particularly necessary to building a sustainable settlement.

2.5 Difficulties in Managing Identity-Related Conflicts

2.5.1 Indivisibility

A central problem in trying to manage or transform identity-related disputes is the "indivisibility" of such conflicts: they are often not amenable to split-the-difference, cake-cutting solutions based on compromise. Conflicts based upon historical identities, religious beliefs, language or symbolic territory are particularly difficult: it is hard to compromise over a question as basic as the nature of the one true God, for example, or whether a particular sacred site is to be the property of one group or another (e.g., the conflict between some Moslems and Hindus in India over the Ayodhya mosque). Moreover, the very nature of identity-related appeals, what one scholar calls the "relentless drumbeat of ethnic propaganda", itself tends to distort the usual modes of political discussion.

2.5.2 Escalation

A second problem is the cyclical nature of many deep-rooted conflicts. Mobilization of groups by one side of a conflict typically leads to a corresponding counter-mobilization by their opponents. Escalation of a conflict on one side almost guarantees a countervailing reaction on the other. The actions of one group are responded to by their opponents: violence begets violence, and the conflict steadily escalates in a series of tit-for-tat exchanges, as in Burundi. The originally divisive issues get augmented, often even replaced, by new and more intense issues arising out of this intensification process. Such issues are amenable to manipulation by leaders and politicians, who may use them to mobilize communities on ethnic or other fault-lines. It

Two recurrent problems make it extraordinarily difficult to manage identity-related disputes: their indivisibility and their tendency towards escalation.

37

is extremely hard to break these cyclical patterns and de-escalate back to the original issues.

2.5.3 Leadership

Managing deep-rooted conflicts requires far-sighted leadership. Just as many conflicts are exacerbated by ethnic entrepreneurs who fan the flames of group animosities, so to bring conflicts to a sustainable settlement requires leaders who are prepared to do just that – lead. To do this, they must often be ahead of the sentiments of a large portion of their followers in counselling for peace, and they must have the authority to carry their supporters with them through difficult times. This is especially difficult when the leaders at the negotiating table are often the very same ones who provoked or maintained the conflicts in the first place. It also requires leaders to put the long-term interests of their nation in achieving a durable settlement before the short-term gains that could be achieved by prolonging the conflict. This handbook carries a number of instances of such behaviour, with the examples of South African leaders Nelson Mandela and F. W. de Klerk particularly apposite. This is not to suggest that leaders will do other than make rational decisions about their own group's core interests when negotiating a settlement. All the negotiating techniques outlined in Chapter 3 are based upon this assumption, as are the designs of the democratic institutions in Chapter 4.

Our attention now turns from the macro-level to the micro-level, from looking at how conflicts in general are expressed, to examining how a particular conflict can be understood by examining its component parts. Successful analysis of a specific conflict in terms of its generic structure enables us to diagnose appropriate methods to successfully negotiate a lasting settlement.

2.6 Analysing Conflict

Before an outcome to conflict can be considered, before even a process to reach that outcome can be designed, we need to have a clear view of the conflict. That sounds like stating the obvious. Actors in a conflict are intimately acquainted with their particular conflict, from possibly a lifetime of involvement in it. They have consciously struggled with it, and with attempts to end it, for prolonged periods of time.

This in-depth knowledge of the conflict is vital. But, for completely understandable reasons, combatants in prolonged and

2.6 Analysing Conflict

deep-rooted conflict have a particular view of the causes, dynamics and effects of their conflict. For very good protective reasons, they have a partisan view of things. This is as it should be: their job has been to be partisan, to represent, support, direct and sustain their community and their struggle.

But we are assuming with this handbook that the conflict phase is reaching a hiatus. Negotiations are at least looming, if not actually in process. To move straight from struggle into dialogue, with the same aims and attitudes intact, will almost guarantee failure. Completely partisan approaches will produce completely competitive talks, with each side still as committed to winning the peace as they were to winning the war. Such negotiations are simply war by other means. But peace, by definition, is not winnable in the same terms as war. To make negotiations work, we must supplement competition with co-operation. Negotiation, by its very nature, implies movement: it is a process in which people, their attitudes and their positions move and change. Negotiation is not merely a matter of convincing the opposition that your position is right: it demands a degree of co-operation with that opposition to move creatively from stalemate towards a new position.

Conflict analysis is not about learning something new. It is about understanding the same thing in different and deeper ways.

To engender that co-operation, in oneself or in others, is not easy, nor automatic. It requires, as a first step, a wider view of the conflict than the strictly partisan one that served during the war. It is a basic requirement of conflict management to try to better understand each other's motivations. Not to agree with each other's viewpoint, not to give up any cherished beliefs about the causes and blame involved in the conflict, but simply to approach an understanding of the opposite viewpoints, without necessarily in any way endorsing them.

This requires adopting new models for thinking by the actors: looking at their subject matter through new lenses. Conflict analysis here is not about learning something new (although that might happen). It is about understanding the same thing in different and deeper ways. This section offers some lenses to facilitate such understanding. One lens concerns how we actually go about the analytic process itself. Quite irrespective of the content of the conflict and the subsequent analysis, this model argues that our attitude and approach in coming to analysis itself significantly affects the results. In brief, there are three ways for actors to analyse their conflict: the *adversarial* way (blaming everything on the other side); the *reflexive* way (looking inward to reflect on one's own sides position in the conflict); and the *integrative* way (looking both at one's own side and at the need to also understand the views of the opposition).

The latter approach (integrative) is really one that proposes that there be movement away from the entrenched attitudes and positions of the parties towards a situation where the real needs and interests of the parties are focused on. There needs to be an acceptance by the parties that there should be movement from what is known as "positional-based" negotiation to "interest-based" negotiation. In reality, however, the ebb and flow of negotiations tends to take the parties through a number of phases, attitudes and positions that will impact on their tactics. Depending on the nature and maturity of the parties, they will generally include a range of elements from all three approaches in their negotiation strategy.

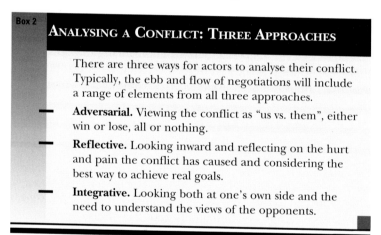

Box 2

ANALYSING A CONFLICT: THREE APPROACHES

There are three ways for actors to analyse their conflict. Typically, the ebb and flow of negotiations will include a range of elements from all three approaches.

— **Adversarial.** Viewing the conflict as "us vs. them", either win or lose, all or nothing.

— **Reflective.** Looking inward and reflecting on the hurt and pain the conflict has caused and considering the best way to achieve real goals.

— **Integrative.** Looking both at one's own side and the need to understand the views of the opponents.

Entering negotiations, as Chapter 3 will emphasize, involves swallowing the bitter pill of co-operating with what used to be the enemy. In preparation for this, assembling a broad analysis of the conflict is a crucial first step. If one is truly committed to negotiation as a way of solving the problem, then a step away from adversarial approaches is a necessary starting point. The closer one can get to an integrative analysis, the better the prognosis for those negotiations.

One of the results of the integrative approach is that it encourages creative negotiation. Parties are more likely to build on each other's proposals than be preoccupied with advancing their own. A full analytic understanding of the conflict is both a prerequisite for going into the process of negotiation – negotiators need to know their subject matter – and a valuable resource to keep in mind during negotiation. First, it is important to grasp and analyse all the relevant factors that go to make up the conflict and give it its shape.

2.7 Factors for Analysis

In this section, our aim is not to solve the conflict, merely to draw out all the elements that must be part of the subsequent solution. Outlined below are some of the questions that need to be asked and answered. Consideration of these various elements will better equip negotiators to devise appropriate strategies to manage the conflict.

ACTORS

Who are the various *actors*, internal and external, in the conflict?

- What are the *identity groups* involved? How do they define themselves, and what are the core features that make up their identity?

- Who are the real *leaders* of these groups? Are they politicians, soldiers, religious leaders, intellectuals, etc.? What pressures are they subject to from followers and opponents?

- How do these identity groups *mobilize*? How do they pursue their needs as communities (i.e., political parties, paramilitary groups, armies, etc.)? What *alliances* have they forged? What interests do they serve (external, regional, global)? What pressures are they subject to?

- What *factions* exist within parties?

- Are there *spoilers* (groups opposed to the peace process)? How great a threat do they represent? What resources exist to deal with them?

- Are there *single-issue groups* (those who represent a strong opinion on a particular aspect of the conflict)? Are there actors who remain internal geographically, but are removed from, or opposed to, the conflict (e.g., peace groups, business interests. etc.)?

- Who are the *external actors* (governments, states, regional blocs, etc.)? Which *outside interests* and groups affect the conflict?

The first step in analysis is acquiring all the raw data, making sure everything relevant is included, the better to see the scope and shape of the problem.

ISSUES

What *issues* are involved in the conflict?

– What issues arise over the *distribution* of economic, social and political resources?

– What is the conflict about in *political terms*?

– Is there *discrimination* at work in the distribution process?

UNDERLYING FACTORS

What are the *needs* of the parties? What are their *fears*?

– What *drives* each of the parties and why? (For example, do they really want secession, or is it an expression of a deeper need for security?)

– What do they *fear* under the present situation? What are the fears each group currently has of the other groups?

SCOPE

What is the *extent* of the conflict's effect, both within and outside the conflict area?

– What is the *scope* of the conflict in its effects on the population? Which sections suffer most, and why? Are some sections of the country relatively untouched, and why?

– What are the implications of the conflict for other states? For regional or global alliances?

– Who is affected by the conflict's continuance, and who might be affected by its settlement?

PREVIOUS ATTEMPTS AT SETTLEMENT

What is the *history* of the conflict regarding attempts to resolve it?

– What structures were previously tried? Why did they fail? Do the flaws relate to who authored the settlement, or with how it was implemented, or what it contained?

– Can *patterns* be identified among previous attempts at settlement?

2.7 Factors for Analysis

PHASES AND INTENSITY

Is it possible to identify *phases* of the conflict?

- Does the conflict have distinct *phases*, for example in relation to experiments in particular forms of governance, patterns of violence, or outside influences?
- Did the *intensity* of the violence shift over time?

BALANCE OF POWER

What is the nature and extent of the *balance of power* between the parties?

- Who is *stronger*? Who has more support? (The perception of the parties of their own power and their own estimation of the "balance" between them is critical.)
- Has this balance changed over time, or has it remained constant?
- Is the dominant position of one party *sustainable*?
- Is it possible that one party may win outright victory in the near future?

CAPACITY AND RESOURCES

What are the current *capacities and resources* of the parties?

- Have the resources shifted for each side over time? Will they change in the near future? Are they internal sources or external?
- What is the *financial situation* of the differing parties?
- What resources will they need to conduct effective negotiations?

STATE OF THE RELATIONSHIP

What is the nature of the *relationship* between the adversaries?

- What is the nature of the relationship between leaders?
- What are the *mutual images* of one another that the parties hold?
- Where do they get information about each other? How accurate is their information?
- What *communication channels* are available between the groups?
- What, if any, degree of trust exists?

2.8 Analytic Lenses

What follows is designed to help put some structure, some organization on the raw data generated by the questions of the previous section. Most of the ideas presented here originated from academic research. The aim is to extract some of the better academic thinking on conflict analysis, and to present it in a useful and practical manner.

As soon as one analyses anything, one simplifies. This is an occupational hazard and necessary element of the analytic process. As long as one recognizes the limitations this implies, then analysis can still be a very useful tool for gaining perspective, for organizing information, for reaching a coherent understanding of the conflict. Simplicity is sometimes a strength, even with the most complex subject matter.

What is offered here are a few simple analytic tools – sometimes called models or theories by their originators. But they are not panaceas: if a model seems inappropriate to the subject matter, one should know when to drop it in favour of another. Again, no one model will explain everything; one chooses models as they work and replaces them when they don't.

Moreover, conflict has a constantly shifting dynamic. Many of the factors outlined in the previous section may change in themselves and alter in their relative importance over time; wholly new factors may arrive and previously important factors disappear. So the analysis process is never completely over. There is a need to go back to it and reassess it regularly. Likewise, the analysis must be projected into the future, to see which current factors will persist, and which will shift with time, over the short, medium and long term.

2.8.1 The conflict triangle

One of the simplest ways to look at conflict is to imagine it as a triangle, with three points:

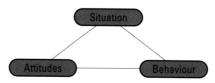

It thus has three elements, any one of which can generate conflict:

Situation. The situation refers to the objective positions that can cause conflict. For instance, if political power resides in the

One of the simplest ways to look at a conflict is to imagine it as a triangle with three points – situation, attitudes and behaviour – any one of which can generate conflict.

hands of one section of a population, to the exclusion of the other; or if one group has exclusive access to all the natural resources in an area; or if a country is partitioned in such a way as to privilege one group over another. Eventually, the groups involved find that the situation has brought them into conflict.

Behaviour. Behaviour relates to the actions of people. One group acts in an aggressive manner towards another: killing their members, or oppressing them, or discriminating against them. Perhaps the second group retaliates. Eventually the behaviours of both spiral into war. Thus the behaviour of those involved, action and reaction alike, generates a context of conflict.

Attitudes. Here, we speak of the attitudes and perceptions of groups, particularly their images of, and attitudes towards, each other. A belief that another group is less valuable than our group, or that they are plotting our destruction, or that their own beliefs offend our moral code, or that they generally are a danger to us, will generate conflict between them and us.

These three elements, then, can each be the root of conflict: the situation people find themselves in, the behaviour they demonstrate, or the beliefs and perceptions they hold about each other. Conflict can begin at any of these points on the triangle. Once conflict begins from one point, however, it quickly spreads to the others. Indeed the three points become mutually reinforcing elements in the conflict. We can then more accurately portray them as interconnected, and reinforcing in both directions:

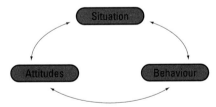

Wherever the conflict originates in the triangle, it begins to circulate in both directions. Aggressive behaviour will reinforce negative attitudes; negative attitudes will make the situation worse; a worsened situation will stimulate more defensive or aggressive behaviour. And likewise, aggressive behaviour will make the situation worse, a worsened situation will reinforce negative attitudes, and negative attitudes will be expressed in more aggressive behaviour. (Despite the danger of overloading such a basic concept as our triangle, this model can then be reversed to show that a reduction in aggressive behaviour, or an easing of negative attitudes, or an improvement in the material situation will logically lead to a reduction in tension and conflict.)

This is a very simple tool. Its purpose is less to do with tracing the origins of a conflict – in prolonged conflict, the cyclical interaction around the triangle in both directions may very quickly muddy any possibility of pinning down a single source. More pertinent is the simple lesson that these three elements add together to form conflict, and that their interaction and interdependence fuel the dynamic of its growth and intensity. Using the triangle as a basic framework may help to separate the complex elements of conflict and to see a little more clearly where the pieces fit.

2.8.2 Stages of escalation

Conflicts tend to escalate and de-escalate over time, bursting out into violence, retreating into latent periods, and so on. It is a vital piece of information, in analysing a conflict, to know where in the escalatory spiral the conflict currently stands, and in which direction it may be heading. Another tool offers a way of doing this. This model says that there are four basic stages that a conflict moves between, listed in rising order of escalation: Discussion, Polarization, Segregation and Destruction.

Discussion stage. Parties are disagreeing, but still close enough to work together. Communication hopefully consists of direct debate and discussion between parties. Mutual perceptions are both accurate and reasonably benign. The relationship is one with a modicum of trust and respect. The issues being emphasized in the dispute are substantive, objective ones. The possible outcome is assumed to be one that can please both sides: a win-win solution. The preferred method for managing the conflict is through co-operation to reach a joint solution. For instance, Canadian-Quebecois tensions over linguistic and cultural rights are deep, abiding and complex. But, by and large, the argument is waged within the parameters of low-escalation discussion.

Polarization stage. The parties have started to put distance between them, to withdraw and turn away from each other. Because of that distance, communication is now more indirect and reliant on interpretation (or, increasingly, misinterpretation). Mutual perceptions of each other are hardening into rigid stereotypes, especially since these are no longer challenged by the evidence of direct interaction with each other. The relationship has deteriorated from one of respect to a cooler one where each sees the other as still important but increasingly unreliable. The

2.8 Analytic Lenses

emphasized issues have moved away from the objective elements to the more psychological concerns about the relationship. The possible outcome is no longer one where everyone wins, but one where each must compromise to win some things and lose others. The preferred method of managing the conflict has moved from co-operative decision-making to competitive negotiation. The Soviet-US relationship during periods of Cold War detente fits the polarization stage fairly closely.

Segregation stage. The parties have moved away completely from each other. Communication is now restricted to the issuing of threats. Mutual perceptions have hardened into a picture of us-as-good and them-as-evil. The relationship is now one of mistrust and disrespect. The issues now being emphasized in the dispute are the core needs and values of each group: thus the stakes have been rapidly raised in this stage. The outcome is now perceived as a zero-sum calculation: a simple win-or-lose situation. And the preferred means of managing the situation has become one of defensive competition, where each protects its own interests above all, while trying to outwit or outsmart the other side. To a degree, the tense stand-off in early 1998 between Iraq and the US over UN weapons inspections reflected an instance of escalation up to the polarization stage, but one which then de-escalated without tipping over into the outright violence of destruction.

Destruction stage. This is one of all-out antagonism. Communication now merely consists of direct violence or complete silence. In order to justify violence, perceptions of the other side have become abusive descriptions of them as non-human, psychopaths, and so on. The relationship is seen as being in a completely hopeless state. The only issue being emphasized now is the ultimate survival of one's own side in the face of the other's aggression. Perceived possible outcomes now are all lose-lose: the situation is so bad that both sides will bear a heavy cost. The chosen method of managing the conflict at this stage is simply that of trying to destroy the opposition: we are in a state of war. the world sadly abounds with examples of conflicts manifestly in the destruction phase.

2.9 Conclusion

Conflict analysis is not easy. At the very beginning of it, adopting the integrative analytic approach is itself a challenge. It is a difficult process, requiring time and effort to unpack the complexities and multiplicities of this kind of conflict. Indeed, it can seem extremely daunting. But it must be borne in mind that, more often than not, what we are in fact looking at is complexity rather than impossibility.

Analysis is complete when we have become aware of all the elements and factors – the actors, the issues, the relationships, and so on – which will need to be taken into account in order to develop a process for managing the conflict peacefully.

Analysis is complete when we have become aware of all the elements and factors – the actors, the issues, the relationships, and so on – which will need to be taken into account in order to develop a process for managing the conflict peacefully. From the analysis, in other words, we can then move to a consideration of all the ingredients which must be part of (a) a workable process for reaching agreement among all those involved, and (b) a viable outcome which covers all the elements, needs and interests identified. We move on now to the first of these – process design – in the next chapter.

REFERENCES AND FURTHER READING

Azar, Edward E. 1991. "The Analysis and Management of Protracted Conflict". In V. Volkan, J. Montville and D. Julius. eds. *The Psychodynamics of International Relationships. Volume 2: Unofficial Diplomacy at Work.* Lexington, MA: Lexington.

Bloomfield, David. 1996. *Peacemaking Strategies in Northern Ireland: Building Complementarity in Conflict Management.* London: Macmillan.

Deutsch, Morton. 1991. "Subjective Features of Conflict Resolution: Psychological, Social and Cultural Features". In Raimo Vayrynen. ed. *New Directions in Conflict Theory – Conflict Resolution and Conflict Transformation.* London: Sage/ISSC.

Mitchell, Christopher. 1981. *The Structure of International Conflict.* London: Macmillan.

Rothman, Jay. 1991. "Conflict Research and Resolution: Cyprus", *Annals of the American Academy of Political and Social Science*, vol. 518. pp. 95–108.

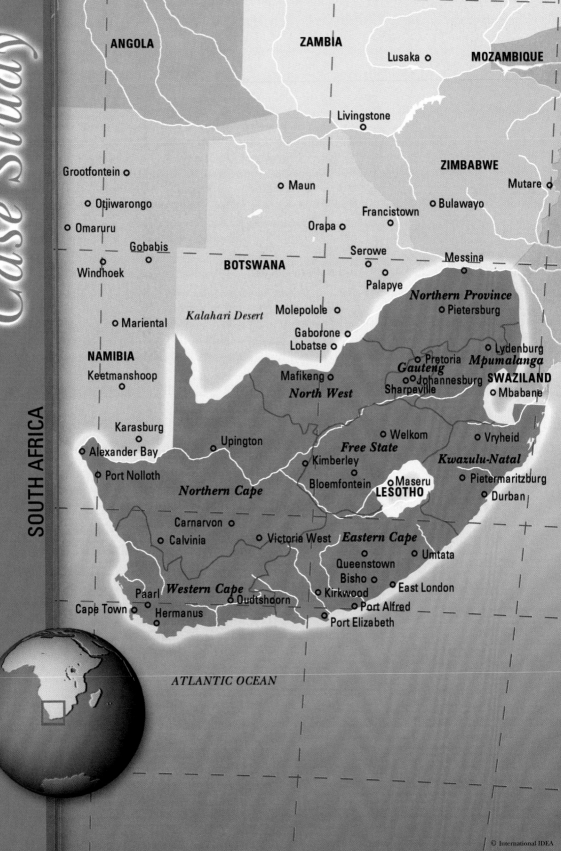

SOUTH AFRICA

ANGOLA

ZAMBIA

Lusaka ○

MOZAMBIQUE

Livingstone

Grootfontein ○

ZIMBABWE

Mutare ○

○ Maun

Bulawayo

Otjiwarongo ○

Francistown

○ Omaruru

Orapa ○

Gobabis

Serowe ○

Messina ○

BOTSWANA

Windhoek

Kalahari Desert

Northern Province

Molepolole ○

Palapye ○

Pietersburg ○

○ Mariental

Gaborone ○

Lobatse ○

Lydenburg ○

NAMIBIA

Pretoria ○

Mpumalanga

Gauteng

Keetmanshoop

Mafikeng ○

Johannesburg

SWAZILAND

North West

Sharpeville

○ Mbabane

Karasburg ○

○ Welkom

Vryheid ○

Upington ○

Free State

Alexander Bay ○

Kimberley ○

Kwazulu-Natal

○ Port Nolloth

Northern Cape

Bloemfontein ○

Maseru ○

Pietermaritzburg ○

LESOTHO

○ Durban

Carnarvon ○

Eastern Cape

Calvinia ○

Victoria West ○

Umtata ○

Queenstown ○

Bisho ○

Paarl ○

Western Cape

Kirkwood ○

East London ○

Cape Town ○

Oudtshoorn ○

Port Alfred ○

Hermanus ○

Port Elizabeth ○

ATLANTIC OCEAN

© International IDEA

Mark Anstey

Case Study: South Africa

SOUTH AFRICA

Introduction

Conflict was evidenced early in South Africa's recorded history, both between and within racial groupings. Migrations by black and white groupings took place under Zulu and British expansionism, and black tribes engaged in a series of skirmishes and battles with Boers (Afrikaners) and British settlers throughout the 1800s. Tensions between the British and the Boers culminated in The Boer War (1899–1902). The discovery of diamonds (1867) and gold (1886) opened the economy and added to the competition over resources and power.

In 1910, the Boer republics (Transvaal and Orange Free State) and the British colonies (Natal and the Cape) were unified, a tenuous white unity achieved at the expense of black suffrage. The exclusion of blacks however sparked the formation of the African National Congress (ANC) in 1912, and the beginnings of a long struggle for political participation.

During the 1930s several investigative commissions questioned the sustainability of economic growth in a system founded on racial discrimination. A degree of liberalization resulted in relaxation of the pass laws, an erosion of the job colour bar, moves towards a closure in the racial wage gap, and some extensions of labour rights. But this stalled after 1945. The National Party (NP), elected in 1948 on a wave of Afrikaner nationalism, enforced a hardline policy of formal racial separatism: *apartheid*. African, Asian and coloured resistance strengthened. In 1957, Africanists opposed to non-racialism split from the ANC to establish the Pan Africanist Congress (PAC), pursuing a more militant line of resistance. The shooting of pass-law demonstrators in Sharpeville by police sparked strikes and riots nationally, an international outcry and a flight of capital from the country. The government hardened its stance, banning the ANC and the PAC, which went underground and shifted their strategies from passive resistance to violence against the state.

But social and economic realities eroded the apartheid dream. Rapid economic growth during the 1960s produced a shortage of workers and demanded more rather than fewer black urban dwellers. Manufacturing required a literate, technically capable workforce. Economic development requirements ran counter to population, labour and education policies. Economic growth stalled as security and military expenditure rose sharply during the 1970s to cope with internal unrest, increasingly costly border protections, and investment in the Angolan conflict.

Heavy-handed and violent repression of demonstrations sparked widespread unrest and resistance which escalated through the late 1970s. On 12 September 1977, Steve Biko, the Black Consciousness leader, was assaulted and died violently in police detention. By the mid-1980s a massive groundswell of resistance was in evidence, led by student and worker activists. South Africa's isolation increased across

South Africa

a broad front of sporting, economic and cultural activities. Multinational companies started to repatriate earnings rather than reinvest and major capital flight became evident.

In the face of internal and international pressure, the government embarked on a confused route of repression and reform, coercion and liberalization. A fast-growing and increasingly militant labour movement escalated strike action. Guerrilla attacks and consumer, rent and school boycotts proliferated. A government initiative to introduce a tricameral parliamentary system excluding blacks but incorporating Asian and coloured populations was rejected with massive demonstrations, but nonetheless forced through by the government.

The Conflict Management Process

High levels of militance both energize progress in political transition and put it at risk. Not uncommonly, countries in transition utilize short-term pacting arrangements at military, political, and social-economic levels to stabilize the change process even as they struggle over its final outcome. In effect, pacts represent mutual guarantees on the part of powerholders to temporarily restrain their capacity for inflicting damage on each other in their own and others interests, and to foster progress in the transition. They represent the moment of interaction at which all major stakeholders realize that they are at risk – there is no returning to the previous system and power needs to be carefully used in order to secure their future. Neither retreat nor outright confrontation is feasible for either party.

The South African case reflects such a *"pact-building process"* – firstly it to open the door to negotiations, and then it to manage the negotiation process itself. This produced a network of stabilizing forums and institutions through which negotiations could occur and conflict could be better regulated. These arrangements were fragile. Progress was continually threatened by suspicions of treachery, by violence and by breakdowns in the negotiation process itself. When this occurred, the scale of violence, and the threat of chaos were such as to oblige parties back to the table.

President de Klerk's opening speech to parliament in February 1990 opened the door to a complex transition process in which stakeholders had to convince themselves and each other of their shared commitment to a jointly negotiated future. De Klerk removed bans on political parties, and signaled new freedoms in political activity. The leader of the ANC, Nelson Mandela, was released from prison, immediately making statements to reassure and cohere his constituency.

Key leadership figures of the ANC were flown into the country to work in a joint committee with government representatives on an indemnity arrangement, but deep suspicions continued to shroud dealings. The ANC group feared that it was being "tricked" into the country under false pretences and would be arrested; the government team feared that amnesty arrangements would be used as a smoke-screen to cover ongoing infiltration and a major revolutionary onslaught. Both sides

South Africa

Case Study: South Africa

hedged and kept contingency plans in place.

Nevertheless the process was sustained and a three-day meeting ended in the Groote Schuur Minute, which facilitated the release of political prisoners and the return of exiles, and amended security legislation. This was followed by the Pretoria Minute in which Mandela announced the suspension of the armed struggle. Conservative elements on both sides feared that too much had been conceded. Previously banned liberation groups had the problem of transforming themselves into legal actors in a country still under the control of the Nationalist Party Government. The government faced problems in moving from an approach of vilifying the ANC as "communist terrorists", to one which acknowledged it and other political groupings as legitimate political players. Partly to contain these problems, the ANC and the NP entered a deal – the DF Malan Accord in February 1991 – in which the government accepted that Umkhonto We Sizwe, the armed wing of the ANC during the struggle, would not be disbanded before transition to a democratic government.

The government wanted a new constitution to be negotiated by a convention comprising all political groupings. The ANC held that it should be carried out by "legitimate representatives" of all the people. The NP recognized that in the ANC scenario it would be reduced to the part of small player. The ANC recognized that in the NP scenario it would be participating with players whose constituencies were either very small or nonexistent (as illegitimate products of the apartheid system) and its own influence would be reduced. This impasse was broken through a compromise in which the "either-or" scenario was transformed into an "order of events". An all-party convention would negotiate the route to a constituent assembly and an interim constitution, leading to the election of the assembly by universal franchise. The assembly would then negotiate the final constitution, but on the foundation of binding principles laid down in the interim constitution on the question of majorities required for decision-making purposes. The Convention for a Democratic South Africa (CODESA) convened late in 1991 to initiate discussions.

It was quickly recognized that building a viable democracy would require institutions and forums for consensus building at all levels within a fractured society. These assumed the major task of institutionalizing the transition, and of managing associated tensions in a manner which would support and indeed carry the political process. Their very existence was confirmation in many ways that change was irreversible. Management of the process was not simply in the hands of the regime. Steadily it moved into a period of joint control through peace accords, economic pacts, local government forums and a transitional executive council which laid the foundation for the advent of majority rule.

In 1992, after lengthy behind-the-scenes discussions and in the context of progress on the political front, the trade union movement entered the National Economic Forum (NEF) with the government of the day and business. Its purpose was to seek consensus over economic policy, especially during the transition period. In this

South Africa

forum, organized labour rather than political opposition groups held sway and sought to entrench their influence over economic and social policy-making. In making these moves the trade unions made the decision to retain an identity separate from that of government and to participate in the change process on its own terms, even as it supported opposition political parties. This strategic move laid the base for a later post-election social corporatism.

Pacting extended to areas of government as well. In 1992, representatives of central, provincial and local government established a Local Government Negotiating Forum to devise a viable and democratic future local government system. A National Education and Training Forum was founded to seek agreement on restructuring the education system to meet the country's development needs. All these forums embedded democratic values and processes of negotiation in the wider society and supported the unfolding political process.

Of central concern was the role and legitimacy of police and security forces. How could they be entrusted as custodians of transition to a new democracy – and what were the alternatives? Several important steps were taken to address this dilemma. A Police Board comprising representatives from political parties, civil society, government and the police was established in 1991 to review police policy and structure and recommend changes for a police service into the future. A National Peace Accord was achieved as a non-aggression pact between key stakeholders involved in the transition process. A detailed written agreement brokered by the churches, the Congress of South African Trade Unions (COSATU) and big business, the Accord sought primarily to end political violence in the country, making provision for codes of conduct for political parties and organizations, a code of conduct for police and the security forces, guidelines for the reconstruction and development of communities, and mechanisms to implement its provisions. It committed parties to a multiparty democracy and to respect for the fundamental rights and freedoms underpinning a democracy, and provided for a system of peace committees at all levels of society to monitor adherence to the Accord and resolve disputes using mediation and arbitration. The Police Board was entrenched as a measure of civilian control over policing activities.

The effectiveness of the Accord has been questioned. High levels of violence continued, particularly in Kwazulu-Natal and the East Rand. If the Accord failed to stop violence, it at least reduced it, and certainly through its conflict resolution mechanisms in the regions, it saved many lives. It contributed to the building of grass-roots peace structures, brought hope and participation in the transition process to many people otherwise alienated from the larger political exchange, and defused many volatile, and potentially fatal, political confrontations. Most importantly however, it represented a joint commitment on the part of all the stakeholders to values and standards which were difficult to walk away from or openly reject.

South Africa

The Political Negotiation Process

CODESA's beginnings were unsteady. The Inkatha Freedom Party (IFP) leader Chief Buthelezi personally boycotted the process. De Klerk and Mandela opened with a heated exchange, accusing each other of bad faith. And so it continued. The ANC wanted a short "phase one" leading to elections and democratic government. The NP, recognizing that its major influence lay in the front rather than the back end of negotiations, wanted a more detailed and protracted process. Increasingly, opposition groups suspected the NP of deliberate stalling tactics, and uneasiness developed as to whether the process was in fact irreversible. De Klerk called a referendum amongst whites in March 1992, and achieved a resounding two-thirds majority for continuing negotiations. But when he returned to the bargaining table, it was with a tougher, rather than a softer line.

Negotiations bogged down on the issue of which matters were "basic principles" to be enshrined as constraints in the final constitution. The NP in effect wanted as much binding agreement as possible up front. The ANC wanted as much latitude as possible retained for a later, more "legitimate" process following elections. The major deadlock was over percentages required for a majority to change the constitution. The ANC demanded two thirds as the international norm; the NP wanted 75 percent. Deadlock continued, and in June 1992, in the township of Boipatong, armed IFP supporters massacred 38 people in their homes. Serious allegations were made that security forces had assisted in the massacre, and there were signs of a police cover-up. De Klerk's visit to the township to placate residents deteriorated into violence, further angering the populace and pushing the ANC to a more militant public position. CODESA collapsed with the ANC withdrawing from the process.

Following the breakdown of CODESA, the ANC, responding to a rising level of grass-roots militance, embarked on a campaign of mass action. Tensions between the IFP and the ANC sparked massive violence in Kwazulu-Natal and the East Rand. Police and security forces were accused of either assisting IFP forces or simply standing by. ANC suspicions of a "third force" were voiced, reflecting a strong view that there were deliberate efforts to sabotage the negotiation process and the ANC's mobilization campaign.

The ANC responded with a formalized "rolling mass action" campaign of strikes, stayaways and boycotts. They turned their attention to the homelands and on 7 March organized a march on Bisho, the Ciskei capital. Ciskei troops opened fire, killing 28 people.

Tragically it was the rise in political deaths, culminating in the Bisho killings, which sobered relations, facilitating the return to prominence of softliners and a reconvening of talks. It obliged the leadership on all sides to face the realities of fail-

South Africa

ing to achieve a political accord. Mandela and de Klerk reduced preconditions for a resumption of negotiations, and talks restarted.

The political violence continued right up to the election period, with the white right playing an increasing role as it sensed the negotiations moving to a close. The threat of rightwing action was ever-present in the process, given the unresolved question of who was really in charge of the country at the time – the government was in place but a Transitional Executive Council (TEC) had established mechanisms to ensure that in effect it governed by consent in the lead-up to elections.

The peace process was conceived in two phases – an interim constitution leading into elections, after which a final constitution would be negotiated. The *interim constitution* provided the foundations for a constitutional democracy, guaranteeing universal suffrage and fundamental democratic rights to be guarded by a constitutional court. The final constitution was to be approved by the *Constitutional Assembly* (national assembly and the senate), and checked by the constitutional court against constitutional principles before being adopted.

The interim constitution provided wide-ranging protection of human and civil rights. It provided for a parliament comprising a *National Assembly*, with 400 members elected by proportional representation; a *Senate* comprising 10 senators for each of nine provinces, also elected by proportional representation, and a *National Executive* headed by a president elected by a majority in the national assembly. The president could appoint two deputies and a cabinet. All parties achieving more than a five per cent vote had a right to be part of the cabinet, and cabinet posts were allocated in proportion to national assembly seats.

Provincial governments were to have their own legislatures elected on the basis of proportional representation, making decisions by simple majority vote. They could pass laws for their provinces, but they could not exceed powers granted by the constitution. Should national and provincial laws clash, the provincial one was to prevail. *Local governments* were to be autonomous according to conferred powers. A *Council of Traditional Leaders* at national level, and *Houses of Traditional Leaders* at provincial level, would advise parliament on traditional and customary law. By agreement the interim constitution was to come into effect on the day of the elections of the national and provincial parliaments.

Founding Elections

During the transition process, the existing government remained in office but acted in consultation with the Transitional Executive Council (TEC) drawn from the parties involved in the negotiating process. An *Independent Electoral Commission* (IEC) was appointed to conduct the country's first democratic elections in April 1994. Its first meeting was held on 20 December 1993 and the actual work of setting up systems of delivery at grass-roots level was only started two months before the elections. Constraints included not only an unreasonably short timeframe, and the

Case Study: South Africa

absence of a voters roll, but the absence of infrastructure in large areas of the country, a lack of trained personnel, few existing administrative structures, and inadequate demographic data. Over the four days of the April 1994 elections, 8,493 ordinary voting stations supplemented with 950 mobile, 1,047 special, and 187 foreign voting stations were in operation in South Africa, and in 78 other countries. A third of the voting stations had no electricity or regular telephone service. It was a difficult process with shortages of materials, logistical problems, sabotage of the counting process, and systems failures. The IEC were acutely aware that failure to deliver a free and fair election might lose South Africa's democracy at the very moment of its delivery. Efficient and credible internal and external (United Nations, European Union, etc.) monitoring was important, as was the creative capacity of the IEC to respond to last minute crises in administration and counting processes.

Consolidating Democracy

South Africa has taken important steps to embed its democracy in political and civil life. A final constitution confirming the spirit of the interim constitution has been negotiated. A number of state institutions exist to strengthen and protect the new democracy, including: a Public Protector; a Human Rights Commission; a Commission to Promote and Protect Rights of Cultural, Religious and Linguistic Communities; a Commission for Gender Equality; an Auditor General; and an Electoral Commission. The public service is being transformed to more fully represent and serve the country's population; new labour legislation adhering to international standards has been introduced and a National Economic, Development and Labour Council has been established to seek consensus on social and economic policy.

An important initiative has been the Truth and Reconciliation Commission (TRC). The TRC offered a means of surfacing the atrocities of the apartheid system in a manner directed at reconciling a deeply divided nation rather than simply exacting revenge or seeking retribution. It has given people at all levels and on all sides the opportunity to declare their part in the conflict, to shed light on disappearances, murders, tortures and lesser human rights transgressions, and importantly to express regret and seek forgiveness and amnesty.

Lessons for Managing Transitions to Democracy

Building and sustaining a democracy in the context of deep-rooted conflict with limited violence is a tough task. The South African experience described here offers some lessons including the importance of:

– A precipitating crisis in the authoritarian system (internal and external pressures);

– A recognition of power realities by leadership (joint acknowledgement that negotiated change offers the best option to all parties);

– An extensive period of pre-negotiation;

– A significant gesture on the part of the government to break the deadlock of

South Africa

preconditions (the extension of meaningful political freedoms/suspension of armed struggle);

- Integrity of leadership and willingness to take risks for peaceful over violent change;

- Reframing deadlocks into common problems (e.g., changing "either-or" into sequence options);

- Pacting on multiple fronts to stabilize the change process and manage conflict relations;

- Embedding democratic participation (civil society participation beyond the political elites);

- The negotiation of a constitution which provides sufficient security for a governing regime to cede power through elections;

- Properly resourced electoral processes;

- Effective institutions for consolidating a new democracy and reconciling interests, moving from a past of deep and often violent division.

Although the tendency is to dissect constitutions and bargaining structures for lessons in managing transitions to democracy, perhaps the really important lessons lie less in these areas of analysis, and more in the attitudinal elements of key stakeholders, the quality of leadership and the skills they reveal in managing processes of negotiation and problem-solving both with adversaries and within constituencies. South Africa was indeed fortunate in these areas. The protracted process which facilitated the development of trade unions, the emergence of struggle structures and leaders with developed bargaining skills before political change was entertained may not have motivated early reform initiatives but, in the end, served the country well in the search for a viable democracy.

South Africa

CHAPTER

3

If a process is designed
that is not appropriate to
the context, then it is
defeated before it begins.

Our focus now turns to process — the question of designing best how to reach a settlement. What is offered in this chapter is a range of negotiation techniques and procedures which can be selected, rejected or adapted depending upon what contending parties regard as most helpful in advancing the management of their conflict.

David Bloomfield,
Charles Nupen and
Peter Harris

Negotiation Processes

3.1 Introduction

C onflicts differ so markedly in history and context, issue
and character, intensity and outcome, that processes to
address them must be responsive to each circumstance. If
a process is designed that is not appropriate to the context, then
it is defeated before it begins. This assertion comes from a recognition of the uniqueness of each situation, which should save us
from universal prescriptions. But the process of comparison can
still be invaluable. The fact that an approach works in, say,
Eritrea is no guarantee that it would be in any way effective in
Palestine or Fiji. But certainly at a more specific level we might
well look at the elements of a cease-fire in Chechnya for clues as
to how to achieve a cease-fire in the Philippines. For all their differences, there are also common or comparable elements: regional armed insurrection against a central government, claims for
self-determination, deep-rooted identity issues intertwined with
perceptions of social and economic discrimination, a recent end
to authoritarian structures of government, and so on. So while
respecting the uniqueness of a particular conflict, we can still
learn important lessons from other situations. Even developing
an answer to the question, "Why *wouldn't* that work here?" en-
genders an analysis of the situation that promotes definition of
what could succeed.

3.2 Key Issues in Process Design

3.2.1 Commonly perceived deadlock

Conflicting parties come to the table only when they perceive
it – willingly or grudgingly – to be in their interests. A confluence of factors must be operating to make this so. In particular,
negotiation only tends to come about when there is a mutually
perceived notion of deadlock. This is often referred to as a
"hurting stalemate". In many cases, only when the conviction
grows on both sides that neither will win outright and that to
continue with violent means will be costly without achieving victory, does the option of negotiation gain attraction. This does
not require that the two sides be evenly matched in their military
power and resources. That is rarely the case in internal conflict.
All it requires is that the weaker can at least prevent the outright

victory of the stronger – this is the rule rather than the exception in most internal conflicts.

Various internal and external factors produced this kind of stalemate in South Africa. The rapprochement between the US and the Soviet Union, followed by the latter's eventual break-up, was highly significant. As the East-West dichotomy began to crumble, some of the traditional support bases for both sides were removed. The international imposition of punitive sanctions and "pariah status" was chipping away cumulatively at the economic viability and moral legitimacy of the South Africans State. Internally, the costs of sustaining apartheid and separate development were spiraling. Population shifts to urban centres made implementation and control more problematic than ever, while the development of the various homelands and assorted separate councils and assemblies produced a vast and hopelessly inefficient bureaucracy. Internal and external resistance to the state escalated and gained huge momentum through the 1980s, proving ever more difficult and expensive to repress.

An effective process is one that will prove itself resilient and durable in the face of delays, deadlocks, walkouts, raised hopes, false expectations and angry words.

Similarly, after 25 years of continuing violence in Northern Ireland, by the 1990s both the paramilitary forces of the Irish Republican Army (IRA) and the generals of the British Army realized that neither side was capable militarily of securing total victory. The best each could do was to prevent the other from winning. The choice then became one between continuing to fight without hope of victory and at continuing high cost in human and financial terms, or to look at other non-military options.

So together a range of factors acted in both South Africa and Northern Ireland to bring about perceptions on all sides both of the pain of continued stalemate and of the attraction of negotiation. The second does not, of course, follow automatically from the first. In Sudan, in terms of human lives and suffering, environmental degradation, internal and external economic burdens, and so on, the cost of remaining in an ongoing stalemate has been huge; and yet, in the words of one scholar, even though Sudan "is a nation at the brink of total collapse ... leaders themselves have apparently not felt the personal threat of imminent demise".

3.2.2 Seizing opportunities

Just the existence of stalemate, then, is not enough. It can produce a window of opportunity, a "ripe" moment for solution, but ripe moments must be recognized, seized and used. Negotiations do not simply emerge from the ashes of conflict. A commonly perceived notion of deadlock leaves contending parties with a perspective that they cannot win by war, but not necessarily with incentives to search for peace. So acknowledging stale-

3.2 Key Issues in Process Design

mate is one thing. But other factors must act on the parties to move them towards negotiation. Stalemate is usually experienced as a sterile situation, which, by definition, precludes any opportunities for change or progress. But almost paradoxically, stalemate can be precisely the beginning of opportunity. That depends on the confluence of factors operating that will make negotiation viable. These factors can come from any aspect of the process, internal or external.

In Mozambique, the intervention of the Roman Catholic church, using the organization Sant'Egidio, via pastoral letters, its own contacts, and its active encouragement and persuasion of the actors, led to its success in facilitating talks involving FRELIMO and RENAMO in Rome between 1990 and 1992. In the Angolan context, the Bicesse accords of 1991 grew directly out of a major shift in superpower perspective which led to Soviet pressure on the MPLA, and US (and South African) pressure on UNITA to go to the table. In South Africa in 1990, President de Klerk abruptly announced the release of political prisoners and the unbanning of the ANC and other outlawed parties. Similarly, Anwar Sadat's famous "flight to Jerusalem" in 1977 stunned the world by breaking the universal Arab taboo on Israeli recognition: he flew to Jerusalem and addressed the Israeli parliament. So much was implicit in the gesture – putting a huge crack in the universal Arab rejection of Israel's right to exist, putting an equally heavy burden of reciprocation on Israel, and so on – that, like de Klerk's speech, new possibilities and parameters for movement were developed out of long-standing stalemate.

So, while stalemate often comes about because of the absence of change, negotiation becomes an attractive proposition precisely because of changes in context – a new government or leader, a shift in support for one side or the other, a unilateral "circuit-breaking" initiative, and so on. Such a turning point in perceptions is required to transform a stalemate into a search for alternatives. There has to be a perception, originally conceived or induced, of the distinct possibility of a negotiated solution.

It is therefore important that an ongoing conflict be constantly evaluated and assessed to ensure "windows of opportunity" are not lost. Generally, such opportunities are rare and should be seized. The parties themselves, because of their proximity to the conflict, may not see such openings, and it may therefore require a third party to take the initiative.

3.2.3 The importance of trust

Negotiations tend to focus on issues, but their success depends on people. So good process also seeks to enhance the relationship between the conflicting parties. This is not a matter of asking enemies to become friends. But there must be a functional working relationship between the parties so that, minimally, they can negotiate with a degree of good faith. To reach that minimal working level of respect is often an incremental process between old enemies. During violent struggle, demonization of the enemy is a standard tactic: visions of the other side as "psychopaths", "terrorists" and "evil empires" help to legitimize the use of violence against them. But such visions must be dismantled in order to hold dialogue. Perceptions must be changed. Small concessions, often with low intrinsic value in themselves, can serve as tokens to demonstrate both one's commitment to the process and one's inclination and ability to deliver on one's promises. When that is done reciprocally, both sides can be seen to be mutually as good as their word. The role of accurate information and the manner of its presentation to the parties can greatly assist the breaking down of incorrect perceptions.

In other words, good process moves the parties beyond an exclusive focus on the competition of bargaining to include a degree of co-operation: without co-operation, there will be no satisfactory outcome. Negotiation, in itself, implies movement and should be a problem-solving process. Participants must, to some degree, co-operate to find a solution to their problem.

The classic example of such a working relationship was that which grew between the chief South African negotiators, Roelf Meyer for the National Party and Cyril Ramaphosa for the ANC. Such was the substance of their relationship that it arguably salvaged the peace process in its darkest days. In the midst of negotiations, a serious outbreak of violence at Boipatong in June 1992 led the ANC to break off all contact with the government. For almost 18 months thereafter, the "Roelf and Cyril show' remained the only open channel of communication between the sides. Meyer himself reflects on this point:

Negotiators need to develop a common understanding of each other's positions. In the case of Cyril and myself, that common understanding led to friendship. But what is very important in this process of coming to understand each other is that you have to put yourself in the shoes of the person on the other side ... The personal chemistry between negotiators is ... a very important ingredient of successful negotiations.

3.2 Key Issues in Process Design

In deep-rooted conflict, parties who come to the negotiating table carry with them an abiding experience of conflict, struggle and war. The exercise of force has been their dominant, perhaps only, mode of engagement. The key challenge in process design is to invert that experience, to get the contenders focused on fears, concerns and interests and the importance of reconciling them, on issues and the importance of resolving them. An effective process is one that will prove itself resilient and durable in the face of delays, deadlocks, walkouts, continuing violence, raised hopes, false expectations and angry words.

3.2.4 Flexibility

Negotiation is a creative process, a precarious journey of discovery. This means that the final outcome cannot always be foreseen at the beginning of the process. Clearly, the parties will have their own views on what they want to achieve, their own "models" of desirable settlements, but only those in a privileged or extremely powerful position will be able to define their objectives and get one hundred per cent of what they want. This is a daunting prospect for a negotiator or process designer. Consequently, while the parameters for the process need careful design and agreement (and will be examined in this chapter) the process needs to be flexible enough to cope with the unforeseen. A naturally protective mind-set at the start of negotiations means that negotiators often look to establish *preconditions for dialogue* – but too many preconditions make the process brittle and can inhibit or even throttle it at birth. Preconditions have a habit of turning around to bite their promoters. In some cases, negotiators have had to go back to their constituencies and attempt to persuade them that the conditions that they were so firm and voluble on were now not so important after all. If the negotiations really move into new territory, then pre-conditions, which made sense at the start, may become irrelevant or worse.

During the talks process, goals and targets can change, and the basic parameters and ground-rules of the process may need to be adapted. Over several years, for example, Sinhalese-Tamil dialogue in Sri Lanka shifted, according to what was possible, acceptable or appropriate, from bilateral negotiations through third-party mediation and an all-party conference, to informal and private engagements and subsequently to formal talks brokered by India. Needs will change, and so must process. Flexibility in process design does not mean lack of resilience or even a lack of guiding principles. But it does require that parties consciously avoid painting themselves into corners, or leaving themselves no alternative to breaking off dialogue. By taking a wider view of the whole peace process, what looks like the end of talks can often prove to be a catalyst that reinforces efforts to get negotiations back on track. Then we may be able to recognize what has been called a step-break-gesture-step pattern. Conflicting parties enter negotiations and take a step towards progress; then the negotiations are broken off over some disagreement; later, outside the talks process, some gesture is made that facilitates a resumption of talks and a further step of progress at the table, before another break occurs, and so on. While not easy to achieve, the greater the flexibility in the design, the greater the chances of progress.

Box 3	**KEY ELEMENTS IN DESIGNING A NEGOTIATION PROCESS**

1. **Commonly Perceived Deadlock**. Negotiation tends to come about when there is a mutually perceived notion of deadlock, often referred to as a "hurting stalemate".

2. **Seizing "Windows of Opportunity"**. But the existence of stalemate is not enough. It can produce a "ripe" moment for solution, but ripe moments must be recognized, seized and used. An ongoing conflict must be constantly evaluated and assessed to ensure "windows of opportunity" are not lost.

3. **Importance of Trust**. Enemies do not need to become friends. But negotiation does demand a minimum of co-operative effort.

4. **Flexibility**. The process of negotiation needs to remain flexible. Too many preconditions can become obstacles to dialogue.

3.3 Pre-Negotiation

Pre-negotiation is, in the Irish phrase, "talks about talks". It is concerned with setting up the framework within which issues can subsequently be discussed, not with the issues themselves. In this handbook's terms, pre-negotiation does not address the design of an outcome – that will wait until the forthcoming talks actually begin – but focuses on process. It is, in effect, *negotiation*

3.3 Pre-Negotiation

over process. Its subject matter will concern procedures, structures, roles, and agendas. One aim of pre-negotiation is to reach a joint definition of the problems and subject matter that will have to be addressed – but it does not tackle those issues beyond defining them for future reference. It can be carried out by very small delegations (or even individual representatives) either talking face-to-face or through a third party.

The importance of pre-negotiation cannot be overstated. Bad process will almost definitely lead to failure: what may seem dry and technical procedural questions need to be resolved prior to talks, otherwise they can become hugely significant or symbolic issues which may abruptly derail the process. In the handbook's terms, good process facilitates good outcome; in practical terms, good procedural pre-negotiation facilitates good substantive negotiation. Additionally, an effective pre-negotiation phase helps to develop the vital working relationship discussed earlier. Especially if it is held out of the glare of publicity, quiet pre-negotiation offers an all-important opportunity to develop the habit of dialogue between opponents while no substantive issue is at stake.

Pre-negotiation is, of course, less neatly distinct in the real world than in this analytic presentation. Pre-negotiation can shade into negotiation if it goes extremely well, or substantive negotiation may need to recede back to procedural pre-negotiation temporarily. Like the entire dialogue process, it can arise through a voluntary desire among conflicting parties, or it can be imposed from outside by a powerful third party who enters the conflict and sets the terms for engagement.

Pre-negotiation can take place even if there is no intention to move on to full negotiations. Perhaps the sides are still too far apart for proper negotiation. Nonetheless initial contacts, aimed at simply increasing mutual understanding of the issues that divide through joint definition of the problem, can establish progress that may make negotiation more feasible at some future stage, or even bring the possibility of direct talks closer to reality. The Norwegian back-channel negotiations to broker the 1993 Middle East peace accord is an example. Initiated by a Norwegian diplomat, this involved highly confidential meetings in the diplomat's private house in Norway between a high-ranking PLO member and an Israeli adviser. The two protagonists acted in completely unofficial capacities. Their conversations focused

Pre-negotiation is concerned with setting up the framework – the procedures, structures, roles and agendas – within which issues can be discussed. Its importance cannot be overstated.

on exploring mutual definitions of their problem, and then examining the obstacles to settlement and the possibilities for overcoming such obstacles. Such matters were in reality the ingredients of the pre-negotiation process of defining the agenda. The talks were exploratory, unofficial, deniable, without formal sanction, and included no expectation or commitment that they should lead further. However, when this pre-negotiation took on its own momentum (not least because of the developing trust between the two interlocutors), it made sense to feed it back in to their respective formal structures: the PLO and the Israeli government. In the end, the dialogue led to full-blown negotiation within the official peace process. The point is that the small, private, exploratory pre-negotiation initiative had no conscious goal of a peace agreement at the time.

In a more formal example of pre-negotiation, the agenda for talks in South Africa was effectively outlined in preparatory form in three important statements that, to a large degree, outlined the agenda and the process for discussion. As one participant noted:

> *A common perception of deadlock seems to be critical, and the first phase of negotiation [i.e., pre-negotiation] seems to be taken up in exploring this deadlock and developing a common mental map. In the South African case the Groote Schuur Minute, the Pretoria Minute and the Record of Understanding were key moments when the major parties to the conflict spelt out their common perception of deadlock, and how to proceed away from it.*

3.3.1 The pre-negotiation agenda

Developing a "common mental map", and then devising the means to travel is the business of pre-negotiation. Putting the design of the negotiations together requires careful consideration and planning. The resulting process should be accepted by all parties as legitimate.

3.4 Developing a Specific Negotiation Process

Box 4

MAJOR ELEMENTS FOR PRE-NEGOTIATION

The following list represents the major elements to be pre-negotiated, from the hugely complex to the apparently straightforward:

- agreeing on the basic rules and procedures;
- participation in the process, and methods of representation;
- dealing with preconditions for negotiation and barriers to dialogue;
- creating a level playing-field for the parties;
- resourcing the negotiations;
- the form of negotiations;
- venue and location;
- communication and information exchange;
- discussing and agreeing upon some broad principles with regard to outcomes;
- managing the proceedings;
- timeframes;
- decision-making procedures;
- process tools to facilitate negotiations and break deadlocks;
- the possible assistance of a third party.

We will examine each of these issues in turn, presenting a menu of options for developing a negotiation system. At all times bearing in mind the influence of context and its potential to inspire completely novel options, parties should be able to design a process which will prove both resilient and durable. They must also, of course, be aware of the possibility that there exists within their own culture indigenous dispute resolution mechanisms: these can be adopted or adapted to further strengthen the whole design.

3.4 Developing a Specific Negotiation Process

3.4.1 Participants

In Nelson Mandela's famous advice to Northern Irish politicians, "You don't make peace by talking to your friends; you have to make peace with your enemies". While it is tempting to exclude more extreme parties from the process, for fear of their disrupting or obstructing talks, the risk then increases that they will act as spoilers in undermining the agreement reached. Moderates will negotiate more easily, but what is implicit in Mandela's words is the need to deal directly with those who are causing trouble, rather than to exclude and subsequently try to marginalize them. This was one reason for the failure of Northern Irish negotiations in 1991 and 1992. While the moderates tried to negotiate agreement around the table, armed extremists on both sides were excluded. The surrounding atmosphere, heavy with the threat of paramilitary violence, undermined the significance and efficacy of the talks.

Reviewing negotiation processes between various permutations of the parties to the Lebanese conflict since the mid-1970s, two leading scholars make the point convincingly:

In terms of structure, the most important deal in the Lebanese conflict revolved around who was included in the negotiations and who was excluded or chose not to join ... [N]o solution to the conflict is likely to be successful if all the major parties to the conflict are not involved in the negotiations. Nor are substitutes likely to succeed ... because they do not have the real power to implement the agreements.

The need to be inclusive refers not only to differing parties, but also to different opinion strands *within* parties. Especially for outsiders, it is tempting to see the sides to a conflict as homogenous, monolithic blocs. This is rarely the case. There are usually a variety of constituencies within any one disputing party – political factions, old and young generations, gender groups, radicals, fundamentalists, peace-activists, business interests, military interests, and so on. Spoilers can come from within one's own broader community – whether they are more extreme or more moderate members than one's own faction – just as easily as from some totally excluded conflicting party.

Furthermore, those who carry out the negotiations must possess – and be seen by the opposition to have – adequate power and authority mandated to them from their own side. They need to be able to speak with authority, to offer deals with the capacity to deliver. To be, in short, the legitimate representatives to the talks. Often the most obviously powerful individuals for this role would seem to be the party/faction leaders themselves.

3.4 Developing a Specific Negotiation Process

However, their own public personas and positions may in fact constrain their capacity to talk flexibly: their role outside the talks requires an integrity of position that cannot appear negotiable for fear of appearing "weak". The judicious selection of negotiators who can bring to the table their leaders' authority while retaining their own capacity for flexibility is a vital ingredient.

It simultaneously makes life at the negotiating table more difficult, but increases the chances of producing a successful outcome, to include all those who can influence the process. But realistically, the minimum requirement is to include the mainstreams from all sides. Subsequently, those included either can strive to bring more of their excluded or unwilling strands into the process as talks gather momentum, or ultimately they can persuade, cajole or coerce their respective extremes into acceptance of the final outcome.

One element of inclusion is to forge *cross-party coalitions* among those in favour of the talks. Within any one camp in a conflict, there are likely to be differing opinions about the value of negotiation. To make the process work, it is important to build a coalition with all who support the *process*, however much they may still disagree about outcome. This applies not only within one's own party, and among one's allies, but – just as importantly – between opposing sides. Building momentum in favour of negotiation across the divide increases the possibility of effective outcomes, and feeds into the process of building trust and a good working relationship between opponents.

"You don't make peace by talking to your friends; you have to make peace with your enemies."

Nelson Mandela

All those parties with a genuine stake in the conflict have a claim to be included, as have those whose co-operation and endorsement is needed to ensure that the outcome of talks becomes a reality. If they are not drawn in, they remain outside the camp, temporarily sidelined but ready (and motivated) to undermine the outcome. The list of participants may thus be extensive: political parties, faction leaders, external actors, and so on. Bigger numbers usually mean a slower process, but there are methods outlined in subsequent sections which will offset the tendency of size to work against efficiency.

Participation is a core issue, and remains a difficult one to resolve. Not only are there usually multiple parties and opinions within any deep-rooted conflict, but additionally both the nature of those parties and their permutations alter over time. An extreme example of an inclusive definition of participants is the number of participants in the Basque conflict in Spain. As many as two dozen identifiable groups had a stake in the negotiations, which could be grouped into four categories: ETA itself, with all of its factions, members in prison or in exile, and their families; other Basque groups, including the Basque autonomous regional government and the political parties and media associated with it; the Spanish government and its associated political parties and media; and international groups, including governments of other nations (neighbouring France, which also has a Basque population, and Algeria) and organizations such as Amnesty International and Interpol.

Such a bewildering "universe of parties" is typical of the complexity of long-standing and deep-rooted conflicts. This may indicate a need to subgroup the participants, for example into external and internal parties, or to subgroup the issues around which negotiations can be structured. Techniques to do this are addressed in later sections. To take the Ethiopian example, the deep divisions between the groupings fighting for self-determination produced a situation in 1989 where two separate and distinct sets of dialogue processes were opened with the government: one with the EPLF and one with the TPLF. To divide the talks groups in this way can be effective, as long as its overall effect is not divisive. But the main point remains that exclusion, abstention or withdrawal of parties needs to be acknowledged, addressed and provided for during the pre-negotiation phase of process design.

A related and pressing question refers to the proportions in which parties should be represented. Does every party get an equal number of delegates? Or do bigger parties get more? Is there a good reason to assign spokesperson roles to some parties or some negotiators, and observer status to others? Is there a basic accreditation process which determines entry to talks?

AMONG THE OPTIONS FOR RESOLVING THE QUESTION OF PARTICIPATION ARE:

- to open channels of communication, however small or informal, in an attempt to start the contact and communication;
- to take the time to include all parties with a serious claim to be involved;
- to build a sufficient mainstream-based pro-negotiation coalition to open talks with some substantial hope of

---

3.4 Developing a Specific Negotiation Process

> achieving an outcome, and hope to co-opt abstainers, or persuade excluded parties to adapt their behaviour to fit the rules of entry;
>
> – to open negotiations with a less than comprehensive range of parties, with the aim of achieving a settlement that excluded parties can be persuaded to live with;
>
> – to limit participation only to those parties who enjoy substantial support, whether that is defined electorally or otherwise;
>
> – to specify equal numbers of delegates per party;
>
> – to allow variable delegation sizes based on electoral strength or status (where elections have been held);
>
> – to place an electoral or other threshold to restrict or enable participation;
>
> – to allow for different degrees of status in the process (e.g., participant and observer) for different parties;
>
> – to distinguish any groupings within the negotiation process who may be opposed on some, possibly major, issues but share positions on others.

3.4.2 Preconditions and barriers to negotiations

Preconditions are core areas of concern that must be dealt with before initiating negotiation on the substantive issues. The early settling of certain preconditions – particularly regarding the use of violence – are frequently a necessary part of bringing negotiation into being. For many "rebel" groups in conflict with a government, the precondition of a cease-fire, or of disarmament, is deeply threatening. And yet it can be a vital requirement for the government, who may see it primarily as a question of legitimizing their opposition. But for the rebels, participation in their rebellion has become a defining element of their identity. To give that up threatens their sense of self, their group coherence, the core of their existence, and the source of their power. Nonetheless, in various contexts, solutions to these core concerns have been devised.

In South Africa, the ANC's agreement to *suspend* their armed struggle – notably and consciously distinct from abandoning it – facilitated a move towards dialogue. A government insistence on permanent disarming would have made progress impossible at that stage. In Angola, El Salvador and elsewhere the UN has effectively acted as a third-party recipient of decommissioned weaponry. In Northern Ireland, the question of paramilitary disarmament stalled negotiations for two years. Eventually, an independent commission devised a set of six principles of non-violence that every party would have to endorse to gain access to the negotiation process. These included a commitment to exclusively peaceful means of resolving political issues, and – significantly – a renunciation of force either to influence the negotiations or to alter their outcome. With all parties signed up to the principles, the obstacle of the disarmament precondition was bypassed, and its significance reduced to more manageable proportions. Inclusive talks began.

A similar, yet slightly different, problem can produce *barriers* to negotiation. This is where a party refuses to enter negotiations for one of two reasons: a refusal to talk to a particular person or group, or a refusal to accept a particular issue as negotiable. The first problem, rejection of a person or group, is usually based upon their actions in the history of the conflict. Someone now in a negotiating team is seen as responsible for inflicting particular wounds, physical or otherwise, on their opponents. The opponents feel they will not, or cannot be seen to, deal with such a person. They may be reacting to a past leader of a violent guerrilla campaign, or perhaps to a government minister who was responsible for particularly harsh oppressive measures. For whatever reason, something in the person's past actions makes him or her unacceptable. It may be that persuasion, or pronouncements by the person concerned, will be enough to remove the objection. Perhaps some actions by them in the present can go far enough to soften the perception of them. But perhaps not.

Mandela's words come to mind again in this instance: that one must make peace with one's enemies. By definition, in this kind of context, enemies tend to have blood on their hands. One approach to this barrier is to set the personalities aside long enough to discuss and agree the general terms for admission to talks. Britain's refusal to negotiate with the IRA in formal session was based in large part on the IRA's history of killing British soldiers and the British tradition of, in the Thatcherite mantra, "not talking to terrorists" (or at least not being seen to be doing so). As noted, this proved an insuperable obstacle to progress until the issue was broadened to the more general level of the terms of admission to which all parties, including the IRA's political party Sinn Fein, could agree.

3.4 Developing a Specific Negotiation Process

There is a need to be creative when it is clear that the presence of a party is critical to the success of the talks and there is a refusal on the part of one party to even talk to the other. Thus the refusal by the Indonesia's Suharto Government to enter into talks with the East Timorese over the issue of independence has led to a situation where the talks are now between Portugal and the Indonesian Government. Clearly the exclusion of the East Timorese is a major hurdle to the conducting of effective negotiations and needs to be addressed before substantive progress is likely to be made.

The problem can be just as difficult when one side identifies a particular issue as *non-negotiable*. They will talk with the opposition about a variety of other subjects, but this one in particular is too precious to them and they cannot compromise. Governments tend to feel this way about territorial integrity: rebels demanding secession are, to the government, asking the impossible. Conversely, anything that can be interpreted as surrender – including the handing in of weapons prior to a settlement – may be an impossibility to the rebels. No facile technique can be prescribed for progress. Either compensation can be offered, so that both sides resist or yield equally on the issue, or a broader debate on the underlying issues can bring wider perspective and redefinition of the terms for entry. But at bottom, the readiness or otherwise to enter talks with the enemy comes down to the parties' real readiness to make peace or their depth of frustration in continuing to make war. Indeed, such barriers may be an expression that parties are not ready to enter a full talks phase.

Rather than try to achieve a settlement while such subjective and perceptual antagonisms remain strong, time might be best spent by a third party, through unofficial communication channels, facilitating intra-party discussion on the potential benefits of talks and the distance yet to be travelled before those benefits materialize. A parallel pre-negotiation process focused only on procedural issues may help to build the foundations of a working relationship and place distance between the violence of the past and the potential of the present.

On the other hand, there may be issues which are important to the parties and which can be agreed in advance as guiding principles that may serve as the basis for further possible discussions. In the conflict in the Sudan, which is still continuing, the contending parties nonetheless reached agreement in September 1994 on a "Declaration of Principles", including matters such as the maintenance of the unity of the Sudanese State and rights relating to self-determination.

> ### THE OPTIONS REGARDING PRECONDITIONS COMPRISE:
>
> – to drop preconditions to negotiations, and accept all comers and issues;
>
> – to use the pre-negotiation process to work through preconditions and questions of legitimacy and recognition of spokespersons;
>
> – to open out preconditions initially aimed at one party into a principled statement to which all parties can and must agree;
>
> – to address preconditions and the commitment to the negotiation process in an unofficial discussion process prior to formal negotiation.

3.4.3 Levelling the playing-field

All too often, conflicting parties approach the end-game of conflict – the hurting stalemate – in an *asymmetrical* relationship. Asymmetry refers to their relative power positions: one is disadvantaged where the other holds formal power. They are not evenly matched, not symmetrical. William Zartman offers the classic scenario of asymmetrical power, where rebels contest with government: "The government has ... sovereignty, allies, arms, and access to resources. The insurgents have to fight for all of these. Moreover, the government determines ... the rules of the game for the rebellion's struggle ... It is both participant and umpire".

So while a government or central authority has ready access to power, controlling the nation's financial and military resources, their opponents' access to resources is usually a more difficult matter, often reliant on covert sources. But at the same time, the asymmetry is modified by several factors. First, the rebels' intense commitment to their cause as the single defining mission of their existence creates an obvious challenge to the other's straightforward application of its power. As any government knows well, a very small force, given adequate arms and training, can create a destabilizing effect out of all proportion to its size. That potential, of the small to thwart the powerful, constrains in very practical terms the government's ability to exer-

3.4 Developing a Specific Negotiation Process

cise its considerable power. Second, most governments have a multifaceted agenda whose scope reaches well beyond just containing or ending the rebellion; with their responsibility for all the other business of governing, their resources are spread broadly over a wider range of interests. Third, external factors can work indirectly to mitigate the differences in the power relations. An international perception of the justness of the rebel cause can constrain the government's wielding of its power. Economic and other sanctions exercised against the South African and Rhodesian (Zimbabwean) regimes are clear examples of this. Fourth, weaker parties themselves often address the question by finding powerful allies, sometimes internal but more frequently external, to the conflict. The Liberation Tigers of Tamil Eelam (LTTE) drew at one stage of their struggle active support from powerful elements in India, including elements within the Indian Government itself. Similarly, in the cases of UNITA in Angola and of RENAMO in Mozambique, their continued ability to fight depended for some considerable time on the support of the South African regime. In a reverse example, in 1991 the PLO suffered a considerable setback and lost considerable resources from traditionally supportive Arab states when it declared itself in favour of Iraq during the Gulf War.

How do we make the playing-field level? How do we ensure that all parties regard the process as legitimate? The main concentration here is not in the power balance in the great scheme of things, but in the situation at the negotiating table. One levelling effect comes from the parties' acceptance of each other's right to be at the table. Simply agreeing to talk confers recognition and legitimacy on spokespersons. This mutual acceptance is an admission of some kind of equality. And even if that equality exists only while the parties are in the negotiation situation (and it may often be impossible for a powerful party to acknowledge such legitimacy anywhere else) that may be enough to facilitate talks.

However, simply within the talks context, there will often still remain a *resource asymmetry*. Good process design entails ensuring that resources on all sides are distributed equitably. That will mean allowing time for preparation, education and familiarization with the process of negotiation. A government with its full-scale administrative capacity, advisors and resources, is obviously at a huge negotiating advantage over a small insurrectionist movement with a handful of lieutenants more familiar with military tactics than political discourse. Suddenly, they must act as a

for the presentation of a final settlement. They do not in general facilitate substantive discussions and deal making, because of their size and formality. (However, see the section on National Conferences in the following chapter for some counter-examples).

Summits of key spokespersons – high-profile short-term events with small numbers of delegates – can be useful for talking through key issues. The high rank of those present can guarantee their immediate official endorsement of any agreement. The public nature, however, raises the stakes considerably by putting extreme pressure on the participants for a result by the end of proceedings.

Round table discussions including all parties are a key element of any negotiation process. But the breadth of attendance and the formality of proceedings can encourage a stiff, rhetoric-based atmosphere not particularly conducive to real deal-making. Plenaries, however, can be the ideal place in which to formally endorse conclusions and agreements reached on agenda items.

Subgroup or subcommittee discussions – where each party is represented but in much smaller numbers than in plenary – facilitate substantive negotiation over specific agenda items, while also allowing a much faster process of information exchange and decision-making. They can also be the place for more plain speaking than formal meetings. But their smallness of scale and narrowness of agenda means they need to be backed up with endorsement from the fuller plenaries.

Shuttle mediation – meetings between the mediator and one party at a time – is a very useful way of indirectly channelling information through the third party to the other conflicting parties. It also provides an opportunity to make clear one's own point of view without argument from opponents, in the knowledge that the clear expression of that view will reach them via the chair or mediator. If there is a problem bringing the parties into a face-to-face situation, either for the first time or because of some impasse reached in direct talks, then shuttling can be a very useful exercise in clarifying positions and maintaining contact. There is no strict rule here and the mediator may decide if it is necessary to put the parties together at any stage of the proceedings in order to clarify issues or to debate a point. *Proximity talks* are a similar, if not identical, version of this procedure: parties are located close by, in different rooms of the same building or perhaps in adjacent buildings. A chair shuttles between them one at a time, or calls them in separately for talks.

3.4 Developing a Specific Negotiation Process

Bilateral discussions – i.e., face-to-face talks between two parties directly – can be official or unofficial. When they are unofficial, co-ordinated through confidential third parties, through unofficial communication channels, or in secret face-to-face encounters, they may have great value in clarifying perceptions of one side by another, and in defining the priorities of each and the distance between them. Once that has been achieved, though, unofficial talks lack the official imprimatur necessary to produce any formal or lasting agreement. But they can be a vital requirement in paving the way toward that goal.

Disaggregation – i.e., a mixture of plenaries and subgroups – involves dividing the workload between subgroups whose task is to prepare specific proposals on particular parts of the agenda, for consideration in plenary sessions. It is still important that all parties should be involved at all levels of the negotiation process. Every effort should be made to resolve differences at the disaggregated level because resolution becomes more difficult in larger and more formal forums. But the plenary sessions still carry more formality and official sanction, and should remain the ultimate authority for approving subgroup proposals. The subcommittees can work on a much smaller scale to deal with a specific issue, and report back to the fuller table. This not only saves time and avoids rhetoric, but additionally functions to chip off workable pieces of what can seem an overwhelmingly complex and daunting agenda.

The Northern Ireland talks process of 1997–1998 is an example of disaggregating agenda items according to which parties they pertain most closely to. The agenda was separated (during previous pre-negotiation efforts) into three strands. Strand One, concerning power-sharing structures within Northern Ireland, involved the Northern Irish political parties and the British Government; Strand Two, concerning the relationship between the two parts of Ireland, also brought in the Irish Republic's Government; while Strand Three, focusing on a new British-Irish treaty, involved only the Irish and British Governments, with other parties included only as observers. The three strands were designed to run simultaneously, each with a different independent chair, and with regular reporting to full plenary sessions for appraisal.

In South Africa, a comprehensive disaggregating process was initiated in the Convention for a Democratic South Africa (CODESA), with three main elements. The negotiating forum formed the overall plenary authority in the process. Then five working groups were given responsibility for specific elements of the agenda, reporting ultimately to the plenary forum. At a third level, technical committees, unlike the other elements, were explicitly *not* negotiating forums. They comprised not party negotiators, but rather non-party experts on the topic at hand, who were requested to prepare proposals for consideration by the plenary forum. Interestingly, while ultimate authority remained with the forum, the other levels exercised great influence on the process, with a "timeframes working group" virtually imposing deadlines on the process, and a "constitutional technical committee" completing the bulk of the all-important drafting of the new constitution.

Where disparate views emerge in subgroups, they may be reflected in alternative proposals that can be debated and decided upon in plenary session. Another strategy, although a potentially divisive one unless circumstances particularly encourage it, is to produce both majority and minority proposals or reports, which represent both the greater opinion grouping and the dissenting voice.

A WIDE VARIETY OF OPTIONS FOR THE FORM THAT NEGOTIATIONS CAN TAKE INCLUDE:

- Large-scale conferences;
- Summits of key spokespersons;
- Full round table sessions;
- Shuttle mediation;
- Bilateral discussions;
- A mixed formula of plenaries and subgroups;
- Acknowledgement of dissenting coalitions by means of minority reports;
- Defining different roles and capacities for negotiators and observers.

3.4.6 Venue and location

While the question of where to hold talks seems a straightforward consideration, it can become a highly divisive issue. A venue can carry deep symbolism. If talks are held on the "home territory" of one side, the other side may perceive an unfair bias against them. As with so many issues in the delicate dance of negotiation, even if in reality such a venue offers little or no advan-

3.4 Developing a Specific Negotiation Process

tage to the "home team", the perception of bias can be enough to obstruct progress.

A *neutral venue*, of course, circumvents this problem. But care needs to be taken in defining such neutrality. If talks are held in a third country, quite outside the conflict territory, is that third country perceived as being more friendly to one side than another? If so, neutrality disappears again. Even if the neutrality is accepted all round, is access to the host country evenly distributed? In a situation where the conflicting parties are a government and an insurgent movement, how free are the insurgents to travel across borders, in comparison to government personnel? While a government will usually have access to all the resources necessary – air transport, travel documents, finance, and so on – insurgents may, by definition, be denied passports and have limited resources for international travel. This was the position of West Bank/Gaza Palestinians for many years; since they were not permitted Israeli passports, unless they themselves possessed other nationalities which provided them with passports, it was difficult for them to travel to or from outside countries.

The arrangements at the venue itself need some consideration. The general principle holds that all manner of resources – from secretarial help to communication access, to private space, and so on – need to be seen to be provided equally to all. And thought needs to go into the situation beyond the formal facilities. Is there room for the equivalent of what was known at the 1978 Camp David talks between Israel, Egypt and the USA as a "walk in the woods"? This was the term coined for quiet, confidential and unofficial discussions between individuals away from the negotiating room. Former Finnish President Kekkonen was famous for holding sensitive foreign policy discussions with Soviet leaders in the relaxed and private environment of his estate's sauna. Such unofficial exchanges do much to lubricate the wheels of the formal negotiation process. This is what former Norwegian diplomat Jan Egeland said of the talks in Oslo:

One of the advantages of the Oslo channel over the traditional conference diplomacy was the informal and undisturbed venue… an atmosphere of mutual trust and affinity was allowed to develop between people who spent hundreds of hours working, quarrelling and eating together in front of Norwegian fireplaces and surrounded only by peaceful countryside.

In general, then, both location and venue itself must be appropriate in terms of:

- *size* and *suitability*: from adequate space for plenaries and for formal as well as informal small-group work to such simple details as catering;
- *security*: of personnel as well as regarding confidentiality of discussions and papers;
- equal *accessibility*: to the venue as well as to means of travel to and from the location.

Some examples of differing venue formulas include the 1978 talks at Camp David, the isolated and well-protected presidential retreat in the US, where Israeli and Egyptian delegations could be housed in separate buildings within the compound, meeting in President Carter's building; the 1991 London conference on the Ethiopian conflict, hosted by Britain but mediated by the US; the neutral location of Geneva for a 1983 conference on Lebanon mediated by Saudi Arabia; the 1991 Madrid conference which launched the Arab-Israeli peace process; Northern Ireland negotiations in 1992 which moved between locations in Belfast, Dublin and London to satisfy competing aspirations over the symbolism of location; and the 1990 church-hosted talks in Rome on the Mozambique conflict.

OPTIONS FOR VENUE CONSIDERATIONS COMPRISE:

- identifying a neutral venue, of no particular symbolism or support to any one party;
- agreeing on a domestic venue acceptable to all parties;
- assuring equal accessibility to the venue for all parties;
- the supplementing of official or formal discussion forums by unofficial, off-the-record and possibly deniable channels of communication outside and around the formal table.

3.4.7 Communication and information exchange

Transparency and confidentiality produce a difficult tension in the negotiating process. But whether proceedings are open or closed, in whole or in part, will depend upon how the parties

3.4 Developing a Specific Negotiation Process

choose to reconcile the interests of keeping the public informed with that of creating an environment where they can explore options and proposals in a secure and uninhibited way. Public support may be a necessary spur to the momentum of the talks process, or an obstacle that reduces the freedom of parties to engage in serious negotiation. Transparency helps reduce outside suspicion aroused by the confidentiality of the process, and it can be a vital preparation to "selling" the resulting outcome to the population at large.

Where the media is excluded, and the talks held in complete confidentiality, participants are obviously more free to speak openly, and more able to explore positions and outcomes without committing themselves. As long as the end result of the negotiations is agreed by all, confidentiality during the process permits a party to accept a loss on today's agenda item in order to gain on tomorrow's, without any accusations from outside of weakness in concession. One's constituency outside the talks cannot constrain one's freedom of operation.

This was a major advantage in pre-negotiations during the "Oslo channel" talks between Israel and the PLO. But that final result may be more of a surprise to constituents when presented as a *fait accompli*, which may breed resentment. Caught up in the momentum of positive but confidential talks, a party can find they have a "re-entry problem" when they leave the heat of negotiations in order to explain an agreement, which may contain compromises, to their larger constituency. This aspect, which we shall call "constituency lag", can hold implications for the structure of the talks: it may be necessary to take frequent breaks to enable consultations with constituents.

On the other hand, the media can be actively used in order to make official one's bargaining position at any given point, and also to help keep one's constituency informed and abreast of progress. Regular media reports also serve to reduce suspicion among the public of "deals behind closed doors". In particular, if there are excluded fringe elements outside the talks, the appearance of secret negotiations might well fuel their antagonism; greater transparency, by keeping the public informed, can be a strong defence against such antagonism and help to defuse the spoilers' capacity.

The obvious way to inform the public is via the media. So the question of who deals with the media, and through what channels and processes, needs agreement prior to the beginning of the process. The importance of this cannot be overstressed: lack of forethought on the topic in Belfast in 1991, beyond a hastily agreed press embargo, led to a situation where parties manipulated the news-hungry media to their own ends, leaking (and in some cases selling for cash) their opponents' confidential position papers.

Secondly, what facilities are there for communication *between* the conflicting parties? Away from the formal table, they may well need to communicate their thoughts on various topics to each other. This is often done by circulating position papers for consideration. Will a central secretariat fulfil such a function? Or can a subcommittee with members from all parties do the job?

DEPENDING ON THE SPECIFIC SITUATION, PROCESS DESIGNERS CAN CHOOSE AMONG THE FOLLOWING PROCEDURES WITH RESPECT TO COMMUNICATION AND INFORMATION EXCHANGE:

- secret negotiations out of all sight;
- closed negotiation sessions, with occasional or regular progress reports to the outside world, agreed by all parties;
- an agreed press embargo among all participants (with enforcement mechanisms to be negotiated among the parties);
- relations with the media being at each party's discretion;
- ceding the public relations role by agreement to the chairperson or mediator;
- establishing a permanent press secretariat to manage media relations on behalf of all;
- establishing a central secretariat to channel information between the parties;
- forming a subcommittee with responsibility for inter-party communication.

3.4.8 Setting the agenda

Participants need to know and agree in advance the broad subject matter of the negotiations. It can be completely destabilizing to open up new and unforeseen substantive issues in the

3.4 Developing a Specific Negotiation Process

midst of the negotiation process (unless, of course, it is part of extending or deepening the process by building on initial negotiating successes). So it is important to define the shape of the agenda, whether in a distinct pre-negotiation process, or in an initial phase of the formal negotiations. This does not involve actually addressing the substantive issues, but it does mean defining, listing and ordering them to the reasonable satisfaction of all.

The agenda for negotiations obviously depends very closely on the specific conflict. But at this preparation stage, it is important to agree at least minimally what the problems are, and what the requirements of their solution must cover. A generic example of the kind of basic structure needed is offered bellow.

---

1. MEASURES TO ESTABLISH PERMANENT PEACE:

- Reconciliation
- Reparation
- Restoration
- Security
- Boundary drawing (where relevant)

2. MEASURES TO ESTABLISH A DEMOCRATIC STRUCTURE AND TO PROMOTE HUMAN RIGHTS:

- A Constitution
- A Bill of Rights
- Institutions and levels of government

3. MEASURES TO PROMOTE ECONOMIC RECONSTRUCTION AND DEVELOPMENT:

- Aid
- Inward investment
- Strategic deployment of resources
- External relations

Beyond the ingredients of the agenda, agreement is needed on how to address it. Can "easier" and more "difficult" items be identified? If so, context alone can tell whether it will be more productive to tackle easier items first, the better to build momentum and co-operative attitudes, or whether difficult but key issues, on which there is little current agreement, must be tackled first because other issues cannot become clear except in the light of agreement over the core issues. A further aspect is what should happen if there is deadlock on a key issue: should it be deferred out to a separate structure for discussion or does it have to be resolved there and then? What is the correct approach to be taken? Is it desirable to start with "soft" issues to show the parties that the process can deliver, or is that not possible?

CHOICES ON AGENDA SETTING WILL HAVE TO BE MADE BETWEEN:

– establishing pre-negotiation processes, either public or private, and possibly with a reduced number of delegates, to define the agenda prior to formal negotiation;

– using the formal negotiation process to resolve procedural and agenda matters;

– ordering agenda items according to contentiousness and importance;

– adopting a long-range policy of a series of negotiations, each building on the achievements of the last.

3.4.9 Managing the proceedings

Who will chair and referee the proceedings? Under what standing orders? How will time be allotted to speakers? Is there a finite deadline for the end of talks? What ground-rules need to be agreed? What recording process will be used? Who will be responsible for it?

The key question of *who chairs* the proceedings needs to be agreed early on. Parties may devolve the responsibility on a rotating basis among themselves, or the responsibility may be assumed by an acceptable individual, a representative from an international agency, a friendly country, a wholly non-involved state, or from the country hosting the negotiations. Elements that must be considered will include not only the acceptability of the individual, organization or state to all participants, but also the relevance and particular suitability and skills of the individuals concerned. Of course, sometimes the question of a chair is not a matter of choice for the conflicting parties but is imposed upon them by an external sponsor or mediator.

In South Africa, a system was devised of rotating the chair among all parties equally. In Northern Ireland, a former US senator was installed as overall chair of the process, with a Canadian and a Finn as vice-chairs. For Bosnia, the chair/mediator was a state – the US at Dayton. In Mozambique, the chair was a religious NGO, Sant'Egidio.

CONTEXT WILL SUGGEST WHICH IS THE MOST SUITABLE WAY TO MANAGE THE PROCEEDINGS:

- negotiation of a system of sharing the chair in such a way that no one party can benefit from their chairing either in general or on key specific agenda items;
- selection of a party totally suitable to all concerned;
- selection of a party minimally acceptable to all concerned;
- identification of the key skills necessary for the function;
- selection of a party with authority to overrule all concerned if necessary;
- selection of an unempowered party dependent on continuing consensus among all concerned.

3.4.10 Timeframes

The question of *time* is central. Are the negotiations to be limited by a prearranged deadline? Or are they to be open-ended, continuing for however long it takes to build an outcome? This varies depending on the context, but "ripe moments" for negotiation tend to be short-lived, in effect providing their own deadline.

One side of the argument insists that deadlines are necessary to push people towards success. The other side of the argument is that with endless time available, the urgency to pressure participants into concessions and agreement is missing. Moreover, participants may be tempted to use delaying tactics if there is little or no time pressure. A party which is a reluctant participant – which sees the *status quo ante* as at least no worse than a likely outcome – can effectively draw out discussions and delay progress, if there is no pressure on them to make progress or take the blame for failure. This is what Unionists did in Northern Ireland in 1991 (partly because they did not believe the seriousness of the official deadline), and arguably what Israeli Prime Minister Netanyahu has done regarding talks with the Palestinians.

On the other hand, deadlines may force people to move faster than they are comfortable with, producing a rushed and incomplete outcome. Surprisingly often, negotiations are given only days or weeks to put an end to years or even decades of bitter conflict. The fear of appearing to be the party who blocked a successful outcome by refusing to compromise can be a healthy spur, but it can also force an unwilling outcome which is subsequently undermined or disowned.

If there truly is a very limited time available, one response is to set limited goals for the negotiations – the establishment of a truce and verification mechanism, or the establishment of a body (agreeing on its participants, its procedural rules, defining its remit, and so on) which will subsequently continue the work. Achieving such limited but significant success can in itself renew the momentum for further negotiations and thus extend or enlarge the window of opportunity. The process becomes in effect one consisting of several negotiating stages.

The Dayton conference, hosted and tightly controlled by the US at all times, became almost the quintessential example of heavy deadline pressure being imposed from a third party (the US) on the negotiating Bosnian leaders. While the effect was to produce an agreement by the deadline, the quality, depth and applicability of the agreement, and the commitment of participants to its implementation, suffered as a result (see Bosnia Case Study). Similarly, the 1978 Camp David Accord was produced under very strong pressure from Carter on both Sadat and Begin to reach agreement before the end of the session or take the blame for failure. Such pressure has a positive side, focusing minds on the task at hand, and increasing the chance of concessions in order to avoid perceived failure. But again at Camp David, the breadth and long-term substance of the agreement suffered as a result.

OPTIONS ON TIMEFRAMES INCLUDE:

- no time-limits: participants remain until the job is done;
- a pre-agreed time-limit;
- a realistic limit on the goals to be achieved within the time available;
- aiming for a comprehensive settlement of all aspects of the dispute;
- an option for further negotiating period/s following success in the initial period.

3.4.11 Decision-making

At regular intervals during negotiations, decisions will have to be made. Are we agreed on this agenda point, and can we then build on that agreement to move on? Decisions must be reached in such a way that all – or most – of the parties accept the legitimacy and binding nature of the agreement. But it is important to establish this in advance. If a party can renege on an earlier agreed point at a later stage, there is a danger of the entire process falling apart before completion. Some mechanism must be established for defining binding agreement in the negotiation process.

Further, how is agreement to be confirmed? Do parties have an overnight period to confirm acceptance of the point by others (perhaps their political leaders) not present at the table? Again, is each point agreed permanently before moving on to the next? If that is so, it may mean that even if talks fall apart later, all the agreements established prior to the break-up remain. Or is there a banking principle at work, as in Northern Ireland? Under that system, "nothing is finally agreed until everything is agreed". The parties put the agreed points "in the bank" for future reference, only to be finally agreed when the agenda had been completed.

The plus side of this is that a party can see the value of conceding on one point in order to gain on another, on the understanding that they will be able to calculate the balance of concessions and gains before finally approving the whole agreement. The down side is that this tends to produce an all-or-nothing character to the talks: if negotiations break off before full completion, then most or all of the agreements reached up to that point may be disowned, and any future process will have to begin all over again.

Cyril Ramaphosa described the South African decision-making formula thus: "All agreements and decisions were to be arrived at by general consensus among all the parties. When general consensus couldn't be achieved, decisions were to be taken on the basis of sufficient consensus. Sufficient consensus was defined as a process of reaching agreement that would take us to the next step. Essentially, it finally meant that there had to be sufficient agreement between two parties or within two parties. Those parties were the National Party and the ANC. The parties who disagreed with the decision could have their objections formally recorded, but in the spirit of co-operation they understood that they could not hinder the process from moving forward." Ramaphosa is quoted elsewhere more succinctly, admitting that, "sufficient consensus means if the ANC and the NP agree, the rest can get stuffed".

The point is well made that "sufficient consensus" needs to be worked out for the specific context, with regard to the number of parties present, their relative strengths, commitment to the process and potential for disruption. Effectively, in this instance, it was the reality that if the two mainstream parties managed consensus, it was difficult for the other, much smaller, parties to challenge it in any effective way.

Similar considerations about facilitating the mainstreams on both sides led to a more intricately defined formula in Northern Ireland in 1997. There, "sufficient consensus" was calculated according to the electoral strengths of the negotiating parties assessed at the pre-talks election, and boiled down to the requirement that any decision had the support of a straight majority on each side – that is, the support of parties representing more than 50 per cent of Unionist voters as well as more than 50 per cent of Nationalist voters.

And how will the final agreement – the completed and agreed outcome – be officially endorsed or ratified? Is it enough if all parties make a joint announcement giving their approval to the result? Or is a referendum necessary among all the represented constituencies in order to bestow public and official endorsement on the outcome? There might need to be a calculation of the risk involved in taking the agreement to the people. They might possibly reject it (but that would indicate its unsuitability, in any case). Or the debate leading up to such a referendum could give excluded or spoiling parties the chance to forge support for their arguments in public in order to undermine the outcome. But certainly such public endorsement gives the outcome an unquestionable legitimacy, as demonstrated by the overwhelming support for the Northern Irish settlment in a referendum in 1998.

> THE MOST SUITABLE FORMULA FOR DECISION-MAKING MUST BE AGREED AMONG THE NEGOTIATING PARTIES. BUT SOME OF THE OPTIONS WILL INCLUDE:
>
> – Total agreement: all parties must endorse a point for it to be agreed;

3.5 Basic Techniques for Negotiation

> - Simple majority acceptance: more than half the parties or delegates agree;
> - Consensus: the point is defined and refined until all can agree to it;
> - Sufficient consensus: a certain specified proportion of the parties or delegates must agree to the point (the exact proportion or criteria to be pre-agreed, and dependent on the number of parties, their relative sizes, and their ability to "sell" the agreement to their broader constituencies);
> - Secret ballots to discover the degree of consensus;
> - An open show of hands to discover the voting preferences;
>
> (NB: there is a slight difference between agreement and consensus. The latter implies that discussion continues until the parties find the best compromise that they can all live with. Agreement, of course, can be exactly that, but may also constitute the preference of one party who prevails over others, as opposed to a genuine compromise).
>
> - Final ratification by parties, or endorsement by referendum of the final outcome.

3.5 Basic Techniques for Negotiation

Techniques and strategies for negotiation are highly dependent on context. Both the context and the creativity of the participants must guide and provide the choice of on-the-spot re-action to the specific situation. Extensive, high-quality books on the topic already exist (see "References and Further Reading" at the end of this chapter). However, some general, simple advice can be offered which may prove useful and applicable in a negotiation. Some are very personal and individual tips; others are simple tactics for improving one's performance in talks. Depending on the situation, some are relatively straightforward while others will prove difficult. But all are worth considering throughout the process.

This advice is not aimed at helping a conflicting party win at the expense of the opposition. It is concerned with implementing good process, to the advantage of all. Underpinning every point mentioned in this section is one simple principle: good

Underpinning every point mentioned in this section is one simple principle: good process helps everyone involved, because good process increases the chances of good outcome.

93

process helps *everyone* involved, because good process increases the chances of good outcome. Good process complements the natural competition of negotiation by generating co-operation. These aspects will help nurture and sustain the difficult process of negotiation.

3.5.1 Promote confidence building between the parties

Negotiators need to have some confidence in each other and in the process. This does not rule out skepticism on both counts, but there must be a degree of mutual trust that permits a basic working relationship, and there must be at least a minimal expectation that a quality outcome can result from the process. The following are some basic rules of the negotiation game:

Ensure confidentiality. A standard ground-rule for negotiation is that what is said is not repeated outside the negotiating room without permission. Each side needs that reassurance in order to discuss serious and sensitive issues with confidence. This should be agreed beforehand and reassurance on this subject must come at repeated intervals from all sides, and be demonstrated by subsequent behaviour. Confidentiality is a keystone of negotiation.

Demonstrate competence and commitment. Mutual respect grows from an awareness of the opponent's ability to do the negotiation job and their willingness to stick with the process until the job is done. Competence and commitment in the negotiation process leads to confidence in the outcome. A party needs to demonstrate these qualities, early and repeatedly, in their behaviour, just as it needs to look for it in the other parties.

Empathize. Relating in a human way to old enemies is supremely difficult. There is no simple way to wipe out the history of previous warfare and the deeds it entails. But if one sees only demons across the table, agreement will never be reached with them. Although the effort required is often immense, it is important to view the opposing parties as human beings, to try at least to understand that they too have pain and anger stored up from the past, and to realize that they too must make the effort to overcome the same preconceptions of other parties.

Retain belief in a solution. If the frustrations of the process grow too great, consider the alternatives to negotiation. They will almost certainly be much worse than unpleasant and incessant talking. Remember the reasons that brought one's party to the table, and the unpleasant consequences of a hasty departure. Expect bumps in the road, but maintain a commitment to keep travelling.

3.5 Basic Techniques for Negotiation

3.5.2 Promote clarity

Accurate information, even unpleasant information, is vital. Without full information no comprehensive and lasting decision can be reached on any point. And without lasting decisions, no solution will be achieved.

Question the other parties. To avoid the appearance of interrogation, use open questions where possible. Closed questions invite simple, yes-or-no answers: for example, "Do you want a new constitution?" is unlikely to elicit much useful discussion. In contrast, open questions demand complex answers, and draw forth richer information: for example, "What sort of constitution do you envisage?" Open questions often begin with "why?", "how?", "what if?", and so on.

Paraphrase, clarify and summarize. After an open question is answered, play back a summary or a paraphrase to the responder, and check for accuracy. Paraphrases begin with, "So what you're saying is...", or "Am I right to summarize your point as...?", and so on. Ask further questions for clarification. Continue the process until the responder is satisfied. This not only elicits accurate information, it reassures the responder that their argument has been heard and understood – exactly the situation that has been missing during the rhetoric of conflict.

Maintain focus on the issues. For the conflicting parties, the bedrock issues are deeply significant beyond their objective content. Each side will have years of pain and anger interwoven around the issues. Those emotions need to be expressed and understood. But for clarification purposes, cool question-and-answer sessions that remain focused on the substance of the issues help to extract vital information without raising the emotional temperature.

Defuse anger. Anger will appear in the negotiation process. It is only natural that it should, given the importance of the issues at stake. Simple de-escalating manoeuvres can defuse the anger without detracting from the significance of the issues: taking a short break to let tempers cool; mutually acknowledging the emotions on both sides; recognizing deep-seated fear, pain and anger in all the communities involved as a mutual problem for the negotiation process, and so on.

3.5.3 Promote understanding

Without full understanding, the process is doomed to failure. All issues must be understood fully by all in order to begin the problem-solving phase of building a solution. Most of this will come from the parties themselves. Additional information can be gathered from outside. Suggested techniques include the following:

Differentiate perceptions from issues. Naturally, many of the issues at stake in the conflict have deep emotional or psychological reverberations for the parties involved. These should not be excluded or de-emphasized. But it is vital that, first, all objective issues of substance in the conflict are laid out for all to see and understand; second, that perceptions – feelings, memories of hurt and sacrifice, mutual views of each other – are also expressed and heard; and, third, that the difference between the two is made abundantly clear. It may be useful to distinguish between these in terms of *objective* issues (resource discrimination, territorial disputes, and so on) and *relationship* issues (perceptions, beliefs and images held by one side of and about another). Building a settlement in the negotiation process will concentrate on the former; but attention to the latter will need to be addressed at some stage and in some way, and the parties need to understand this. As the working relationship develops in a good process, these issues may indirectly be defused to some degree. A good mediator will be able to judge the appropriate moment when it may be either necessary or desirable for one or both parties to blow off steam, or "let a little blood" as it is sometimes known.

Identify needs and interests. Deep-seated needs underpin the expressed issues and demands in identity-related conflict. Listen carefully to the other parties talk and try to dig below and identify these needs. A demand for self-determination may reflect a deep-seated insecurity about a community's future. A demand for political control may reflect an underlying need for recognition of identity through political participation. Political interests and issues are the stuff of political negotiation and settlement; but attention to and recognition of underlying needs can bring the parties to a fundamentally deeper understanding of their positions and their conflict. Additionally, often the underlying needs of all sides to the conflict, once reframed in terms of security or expression of identity, may be similar. This new perspective can provide important new information to parties, assisting the search for common ground and the drawing of parties into co-operative processes. By way of illustration, there is a tendency on the part of external actors, and, particularly the interna-

tional community, when an identity-based conflict arises to immediately jump to the conclusion that some kind of territorial
autonomy may be the solution. This is sometimes a dramatic response to an issue which may have as its real cause a resource or
security issue, and which could be addressed by mechanisms
which do not necessarily go to the heart of the state and its territorial integrity.

Take expert advice. Look outside the negotiating process for
information, if necessary. This may be especially relevant to information about possible future scenarios or structures that are
being debated at the table. This does not refer to information as
ammunition to use against opponents, but rather information
that can be shared and will enlighten discussions. By agreement
with other parties, commission outside studies or reports for the
negotiation process. *Fact-finding* projects can produce cool and
impartial reports on subjects of contention within the talks. *Expert working groups* can take a contentious issue from the talks
agenda, and produce clear proposals and possibilities for solution on the issue.

3.5.4 Promote movement

Eventually, when information gathering is over, when basic
respect has been developed, and when positions have been made
abundantly clear, the problem-solving phase begins. Some small
techniques can simplify the daunting task in this difficult phase.

Fractionate. Often a major obstacle to movement is a sense of
the overwhelming complexity of the agenda. Fractionating
means to break down the elements of the agenda into smaller,
more addressable issues. These can then be tackled in sequence
across the table, or mandated to issue-oriented subcommittees
for discussion and proposals, or delegated to outside working
groups for attention and reports.

Prioritize issues. Another means to clarify a complex agenda
is to order the items according to priority. They can then be addressed in order of importance, or in reverse order of difficulty,
as the parties agree.

Separate proposals from authors. It is a characteristic of competitive negotiation that one side's proposal for solution can be
unacceptable to another side simply because of its origin. It may
be eminently sensible in its content, but impossible to accept,
because to do so would feel like conceding or losing a point. Try
to assess an opposition proposal on its merits, not its origin.

Box 5 **NEGOTIATING TECHNIQUES: SOME BASIC PRINCIPLES**

1. Promote confidence building between the parties – There must be a degree of mutual trust which permits a basic working relationship. This can be fostered by:
- *ensuring confidentiality;*
- *demonstrating competence and commitment;*
- *empathizing; and*
- *retaining belief in a solution.*

2. Promote clarity – Without full and accurate information, no comprehensive and lasting decision can be reached. Elicit useful and clear discussions by:
- *Asking open questions* (i.e., "What sort of constitution do you envisage?"), rather than closed or interrogative questions (i.e., "Do you want a new constitution?");
- *Paraphrasing or summarizing* the responder's answers to ensure accuracy, and asking further questions for clarification;
- *Maintaining focus* on the substance of the issues;
- *Defusing anger,* by taking short breaks and mutually acknowledging emotions on both sides.

3. Promote understanding – All issues must be understood fully in order to begin the problem-solving phase of building a solution. This can be furthered by:
- *Differentiating perceptions from issues.* First, all objective issues of substance must be spelled out and understood; second, perceptions, fears, mutual views of each other must be expressed and heard;
- *Identifying needs and interests.* Focus on and recognize the underlying needs of all sides;
- *Taking expert advice.* Outside information can be commissioned to enlighten discussions, through fact-finding projects or expert working groups.

4. Promote movement – Once information is gathered, respect has been developed, positions have been made clear – then problem solving can begin. This difficult phase can be facilitated by:
- *Fractionating,* or breaking down the elements into smaller, more addressable issues;
- *Prioritizing issues* either in order of importance or in reverse order of difficulty;
- *Building on other parties' proposals;*
- *Identifying common ground,* even small areas of commonality, which can serve to encourage all participants and generate momentum;
- *Brokering concessions,* particularly if views on all sides have hardened into set positions on a question.

A further mechanism to be considered is for a mediator or independent third party to listen to the parties and then prepare a draft for discussion, so that it is not perceived as coming from one particular party.

Build on other parties' proposals. If an opposing party offers a proposal with at least some merit, they are likely to agree more easily to another proposal that both builds on and acknowledges their input.

Identify common ground. While on occasion it may feel like the negotiation process is merely underlining the differences between opposing sides, it is still valuable to cast the net widely and search for even small areas of common ground. A pre-agreed agenda, or a joint definition of the problem, are examples of such common ground, and proof that commonality can and has already been built among former enemies. Identifying even small areas of common ground during negotiations can be surprising and encouraging to all participants, helping to generate momentum towards co-operation and further commonality.

Broker concessions. Particularly if views on all sides have hardened into set positions on a question, unofficial channels may be the appropriate place to take on a brokering role. Try to look for compensations, *quid pro quos*, tit-for-tats. Deal making and compromise is the life-blood of negotiation.

3.6 Tools to Break Deadlock

With or without third parties, whether motivation is low or high, negotiations can hit moments of deadlock. In general, if the process design has incorporated sufficient flexibility, deadlock is easier to address. But additionally, there are tried and tested techniques which may be useful for overcoming such situations.

3.6.1 Coalition building

The idea of building a coalition of commitment between all those who value negotiations was mentioned before in Section 3.4.1. Such a coalition should cross all boundaries: intra-party as well as inter-party. It will also benefit if it includes sections of the negotiators' wider constituencies: public opinion in favour of a negotiated settlement can be a powerful source of pressure, especially on politicians who need to court that public. Those who believe in the value of continued negotiation will be less strict about concessions than other less committed members. A strong pro-negotiation coalition can increase pressure on those causing

A number of tools can help break deadlock, including coalition building, unofficial channels and shuttle mediation.

99

deadlock by the implicit threat that they will take the blame if talks stall or collapse. More positively, members of a cross-party coalition can co-operate in pressing their respective backers to do what is necessary to facilitate a solution to the problem.

3.6.2 Unofficial channels

Also mentioned earlier, in Section 3.4.6, was the need for unofficial channels of communication. These channels supplement and can at times circumvent the more official channels across the table or through a secretariat. They can take any appropriate form, but the more they exist the easier it is to continue discussion of a problem that, in the official setting, cannot be openly negotiated. At Camp David, the "walk in the woods" served this valuable purpose for a variety of permutations of participants. (The term was quite literal: the venue was surrounded by forest, which provided the ideal place to take a break.) In Northern Ireland, the indoor version of the same thing was termed "voices in the corridors". In South Africa, the unofficial friendship that resulted in the "Roelf and Cyril show" permitted the development of what was somewhat prosaically termed "the channel": a parallel conduit for communication to supplement the official process. In Finland, the sauna became the channel. In Norway, it was a fireside chat.

These kinds of channels evolve organically through the pre-negotiation and negotiation processes, and cannot in any real sense be predicted or prescribed. But it is vital that participants both recognize the importance of such mechanisms to lubricate the formal talks process, and remain aware of their possibilities as the opportunities occur. These channels may need to be deniable, and therefore may not involve party leaders or those with a high profile, unless a particular personal chemistry permits it. More often, they are quiet, behind-the-scenes chats between second-tier delegates, for the purpose of explaining in fuller terms the positions, problems, restraints and perceived obstacles between rival parties.

3.6.3 Subgroups

The idea of subgroups or subcommittees has been mentioned at various times as a means to fractionate or subdivide the agenda into more manageable ingredients. More specifically, when a particular obstacle creates deadlock over a certain agenda item, an *ad hoc* subgroup may be usefully convened to address the point. Away from the formal table, the smaller group can discuss

3.6 Tools to Break Deadlock

the problem in more forthright terms, and speculate more freely about ways to overcome it. The members will of course report back to their respective delegations, but the subgroup's lack of formal minutes, the reduction in rhetoric, the removal of the need to protect public positions and the specificity of the one-item agenda can facilitate speedy, honest and co-operative deal making. In the words of one Northern Irish negotiator:

> *When you get three or four people sitting down with one chairperson, you can get stuck in to the business. Because you have an opportunity to say, 'Look, stop —ing around here, what is the problem with x?' And the other guy says, 'Well, what we're really bothered about is a, b and c.' And then you start addressing the issues. When you're sitting with 40 people in a room, it's much harder to say that.*

3.6.4 Shuttle mediation

When the formal plenary session of talks runs into problems over a particularly divisive issue, it may be best to leave the formal setting and enter into shuttle mediation: discussions held between the chair or mediator and one party at a time. This allows for a process of clarifying a given party's stance on the subject, communicating accurately other parties' positions (gained through other shuttle discussions) and defining each party's needs, expectations and possibilities around the deadlocking issue. The chair or mediator, by this means, may well be able to draw a clearer picture of the situation than can be done in plenary, and can then communicate this picture in further bilaterals, along with possibilities for movement.

3.6.5 Proximity talks

A similar procedure to shuttle mediation is proximity talks. The difference here is that the parties actually move to the same specific location for the purposes of the talks, rather than remain in their own geographical bases to be visited by a mediator. Here, the party delegations reside close by each other, possibly in different rooms of the same building, but communicate entirely through bilateral discussion with the chair. This can be particularly useful as a prelude to face-to-face negotiation or for pre-negotiation. The nearness and accessibility of the parties makes it feasible, without the need for actual meeting (which may be publicly unacceptable at this stage). But it can also be a means to relax the pressure when deadlock is blocking plenary discussion. Proximity keeps the focus on the subject matter, in a way that would be lost if the parties actually left the negotiation venue.

3.6.6 Referendums, consultations and mandates

On a rather larger scale, but nonetheless pertinent in the right situation, parties may want to seek wider endorsement of a proposed move. Particularly if progress in negotiation has been substantial up to this point, the deadlock may be caused by a fear of the reception which a particular concession or agreement might receive in the broader constituency which negotiators represent. Fearing to go too far without the express support of their constituency, a delegation may need to seek approval from a wider membership of their party or movement, or indeed from their supporters or their public at large. While this can be time-consuming and complicated, it may be worthwhile to produce an energizing endorsement for change and progress which can move the negotiations on to the fast track. An example is the 1992 whites-only referendum called by South African President F. W. de Klerk to renew his mandate for negotiating with anti-apartheid organizations. The referendum result, a decisive vote in favour of continued reform, provided an important boost to de Klerk and served to renew confidence in the reform movement.

Such referendums, of course, must be approached with great care. Despite the best-laid plans, referendums always carry the risk of rejection: the calculation must be made carefully, since a negative response will hugely hamper, or altogether destroy, the negotiation process.

3.6.7 Unofficial supplements to negotiation

Well beyond the negotiation process, including any unofficial or ad hoc channels, there usually exists a broader population which comprises the civil society of the country in conflict. These people are normally not part of the negotiation process, and yet they are part of the conflict and part of its potential solution. Among that population will be organizations, groups and individuals who have their own processes and communication channels – and their own expertise – of which negotiators can avail themselwes. Such elements include religious institutions and

3.6 Tools to Break Deadlock

leaders, business interests, academic institutions, labour interests, peace groups, cross-community co-operative ventures, and so on. When deadlock ties the negotiations down, these elements remain available. They can function as supports for, or alternatives to, the talks process itself.

Box 6

BREAKING DEADLOCK

The following are some tried and tested techniques which may be useful in breaking deadlock:

1. **Coalition building** – Build a strong coalition of commitment between all those who value negotiations.

2. **Unofficial channels** – unofficial channels, such as the "walk in the woods" at Camp David, can supplement and at times circumvent the more official channels. The more they exist the easier it is to continue discussion of a problem that, in the official setting, cannot be openly negotiated.

3. **Subgroups** – When a particular obstacle creates deadlock over a certain agenda item, subgroups or subcommittees can discuss the problem in more forthright terms, away from the formal table.

4. **Shuttle mediation** – Discussions between the chair or mediator and one party at a time, which allows for a process of clarifying a given party's stance on the subject, communicating accurately other parties' positions, and defining each party's needs and expectations around the deadlocking issue.

5. **Proximity talks** – Party delegations reside close by each other, possibly in different rooms of the same building, but communicate entirely through bilateral discussion with the chair.

6. **Referendums, consultations and mandates** – Parties may want to seek wider endorsement of a proposed move, for example through referendums, before going too far without the express support of their constituency.

7. **Unofficial supplements to negotiation** – The broader civil society in a country, including religious institutions and leaders, business interests, labour interests and peace groups, can function as supports for, or alternatives to, the talks process itself.

There may be good reason to utilize the services of an academic institution to facilitate, say, a problem-solving workshop on the point in question, where a small group of representatives can meet to discuss the subject matter in neutral surroundings and try to use co-operative analysis to produce new alternatives to deadlock. Religious leaders or groups may be able to venture across boundaries where official negotiators cannot to keep communication alive. Business interests may have very practical and well-established bases of communication and co-operation which can be called upon to assist in breaking the deadlock.

Again, the possibilities for the use of such unofficial entities depends on what is available in the given situation. But parties need to be aware of these possibilities, alive to the opportunities to use them, and in general on the lookout for any available additional means to supplement the more official processes at the negotiating venue.

3.7 Third-Party Assistance

3.7.1 Introduction

Third-party intervention is increasingly popular in negotiation, either as a central feature of a talks process or as an ad hoc deadlock-breaking tool. Because of its wide potential applicability, it deserves attention as a mechanism in its own right.

A third party – a person, group, institution or country that is not identified directly or indirectly with any of the parties or interests to the conflict – can be very effective in chairing or facilitating the talks process. And a long-standing conflict, especially where there is considerable stalemate or just staleness of view, can benefit from the fresh perspective of newcomers. The first two important questions are: Do we need a third party? And, if so, who?

The South African peace process reached settlement without formal intervention by any third parties in the negotiation process itself, although third-party intervention did take place in relation to the participation of Inkatha in the election in 1994. A high-profile intervention by two former foreign policy heavyweights, Lord Peter Carrington of the UK and Henry Kissinger of the US, produced little result, while a lower high profile intervention by a Kenyan, Mr Okumu, was very successful. There is an increasing trend, voluntary or otherwise, to utilize intervenors or mediators from outside the conflict. Part of this trend must be attributed to a growing keenness in the international communi-

3.7 Third-Party Assistance

ty to play such roles, and the new context in which they have found themselves since the end of the Cold War. Moreover, intervenors increasingly operate in coalitions (for example, the collaboration of the Contact Group of States, the Organization for Security and Co-operation in Europe, the United Nations High Representative, the United States, the European Union and various NGOs in Bosnia).

Even if a third party is not used during negotiations, there may be a limited but effective role for such a person or group in enabling low-key discussion of a problem or sticking point. An independent mediator may well be ideal for this. The mediator will simply facilitate focused discussion of the deadlocked point, in order to increase communication and understanding and to generate possibilities for agreement. Again, small delegation sizes will help. Even where a third party mediates the formal talks, a small-scale subgroup discussion with a different mediator (or a secondary member of the official mediation team) can be useful.

Another way to use intervention is to seek arbitration on the sticking point, either by the existing mediator or, more effectively, by an outside person or group particularly relevant to the point in question. While arbitration can often be criticized for the impositional nature of its solutions, if deadlock is genuinely produced by a mutual despair, it may be seen as both necessary and acceptable by the parties as an alternative to a breakdown in the entire process.

In general, mediation is as much a tool as any other in negotiations. If it is inappropriate for the process as a whole, ad hoc mediation in a variety of forms can be brought in for particular problems. The problem itself will, as always, define the characteristics of the most suitable mediator or arbitrator.

First and foremost, third parties must be generally acceptable to all sides. Usually, this is voiced in terms of the third party's neutrality or impartiality. But no third party is truly impartial or neutral, since they will carry with them an agenda of their own – whether this is an external state with regional interests in the conflict, or simply an individual who may want to take credit for a successful outcome.

As important as impartiality or neutrality is the *acceptability* of the person or agency. Third parties can even come from within the conflict, even from one side of it – for example, religious figures or business or civil leaders – as long as there is sufficient

First and foremost, third parties must be generally acceptable to all sides.

respect for them from all sides and for their capacity to act in a neutral manner. Perhaps the easiest way to summarize this quality of acceptability is to talk in terms of building the same kind of trust which, we argued earlier, must be developed between conflicting parties in order to develop a satisfactory working relationship. The intervenor needs the working trust of all parties in order to function.

3.7.2 Types of intervention

Third-party intervention is a wide-ranging concept. We will borrow the work of leading scholars to get a more focused picture of what it can entail, while always remembering that such a neat analysis is a simplification of the real world. The terms used in the following discussion are somewhat arbitrary; we use them here to clarify distinctions between types of intervention, rather than as recognized definitions.

Essentially, we identify five different, if overlapping, intervention roles, each appropriate at different stages and phases, or for different elements, of the process. Each can be played by separate parties or, more likely, an intervenor will find themselves moving between, or combining, several roles.

Conciliation

A conciliator provides a communication channel between the parties. The main aims of conciliation are to help identify the major issues of contention, to lower tensions between parties, and to move the parties closer to direct interaction (i.e., negotiation) over the identified issues. In our framework, conciliation is particularly beneficial at the *pre-negotiation* stage, where it has the effect of clarifying the agenda for subsequent discussion, encouraging the building of a "common mental map"; reducing tensions and facilitating greater understanding of each other's aims and goals; and building the initial stages of a bridge between adversaries that will lead to more co-operative approaches. There is no requirement that the protagonists actually meet together during conciliation.

The work of the Quaker Adam Curle in the Nigerian conflict of 1967–1970 is an instance of conciliation. Although Curle and his colleagues never brought the Nigerian Government or the Biafran rebels together, they shuttled between the two sides with messages, engaging in bilateral discussions with each side in order to help them get a clearer picture of their position, their view of the issues and their ideas for solution, floating possibilities for progress to each side, and so on.

Facilitation

A facilitator addresses the relationship and issues between conflicting parties. The facilitator brings representatives of the parties together, usually in a neutral environment. The facilitator chairs joint or separate meetings in order to examine mutual perceptions, and encourages communication in a safe and non-threatening way and joint analysis of the problem. Each party is encouraged to express its perceptions of the other, as well as its notion of the other's perception of it. The facilitator assists the setting of ground-rules and manages the process of the discusions; the participants retain control of the content. This can take place when the parties are not able to agree on a chair for the meetings or the process. With mutual understanding thus increased, the parties move on to joint discussion of their situation and their problem, and eventually to joint co-operative analysis and problem-solving. Facilitation assumes that improved mutual knowledge, improved understanding and trust, and strengthened communication channels will assist in clearing the way for the parties to engage in direct substantive negotiation over the issues that divide them.

The Norwegian back-channel arguably functioned as facilitation – confidential, unofficial discussion and relationship-building in a neutral venue, with no expectation that agreement had to be reached. The problem-solving workshops facilitated by Herb Kelman, a US academic, between Israeli and Palestinian groups over a twenty-year period are excellent examples. Kelman identifies individuals with influence within their communities – policy advisers, second-tier politicians, academics, opinion-formers, and so on. He hosts three- to five-day joint meetings with them on neutral ground. Importantly, they come as individuals, whatever their official status at home. Led by a team of facilitators, they work through the agenda of swapping understandings of the conflict and of each other, of identifying and discussing obstacles to progress and then jointly brainstorming possible solutions to those obstacles. The confidentiality of the meetings, and the control of process retained by the facilitators, make the meetings non-threatening. They contribute to issue clarification as well as relationship building. The individuals take the results of the workshop – increased understanding and respect, clari-

fied issues, scenarios for progress – back with them to feed into
their official apparatus.

Arbitration

A third party that functions as an arbitrator brings authority
and legitimacy to the proceedings which permit the arbitrator to
impose a solution equally on all the conflicting parties. The arbitrator listens to all sides of the argument, considers the merits of
the respective cases, and then constructs a settlement in a fair
and just way. The key distinctions of arbitration are two-fold.
First, the solution comes from the third party, not the conflicting parties. They do not necessarily engage in discussions to construct that solution, beyond advocating their own point of view
to the arbitrator. Second, the authority of the arbitrator is such
that the conflicting parties are bound to the ruling its solution
as binding. They may well be faced with rewards for compliance
and punishments for non-compliance.

Arbitration rarely, if ever, serves as the sole approach to
managing deep-rooted conflict: because of the depth of feeling
involved in such conflict, solutions which are not "owned" by the
disputants are usually inappropriate. The legal nature of arbitration can, however, be useful in contributing to a settlement.
Regional and international intergovernmental organizations,
(such as the United Nations, Organization of American States,
and so forth) and regional and international courts (such as the
European Court of Justice, the International Court of Justice,
etc.) can sometimes play an arbiter's role on more straightforward
aspects of the conflict.

One recent example of the use of arbitration in a deep-rooted
conflict situation was the appointment of an Arbitral Tribunal
for Brčko, a war-ravaged multi-ethnic municipality in the north-
east of Bosnia. When the Dayton peace agreement was signed,
the issue of Brčko's status was considered too contentious to be
settled, and was left to later arbitration. Although the Brcko
Arbitral Tribunal was not without its problems, its establishment
did have the useful effect of defusing the issue and removing a
potential stumbling block from the original Dayton agreement,
to be dealt with at a later time.

Pure mediation

A pure mediator's role is to facilitate direct negotiation on
the substantive issues, with the aim of producing a lasting settle-

3.7 Third-Party Assistance

ment. The use of the word "pure" implies no judgement as to its quality or morality. Put simply, the pure mediator has no power outside the negotiation situation, and any power within the negotiations rests at all times on the continued permission of the conflicting parties. Pure mediation involves the use of process skills, techniques and experience to urge the parties on, or ease their path, towards a solution which they themselves design, refine and ultimately implement. The conflicting parties at all times hold the initiative. The mediator merely uses reasoning, unforced persuasion, the control of information and the generation of alternatives to encourage them to reach agreement.

Additionally, the mediator can play a vital role in outlining the consequences of proposals and options: by putting him or herself in the shoes of the other side, a mediator can effectively "reality-test" a party's proposal in advance. Throughout the process, the pure mediator's role is a major one, but their status is minor in comparison to the conflicting parties. The pure mediator controls process but, beyond suggesting options and scenarios, has little or no direct input into the substance of the outcome. Jimmy Carter's interventions in the Eritrean conflict, the Catholic church's facilitation of talks on Angola, and many other behind-the-scenes dialogue processes are examples of pure mediation.

Power mediation

This builds on pure mediation, but with one huge difference: the mediator has power, drawn from its position outside the negotiation situation, to persuade the parties to obey. The power mediator shares all the aims of the pure mediator, but the means are different: the power mediator has leverage over the conflicting parties. It uses incentives and punishments – carrots and sticks – to persuade the parties to yield inflexible positions and to embrace compromise. But such movement is based on the power relations between the mediator and each party, rather than on the inter-party relationship. The power mediator takes the initiative in the process, rather than leaving it with the conflicting parties. The mediator's status at all times constrains the activities of the conflicting parties; they need to consider carefully their relationship with the mediator, and the consequences of endangering that relationship. The power mediator has its own agenda, and frequently its own preferred outcome. And it has a degree of influence over the parties to move them towards that outcome. Furthermore, unlike all the other intervenor roles except the arbitrator, the power mediator has the leverage to provide subsequent incentives (or punishments) to guarantee the agreed outcome and to ensure continued compliance.

Many examples exist. Indeed, most instances of hosted negotiations in the international arena tend to involve predominantly power mediation: President Carter at Camp David, US diplomats such as Richard Holbrooke at Dayton, joint US-Soviet influence at Bicesse, the UN Special Representative in the Iran-Iraq War, and so on. In reality, pure and power mediation are often not quite as distinct as our definitions here might suggest.

3.7.3 Official and unofficial intervention

The preceding five-part terminology, in which mediation represents only two types of intervention among five, is presented here in order to highlight the various approaches to third-party intervention. Another, simpler, way to distinguish between types of third-party roles is to group them under *official* and *unofficial* headings. Once again, such terms are offered only for the specific purpose of maintaining clarity in this discussion. *Official* intervention is also termed "track one" diplomacy (that is, part of the official international diplomatic discourse), in contrast to "track two" diplomacy, which is more of an *unofficial* or informal complement to the formal diplomatic process. Thus, formal negotiations convened between disputants by, say, a head of government are an instance of official intervention; informal dialogue between them assisted by, for example, a Quaker group, would constitute more unofficial intervention, which might supplement or lead to more formal dialogue.

Clearly facilitation, conciliation and, in particular, pure mediation have in common one central factor: the intervenor brings no real power or influence to bear on the proceedings, beyond that which is voluntarily given to them by the conflicting parties. In that sense, the mediator has no "official" status or power outside the negotiations.

By contrast, arbitration and power mediation base their authority on the "official" status and power levels which the intervenor wields in the outside world: as a judge, a regional leader or the head of an influential state, for example. To oversimplify for a moment, an unofficial intervenor might arrive and say, "I'm Bill, and I'm here to help". An official intervenor might say,

3.7 Third-Party Assistance

"I'm President Bill Clinton, and I'm here to help". Immediately, the latter brings with him all manner of influence and leverage over the conflicting parties that the former will not have. This is not to say, however, that the unofficial intervenor cannot have an influential effect on negotiations. Precisely the fact that they are unempowered from outside can give unofficial intervenors more ready access to the process – more acceptability to all sides – as well as free them to make suggestions without being suspected of ulterior motives or agendas. The point of being an official intervenor is to bring outside influence and legitimacy to bear on the negotiation. The point of being an unofficial intervenor is to operate free from such influence.

Both official and unofficial intervention – power and pure mediation – are valuable. Where all parties are anxious to reach agreement, unofficial intervention by a pure mediator might be best suited. Where there is reluctance to enter negotiations, or to offer substantive compromise towards an outcome, intervention by a power mediator may supply the muscle to overcome such obstacles. In the negotiation process, it is very important that the mediator's role is recognized and its terms of reference are accepted and agreed at an early stage, even if that includes an acceptance that different status and different terms may be needed at different stages. Naturally, the terms of reference of the mediator are set by the parties.

There is no set protocol for the way in which mediators go about their work, but in general terms they will clarify the issues that divide parties, determine the degree of flexibility which parties have on those issues and the importance which parties attach to them, identify interests that lie behind parties' stated positions, generate options and assist parties to formulate proposals, suggest trade-offs, communicate messages, reduce tensions, and encourage a rational appreciation of proposals that may be forthcoming. They will encourage concentration on the issues and constructive engagement between the parties. They may develop their own proposals for consideration by the parties which the parties do not own and therefore do not need to defend. They will reality-test parties' perceptions, positions and proposals, to develop a realistic appreciation of whether these things are tenable. Good mediators will have sophisticated problem-solving skills which enable them to help parties to determine key problems, diagnose them, develop a range of approa-

Box 7

FORMS OF THIRD-PARTY INTERVENTION

The following are five different, if overlapping, intervention roles, each appropriate at different stages of the negotiating process. The terms used are to clarify distinctions between types of intervention, rather than as recognized definitions.

"Track One" Diplomacy (official intervention): intervenor holds "official" status and power internationally.

1. **Arbitration** – The arbitrator listens to all sides of the argument, considers the merits of the respective cases, and then constructs a settlement in a fair and just way. In an arbitration, the solution comes from the third party, not the conflicting parties; and the authority of the arbitrator is such that the conflicting parties are bound to accept its solution as binding.

   For example: the Brčko Arbitral Tribunal in Bosnia.

2. **Power mediation** – In this case the mediator has power to persuade the parties to obey. It uses incentives and punishments to persuade the parties to yield inflexible positions and to compromise.

   For example: President Jimmy Carter at Camp David and US negotiators at Dayton.

"Track Two" Diplomacy (unofficial intervention): intervenor brings no real power or influence to bear on proceedings.

3. **Conciliation** – The conciliator provides a communication channel between the two parties. He or she helps to identify the major issues of contention, to lower tensions between parties, and to move the parties closer to direct interaction. There is no requirement that the protagonists actually meet together during conciliation.

   For example: the work of Quaker Adam Curle in the Nigerian conflict of 1967–1970.

4. **Facilitation** – The facilitator brings representatives of the parties together. He or she chairs joint or separate meetings in order to examine mutual perceptions and encourages communication in a safe and non-threatening way.

   For example: the problem-solving workshops facilitated by Herb Kelman, a US academic, between Israeli and Palestinian groups over a twenty-year period.

5. **Pure mediation** – A pure mediator's role is to facilitate or direct negotiation on the substantive issues, with the aim of producing lasting settlement. The pure mediator uses process skills and experience to urge the parties on towards a solution that they themselves design, refine and implement.

   For example: the Catholic church's facilitation of talks on Angola.

ches to address them, and then settle on a way forward. Problem solving is the core skill of the mediator. Finally, they will assist the parties in recording outcomes in language which permits no ambiguity or consequent conflict of interpretation.

Mediation may add value in a number of respects to negotiation. By managing the manner of engagement between the parties, it can significantly enhance the quality of the engagement. Mediators will work with parties, in joint session or separately, and may bring chief negotiators together in one-on-one meetings. The simple test will always be what process design is most likely to enhance the prospects of progress.

3.8 Conclusion

This single chapter perhaps belies the amount of work required in process design. A wealth of detail needs to be addressed in order to get the optimum design for the circumstances. Nevertheless, the effort is vital. Without a properly designed and maintained process vehicle, the negotiations will never complete the journey towards a sustainable outcome. However, with sufficient work completed in analysing the conflict, and then in designing the process, we can finally move on to consider the question of designing an outcome. The contents of this outcome – the institutions and mechanisms which can be put in place to promote a sustainable democratic settlement – will be examined in the following chapter.

A wealth of detail needs to be addressed in order to get the optimum design for the circumstances. Nevertheless, the effort is vital.

DEVELOPING A NEGOTIATION PROCESS

Below we outline the major elements that need to be pre-negotiated and present a menu of options for each.

1. PARTICIPANTS

- Open channels of communication, however small or informal, in an attempt to start the contact and communication;
- Include all parties with a serious claim to be involved;
- Build a sufficient mainstream-based pro-negotiation coalition to open talks with some substantial hope of achieving an outcome, and hope to co-opt abstainers, or persuade excluded parties to adapt their behaviour to fit the rules of entry;
- Open negotiations with a less than comprehensive range of parties, with the aim of achieving a settlement that excluded parties can be persuaded to live with;
- Allow equal numbers of delegates per party;
- Allow variable delegation sizes based on electoral strength or status (where elections have been held);
- Set an electoral or other threshold to restrict or enable participation;
- Limit participation only to those parties who enjoy substantial support;
- Allow for different degrees of status in the process (e.g., participant and observer) for different parties;
- Distinguish groupings within the negotiation process who may be opposed on some, possibly major, issues but share positions on others.

2. PRECONDITIONS AND BARRIERS TO NEGOTIATION

- Drop preconditions to negotiations, and accept all comers;
- Use the pre-negotiation process to work through preconditions and questions of legitimacy and recognition of spokespersons;

- Open out preconditions initially aimed at one party into a principled statement to which all parties can and must agree;
- Address preconditions and the commitment to the negotiation process in an unofficial discussion process prior to formal negotiation.

3. LEVELLING THE PLAYING-FIELD

- Accept, at least within the negotiation context, the right of all sides to be present;
- Agree on procedures permitting the involvement of previously excluded or restricted persons;
- Schedule time and resources to permit all parties to come to the table prepared;
- Make contact with, and learn from, counterparts from other contexts;
- Look to an external powerful mediator or chairperson both to bestow at least temporary legitimacy on all parties equally for the duration of talks, and to underwrite the equality of all parties at the table.

4. RESOURCING THE NEGOTIATIONS

- Negotiations which are self-funded by each side;
- Negotiations in which one party offers to resource most or all of the negotiations;
- Negotiations in which contributions from other domestic actors are sought;
- Negotiations funded by international bodies.

5. FORM OF NEGOTIATIONS

- Large-scale conferences;
- Summits of key spokespersons;
- Full round table sessions;
- Shuttle mediation;
- Bilateral discussions;
- A mixed formula of plenaries and subgroups;
- Acknowledgement of dissenting coalitions by means of minority reports;
- Defining different roles and capacities for negotiators and observers.

6. VENUE AND LOCATION

- Identify a neutral venue, of no particular symbolism or support to any one party;
- Agree on a domestic venue acceptable to all parties;
- Assure equal accessibility to the venue for all parties;
- Supplement official or formal discussion forums by unofficial, off-the-record and possibly deniable channels of communication outside and around the formal table.

7. COMMUNICATION AND INFORMATION EXCHANGE

- Secret negotiations out of all sight;
- Closed negotiation sessions, with occasional or regular progress reports to the outside world, agreed by all parties;
- An agreed press embargo among all participants (with enforcement mechanisms to be negotiated among the parties);

- Relations with the media being at each party's discretion;
- Ceding the public relations role by agreement to the chairperson or mediator;
- Establishing a permanent press secretariat to manage media relations on behalf of all;
- Establishing a central secretariat to channel information between the parties;
- Forming a subcommittee with responsibility for inter-party communication.

8. SETTING THE SUBSTANTIVE AGENDA

- Establish pre-negotiation processes, either public or private, and possibly with a reduced number of delegates, to define the agenda prior to formal negotiation;
- Use the formal negotiation process to resolve procedural and agenda matters;
- Order agenda items according to contentiousness and importance;
- Adopt a long-range policy of a series of negotiations, each building on the achievements of the last.

9. MANAGING THE PROCEEDINGS

- Negotiation of a system of sharing the chair in such a way that no one party can benefit from their chairing either in general or on key specific agenda items;
- Selection of a party totally suitable to all concerned;
- Selection of a party minimally acceptable to all concerned;
- Identification of the key skills necessary for the function;
- Selection of a party with authority to overrule all concerned if necessary;
- Selection of an unempowered party dependent on continuing consensus among all concerned.

10. TIMEFRAMES

- No time-limits: participants remain until the job is done;
- A pre-agreed time-limit;
- A realistic limit on the goals to be achieved within the time available;
- Aiming for a comprehensive settlement of all aspects of the dispute;
- An option for further negotiating period/s following success in the initial period.

11. DECISION-MAKING PROCEDURES

- Total agreement: all parties must endorse a point for it to be agreed;
- Simple majority acceptance: more than half the parties or delegates agree;
- Consensus: the point is defined and refined until all can agree to it;
- Sufficient consensus: a certain specified proportion of the parties or delegates must agree the point (the exact proportion or criteria to be pre-agreed, and dependent on the number of parties, their relative sizes, and their ability to "sell" the agreement to their broader constituencies);
- Secret ballots to discover the degree of consensus;
- An open show of hands to discover the voting preferences;
- Final ratification by parties, or endorsement by referendum of the final outcome.

Negotiation Processes

REFERENCES AND FURTHER READING

Anstey, Mark. 1991. *Negotiating Conflict: Insights and Skills for Negotiators and Peacemakers*. Kenwyn, SA: Juta and Co Ltd.

Anstey, Mark. 1993. *Practical Peacemaking: A Mediator's Handbook*. Kenwyn, SA: Juta and Co Ltd.

Bloomfield, David. 1997. *Political Dialogue in Northern Ireland: the Brooke Initiative 1989–92*. London: Macmillan.

Clark, Robert P. 1995. "Negotiations for Basque Self-Determination in Spain". In William Zartman, ed. *Elusive Peace: Negotiating an End to Civil Wars*. Washington, DC: Brookings Institute.

Deeb, Mary–Jane and Marius Deeb. 1995. "Internal Negotiations in a Centralist Conflict: Lebanon". In William Zartman, ed. *Elusive Peace: Negotiating an End to Civil Wars*. Washington, DC: Brookings Institute.

Deng, Francis Mading. 1995. "Negotiating a Hidden Agenda: Sudan's Conflict of Identities". In William Zartman, ed. *Elusive Peace: Negotiating an End to Civil Wars*. Washington, DC: Brookings Institute.

Fisher, Ronald J. and Loraleigh Keashly. 1991. "The Potential Complementarity of Mediation and Consultation within a Contingency Model of Third Party Intervention", *Journal of Peace Research*, vol. 28, no. 1. pp. 29–42.

Kelman, Herbert C. and Stephen Cohen. 1976. "The Problem-Solving Workshop: a Social-Psychological Contribution to the Resolution of International Conflicts", *Journal of Peace Research*, vol. XIII, no. 2, pp. 79–90.

Lederach, John Paul. 1995. *Preparing for Peace: Conflict Transformation Across Cultures*. Syracuse, NY: Syracuse University Press.

O'Malley, Padraig. 1996. *Ramaphosa and Meyer in Belfast: the South African Experience: How the New South Africa was Negotiated*. Boston, MA: University of Massachusetts.

Ottaway, Marina. 1995. "Eritrea and Ethiopia: Negotiations in a Transitional Conflict". In William Zartman, ed. *Elusive Peace: Negotiating an End to Civil Wars*. Washington, DC: Brookings Institute.

Princen, Tom. 1991. "Camp David: Problem-solving or Power Politics as Usual?", *Journal of Peace Research*, vol. 28, no. 1. pp. 57–69.

Rothman, Jay. 1990. "A Pre-Negotiation Model: Theory and Training", *Policy Studies*, No. 40. Jerusalem: Leonard David Institute.

Slabbert, Frederick van Zyl. October 1997. "Some Reflections on Successful Negotiation in South Africa". Paper presented in Liverpool, Dublin and Belfast.

Spencer, Dayle E., William Spencer and Honggang Yang. 1992. "Closing the Mediation Gap: The Ethiopia/Eritrea Experience", *Security Dialogue*, vol. 23, no. 3. pp. 89–99.

Wriggins, Howard. "Sri Lanka: Negotiations in a Secessionist Conflict". In William Zartman, ed. *Elusive Peace: Negotiating an End to Civil Wars*. Washington, DC: Brookings Institute.

Zartman, William. ed. 1995. *Elusive Peace: Negotiating an End to Civil Wars*. Washington, DC: Brookings Institute.

Zartman, William, and Saadia Touval. 1985. *International Mediation in Theory and Practice*. Boulder, CO: Westview Press.

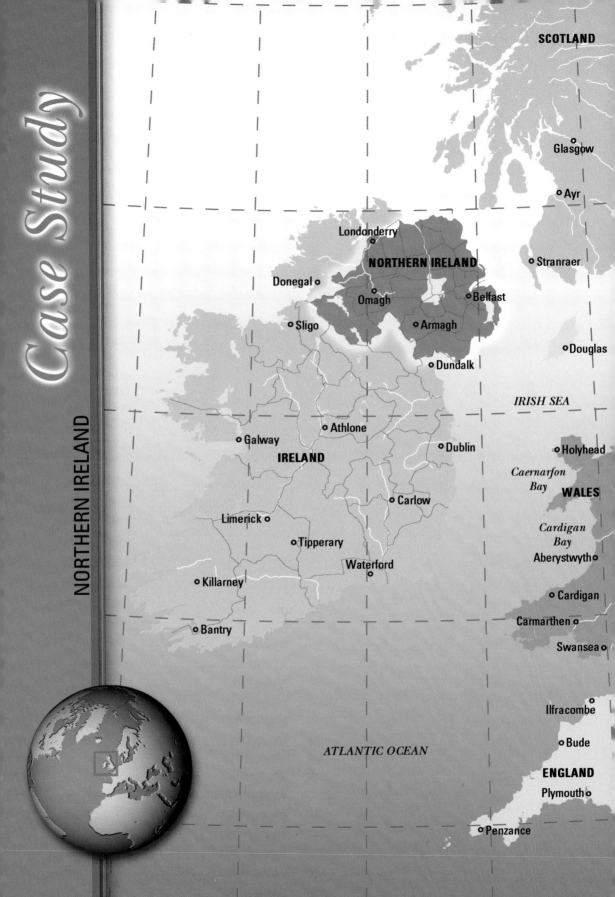

Case Study

NORTHERN IRELAND

SCOTLAND

Glasgow

Ayr

Stranraer

Londonderry

NORTHERN IRELAND

Donegal

Omagh

Belfast

Sligo

Armagh

Douglas

Dundalk

IRISH SEA

Athlone

Dublin

Holyhead

Galway

Caernarfon Bay

IRELAND

WALES

Carlow

Cardigan Bay

Limerick

Aberystwyth

Tipperary

Waterford

Cardigan

Killarney

Carmarthen

Swansea

Bantry

Ilfracombe

Bude

ATLANTIC OCEAN

ENGLAND

Plymouth

Penzance

© International IDEA

David Bloomfield

Case Study: Northern Ireland

NORTHERN IRELAND

The Plantation

Since English forces first arrived to claim the island of Ireland around 1170–1190 CE, centuries of complex Anglo-Irish history have produced Europe's longest-standing identity-related conflict. Space permits no more than a sadly inadequate nod to that rich narrative.

The indigent population at the time of the English invasion were descendants of the Celts who had swept westward across Europe in the pre-Christian era. They had been converted to Christianity during the 5th and 6th centuries. They were rural, agriculturally based and formed a largely decentralized society. The Protestant reformation which took deep root in England mostly passed Ireland by, and its population remained almost wholly Catholic.

As a means of later subjugation, the English introduced the Plantation, an early but obvious form of colonialism. From the early 1600s, hundreds of thousands of settlers from England and lowland Scotland were offered plots of fertile agricultural land if they agreed to be permanently "planted" in Ireland. In the process, most native Irish were displaced from their homes into the barren hills.

The Plantation had two key effects. First, the land displacements created a deep and abiding Irish sense of criminal injustice on the part of the English. Second, the native population was completely Catholic while the settlers were overwhelmingly Protestant. In the context of the times, religion was a central defining factor of culture and politics, and so the two groups, natives and settlers, were instantly alien to each other. Matters were not helped by the Protestant zeal with which the Planters set about subduing the angry but powerless Irish. Oliver Cromwell – in the British context, an heroic revolutionary figure in the development of western democracy – slaughtered Irish Catholics by the thousand in a vicious programme of ethnic cleansing.

The Plantation flourished best in north-east Ireland. For the next 250 years, the history of Ireland developed along two main themes. On the one hand, there were regular but unsuccessful attempts at rebellion by the dispossessed Catholic Irish, during which a cumulative sense of Irish nationalism developed. On the other, the British-sponsored industrialization and economic development of the north-east raced ahead. The region's central city, Belfast, became two things by Victorian times: a heavily industrialized port as integral to the British empire as Liverpool or Southampton (producing ships, textiles, heavy machinery, armaments and, later, aircraft) and a centre of strongly British-oriented culture dominated largely by Protestants. This abiding sense of a British identity translated itself politically into Unionism – support, that is, for the continued Union with Britain.

Northern Ireland

While Irish nationalism spread throughout the rest of Ireland, in the industrial north-east the Unionist focus remained resolutely tied to the British empire as the predominant source of wealth and international and domestic markets and as the channel of access to the outside world. While Irish Catholics increasingly mobilized around the cause of Irish independence, northern Protestants rallied to the cause of the British empire, busily filling its factories and patriotically fighting its wars. Religion had long ceased to be the issue of conflict between these two fundamentally opposed cultural communities, but continued to serve as the badge of identity for both sides.

So by 1900, there existed in Ireland two deeply separated communities, both with long-standing historical claims to the territory, both divided not only by religious labels but also in their politics, history, heritage, culture and economy, who saw their sources of support as different, their relationships to Europe as different, and especially their relationship with the superpower of the day (Britain) as diametrically opposed.

Partition

By the turn of the 20th century, Irish pressure for independence became irresistible. Northern Protestant opposition to the idea was equally strong. Both sides began to arm, each prepared to fight their cause against the British. Heavy-handed British suppression of an abortive 1916 rising in Dublin, the Irish capital, by rebels of the Irish Republican Army (IRA) produced the martyrs who inspired a mass liberation movement. In 1920, limited independence was granted to all 32 counties of Ireland, but the nine counties of the north-east (the province of Ulster) were given the option to opt out of the arrangement. Six of the nine, the ones with Protestant majorities, chose to remain with Britain in the UK, and the island was partitioned in 1921 between the 26 counties of the Irish Free State to the south, and the six counties of Northern Ireland. The Free State fought a bloody internal civil war for a year, before accepting the less-than-total independence on offer. (The Irish Republic declared full independence in 1937.)

Northern Ireland was given its own regional parliament in Belfast. Westminster, while retaining overall sovereignty, adopted a *laissez-faire* attitude and largely ignored Northern Ireland for the next 40 years. The 1.5 million population of the new sub-state had a 2:1 Protestant majority, reflected in its majority-rule parliament which effectively operated under permanent Unionist control. The discontented Catholics of Northern Ireland were viewed by this parliament – with some justification but much exaggeration – as subversive agents of the new and hostile foreign state to the south: they were not to be trusted or worked with, they were to be feared, controlled and excluded.

Northern Ireland

Case Study: Northern Ireland

With its permanent majority, and its deep-seated insecurities, the Northern Ireland State practised decades of discrimination against Catholics in employment, voting, education, housing, and so on. A highly segregated society developed, ruled by a permanently Unionist government who controlled a highly armed and 90 per cent Protestant police force. For 40 years, the society remained stagnant, with two almost totally separate communities living parallel lives in a patchwork of small segregated areas, each with their own housing, schools, shops, churches, factories, clubs, sports, etc.

The Troubles

The stagnation ended in the 1960s. Catholic university students, influenced by the US civil rights movement, took to the streets to demand an end to the discriminatory practices of the Northern state. The "Troubles" thus began as a conflict between Catholics and the state over civil rights. It escalated rapidly as the state and police responded brutally to a largely peaceful protest movement. In 1969, the Unionist Government realized that the situation was out of control, and requested the British army to intervene. A burgeoning of hard-line Unionism frustrated any last-minute attempts at moderate reform which might have quelled unrest. By 1972 the government was in complete disarray, but still resisting demands for reform, and Westminster stepped in to close down the Belfast Parliament and assume direct rule over Northern Ireland.

Britain moved rapidly to redress the more glaring civil rights grievances; but the British army acted towards the Catholic community in extremely heavy-handed fashion, rapidly alienating the Catholics it had arrived to protect. As Catholics rushed to defend themselves against the threat of armed British troops and a Protestant backlash, the IRA – almost defunct in the 1960s – was reborn. The British army has remained ever since.

From 1972, what had begun as a civil rights protest by the Catholic community towards the Protestant/Unionist Government was transformed into a war of liberation waged by the IRA against the British Government and army, and against the local police.

The next 20 years form a history of failed political initiatives, occasional short-lived cease-fires, an ebb and flow in the level of violence, economic and social devastation to the region, the institutionalization of violence in Northern Irish society, and an eventual military stalemate that neither side could win outright. In the process, both communities grew more polarized than ever, the sense of stagnation prevailed, and more than 3,000 people died violently as each community mythologized its contemporary martyrs and heroes.

The battle-lines were clearly drawn up. Catholics overwhelmingly supported the Irish nationalist cause, which aspired to a united and independent Ireland. The

Northern Ireland

main nationalist political party, the Social Democratic and Labour Party (SDLP),
espoused peaceful means towards a more just political system in Northern Ireland
and towards eventual Irish unity. Within nationalism, the smaller Republican movement, consisting of the paramilitary IRA and the political party Sinn Fein (in the
Irish language, "Ourselves Alone") advocated violent struggle to rid Ireland of the
British presence. Protestants equally fervently supported the cause of Unionism
(that is, a continuation of the union of Northern Ireland with Britain within the
UK). Mainstream political opinion was represented by the Ulster Unionist Party
(UUP), who had controlled the parliament until 1972, tempered by the smaller and
more hard-line Democratic Unionist Party (DUP), formed in the late 1960s by Ian
Paisley in response to perceived weakness within the UUP. On the fringes of
Unionism were the loyalists, paramilitary and political counterparts to the
Republicans, who adopted anti-nationalist violence to protect the Union.

Peace Initiatives

Having assumed direct rule of Northern Ireland in 1972, the British Government
had managed by late 1973 to drag the mainstream political representatives of
Unionism and Nationalism, and the Government of the Irish Republic in the South,
to a shaky political agreement that involved a new power-sharing government in the
North, and a new cross-border Council of Ireland to facilitate Southern input into
the North's affairs. The new government, consisting of both the UUP and the SDLP,
lasted for the first five months of 1974, before massive and militant protest by the
Protestant community, enraged by the proposed Council of Ireland, brought it to
collapse and control reverted to Westminster. Direct rule continued uninterrupted
until 1998.

Throughout the 1970s and 1980s, Britain made several further attempts at
political settlement. From time to time, elections would be held for a new parliamentary assembly, but the resulting bodies were always boycotted by one side or the
other. British policy was two-pronged. One aim was to enable a power-sharing government which would bring nationalists into a share in government within
Northern Ireland. The other aim was known as the "Irish dimension": placating
nationalism by permitting the Irish Republic a degree of influence in Northern
affairs. Unionists might accept some form of the first, but wholly rejected the second; while nationalists were deeply suspicious of the first without the second.

Throughout the period, paramilitaries in general, and Republicans in particular,
were excluded from political consideration. By common consent, their adoption of
violence precluded them from the democratic process. In return, the Republican
movement totally and violently rejected any of the proposed solutions.

In 1981, in the relentless glare of international publicity, 10 IRA prisoners starved
themselves to death in a stand-off with British Prime Minister Thatcher over their

Northern Ireland

Case Study: Northern Ireland

claims to be political prisoners of war (as opposed to criminals). The resulting wave of sympathy for Republicanism bolstered the fortunes of its political party, Sinn Fein which, at the same time, decided to end decades of abstentionism and begin contesting elections in both North and South.

In response to this perceived political threat from a resurgent Republican movement, the political parties of the Irish Republic and the SDLP met in the 1983 New Ireland Forum to develop a new definition of constitutional Irish nationalism. The resulting Forum Report effectively redesigned Irish nationalism, and its language and content were greatly influenced by the SDLP leader, John Hume. Old, simplistic anti-British sentiments were replaced with new tenets of commitment to peaceful politics and respect for the unionist tradition. The Irish Government took the thinking of the Report as a basis for entering negotiations with Britain over what became the 1985 Anglo-Irish Agreement, a melding of both governments' aspirations towards peaceful resolution of the Northern question. The Agreement established several key factors formally: the governments' commitment to work together for peace, an Intergovernmental Conference in which Irish ministers could regularly question and comment upon British policy in the North, and a secretariat of Irish officials located in a Belfast suburb.

This international treaty between the two sovereign nations had two powerful effects. First, it made the Republic of Ireland a partner with Britain in the process, in contrast to their previous history of antagonism over Northern Ireland. Political initiatives would now be authored not by Britain alone, but by both governments in partnership. The "Irish dimension" was thus moving closer to reality. But second, in contrast to Hume's close, if unofficial, involvement in the drafting of the Agreement, Unionists were not consulted about the intergovernmental negotiations. They reacted with shocked anger to an Agreement that had both ignored their opinion in its construction and, in their view, weakened the link with the UK by allowing a "foreign" government to meddle in their affairs. Deeply alienated, Unionist politicians withdrew from all contact with the British Government.

By 1989, however, Unionist opposition had failed to prevent the Agreement from becoming an established fact. The Irish Government was now an engaged partner in the political process with Britain, and Unionist anger, initially and tellingly mobilized around the slogan "Ulster Says No!", had turned to frustration. Realizing that continued non co-operation would only make things even worse, they finally agreed to enter discussions with the British about possible political structures, and eventually in 1991 the UUP and DUP entered British-facilitated negotiations with the SDLP and the small, cross-community Alliance Party. Those talks failed to make much progress, bogging down in early arguments over procedural issues. But they did serve to set and clarify the agenda for future discussions into three strands –

Northern Ireland

power-sharing arrangements for an internal Northern Ireland government under British rule as long as a majority of the Northern population voted to retain the Union; the practical shape of North-South institutions to strengthen the Irish dimension; and a more developed Irish-British treaty to replace the Agreement.

By the consent of all involved, paramilitary political parties from both communities were still excluded, until such times as they would renounce violence.

The following year, talks were resumed for a further four months, and made some progress on all three agenda strands, but eventually collapsed far short of agreement. Meanwhile, Hume had initiated dialogue with Sinn Fein with the ultimate aim of persuading them away from violence and into the political process. During these discussions, and even during subsequent secret British-Sinn Fein communications, IRA violence – bombs and shootings – continued against the British army and the Northern Ireland police, and spread to a devastating bombing campaign in England. At the same time, the two main loyalist paramilitary groups developed a new degree of sophistication both militarily, becoming much more active against Republicans, and politically, developing new political parties to represent their views and try to wean voters away from the mainstream Unionist parties. The Ulster Defence Association (UDA) developed the Ulster Democratic Party (UDP), and the Ulster Volunteer Force (UVF) produced the Progressive Unionist Party (PUP).

Sinn Fein, the UDP and PUP all began to increase their political profile, but all were strictly excluded from negotiations.

By 1994, however, Hume's dialogue with Sinn Fein had developed into a wider nationalist consensus involving their two Northern parties, the Irish Government and Irish America (where a new and much less pro-British President Clinton had been installed). The pressure intensified on Sinn Fein leader Gerry Adams to accept the military stalemate and the necessity to engage democratically in the political process. The result was the IRA's cessation of violence in August 1994, followed a month later by a loyalist cease-fire.

But political progress was too slow to satisfy Republicans. Supported by Unionists, the British at first demanded an IRA statement that the cease-fire was permanent – a concession which the IRA saw as tantamount to a surrender, and refused to give – and then insisted, equally ineffectually, that IRA weapons be handed over before Sinn Fein be permitted entry to negotiations. The British insisted on disarmament and then talks; the paramilitaries on both sides insisted on talks first and then subsequent disarming. All other discussions about progress foundered on this rock of the decommissioning of weapons. Until that issue was resolved, the British and the Unionists refused to admit paramilitary parties to any negotiations. Former US Senator George Mitchell was brought in to chair a commission into the question of

Northern Ireland

Case Study: Northern Ireland

disarmament of paramilitaries as part of the broad peace process. The commission accepted that no group was going to disarm before talks, and suggested two compromises. First, disarming should happen *during* talks, in parallel to political progress and as part of confidence-building measures. Second, a set of six principles of non-violence were established, which all parties would have to endorse on entry to the negotiations. These included a commitment to purely peaceful means, and a renunciation of violence as a means either to achieve political ends or to undermine an unfavourable political outcome.

But attitudes all round had hardened in the period since the cease-fires, with all sides trying to use politics merely to wage war by other means. Eighteen months after the IRA cease-fire, Sinn Fein were no closer to inclusion in any substantive talks process, and in February 1996 the IRA suspended its cease-fire and returned to a limited military campaign, mostly aimed at British military and economic targets. The loyalist paramilitaries edgily maintained their own cease-fire agreement. Elections went ahead to identify participants to a talks process that started in June 1996, but Sinn Fein were excluded once again until such times as the IRA might call another cease-fire. The talks rambled on, but failed to get beyond the continuing procedural wrangles about decommissioning and the terms of Sinn Fein's admission. With his parliamentary majority down to one, Conservative Prime Minister Major could exert little influence over the traditionally conservative UUP parliamentary group led by David Trimble, whose 10 MPs held a potential balance of power.

Agreement

But with the June 1997 installation of a Labour government with an unassailable parliamentary majority, the pace picked up once more. A new IRA cease-fire was called the following month, and inclusive talks began in September under the chair of George Mitchell. No weapons were handed in, but all parties signed up to the Mitchell principles of non-violence. For the very first time, Sinn Fein, the UDP and the PUP were all included around the table. In response, the DUP and another tiny Unionist political newcomer, the UK Unionist Party (UKUP) walked out. Around the table, long-standing suspicions and antagonisms were rife, and progress was interminably slow as historic foes sparred nervously with each other in an uncomfortable process. The two earlier talks attempts had exclusively involved only the four mainstream and non-violent parties and the two governments. This time around, the inclusion of the paramilitary politicians increased the chances that any potential settlement could be more comprehensive in effectively addressing the issues of violence, and in finally removing the gun from Irish politics. But at the same time, inclusiveness greatly widened the distance between the viewpoints represented around the table, and made compromise all the more difficult.

Northern Ireland

Three months of talks became rapidly bogged down once again in procedural issues, with parties fighting every point. Delays and obstructionism continued, as politicians on all sides were deeply challenged at the prospects both of facing their long-standing enemies across the table and of finally accepting a less-than-perfect negotiated compromise after decades of promoting absolutist positions of outright victory. Confidence-building measures ran in parallel to the talks, consisting largely of concessions by the two governments over paramilitary prisoners, and a lowering of the British army profile on the ground.

As the talks inched forward painfully into 1998, frustration grew at the extreme fringes on both sides. New anti-cease-fire paramilitary groupings emerged from both republicanism and loyalism, and bombings and shootings began once more. After a series of murders by the UDA, its political party the UDP was suspended for several weeks from the negotiations for a period of "quarantine" until the cease-fire had been restored. Shortly thereafter, Sinn Fein was suspended for two weeks because of similar IRA activity. The violence of the politically represented paramilitaries again subsided, but that of the uncontrolled extremes continued sporadically.

In late March, Mitchell finally announced a two-week deadline for the talks process. By this stage, he argued, all the relevant issues had been discussed. There was no need for further discussion or elaboration: what was needed now was a demonstration of the political will to reach agreement. He set the deadline of midnight on 9 April for an agreement.

Amidst heightened tension, signs appeared that his ultimatum, backed up by pressure from London, Dublin and Washington, might indeed produce results. Both Irish and British premiers arrived at the talks venue, and a hotline to the White House was established. The midnight deadline passed, talks continued through the night and another day, and finally, to universal surprise, after 32 hours of straight negotiation, an agreement was announced on 10 April.

The Agreement ran to over 10,000 words. It reflected closely the three-stranded agenda upon which it was negotiated. At its heart were the design and fast-track implementation of new core political structures and constitutional changes, supported by various commissions, each with specific deadlines for implementation, to oversee issues whose detail was yet to be filled in. The Agreement would be offered to the people of both North and South in simultaneous referendums in May 1998.

Of the core changes, the first would be the removal from the Irish Constitution of the territorial claim to the North, in parallel with a British repeal of outstanding legislation claiming jurisdiction over Ireland as a whole.

In Strand One, in June 1998, a 108-member Northern Ireland Assembly would be elected by a single transferable vote form of proportional representation, thus enabling the election of smaller parties. The Assembly's consensus voting mecha-

Northern Ireland

Case Study: Northern Ireland

nism would require minimally 40 per cent support from each of the unionist and nationalist blocs, provided that comprised at least 60 per cent of the overall vote. Its early decisions would concern the election of a First Minister, Deputy First Minister and 10 ministers with departmental responsibilities. All these posts would be allocated in proportion to party strength.

In Strand Two, a North-South Ministerial Council would be established consisting of ministers from both the Irish Parliament and the Northern Irish Assembly. (The Assembly will not be permitted to continue in operation unless the Council is implemented.) Once constituted, the Council would devise cross-border implementation bodies with an "absolute commitment" to work together in at least 12 specified areas of common interest. Council decisions will be by agreement, and a strict timetable is specified for the operation of all these arrangements.

In Strand Three, a new Irish-British Treaty would replace and take over the workings of the 1985 Anglo-Irish Agreement, and would permit intergovernmental co-operation on Northern matters (including sensitive ones such as security, etc.) not yet devolved to the Assembly. A British-Irish Council to promote wider regional co-operation would be established, comprising representatives from the Irish and British governments, the Northern Assembly, and the forthcoming devolved assemblies to be established in Scotland and Wales.

Around these key structures, specific timetables were set for establishing other reinforcing mechanisms. The European Convention on Human Rights will be fully incorporated into Northern Irish law. A new Northern Ireland Human Rights Commission will co-operate through committee with its Irish counterpart. Commissions will also be established in Northern Ireland on equality, weapons decommissioning (to be completed within two years of the referendums), police reform, and the criminal justice system. Finally, mechanisms will be put in place by both governments to facilitate the accelerated release (within two years) of all paramilitary prisoners from groups continuing to observe cease-fires.

It was a tortuous document, produced through a tortuous process, and was not without a degree of the fudge that has characterized Irish negotiations for 10 years. When it came to voting in the Northern referendum and the Assembly election, the key divisive issues were not the core political structures that had entailed so much painstaking negotiation. Instead, the predominantly Unionist anti-Agreement vote rallied around the emotive issues of early prisoner release, victims' rights, and doubts over the effectiveness of weapons decommissioning. The referendum revealed fundamental divisions within Unionism. Nationalists, Republicans, Alliance, loyalist parties and moderate Unionists won a 71 per cent pro-Agreement majority in the referendum, and a narrow but workable majority in the Assembly. The UUP's Trimble was elected First Minister, with the SDLP deputy leader as his

Northern Ireland

Deputy. But the DUP, UKUP and significant UUP elements coalesced into a hard-line obstructionist tendency. The situation remained very tense throughout the summer of 1998. Anti-Agreement Unionist's street protests waxed and waned, threatening the fragile majority consensus. A small but well-armed anti-ceasefire group split off from the IRA and embarked on a devastating bombing campaign in the North. As the politicians returned to work in September to begin implementing the provisions of the Agreement, there was still no certainty of success.

Northern Ireland

CHAPTER 4

Appropriately crafted
democratic institutions
are crucial to the
sustainability of any
negotiated settlement.

This chapter addresses the need to inform domestic political actors about the options available to them in terms of democratic institutions. It outlines the way in which basic institutions and policies can be purposely designed to maximize the prospects of democracy taking root in post-conflict societies. It also aims to draw these issues to the attention of interested external actors in the international community, who may be charged with the responsibility of crafting a settlement or supervising a period of state reconstruction. The following constitutional and policy levers are discussed, and the advantages and disadvantages of various options analysed.

Ben Reilly

Democratic Levers for Conflict
Management

Democratic Levers: An Introduction

S ince the early 1970s a revised focus on the possibilities and
prospects of democracy in divided societies has been evident around the world. At the base of this new wave of
interest in democracy has been a recognition that democratic
government, rather than oligarchy or authoritarianism, presented the best prospects for managing deep societal divisions.
Democracy increasingly came to be seen as not just possible, but
necessary, for the peaceful management of divided societies.
This more optimistic assessment of the potential of democracy
was greatly boosted by what has been characterized as the "third
wave" of democratization which, beginning in the 1970s and gaining pace in the early 1990s, has seen a threefold increase in the
number of democratic governments around the world.

This unprecedented expansion of democratic government,
concentrated particularly in the developing world, has led to a
renewed focus on the question of which institutional arrangements are most likely to secure stable and legitimate democratic government in divided or post-conflict societies. There is an
increasing recognition that the design of political institutions is
a key factor affecting the likelihood or otherwise of democratic
consolidation, stability and longevity. A better understanding of
the effects of political institutions also holds out the possibility
that we may be able to design institutions so that desired outcomes – for example, co-operation and compromise – are rewar-
ded. Three broad areas of constitutional design have received
particular attention in this regard: the territorial structure of the
state; the form of the state's legislative and executive functions;
and the nature and structure of a state's rules of political representation. This has meant careful examination of the competing
claims of different forms of power sharing, federalism, the benefits of parliamentary versus presidential government, the political consequences of different electoral laws, and so on. Recent
transitions to democracy in South Africa, Chile, the Philippines
and elsewhere have also focused attention on "extra-constitutional" institutions and policies which may be of particular util-

*At the base of this new
wave of interest in
democracy has been a
recognition that
democratic
government, rather
than oligarchy or
authoritarianism,
presented the best
prospects for
managing deep
societal divisions.*

ity to countries emerging from a period of deep hostility and conflict. These include the use of transitional justice mechanisms such as truth and reconciliation commissions, war crime tribunals, gender commissions, electoral administrations and so on. While there are many devices, these interlocking "constitutional" and "extra-constitutional" mechanisms will be the focus of this chapter.

A basic precept of this handbook is that robust democratic governance is itself a fundamental pillar of building any sustainable settlement of a violent conflict. Democracy is a system by which conflicts in a society are allowed to formulate, find expression and be managed in a sustainable way, via institutional outlets such as political parties and representative parliaments, rather than being suppressed or ignored. It is, in the words of Adam Przeworski, a system for *managing* and *processing* rather than resolving conflicts. Disputes under democracy are never definitively "solved"; rather they are temporarily accommodated and thus reformulated for next time. The best example of this is the electoral process itself, where parties and individuals may "win" or "lose", but where the losers may win next time and the winners know that their victory is only temporary.

Furthermore, the comparative experience of deeply divided societies to date strongly indicates that democratic procedures, which have the necessary inclusiveness and flexibility to manage deep-rooted identity-based conflicts, stand the best chance of delivering a lasting peace. In societies divided along identity lines, for example, the type of political institutions that protect group and individual rights, deliver meaningful devolution and encourage political bargaining are probably only possible within the frameworks of a democracy. Democracy is based, at least in part, on a common conception and adherence to the "rule of law", which protects both political actors and the wider civil society. Ultimately, as democratic practices and values become internalized in the workings of society, democratic governance creates the conditions for its own sustenance. That is why a valuable indicator as to whether a country is likely to continue to be democratic is to look at its history: the longer the democratic history to date, the better the prospects that such behaviour will continue in the future.

A "minimal" conception of democracy, in terms of the right to participate in free and fair elections, has rapidly emerged as a fundamental international norm for states to observe. For democracy to be meaningful, however, these "rules of the game"

Democratic Levers: An Introduction

must have a meaning for political competitors beyond the dry pages of statute books or constitutions. They must be valued, and observed, of and for themselves. This is what is meant by democratic *consolidation*: that democratic practices become so deeply internalized by political actors that acting outside the institutional "rules of the game" becomes unthinkable. This demands a faith in the integrity of the political process that may not always be forthcoming in situations of deep hostility or conflict.

There is a significant caveat concerning this rosy view of democracy, however, and it concerns the nature of democratic institutions. Different types of society require different types of institutions. Federalism, for example, may be irrelevant to small homogenous countries but a virtual necessity for large heterogeneous ones (and it is thus no surprise that many large diverse countries like Canada, India, Australia and the US are all federal states). Different types of electoral systems can ensure the proportionate representation of minority groups or singlehandedly ensure their exclusion. Parliaments and executives can be structured in such a way as to give all groups a share of power, or to enable one group to dominate over all others. The use of truth and reconciliation commissions can be a way to help heal old wounds, or to re-open them. Appropriately *crafted* democratic institutions are thus crucial to the sustainability of any negotiated settlement.

Unfortunately, the significance of institutional design has often been overlooked or ignored by both disputants and negotiators in many recent attempts to resolve conflicts. Indeed, constitution-makers in new democracies have often been content to restore the very institutions that were conducive to the previous breakdown, or else to look for inspiration to the institutions of the apparently successful democracies of the West, even though these have seldom been fashioned for the demands of post-conflict societies. The constitutional choices made at these times can often have major repercussions for a nation's future prospects, so it is important to get them right from the start. We hope this chapter will help political actors make the best choices for their country by clarifying the range and consequences of the different institutional models.

The constitutional choices made during a settlement process can often have major repercussions for a nation's future prospects, so it is important to get them right from the start.

REFERENCES AND FURTHER READING

Diamond, Larry. 1995. *Promoting Democracy in the 1990s: Actors and Instruments, Issues and Imperatives.* New York: Carnegie Commission on Preventing Deadly Conflict.

Huntington, Samuel P. 1991. *The Third Wave: Democratization in the Late Twentieth Century.* Norman, OK: University of Oklahoma Press.

Przeworski, Adam. 1991. *Democracy and the Market: Political and Economic Reforms in Eastern Europe and Latin America.* Cambridge: Cambridge University Press.

Timothy D. Sisk

4.1 Power-Sharing Democracy: An Overview

In power-sharing political systems, decision-making ideally occurs by consensus. All major ethnic groups in the country are included in government, and minorities, especially, are assured influence in policy-making on sensitive issues such as language use and education. Power-sharing democracy is often contrasted with "regular" or majoritarian, winner-take-all democracy in which the losers of elections must wait out-of-power in loyal opposition for a later chance to replace the government of the day.

4.1.1	*Preventing or escaping deep-rooted conflict*
4.1.2	*Group building-block versus integrative approaches*
4.1.3–4.1.4	*When does power sharing work?*

A Menu of Options 2	Power-Sharing Mechanisms (pp. 144–145)

4.1.1 Preventing or escaping deep-rooted conflict

The early introduction of power sharing can potentially prevent identity-based conflicts from turning violent. For example, many believe that getting a power-sharing agreement in Kosovo (an Albanian-majority province in Serb-majority former Yugoslavia) will be critical to keeping identity-related disputes in the region (e.g., education policy) from further escalating into another war in the Balkans. When governments are democratic *and* inclusive, the argument goes, violent conflicts can be prevented because minorities won't need to resort to violence to advance their interests.

Moreover, power sharing is seen as a viable route to escaping deadly conflicts. Following bitter wars such as in Bosnia, most observers agreed that the only way to preserve a united, multi-ethnic country – to keep the country from splitting up altogether – was to create a post-war system of government in which the Bosnian Croat, Bosniac (Muslim), and Bosnian Serb communities could share power (see Bosnia Case Study).

The 1995 Dayton Accord set up a political system in which the three communities would make decisions collaboratively through a joint presidency and a parliament that included, in rough proportion to the population, the three main groups. Although it doesn't function as well as it was designed on paper, Bosnia's nascent power-sharing system appears to be its best chance to create a viable multi-ethnic democracy after such an intense civil war. Power sharing is also seen as a way to end civil wars and get a negotiated settlement – and to build more legitimate democratic institutions – in current conflicts as far afield as Sri Lanka, Sudan and Tajikistan, as it was in other recent conflicts such as Angola, Sierra Leone or Cambodia.

4.1.2 Differences in approach

When governments are democratic and inclusive, the argument goes, violent conflicts can be prevented because minorities won't need to resort to violence to advance their interests.

Policy-makers and scholars differ over whether a *group building-block* approach like that adopted in the Dayton Accord for Bosnia – in which groups (usually ethnically homogenous political parties) are viewed as the building blocks of a common society – leads to better conflict management than an *integrative* approach to power sharing. The latter approach emphasizes levers to build political alliances across lines of conflict.

The group building-block approach relies on accommodation by ethnic group leaders at the political centre and guarantees for group autonomy and minority rights. The key institutions are federalism and the devolution of power to ethnic groups in territory that they control, minority vetoes on issues of particular importance to them, grand coalition cabinets in a parliamentary framework, and proportionality in all spheres of public life (e.g., budgeting and civil service appointments). Like Bosnia, Lebanon has a political system in which representation and autonomy for the country's main religious groups is guaranteed in the constitution.

The integrative approach eschews ethnic groups as the building blocks of a common society. In South Africa's 1993 interim constitution, for example, ethnic group representation was explicitly rejected in favour of institutions and policies that deliberately promote social integration across group lines. Election laws (in combination with the delimitation of provincial boundaries) have had the effect of encouraging political parties to put up candidate slates – if they want to maximize the votes they get – that reflected South Africa's highly diverse society. And the federal provinces were created so as not to overlap with ethnic group boundaries (South Africa's groups are more widely dispersed in any event).

4.1 Power-Sharing Democracy:
An Overview

Thus, the integrative approach seeks to build multi-ethnic political coalitions (again, usually political parties), to create incentives for political leaders to be moderate on divisive ethnic themes, and to enhance minority influence in majority decision-making. The elements of an integrative approach include electoral systems that encourage pre-election pacts across ethnic lines, non-ethnic federalism that diffuses points of power, and public policies that promote political allegiances that transcend groups.

The group building-block and integrative approaches can be fruitfully viewed as opposite poles in a spectrum of power-sharing institutions and practices. Which approach is best? To make such a determination, it is useful to consider power-sharing practices in terms of three dimensions that apply to both approaches: territorial division of power, decision rules, and public policies that define relations between the government and the ethnic groups. With these dimensions in mind, a "menu" of power-sharing institutions and practices is offered (see "Power-Sharing Mechanisms: A Menu of Options", pp. 144–145).

Like any menu, levers of democratic influence can be combined to suit individual tastes. In deciding which power-sharing institutions and practices might work, there is no substitute for intimate knowledge of any given country. In multi-ethnic Fiji, for example, an 18-month expert review of the country's political system produced a set of recommendations for a new constitution that combines measures to guarantee a minimum level of indigenous Fijian and Indo-Fijian representation in parliament (a group building-block option) with electoral incentives to promote the formation of political alliances across ethnic lines (an integrative option).

4.1.3 Promoting power sharing

Often, external parties in the international community have promoted power sharing by offering formulas – institutional blueprints for political structures – to prevent or escape ethnic conflicts. International mediators have also sought to induce the political leaders of contending groups to accept these blueprints through a combination of diplomatic carrots and sticks, such as offering aid or threatening sanctions.

For example, the United Nations secretariat has produced a "set of ideas" for a bi-zonal, bi-federal arrangement for power sharing between Greek Cypriot and Turkish Cypriot communities in Cyprus. Autonomy frameworks have been proposed to help resolve the disputes between majority and minority communities in Indonesia (East Timor) and Sri Lanka. The peace accord for Northern Ireland sets up a number of cross-border power-sharing institutions and creates a new assembly in the disputed territory (see Northern Ireland Case Study). Each of these plans is backed by diplomatic initiatives to pledge international assistance in implementation if the parties agree to share power in parliament instead of contesting it on the battlefields or in the streets.

Increasingly, the international community is using linkages to other issues, such as membership in collective security, trade, and other international organizations, to persuade states to adopt power-sharing practices that promote ethnic accommodation. The European Union has invoked these conditionalities in its relations with some Eastern European states, such as Romania, to encourage management of ethnic-Romanian and ethnic-Hungarian differences through democratic political structures.

Promoting democratic conflict-regulating practices in this manner can be a useful tool of diplomacy to arrest the escalation of ethnic conflicts into violence or to bring them to an end after preventive efforts fail. Moreover, even when democracy may be a long way off, the international community can exert pressure for the adoption of conflict-regulating practices by non-democratic states, such as fair treatment of ethnic minorities and the creation of ethnically diverse security forces.

4.1.4 When can power sharing succeed?

Power-sharing agreements that looked good on paper have failed in recent conflict settings such as Rwanda and Burundi. In both of these countries in which majority-Hutu and minority-Tutsi ethnic groups have a history of violent strife, efforts to find solutions by creating power-sharing democratic institutions proved to be insufficient in overcoming deep distrust and the perception of mutual victimization. In both cases, the power-sharing experiments broke down and violent clashes ensued; in Rwanda, an incipient power-sharing pact was scuttled by the 1994 genocide there, a deliberate move by its perpetrators.

Similarly, before the outbreak of civil wars in Lebanon and Cyprus in the mid-1970s, these countries had power-sharing systems. Lebanon's civil war was eventually ended with a new power-sharing pact (the 1990 Taif Accord), and, as mentioned above, a revival of power sharing seems to be a preferred outcome to Cyprus's long-running communal conflict.

4.1 Power-Sharing Democracy: An Overview

Policy-makers and scholars with difficult choices in complex conflicts rightly ask straightforward questions about experiences with the various levers of democratic practice in divided societies. Under what conditions does power sharing work, and under what conditions does it fail? Under what conditions do power-sharing systems entrench group identities and collapse into violent conflict, and when do they lead over time to more pluralistic and sustainable patterns of democracy?

Naturally, there are no simple answers to the questions posed above, but some conclusions can be drawn. For power-sharing democracy to work, there must be a sufficiently strong core of moderates – including both political elites and the broader civil society – that seeks pragmatic coexistence in a multi-ethnic society. Moderates committed to sharing power in a multi-ethnic democracy must also be able to withstand pressures created by extremist politicians and publics who mobilize on divisive ethnic themes as a route to power. This critical core of moderates appears to exist in South Africa, it might exist or be created in Bosnia, and it is clearly absent in Rwanda and Burundi. Without the existence of a core of moderate voices, multi-ethnic countries are likely to succumb to inter-group violence and, potentially, state collapse or disintegration.

When a sufficiently cohesive core of moderates does exist, power sharing is a viable means of democratic conflict management. Although there is no single, transportable model of power sharing, there is a broad menu of public policies, institutions, and mechanisms to promote democracy in countries with deep-rooted identity conflicts. The actual form of power sharing (group building-block versus integrative) seems to be less important than the extent to which the agreement to create a power-sharing system is the result of good-faith bargaining and negotiation among the contending social forces. The negotiation process itself must be inclusive and legitimate.

Power-sharing systems work best when, ideally, they are a temporary measure to build confidence until more customary, sometimes-win-and-sometimes-lose democracy can be embraced. This appears to be the course that South Africa will take; its final constitution, adopted in 1996, is much more majoritarian even though minority rights are closely guarded. Whether the withering away of power sharing in a more conflicted society such as Bosnia is possible, or whether power sharing will fail leading to the country's dissolution, remains an open question. But the

POWER-SHARING MECHANISMS

POWER-SHARING POLITICAL SYSTEMS

- Decision-making ideally occurs by consensus;
- All major ethnic groups included in government; minorities, especially, are assured influence in policy-making on sensitive issues (i.e., language use, education);
- Can take two forms: *group building-block* approach and *integrative* approach.

GROUP BUILDING-BLOCK

- Ethnically homogenous groups (political parties) form building blocks of common society;
- *Key elements*: federalism and devolution of power to ethnic groups in the territory that they control; minority vetoes on sensitive issues; grand coalition cabinets; proportionality in all spheres of public life;
- *Example:* Dayton Accord for Bosnia.

INTEGRATIVE

- Political alliances across lines of conflict; thus creating incentives for political leaders to be moderate on divisive ethnic themes; and enhancing minority influence in majority decision-making;
- *Key elements*: electoral systems that encourage pre-election pacts across ethnic lines; non-ethnic federalism that diffuses points of power; public policies that promote political allegiances that transcend groups;
- *Example*: South Africa's 1993 interim constitution.

Although the following menu presents two conceptually distinct approaches, it is clear that in the real world, power-sharing options can be pieced together in a number of ways.

FIVE GROUP BUILDING-BLOCK OPTIONS

1. Granting territorial autonomy to ethnic groups and creating confederal arrangements;
2. Adopting constitutional provisions that ensure a minimum level of group representation (quotas) at all levels of government;
3. Adopting group proportional representation in administrative appointments, including consensus-oriented decision rules in the executive;
4. Adopting a highly proportional electoral system in a parliamentary framework; and
5. Acknowledging group rights or corporate (non-territorial) federalism (e.g., own-language schools) in law and practice.

FIVE INTEGRATIVE OPTIONS

1. Creating a mixed, or non-ethnic, federal structure, with boundaries drawn on other criteria such as natural features or economic development zones;
2. Establishing an inclusive, centralized unitary state without further subdividing territory;
3. Adopting winner-take-all but ethnically diverse executive, legislative, and administrative decision-making bodies (e.g., a purposefully diverse language board to set policies on language use);
4. Adopting an electoral system that encourages the formation of pre-election coalitions (vote pooling) across ethnic divides; and
5. Devising "ethnicity-blind" public policies and laws to ensure non-discrimination on the basis of identity or religious affiliation.

LESSONS LEARNED

1. For power sharing to work, there must be a strong core of moderates – both political elite and civil society – that seeks coexistence. Moderates must be able to withstand pressures by extremist politicians and publics.
2. More important than the actual form of power sharing (group building-block or integrative) is the extent to which agreement to create power-sharing system is the result of good-faith bargaining and negotiation.
3. Power-sharing systems work best when they are a temporary measure to build confidence until more permanent structures can be developed.

A MENU OF OPTIONS 2 [P. 145]

present alternative to power sharing in Bosnia is not "regular" or majoritarian democracy, it is the abandonment of Bosnia as a multi-ethnic country altogether. Unfortunately, this is the case in many other deep-rooted ethnic conflicts as well.

REFERENCES AND FURTHER READING

Horowitz, Donald L. 1985. *Ethnic Groups in Conflict.* Berkeley, CA: University of California Press.

Horowitz, Donald L. 1990. "Making Moderation Pay: the Comparative Politics of Ethnic Conflict Management". In Joseph V. Montville. ed. *Conflict and Peacemaking in Multiethnic Societies.* New York, NY: Lexington Books.

Lijphart, Arend. 1977. *Democracy in Plural Societies.* New Haven, CT: Yale University Press

Lijphart, Arend. 1991. "Constitutional Choices for New Democracies", *Journal of Democracy*, no. 2. (winter 1991) pp. 72–84.

Sisk, Timothy D. 1996. *Power Sharing and International Mediation in Ethnic Conflicts.* Washington, DC: United States Institute of Peace Press.

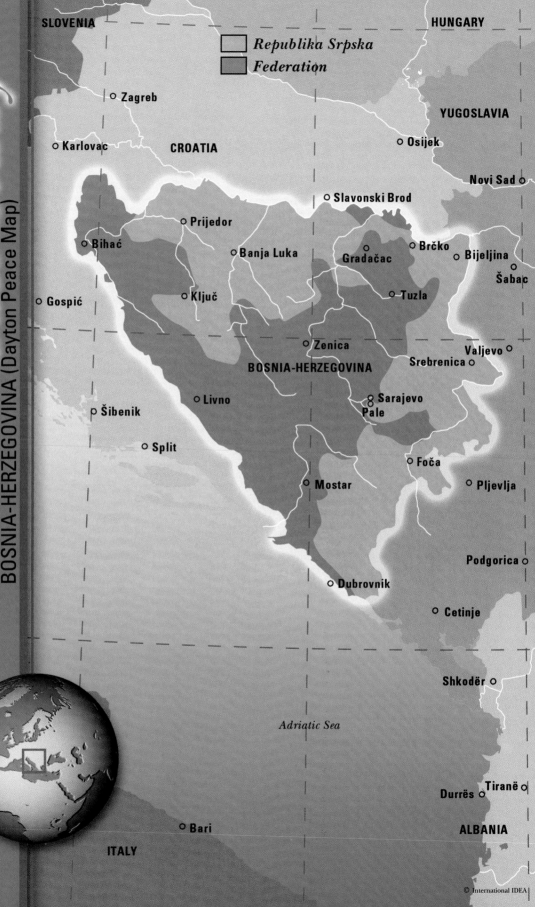

© International IDEA

Christopher Bennett

Case Study: Bosnia-Herzegovina

BOSNIA-HERZEGOVINA

At its simplest, the Bosnian question boils down to two issues: how 2.2 million Muslim Slavs (Bosniacs) can live amid 4.5 million Croats and 8.5 million Serbs in the wider region of the former Yugoslavia; and how 750,000 Croats and 1.3 million Serbs can live together with 1.9 million Bosniacs within Bosnia-Herzegovina (Bosnia) itself. Depending on where borders are drawn and whether they are respected, Bosniacs either form a minority squeezed between two more powerful ethnic groups, or they comprise a relative majority in a territory shared with two large minority communities, both of which consider the neighbouring states of Croatia and rump Yugoslavia (Serbia and Montenegro) their mother countries.

The current arrangement, enshrined in the Dayton Accords, is the result of three years and nine months of fighting within Bosnia – much of it three-sided – and four and a half years of warfare within the former Yugoslavia. It was reached after more than 100,000 deaths (the exact figure is not known) and the expulsion of about half of Bosnia's 4.3 million population from their homes in so-called ethnic cleansing. It was agreed between Bosnia's Bosniac President, Alija Izetbegovic, on behalf of Bosnia; Croatia's President Franjo Tudjman, on behalf of Bosnian Croats; and Serbia's then President Slobodan Milosevic, on behalf of Bosnian Serbs. And it followed several years of failed attempts by international mediators to broker an agreement; massive, belated and concerted international pressure for a settlement; and three weeks of intense negotiations at a US airforce base in Dayton, Ohio during November 1995.

Power Sharing under Dayton

Under Dayton, Bosnia is defined as a single state with three main constituent peoples – Bosniacs, Serbs and Croats – divided into two entities: the Federation of Bosnia and Herzegovina (Federation), comprising 51 per cent of the territory, and Republika Srpska, 49 per cent. Despite being one country, both entities have their own armed forces (and the Federation army is effectively divided into Croat and Bosniac forces), whose strength is regulated and related to that of the neighbouring states. The ratio between the military stockpiles of rump Yugoslavia, Croatia and Bosnia is 5:2:2, and within Bosnia between the Federation and Republika Srpska is 2:1. The country which emerged out of Dayton nevertheless inherited the political independence, territorial integrity and sovereignty of the previous state, the republic of Bosnia-Herzegovina, a former republic of the Socialist Federal Republic of Yugoslavia but internationally recognized and admitted to the United Nations shortly after the outbreak of war in April 1992.

Dayton contains 11 annexes, of which only the first concerns the cease-fire and military matters. The remaining 10 cover civilian aspects of the peace plan, including the right of displaced Bosnians to return to their homes or to be compen-

Bosnia-Herzegovina

149

sated for the loss of their property. And the future shape of the country depends as much on the manner in which the civilian side of the peace plan is implemented, as on the political structures contained within it.

Bosnia's central institutions are weak. They are responsible for foreign policy, various aspects of foreign trade policy – including setting import tariffs (though critically not gathering the revenue) – inter-entity communications and criminal law enforcement. Other matters, including tax collection, are left for the two entities. Although the entities are able to establish "special parallel relationships with neighbouring states", these have to be "consistent with the sovereignty and territorial integrity of Bosnia". With the consent of the Parliamentary Assembly, the entities can enter into specific agreements with states or international bodies. The Federation may, therefore, form special links with Croatia, and Republika Srpska may form special ties with rump Yugoslavia, but neither entity can break away from Bosnia.

The Parliamentary Assembly has two chambers: the House of Peoples and the House of Representatives. The former has 15 members, five from each constituent people – 10 (five Bosniacs and five Croats) from the Federation and five (Serbs) from Republika Srpska. The Bosniac and Croat members are appointed from the House of Peoples of the Federation and the Serbs are nominated from the Republika Srpska Assembly. Nine delegates, with at least three from each community, have to be present for a quorum. The House of Representatives has 42 members, 28 of whom are elected from the Federation and 14 from Republika Srpska. A majority of those present in both chambers is the basic requirement for taking decisions in the Parliamentary Assembly. However, each constituent people has the right to declare any prospective decision "destructive of a vital interest", in which case the proposal requires "a majority of the Bosniac, of the Croat and of the Serb Delegates present and voting". In such a way, decisions are to be made by broad consensus and not against the declared vital interest of any community.

The "vital interest" mechanism is also a feature of the three-person Presidency. This is made up of one Bosniac and one Croat, both directly elected from the territory of the Federation, and one Serb, directly elected from Republika Srpska. Since each voter is only able to cast one ballot at the presidential level, Bosniacs effectively elect the Bosniac member, Serbs elect the Serb member, and Croats elect the Croat member. Although the Presidency should aim to reach decisions by consensus, a majority decision is possible, subject to certain limitations. In the event of a two-to-one decision, Presidency members can, in the following three days, declare a decision to be "destructive of a vital interest", in which case the decision is referred to either the Republika Srpska Assembly or either the Bosniac or Croat members of the House of Peoples in the Federation. A vote of two thirds of the relevant group within 10 days renders the decision null and void. The Presidency appoints the government, or Council of Ministers, of which no more than two thirds of ministers can

Case Study: Bosnia-Herzegovina

come from the Federation and deputy ministers may not be of the same constituent people as the minister.

International Presence

Taken together, all these mechanisms mean that the system requires broad agreement and consensus to function. However, given the existing animosity and absence of trust, and the fact that both Serb and Croat political leaders continue to believe that union with their mother countries is a viable alternative to Bosnia, such consensus does not exist. Indeed, if left entirely up to the former warring factions, Dayton would never be implemented. The accord therefore includes provision for international involvement in all aspects of the peace process – in addition to a NATO-led peace-keeping force (initially consisting of 60,000 troops) – with overall co-ordination entrusted to a so-called High Representative, under the authority of the UN Security Council.

The Organisation for Security and Co-operation in Europe (OSCE) has a three-pronged mandate in Bosnia. It monitors the human rights situation; it oversees arms reduction; and it supervises elections. And a UN International Police Task Force (IPTF), made up of (initially 1,500) unarmed foreign police officers, assists, advises, monitors and observes the work of local police.

Foreign influence is equally crucial in a host of ostensibly domestic institutions. There is, for example, a foreign Human Rights Ombudsman who is appointed by the OSCE for the first five years of Dayton implementation; the Governor of the Central Bank is a foreigner appointed by the International Monetary Fund (IMF) for the first six years; and three out of the nine members of the Constitutional Court are foreigners appointed by the President of the European Court of Human Rights. And this massive presence is cushioned by a five-year $US 5.1 billion reconstruction plan, designed and guided by the World Bank.

Though critical to the peace process, the scale of the international presence is in some ways counter-productive to Bosnia's long-term future. On the one hand, domestic institutions and politicians have to a large extent given up responsibility for governing their own country. On the other, the massive international stake has led key players to declare the peace process a success, irrespective of how it is actually evolving, since failure would reflect badly on those statespeople, organizations and countries responsible for the agreement. For example, elections were scheduled to take place between six and nine months after Dayton came into force and were duly held exactly nine months from the day the agreement was signed. However, even though the poll succeeded only in cementing the results of ethnic cleansing, amounting to an inaccurate ethnic census of the population where more than 100 percent of the electorate voted, the event was hailed as a "triumph of democracy". Moreover, since the poll, the ethnically based parties which dominate

Bosnia-Herzegovina

Bosnian politics have refused to work together; the common institutions – whose formation was ostensibly the reason that elections needed to take place – have failed to function in a meaningful manner; and the international community, in particular the High Representative, has had to take on an increasing role, imposing solutions on recalcitrant Bosnian institutions, and even ruling on issues such as the design of the country's flag.

That the peace remains so fragile is hardly surprising, given the circumstances in which Dayton was arrived at. For the settlement was agreed by the very individuals who were responsible for the war in the first place and who were aiming, above all, to secure their own political future. Moreover, it was brokered by US diplomats, and in particular Richard Holbrooke, whose overriding concern was to stop the fighting and get events in Bosnia off the international political agenda because of the acrimony the conflict had created within the NATO alliance.

Why Dayton Worked

Dayton succeeded where earlier peace plans had failed because of the single-minded determination of the US negotiating team and the backing they received from other countries; because, after years of humiliation, there was a genuine threat that European troops (in particular British and French) who made up the backbone of the UN force in Bosnia would be withdrawn in the event of failure; and because of a fundamental shift in the military balance, which had been in part engineered by US diplomacy. In the course of 1995 the tide of battle changed, first in neighbouring Croatia and then in Bosnia. Two out of three Serb-held enclaves in Croatia were overrun in lightning strikes in May and August and, with the support of Bosnian Croat forces and the predominantly-Bosniac Bosnian Army, the offensive rolled forward into Bosnia reversing many of the early Serb war gains. Diplomatic pressure brought a halt to the offensive when the territorial division within the country corresponded to that envisaged in earlier peace plans proposed by international mediators.

Dayton was but the last in a long line of internationally brokered peace plans, one of which, the Vance-Owen plan (named after Cyrus Vance and David Owen, its sponsors) is worthy of special note. Unlike Dayton, the Vance-Owen plan attempted to build the concept of multi-ethnicity into the system throughout the country. Though it too entailed a territorial division and the creation of 10 regions – nine of which were deemed to have an ethnic majority of one people and one (Sarajevo) to be mixed – it guaranteed minority ethnic representation in each region via a complex constitutional plan designed by the Finnish diplomat Martti Ahtisaari. The Vance-Owen plan failed, however, because it did not receive international, in particular US, backing and was rejected by the Bosnian Serbs. No country was willing to risk deploying forces to reverse Serb military gains.

Bosnia-Herzegovina

Case Study: Bosnia-Herzegovina

When war broke out in the former Yugoslavia in 1991, the international commu-nity had no choice but to become directly involved because the fighting was so geo-graphically close to key western European countries. The former Yugoslavia borders three European Union member states and literally divides 14 of them physically from Greece. International media devoted massive attention to the conflict and hundreds of thousands of refugees fleeing the fighting began making their way to western Europe, and in particular to Germany. But without the political will to address the massive imbalance in fire-power within the former Yugoslavia and neu-tralize overwhelming Serb superiority, the only strategy open to international medi-ators was one of appeasement – determining the minimalist Serb position and attempting to persuade Croats and Bosniacs to accept it. And the minimalist Serb position essentially amounted to the construction of a Serb state comprising all ter-ritory in the former Yugoslavia inhabited by Serbs, irrespective of the wishes of the non-Serb population.

Of Bosnia's 109 municipalities, 37 had an absolute Bosniac majority, 32 an absolute Serb majority and 13 an absolute Croat majority. A further 15 municipali-ties had a simple Bosniac majority, five a simple Serb majority and 13 a simple Croat majority. With the exception of Croat-populated western Herzegovina, an absolute majority rarely accounted for more than 70 per cent of the population, and as often as not neighbouring municipalities had majorities of one of the republic's other peoples. Bosnia could not therefore fragment neatly along an ethnic line, because there was no ethnic line to fragment along. Dividing Bosnia into ethnic territories would inevitably be messy and require massive population transfers.

The fundamental cause of conflict in the former Yugoslavia in the early 1990s was not, however, simply the drive by the country's Serbs to forge their own national state at the expense of their neighbours. Structurally speaking, this was only a man-ifestation of what was and remains a much deeper-rooted problem. For as commu-nism disintegrated in eastern Europe, the gel that had held Yugoslavia together since World War Two disappeared and the country was ill-equipped institutionally to deal with the transition to democracy. Nearly half a century of communism had failed to resolve the national question. Indeed, it may even be argued that commu-nist rule had exacerbated the potential for conflict within Yugoslavia since, in prac-tice, it had stifled open dialogue on ethnic issues. Moreover, the planned economy had failed to sustain prosperity and had been disintegrating throughout the 1980s.

Although Bosnians had appeared to live together in reasonable harmony before the war, ethnic identities formed over centuries of Ottoman rule – when each reli-gious community was governed separately under its own spiritual rulers – remained strong. As a result, when elections took place in 1990, the poll approximated to an ethnic census as the electorate divided along ethnic lines. Though the ethnically based parties were ostensibly in coalition and governing together, they rapidly fell out with each other and politics descended into a "zero-sum" game, much like the

Bosnia-Herzegovina

current situation, as Serbs, and later Croats, decided that they had an alternative to Bosnia. This pattern was repeated at Bosnia's post-Dayton 1996 elections, where the major parties based their campaign almost exclusively on nationalist appeals to their own ethnic group, thus reinforcing the divisions of the war rather than encouraging politics centred on other, less damaging, issues.

Though it is without doubt possible to contain the Bosnian conflict almost in-definitely, this requires policing and is an extremely costly approach. Moreover, international leaders who have troops deployed in Bosnia are acutely aware of the political risks they are running domestically, should, for example, any of their sol-diers be killed. In addition to containing the conflict, therefore, they are hoping to find an exit strategy. Prospects of troop withdrawal or substantial reduction are poor, however, because of instability elsewhere in the region, and in particular in Yugoslavia and the southern Balkans. Indeed, as the predominantly Albanian province of Kosovo disintegrates in ethnic violence, international involvement and presence throughout the region is expanding, not contracting. And whether in Kosovo, Macedonia or Bosnia, the fundamental problem remains of how to recon-cile the legitimate interests of different communities living side by side.

4.2 The Structure of the State: Federalism and Autonomy

Yash Ghai

4.2 The Structure of the State: Federalism and Autonomy

Most solutions to internal conflicts require adjustments to the structure of the state. In this section we discuss how federalist and autonomy arrangements can help defuse tensions within a state by devolving greater powers to ethnic groups.

4.2.1–4.2.2	*Means of devolving power*
4.2.3	*Examples of federalism and autonomy*
4.2.4	*Legal basis for autonomy*
4.2.5	*Advantages of autonomy solutions*
4.2.6	*Resistance to autonomy*
4.2.7	*Structuring autonomous arrangements*

Many conflicts centre on the role of the state in society and emanate principally from its structure and organization. In most countries, the state is the most powerful organization, even when it is not very effective in implementing policy. Control of the state usually provides access to economic power since the state is the major means of the reproduction of capital. Consequently, there is strong competition for control over the state apparatus and this struggle is the cause of many of today's conflicts. These conflicts can be prevented or mediated by re-structuring of the state, or by official policies, such as re-distribution through affirmative action mechanisms, recognition of personal laws and other forms of pluralism, fairer electoral laws and forms of power sharing (these elements are discussed in other parts of the handbook).

Problems also arise from attempts to adopt symbols of the state that are rooted in the religion or traditions of one community (Sri Lanka, Malaysia, etc.) which alienate other communities. A solution might be neutral symbols (like democracy, human rights and the rule of law), secularism as a kind of state nationalism, but many leaders consider that its capacity to inspire loyalty among their supporters is limited. A more productive strategy is often to look at ways of devolving power via federalism, autonomy or other adjustments to the structure of the state.

4.2.1 Means of devolving power

There are a wide variety of arrangements for the devolution of power. In considering these options, it is important not to see them as mutually exclusive or as either/or alternatives. Given the current variations in diversity, in terms of numbers, identity and resources, within one single state some combination of devices may be required (as the Canadian and Indian experiences reveal).

Federalism. The best known arrangement is federalism, where power is devolved equally to all regions and each region has an identical relationship to the central government. While traditionally federalism has not been used to solve problems of ethnic diversity, there have been instances where federalism has proven effective. For example, the adoption of federalism in Switzerland and Canada was partially motivated by the need to accommodate diverse communities. Also, the federal device was used frequently for the settlement of ethnic problems at the end of World War Two, for example in India, Malaysia, and Nigeria. Federalism has been argued for in other contexts as well, such as during the discussions in South Africa leading to the post-apartheid settlement.

If the need is to accommodate only one or two minority groups, however, the federal model may be unnecessary. Also, the federal model may not be seen to be sufficiently sensitive to the cultural and other needs of a community. Consequently, there have been two alternative responses: *asymmetrical federalism* and *autonomy.*

Asymmetrical federalism. In an asymmetrical federation, one or more federal states are vested with special powers not granted to other provinces, to allow for preservation of the culture and language of its settlers. An old example of this is Quebec, and a more contemporary instance is Kashmir's special status within the Indian federation.

Autonomy. An autonomous arrangement, in which only one or more regions have devolved to them special powers, is more common. Autonomy tends by its very nature to be asymmetric. Examples of autonomy include: two provinces in the Philippines (the Cordillera and Mindanao), Zanzibar in relation to Tanzania, Hong Kong in relation to China, Greenland in relation to Denmark, Puerto Rico in relation to the US, the Autonomous Communities in Spain, and Åland in relation to Finland.

There is strong competition for control over the state apparatus, and this struggle is the cause of many of today's conflicts. These conflicts can be mediated by looking at ways of devolving power by federalism, autonomy or other adjustments to the structures of the state.

4.2 The Structure of the State:
Federalism and Autonomy

An important distinction between federalism and autonomy is that in federations the regions participate actively in national institutions and national policy-making, in addition to controlling devolved subjects within the region. In autonomy, the emphasis is on the region's power to control its own affairs, rather than to participate in national institutions. (The case of Zanzibar is somewhat anomalous, given its influence in the national parliament and in the executive disproportionate to its size, resulting in much resentment on the mainland.)

Reserves. These were first used by European settlers in the Americas, to isolate and dominate indigenous peoples, and were subsequently used in Australia, Africa and parts of Asia. The apartheid policy of Bantustans was a modern version. In recent years, however, the aspirations and historical claims of indigenous peoples have been recognized through the transformation of reserves into self-governing areas, particularly in Canada and the Philippines. The extent, however, to which they can opt out of national laws, which may be necessary for the preservation of their political and cultural practices, is variable.

Local government institutions. Another way to devolve power is through local government institutions or forms of decentralization. These differ from federations and autonomy in that they do not have a specific constitutional status or constitutional guarantees. Local government can be an effective way to give certain powers to a group since the geographical scale of local government is small and the population is likely to be homogeneous.

The developments regarding federalism and autonomy outlined above greatly increase the possibilities of devising flexible arrangements for forms of self-government to suit widely varying circumstances and contingencies. (In this section autonomy is frequently used in its generic sense to include all forms of spatial arrangements for self-government.) Added to these broad categories of self-government are variations in arrangements within each category, such as the division of powers between different layers and structures of government, the relationship between these structures at different levels, and the distribution of financial and other resources. While this flexibility is important in the negotiation process and facilitates compromises, there is a danger that it may lead to complex arrangements and systems, leading to a lack of cohesion and governability. Federal or autonomy arrangements are inherently hard to operate, and the embroidery on classical systems that tough negotiations may lead to can undermine long-term prospects of settlement by their sheer weight or complexity (a good example of this experience are the regional arrangements in Kenya's independence Constitution, and more recently of Papua New Guinea's system of provincial government established in 1976).

4.2.2 International regional organizations

A new but uneven element in the spatial organization of government is the emergence of *international regional organizations* in which national sovereignty has been traded for a share in the participation and decision-making in these organizations. Common policies over larger and larger matters are determined by such organizations. In this way a measure of control over the affairs of a national region has been transferred from national to supranational authority. This diminution of national sovereignty opens up possibilities of new arrangements between the state and its regions. The benefits work both ways: the state feels less threatened by regions in a multi-layered structure of policy-making and administration; and the region becomes more willing to accept national sovereignty, which may be the key to its participation in the wider arrangements.

This trend is most developed in the European Union, where it is helping to moderate tensions between states and border regions previously intent on secession. For example, it has facilitated the interesting spatial arrangements for policy, administration and consultation in the two parts of Ireland, each under separate sovereignty, which underlie the new peace proposals (see Northern Ireland Case Study). Attempts to provide for unified Nordic arrangements for the Saami people, including a substantial element of autonomy, regardless of the sovereignty they live under, are another instance of similar kind.

4.2.3 Examples of federalism and autonomy

While, traditionally, federalism has not been used to deal with ethnic issues, there are nevertheless several examples of how federal and autonomy devices have helped to mitigate or even solve internal conflicts or have provided a basis for the peaceful co-existence of diverse communities. A particularly successful example of autonomy is Åland, where a predominantly Swedish-speaking population under Finnish sovereignty has enjoyed a large measure of cultural and political autonomy since 1921. Autonomy has diffused ethnic tensions between Italian-and German-speaking people in South Tyrol. Many of India's ethnic demands have been dealt with in this way, starting with the re-organization of states along linguistic lines in 1956, and the subse-

4.2 The Structure of the State:
Federalism and Autonomy

quent divisions of the former Punjab and Bombay and the accommodation of Assam, Nagaland, and Mizoland as states.

The transition to democracy in Spain after the overthrow of Franco was greatly facilitated by the provision in the 1978 Constitution for the establishment of "autonomous communities". By giving "historic" communities, like the Basque and Catalans, a large measure of self-government, pressures for secession were reduced and terrorist activities consequently declined. In the Philippines, Muslim secessionist activity in Mindanao, lasting for a quarter of a century, has been abated due to an agreement in 1996 between the Moro National Liberation Front and the government. Under this agreement a council will be established under the chair of the leader of the Liberation Front to supervise development of 14 provinces in southern Mindanao island (regarded by it as traditional Muslim homelands), followed by a plebiscite and regional autonomy three years later. There are many lesser-known examples from the South Pacific where autonomy helped to bring disputes to some settlement (prominently the 1975 differences between Papua New Guinea and Bougainville and the francophone claims in Vanuatu).

A novel form of autonomy is represented by the arrangements under which Hong Kong returned to Chinese sovereignty in July 1997 (which Deng Xiaoping claimed had the potential to solve many world problems). Its novelty lies in the arrangements for the coexistence of very different, and in many respects opposed, systems of economy and politics within one sovereign state. Britain was prepared to return Hong Kong to China only on the basis of promises of Hong Kong's autonomy as set out in the 1984 Sino-British Joint Declaration. Macau's return to China in 1999 is based on similar principles.

More importantly, China is pursuing reunification of Taiwan with the mainland on the same policy of "One Country, Two Systems". It is likely that when serious negotiations between the two sides get under way, the principal issue will be the scope and modality of Taiwan's autonomy. Currently there are attempts to solve internal conflicts through autonomy arrangements, such as Sri Lanka-Tamils; Indonesia-East Timor; the Sudan-Southern Sudan; Georgia-Abkazia; and although not a conflict situation, the future relationship between the US and Puerto Rico.

Autonomy is often claimed by the disaffected group: white settlers and minority tribes in Kenya; kingdoms in Uganda; islands in Papua New Guinea, Tamils in Sri Lanka and so on. But sometimes the government offers autonomy as a way to fend off secession or bring armed struggle to an end, as in the Philippines for Mindanao, north-east India, Palestine, Spain, or belatedly in Sri Lanka. The Indian National Congress, for example, was prepared to countenance a high degree of autonomy if the Muslim League accepted a united India; but once partition was declared by the British, it argued successfully for a strong central government, with weak states.

4.2.4 The legal basis for autonomy

Despite the increasing use of autonomy solutions, the legal bases for autonomy remain unclear. There are two principle bases for autonomy:

Minority rights. In recent years, the United Nations has shown more interest in minority rights. It has adopted a *Declaration on the Rights of Minorities* which goes further than Article 27 of the International Covenant of Civil and Political Rights in protecting minority rights (see "Human Rights Instruments" section 4.6.3). In addition, the UN Human Rights Committee has adopted some interpretations of Article 27 that recognize that a measure of autonomy may be necessary for the protection of cultural rights of minorities. Efforts have also been made by that committee and others to interpret the right to self-determination to mean, where relevant, "internal autonomy" rather than secession. The approach of the OSCE (in its various declarations as well as in practice) favours autonomy regimes, and its rules for the recognition of breakaway republics of Yugoslavia included adequate minority protection of this kind. The new *Convention Concerning Indigenous and Tribal Peoples in Independent Countries* (1991) and the draft declaration of the rights of indigenous peoples have endorsed autonomy regimes.

Self-determination. In itself a difficult and controversial concept, self-determination is increasingly being analysed in terms of the internal, democratic organization of a state rather than in terms of secession or independence. The UN General Assembly resolved many years ago that autonomy is a manifestation of self-determination. The increased involvement of the UN and other international organizations in the settlement of internal conflicts has helped to further develop the concept of self-determination as implying autonomy in appropriate circumstances.

Such a view of self-determination has some support in certain national constitutions, but it is no more than a trend at this stage. Often constitutional provisions for autonomy are adopted during periods of social and political transformation, when an

**4.2 The Structure of the State:
Federalism and Autonomy**

autocratic regime is overthrown (when there is considerable legitimacy for autonomy) or a crisis is reached in minority-majority conflicts, or there is intense international pressure (in which case legitimacy is often granted rather grudgingly). Propelled by these factors, a number of constitutions now recognize some entitlement to self-government, such as the Philippines (in relation to two provinces, one for indigenous people and the other for a religious minority); Spain (which guarantees autonomy to three regions and invites others to negotiate with the centre for autonomy); Papua New Guinea (which authorizes provinces to negotiate with the central government for substantial devolution of power); Fiji (which recognizes the right of indigenous people to their own administration at the local level); and recently Ethiopia (which gives its "nations, nationalities, and peoples" the right to seek wide ranging powers as states within a federation and guarantees to them even the right to secession). The Chinese Constitution entrenches the rights of ethnic minorities to substantial self-government, although in practice the dominance of the Communist Party negates their autonomy. In other instances the constitution authorizes, but does not require, the setting up of autonomous areas. On the other hand, it should also be noted that some constitutions prohibit or restrict the scope of autonomy by requiring that the state be "unitary", or some similar expression; such a provision has retarded the acceptance or the implementation of meaningful devolution in countries such as Sri Lanka, Papua New Guinea and China.

The presence or absence of an entitlement in either international or national law to autonomy, as well as provisions limiting its scope, can play an important role in the conduct of negotiations and the relative bargaining position of parties, especially when there is international or third-party mediation.

4.2.5 The advantages of federalism and autonomy solutions

There are several advantages to federalism and autonomy mechanisms:

It ensures minorities a measure of state power. Minorities can enjoy executive, legislative and fiscal powers, not merely parliamentary representation with little prospect of a share in policy-making or distribution of resources.

It offers minorities better prospects of preserving their culture. Enabling minorities to make important decisions for themselves almost always offers better prospects for their own cultural preservation.

It may forestall or terminate demands for secession. The flexibility of the federal device in terms of the division of powers and the structure of institutions enables various kinds of accommodations to be made; it is more hospitable to compromise than other kinds of minority protection.

It can increase the political integration of ethnic groups. Autonomy devolves power to the state, which increases opportunities for people to compete in the political system; this political competition can, in turn, accentuate differences within groups, which can lead to the fragmentation of previously monolithic ethnic parties. The proliferation of parties enables coalitions of similarly situated ethnic parties (i.e., in Nigeria and India) across the state. Local problems that might otherwise have created a national crisis are dealt with by the locality itself. Territorial asymmetrical arrangements encourage demands for similar arrangements by other groups (India, Nigeria, and Papua New Guinea). The proliferation of these arrangements increases the prospects of national unity as it diffuses state power and enables central authorities to balance regional with national interests.

It can contribute to constitutionalism. Autonomy arrangements, and the mechanisms to enforce them, emphasize the rule of law, the separation of powers, and the role of independent institutions. The institutionalization of autonomy, particularly procedures governing the relationship between the centre and the region, must be based on discussions, mutual respect and compromise, thereby reinforcing and strengthening these qualities.

Autonomy enables ethnic problems to be solved without "entrenching" ethnicity, since its focus is on defining a region as a geographic entity and not as an ethnic entity. However, some forms of autonomy may indeed entrench ethnicity, as in the case of reservations where the cultural dimensions and the need to preserve the identity of the group may serve to sharpen boundaries against outsiders. An important qualification on the autonomy device is that it can operate only when a minority is concentrated geographically *and* is a majority in that area. One solution to the lack of geographical concentration is a kind of corporate federalism which can take various forms – the millet system used in the Ottoman Empire, Fijian system of native administration, Indian system of personal laws, consociationalism in Cyprus at the time of independence and now in Belgium. Aspects of this solution are discussed in sections 4.1 of this handbook.

4.2 The Structure of the State: Federalism and Autonomy

Even if autonomy solutions do not last, an end to hostilities provides breathing space. It is also important to recognize that even when agreement is reached on autonomy, the end of tensions or hostilities does not mean that tensions will not resurface, or that one party or the other will not subsequently repudiate or redefine the autonomy arrangements. This happened in many parts of Africa where some measure of regional autonomy was seen as a pre-condition of independence (as in Uganda, Kenya and Ghana). There are many other examples where federal or autonomy arrangements did not last (as in the Sudan, Eritrea and de facto in Kashmir).

However, even where the arrangements do not last or tensions re-emerge, the end of hostilities provides a breathing space, helps to define issues and points of difference, and may even provide the framework for negotiations in the future. The last point can be important since a frequent problem in many ethnic conflicts is finding a framework, and even sometimes parties, for negotiations (as in Sri Lanka, Punjab or Kashmir; India has managed to defuse some of its ethnic problems by providing for elections to provincial or assemblies in the "hill areas" before the start of negotiations). The party that wins also claims a mandate to negotiate (as with the 1996 elections in Kashmir). Sometimes merely the commitment to consider autonomy can serve to defuse tensions, as in South Africa where the agreement to consider a "white homeland" secured the participation of hard-line Afrikaners to the interim constitution.

4.2.6 Resistance to federalism and autonomy

Despite these obvious advantages, there has been resistance to the adoption of autonomy in cases of internal, particularly ethnic, conflicts. It involves the restructuring of the state and requires the redistribution of its resources, which upsets vested interests. Consequences can include:

Majority leaders fear losing electoral support. The leaders of the majority community may be reluctant to concede autonomy, fearing the loss of electoral support among their own community (a problem that has bedevilled Sri Lanka). Majority leaders, even if well disposed to autonomy, may not have the confidence that they would be able to implement the autonomy agreement, especially if it requires amendment of the constitution, a referendum or even merely fresh legislation.

Fears that autonomy will be a spring board to secession. This is seen to be an especially serious problem when the group

163

demanding autonomy is related, and contiguous, to a neighbouring kin state. Autonomy granted to a minority in its "homeland" may in turn create new minorities (as with Muslims in
northeast Sri Lanka which the Tamil Tigers want under their
control, or Christians in Mindanao, or the fear that Malaysian
Borneo states may get too close to Indonesia). This may trigger
demands for autonomy by the "new minorities" and lead to further fragmentation of the state. There may also be anxiety that
the fundamental values of the state may be compromised by the
recognition through autonomy of different cultural or religious
values. There may also be a concern with economic and administrative efficiency that is frequently seen to be jeopardized by
complex autonomy arrangements.

Unpredictability of its consequences. The adoption of the federal
device changes the context of ethnic relations. Territorial or
corporate federal arrangements are not purely instrumental.
Merely by providing a framework for inter-ethnic relations, they
affect and shape these relations. They may fashion new forms of
identity or reinforce old identities. They may enhance or decrease
the capacity of particular groups to extract resources from the
state. They may provide new forms of contention and dispute.

May encourage other communities to mobilize for autonomy.
Connected with the preceding point is the fear that if autonomy
can be justified on ethnic grounds, the rules justifying the granting of autonomy (identity, a sense of discrimination/injustice)
may encourage the mobilization of other communities along
ethnic lines, indeed to manufacture "ethnic communities".

**Autonomy arrangements for ethnic coexistence have not wor-
ked.** The reluctance towards autonomy may be reinforced by a
sense that autonomy arrangements for the purposes of ethnic
coexistence have not worked. There are certainly many examples of failure, abandonment of autonomy, and attempted and
even successful secession on the back of autonomy (as was demonstrated by the break-up of the former Yugoslavia). Even if
such drastic consequences are not envisaged, there may be reluctance on the basis that the relevant political culture is alien to
habits of consultation and compromise necessary for success.

4.2.7 Structuring autonomy arrangements

All of these are legitimate concerns. But they do not dictate
the conclusion that autonomy should not be used to deal with
ethnic conflict. What is necessary is to structure autonomy arrangements so as to increase the advantages and minimize the dis-

4.2 The Structure of the State: Federalism and Autonomy

advantages of autonomy. Below we outline some of the considerations relevant to the design of autonomy. But before that, we make three preliminary points. First, the concept of "success" of autonomy is itself problematic, since there is no clear consensus on the criteria. Second, it is difficult to isolate general factors that affect the operation of autonomy (e.g., a downturn in the economy) from factors that are specific to it. Third, autonomy is a *process* and there are inevitably changes in the context in which it operates, even in the original aims of autonomy. Options for structuring autonomy arrangements include:

Establish autonomy once and for all or through a phased, negotiating process. A choice has to be made between agreeing at one go on all the details of the autonomy system or to establish them through a series of phased negotiations. A middle ground is one where broad principles for autonomy are specified. Each option has its advantages and disadvantages and what is an optimum decision depends on the circumstances of the case. It is desirable to agree on the fundamental principles at least to start with. Experience in several countries has shown that matters left for future settlement are hard to negotiate successfully as immediate pressures, and a sense of urgency, abate. The opponents of autonomy have time to regroup. On the other hand, agreements made in rush without time for proper evaluation of alternatives may contain flaws.

In this context, some mechanism should be set in place to ensure that autonomy arrangements are implemented. Courts can play a role in certifying that the necessary arrangements have been legislated and implemented. Special political or administrative bodies can be set up to oversee the implementation process. Sometimes international supervision or conditionalities can be provided to ensure implementation (as with the Dayton Accord or the Paris Cambodian Accord).

The importance of the procedure. Autonomy established without adequate consultations tends to be controversial and lacking legitimacy. Many systems of autonomy imposed as part of the constitutional settlement at independence were dismantled soon afterwards at the instigation of the majority community. Autonomy may also affect relations in the relevant region and may be internally opposed by significant groups. In principle it is desirable that there should be wide consultations and referendums on autonomy proposals. Several national constitutions which provide for autonomy require that they be approved in a referendum (e.g., Spain, Ethiopia, and in an indirect form, Papua

New Guinea). Occasionally there is a requirement for constituent assemblies, which provide the mandate for negotiations.

While all these methods legitimize autonomy arrangements, there is also the danger that in a nation-wide referendum the proposal would be defeated if the majority community is opposed. Sometimes it is necessary to strike a fine balance between decisions by political leaders and the people.

Degree of entrenchment. Whatever method is used to arrive at decisions about autonomy, it is important that there should be firm legal guarantees for it. In particular it should not be possible for central authorities to unilaterally change the rules regarding autonomy. When the central government can change the rules on its own, the incentives for it to consult with regions diminish and mechanisms for developing consensus do not operate well.

Methods of dispute settlement. In principle the methods of dispute settlement should combine efforts first at consultation and mediation, and if that fails, judicial intervention. If the methods of settlement are impartial and accepted as such by both parties, it is possible to operate on the basis of broad principles (as has been possible in Spain); otherwise there would be pressures towards specification of details tending towards a rigid structure.

Consultative mechanisms. It is useful to provide for mechanisms for consultation between the centre and region/s, in part to avoid litigation, but also in recognition of the dynamics of autonomy. However serious an effort is made to separate off the areas of responsibilities between the centre and the region, there is likely to be some overlap as well as the need for co-ordination.

Problems with asymmetry. A particular problem with asymmetry is that all regions aspire to the completeness of powers that the best placed region has, while that region wants to keep its pre-eminence, as is evident from the experiences of Bougainville, Quebec, the Basque region and Catalonia. This can produce resentment against the privileged region in other parts of the country and put in some jeopardy its status (as with mainland resentment at the special powers of Zanzibar).

Protection of rights. Another problem with asymmetrical autonomy, especially that based on cultural differences, is that the community or region may be allowed to opt out of standard

4.2 The Structure of the State: Federalism and Autonomy

human rights provisions. This is most dramatically manifested in the "notwithstanding" clause of the Canada Charter of Human Rights under which a province can pass legislation in contravention of the Charter by making an express declaration to that effect – a concession at the instance of Quebec. Another example comes from the regime of personal laws in India where Muslim divorced women are subject to *sharia* for the purpose of maintenance from their previous husband instead of the more favourable provisions under the national laws. Problems of differential treatment arise even more extensively in regimes for indigenous peoples.

These provisions can also affect the rights of citizens outside the community. They can be subject to restrictions that do not apply to "locals" of the region (with respect to residence or employment, for example). New minorities that result from the conferring of autonomy on a region may need protection against victimization. The interests of the new minority can be secured through a further tier, that of local government (where they constitute a majority), or through special responsibilities of the central authorities.

Provisions recognizing differential values undermine the basic rights of individuals or groups within the community and cause resentment among the rest of the population. Thus autonomy can become a source of conflict rather than a solution to it. If too much importance is placed on accommodating differences and too little attention is given to building on those traditions, values and aspirations which a people share, it can lead to further fragmentation and weaken the sense of solidarity. While acknowledging cultural differences and sensitivities, it is important to emphasize national values and ensure the protection of human rights to all persons.

REFERENCES AND FURTHER READING

de Villers, Bertus. ed. 1994. *Evaluating Federal Systems.* Dordrecht: Martinus Nijhoff.

Ghai, Yash. 1998. "Decentralisation and the Accommodation of Ethnicity". In Crawford Young. ed. *Ethnicity and Public Policies.* London: Macmillan.

Hannum, Hurst. ed. 1993. *Documents on Autonomy and Minority Rights.* Dordrecht: Martinus Nijhoff.

Hannum, Hurst. 1996. *Autonomy, Sovereignty, and Self-Determination: The Accommodation of Conflicting Rights.* Philadelphia, PA: University of Pennsylvania Press.

Lapidoth, Ruth. 1996. *Autonomy: Flexible Solutions to Ethnic
Conflicts*. Washington, DC: United States Institute of Peace.

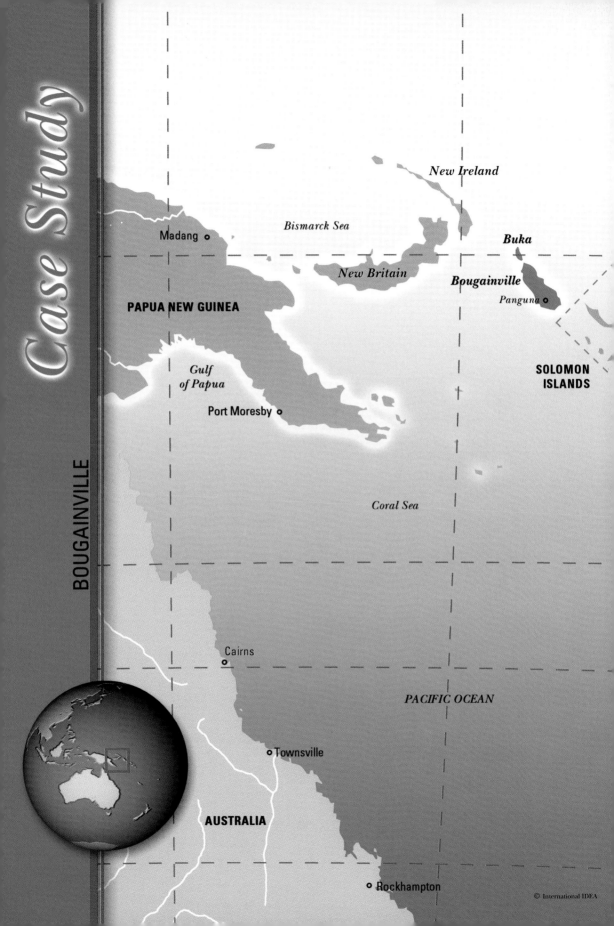

Anthony J. Regan

Case Study: Bougainville

BOUGAINVILLE

The almost 10-year old ethno-nationalist conflict in Bougainville – the most serious conflict in the Pacific island states in the 1990s – made significant progress towards peace in 1997–1998. The Bougainville conflict has had international repercussions, affecting Papua New Guinea's relations with its neighbours, especially the Solomon Islands and Australia, and involving the region in several attempts at conflict resolution. At the heart of the conflict lies the demand for independence made by the Bougainville Revolutionary Army (BRA), a demand opposed by Papua New Guinea and by many Bougainvilleans, including "resistance forces" armed by the government.

Background

Independent from Australian colonial control since 1975, Papua New Guinea (PNG) has a population of about four million people, occupying the eastern half of the island of New Guinea and many smaller islands. The province of Bougainville (population about 170,000) is the most distant from the mainland capital of Port Moresby, about 1,000 km to the east. Before the conflict, Bougainville's substantial initial contribution to the national economy was disproportionate to its small size, due to the enormous copper, gold and silver mine at Panguna on the main island which was operated by Bougainville Copper Ltd. (BCL) from 1972 until 1989.

Papua New Guinea is a country of immense ethnic diversity (it has more than 800 distinct languages, to cite just one example). Bougainville fits this pattern: it has 19 main languages and a population divided into numerous small semi-traditional societies. Bougainvilleans share a strong sense of a separate ethnic identity based on distinctive black skin colour and traditional affinities with the neighbouring Solomon Islands rather than with the rest of Papua New Guinea. Widely shared grievances about both the imposition of colonial boundaries and alleged colonial neglect have contributed to the sense of separate identity.

From the mid-1960s, a new grievance energized the emerging Bougainvillean identity: the imposition of the Panguna mine for the economic benefit of PNG despite detrimental effects on the Bougainville environment and people, and with limited fiscal benefits for the province. Distinct identity and grievances about the mine were factors in the attempted secession of Bougainville in 1975–1976. This was resolved peacefully by national government concessions, which gave Bougainville an effective and relatively autonomous provincial government; this was suspended, however, in 1990.

Rapid economic and social change resulted in major differences in regional economies within Bougainville, and significant economic inequality. Limited secondary education and employment opportunities produced a large pool of under-educated, under-employed and resentful youth. Many Bougainvilleans blamed the

Bougainville

new economic inequalities on the mine operator, BCL, and the influx of non-Bougainvilleans attracted by employment with the mine and on plantations. Outsiders were also blamed for escalating social tensions and law and order problems. These tensions contributed to the eruption of secessionist conflict in 1988–1989.

Conflict Analysis

In 1988, an inter-generational dispute among landowners around the mine led to attacks on BCL property by young men from local landowner groups led by Francis Ona. They demanded the closure of the mine and massive compensation. Poorly judged and ill-disciplined responses by police and, later, the Papua New Guinea Defence Force (PNGDF), resulted in deaths and injuries for many Bougainvilleans and provoked demands for Bougainville independence. As a result, Ona's Bougainville Revolutionary Army (BRA) was able to transform the localized conflict into a wider ethnic uprising. Ona's support came from under-employed youth in many parts of Bougainville.

As the situation slipped out of control, the mine was forced to close in May 1989. All government authority collapsed. A cease-fire and withdrawal of the PNGDF was negotiated, but instead of disarming and negotiating as agreed, the BRA tried to take control. They made a unilateral declaration of independence in May 1990 and appointed the Bougainville Interim Government (BIG), which included some former provincial government figures.

Once the security forces left, the focus of the BRA groups became their perceived enemies *within* Bougainville. The BRA was a loose coalition of semi-independent groups of mainly young men, each group based in its own semi-traditional society, often with differing perceptions of the conflict. Bougainvilleans with wealth, education or status, and many non-Bougainvilleans were harassed, imprisoned, tortured or murdered. Ona developed and propounded an ideology based in part on a return to traditional society and rejection of outside influences.

Armed opposition to the BRA emerged in Buka, north of the main island of Bougainville. Local leaders there requested national government intervention, and after some violent clashes with the BRA late in 1990, government forces took control of Buka. At the invitation of local leaders, government forces returned relatively peacefully to the north and south-west of the main island in 1991–1992. New local governments ("interim authorities") drawing mainly on traditional leadership were also established in those areas.

Armed opponents of the BRA and surrendering BRA elements formed "resistance forces" which received material support from the PNGDF and gave it active support. Bougainville became an increasingly violent place as the BRA, resistance forces, armed criminal groups and – on occasion – PNGDF elements became embroiled in conflict over mainly localized issues, often resulting in spirals of revenge killings.

Bougainville

Case Study: Bougainville

Following national elections in mid-1992, a new PNG government encouraged military initiatives, most notably efforts to re-take the area around the provincial capital and the Panguna mine. Violence elsewhere was escalating as the BRA sought to consolidate its position in areas to which the PNGDF had returned, and resistance groups were also operating. Some Bougainvillean leaders and local associations (especially women's organizations) became increasingly aware of the need to bridge the gaps among themselves if there was to be progress to peace.

Finally in September 1994, the PNG Prime Minister established negotiations in the Solomon Islands. Agreement was reached on a cease-fire, and on the holding of a peace conference, with security to be provided by a South Pacific regional peace-keeping force. When, for some reason, the senior BIG/BRA leaders did not attend the peace conference, the resulting popular frustration led to the emergence of a strong moderate movement in much of the area of BRA core support in central Bougainville. Within weeks the moderates proposed an interim provincial government to act as an umbrella for "moderate" groups (those opposed to secession) and as a bridge to the BIG/BRA, and to negotiate a new political status for Bougainville. The new government – the Bougainville Transitional Government (BTG) – was established in April 1995.

Some in the national government were suspicious of the BTG, afraid it was a "Trojan horse" for the BRA. Building understandings with the BIG/BRA leaders was slow, and the national government had little patience. It did agree to meetings between the BIG/BRA and the BTG in Australia, but became increasingly suspicious that the two groups were becoming too close. In January 1996, as BIG/BRA leaders returned from the talks in Australia, they were attacked by PNGDF troops. The BRA retaliated, and the national government lifted the ceasefire. Both sides now committed themselves to force. The PNGDF launched major military operations against the BRA in mid-1996. Their failure, and subsequent massacres and hostage taking of security personnel, underlined the inability of the security forces to defeat the BRA. Desperate for clear progress towards resolving the conflict prior to impending national elections, in January 1997 the government engaged mercenaries who began to train with the PNGDF Special Forces Unit, intending to crush the BRA and capture the Panguna mine site. But in a surprise move, the PNGDF commander announced the refusal of his forces to work with the mercenaries. They were ejected from the country and the Prime Minister and two key ministers were forced to stand down during a judicial inquiry.

The Conflict Management Process

Interest groups and the issues that divide

The wide range of groups with interests in the conflict or its outcomes include: the BIG/BRA; the BTG; the resistance forces; other less organized Bougainvillean interests; the national government; and other governments in the region.

Bougainville

The key issues include: the future political status of Bougainville and the method (and timetable) to decide it; interim arrangements for the governing of Bougainville in the period before the political status issue is determined; the presence of PNG security forces in Bougainville; arrangements for the disarming of the BRA and the resistance forces and restoration of civilian law; the future development of Bougainville; and the possible re-opening of the Panguna mine.

In Bougainville, three main parties are involved directly in the peace process, a range of interests and localized groups existing within each of them. The BRA and the BIG are concentrated in central and south Bougainville, but with some elements in most parts of the main island of Bougainville. The "hard-line" leadership under Ona is not prepared to negotiate anything other than independence. But during 1997, war-weariness and dissatisfaction with Ona's radical prescription for future development of Bougainville have enabled a relatively moderate leadership to emerge, willing to engage in an open-ended peace process involving other Bougainvillean groups and the national government.

With members from all parts of Bougainville, the BTG provides a focus for Bougainvillean leadership prepared to negotiate special political status for Bougainville within PNG. They include both those with sympathy for the BRA's aspiration for independence but who believe a compromise is needed to end the suffering of ordinary people, and those who are vehemently opposed to the BRA. In general, though, the BTG acts as a bridge between the national government and the BIG/BRA. As such, it tends to be suspected by both sides. The resistance forces constitute a third major group. While represented in the BTG, they have quite distinct structures and interests, in large part related to their combat roles, control of weapons and links to the PNGDF. A complex web of other Bougainvillean interests exists, including armed criminal groups; traditional leaders; women's organizations; churches; secular NGOs; and Bougainvilleans living elsewhere.

At the national government level, numerous ministers and government agencies have roles in the conflict, and conflicting agendas abound. At the international level, Australia has strong political and economic links with PNG, including support to the PNGDF during the conflict, while in the Solomon Islands, there is considerable sympathy for the cause of Bougainville independence.

Through most of the conflict, few democratic political institutions have functioned. Bougainville has elected national parliament members in the 1992 and 1997 elections, but they have all been based in the national capital, and have had limited roles in local politics. Provincial and local governments ceased operating in 1990. Since then, traditional leaders have provided local-level government in both government-controlled and BRA-controlled areas. They have strong legitimacy, reflecting a widespread popular concern for strengthening traditional authority as a means of re-establishing social control. The BTG comprises mainly members elected indirectly by such local government bodies.

Bougainville

Peace-making initiatives

Several sets of negotiations between the national government and the BRA occurred but failed between 1988 and 1994. These efforts failed for a number of reasons: (a) the lack of trust between the main parties resulted in unrealistic assumptions; (b) each side tended to be confident of ultimate success, so contacts between them were often directed at seeking short- to medium-term advantage rather than conflict resolution; (c) differences in understanding about what actually was agreed prevented implementation of some agreements; (d) divisions within particular parties were also a factor, with concessions made by moderate negotiators being subsequently disowned by more hard-line groups.

But after the ejection of the mercenaries and the resignation of the prime minister in March 1997, conditions became conducive to progress. First, more than eight years of conflict had created deep war-weariness and leaders of all main groups were feeling popular pressure for progress towards peace. Second, the actions of the PNGDF in ejecting the mercenaries created more room on all sides for moderate leadership. Third, all parties were conscious of a military stalemate. Fourth, at the national level, the new government were willing to examine moderate alternatives. Fifth, New Zealand emerged as an independent facilitator. Sixth, a newly elected Solomon Islands government favoured resolution of the conflict.

From April 1997, the BTG and BRA/BIG started making direct contact for the first time since 1995. The New Zealand government hosted talks at Burnham military barracks outside Christchurch on New Zealand's south island in July, involving about 70 persons from all main groups. Francis Ona was absent, but key BRA/BIG leaders in attendance used his absence to build a coalition of "moderate" interests.

The resulting Burnham Declaration committed the Bougainvillean leadership to peaceful resolution of the conflict. Four developments at Burnham were crucial. The first was the development of trust and understanding among the divided Bougainville leadership. Second, New Zealand played a key role as neutral facilitator. Third, the timing of the Burnham meeting was fortuitous in building momentum for support for a negotiated settlement among the diverse elements of the PNG government. Fourth, the focus of the meeting was on process rather than outcomes, establishing a process for achieving peace while putting outcomes on the main divisive issues to one side. In past negotiations, efforts to address the key questions of the long-term political status of Bougainville and the BRA/BIG demand for immediate withdrawal of the PNG security forces had resulted in impasse. The focus on process meant that the Burnham Declaration was deliberately vague on the divisive issues.

The Burnham meeting agreed that Bougainvillean delegations should soon meet with PNG officials to plan a major leaders meeting. The meeting with officials was held in October 1997, again at Burnham. It involved over 80 Bougainvilleans, about

Bougainville

20 PNG representatives, and six observers from the Solomon Islands government, including a cabinet minister who ultimately chaired the meetings. Leaders of most BRA "companies" and resistance forces elements attended. Remarkable progress was made at this "Burnham II" officials meeting. The emphasis continued to be on process, leaving outcomes on the most contentious issues to one side. However, contrary to expectations, a "Burnham Truce" was signed.

The Truce was monitored by a multinational unarmed monitoring group under New Zealand leadership and was in place by December 1997. New Zealand, Australia, Vanuatu and Fiji provided the personnel. The truce provided public education about the accelerating peace process, while also providing security for organizing reconciliation ceremonies at the local level, and for organization of the forthcoming leaders meeting. The dramatic progress was welcomed by almost all sides except Ona, who consequently became increasingly marginalized.

The leaders meeting was held at Lincoln University in New Zealand in early 1998, attended by PNG, New Zealand, Australia, Solomon Islands and other Pacific Island states, and representatives of most Bougainvillean interest groups. The meeting produced the "Lincoln Agreement on Peace, Security and Development on Bougainville". The emphasis was still on process, but there was some progress towards agreement on some of the major issues. A permanent cease-fire was agreed. To operate from May 1998, it was to be monitored by a further regional monitoring group with involvement of a UN observer mission. An elected "Bougainville Reconciliation Government" was to be established by the end of 1998. Provision was also made for withdrawal of the PNGDF, subject to the restoration of civil authority. Disarming of the BRA and other Bougainville groups was agreed, although no modalities were provided.

Some implementation of the Lincoln Agreement has occurred, notably with the cease-fire agreement coming into effect on 1 May, and the Truce Monitoring Group under New Zealand leadership becoming a Peace Monitoring Group led by Australia. There has been some progress towards developing civilian policing arrangements. There has been no progress towards establishing the Bougainville Reconciliation Government or disarming, in part because Ona has opposed the cease-fire, and thereby made it difficult for the moderate BIG/BRA leadership to be seen to make too many concessions prior to the leaders meeting expected in June.

Competition for power has been increasing. Both the BTG and the BIG recognize that ultimately there will need to be an elected Bougainville government. There are concerns, however, that it could be difficult to hold full elections without first making considerable progress on existing divisions and outstanding contentious issues. Many BIG/BRA leaders tend to favour a referendum on the question of independence. But that may cause major problems: campaigning could divide people still further.

Ongoing issues

The peace process has not yet touched upon some significant issues. In particular, the question of the future development of Bougainville divides participants. Hard-line BRA elements favour a highly egalitarian society based largely on tradition. More moderate BRA/BIG leaders support a more open society, as do BTG and most other Bougainvillean leaders. However, many otherwise "moderate" Bougainvillean leaders also agree future economic development should be controlled by Bougainvilleans, and that there should be limited freedom of movement into Bougainville for other PNG citizens.

In general the BRA/BIG opposes any future mining or mineral exploration in Bougainville. Many Bougainvilleans support that stand. But there are moderate leaders who privately believe that an independent Bougainville will need mining revenue to develop, and would support re-opening the mine under local control, on fairer terms to landowners and with far greater environmental protection. Although new mining, petroleum and gas projects elsewhere have more than made up for the loss of revenue from Bougainville, there are national politicians keen to see mining activity renewed there.

Bougainville remains deeply divided, and hard-line BRA elements who are still outside the process, or future disagreement within the process, could de-rail progress. Nevertheless, progress in the year to June 1998 has been remarkable. The provision of the unarmed truce monitors has been of central importance in providing security for the process, giving participants confidence to continue. The focus on process rather than outcomes has been crucial in engaging a wide range of leaders in a long-term process where trust can be developed, to enable compromises to emerge. Future progress will depend on keeping them engaged in the process.

Lessons from the Bougainville Conflict Management Process

Some aspects of the Bougainville conflict management process may be of wider application.

– First, in a complex divided situation as in Bougainville, while it may be tempting for a national government embroiled by ethnic conflict to exploit divisions among its potential opponents, the danger is that those divisions themselves become a major obstacle to resolution of the conflict. Processes developed by Bougainvilleans have been crucial foundations for all subsequent progress. This highlights the importance of the national government permitting room for such local involvement.

– Second, conditions which have encouraged the emergence of moderate leadership on both sides have been vital.

– Third, Bougainville demonstrates that a military stalemate offers opportunities for making progress in conflict resolution.

Bougainville

- Fourth, changes of government offer opportunities as new leadership seeks to distance itself from past policies, or seeks to make political capital from progress in resolving the conflict.

- Fifth, neutral outsiders such as foreign governments can play useful roles in creating conditions amenable to negotiations.

- Sixth, there are both advantages and problems inherent in a conflict management approach that focuses on process rather than outcomes. The obvious advantage is that it creates opportunities for building trust and understanding between the parties and engaging them in a process, which they may have difficulty walking away from. The main problem is that at some point the question of outcomes must be addressed. If this is done too early, tensions between and pressures on the parties may be so great that the whole process will be aborted. One solution is to negotiate a process where the key issues are addressed at a later date. In Bougainville, that might be done by establishing a highly autonomous Bougainville government in which all Bougainville factions can participate, whilst postponing a decision on the question of independence.

- Seventh, there may be dangers in pressures for democratization of the conflict resolution process, through acts of self-determination or establishing of elected institutions. In situations where parties are deeply divided, such processes and institutions may themselves exacerbate tensions and conflict.

Bougainville

4.3 Executive Type: Presidentialism versus Parliamentarism

There are essentially three options for constituting an executive government: one based on a parliamentary system, one based on a presidential system, and one based on some combination of the two (sometimes called semi-presidentialism). This section analyses the major competing arguments in favour of and against these three choices.

4.3.1 *Parliamentary systems: advantages and disadvantages*

4.3.2 *Presidentialism: advantages and disadvantages*

4.3.3 *Semi-presidentialism: advantages and disadvantages*

| A Menu of Options 3 | Constituting an Executive Government (p. 189) |

With the possible exception of Switzerland, every established democracy in the world today uses either a presidential, parliamentary or semi-presidential system of government. Parliamentary systems are characterized by the legislature being the principal arena for both lawmaking and (via majority decisions) for executive power. Presidential systems are characterized by the separation of the executive and legislative branches, with executive authority residing outside the legislature, with the president and his or her cabinet. The simplest definition of the differences between the two approaches can thus be summed up by the degree of relative independence of the executive, with pure presidentialism being characterized by executive independence and pure parliamentarism by the mutual dependence and intertwining of a state's legislative and executive capacities.

For the issue of democracy and deep-rooted conflict, however, the key distinction between parliamentarism and presidentialism focuses on the distinction between, on the one hand, the range of parties and opinions that can be represented in the executive under a parliamentary system, in contrast to the unavoidably singular nature of authority represented by the office of the president. Although this comparison is often over-drawn-

– presidential executives can and often do have a range of political and ethnic identities represented in the cabinet, while parliamentary systems are often dominated by a single party alone – it remains central to the debate concerning the relative merits of presidentialism, parliamentarism and semi-presidentialism.

As with many institutional choices, the debate over the merits of parliamentary versus presidential approaches is not so much a question of which is *best*, but rather of the most appropriate choice for a given society, considering its particular social structure, political culture and history. It is essential, before any of the options are examined in any detail, for due consideration to be given to the specific factors that need to be addressed in the country. This may include issues such as the need for a strong government, the degree of trust between the parties, their ability to set aside their differences in the national interest, the levels of checks and balances required, the extent of the trauma that the society has undergone, the presence of dominant personalities and their democratic credentials in the political arena, the need for compromise, the necessity to think long-term as well as short-term, the need for flexibility and so on.

The debate over the merits of parliamentary versus presidential approaches is not so much a question of which is best, but rather of the most appropriate choice for a given society, considering its particular social structure, political culture and history.

4.3.1 Parliamentary systems

In practice, the institutional choices made by most new democracies in the "second wave" of democracy following the World War Two has favoured parliamentary systems as being the best choice for fragile or divided new democracies. Much of the scholarly debate in favour of parliamentarism has focused less on the desirability of parliamentary government than on the inherent difficulties of presidentialism. The majority of the world's "established" democracies use parliamentary systems, while a disproportionately large number of democracies which have experienced authoritarian interludes – especially in Latin America and Asia – use or have used presidentialism. Because of this record, many observers have argued that it is parliamentarism itself that has proved to be a positive factor in consolidating democracy. Under this rationale, parliamentary government has been identified as having a number of moderating and inclusion-promoting features that have assisted nascent democracies.

Advantages

The efficacy of a parliament as a mechanism of democratic governance will be substantially influenced by the composition

4.3 Executive Type: Presidentialism versus Parliamentarism

of that parliament in terms of the number of political parties represented. Therefore, any discussion of the advantages of parliamentary systems must bear in mind that it is closely related to the type of electoral system used in the election of that parliament; this will determine aspects such as inclusivity, particularly in relation to ethnic groupings. Such advantages include:

Ability to facilitate the inclusion of all groups within the legislature and the executive. Because cabinets in parliamentary systems are usually drawn from members of the elected legislature, parliamentary government enables the inclusion of all political elements represented in the legislature, including minorities, in the executive. Cabinets comprising a coalition of several different parties are a typical feature of many well established parliamentary democracies. This means that participation in government is not the preserve of one group alone, but can be shared amongst many, or all, significant groups.

In societies deeply divided by significant ethnic or other cleavages, this principle of *inclusion* can be vital. This is why a number of democratic transitions in recent years (e.g., South Africa) have featured "grand coalition" or "unity" governments – i.e., executives in which all significant political parties are represented in cabinet and take part in executive decision-making. Such arrangements are often made mandatory on the basis of primary electoral support – for example, a constitution may state that all parties which receive a minimum percentage of the vote should be included in the grand coalition executive in proportion to their overall vote share, as in Fiji and transitional South Africa. Grand coalitions are also common in non-divided democracies at times of great stress – such as times of economic crisis or when a country is at war – where "governments of national unity" bring together major parties from all sides into the cabinet.

Flexibility and capacity to adapt to changing circumstances. Because parliamentary coalitions can be made and unmade to suit changing circumstances, and because governments in many parliamentary systems can change on the floor of the legislature without recourse to a general election, advocates of parliamentarism point to its flexibility and capacity to adapt to changing circumstances as a strong benefit. A discredited government can be dismissed from office by the parliament itself, for example, as occurred in Ecuador in 1994. In the same way, many parliamentary systems (e.g., the United Kingdom, Canada, Australia and many others) enable elections to be called at any time, rather than be subject to the fixed terms common to presidentialism.

"Checks and balances". By making the executive dependent, at least in theory, upon the confidence of the legislature, parliamentary systems are said to foster greater accountability on the part of the government of the day towards the people's representatives. Proponents argue that this means that there is not only greater public control over the policy-making process, but also greater transparency in the way decisions are made. However, such arguments often fail to take account of the degree of party discipline in many parliaments, where the legislature acts more as a "rubber stamp" than a check upon the power of the executive.

Relative stability and continuity of new democracies that have adopted parliamentary systems. Of the many states that became independent in the three decades following the end of World War Two, *all* the countries which could claim to have maintained a continuously democratic record to the late 1980s were parliamentary systems. The statistics are illuminating: of the 93 new democracies that gained their independence between 1945 and 1979, all of the 15 countries which remained democratic throughout the 1980s were parliamentary rather than presidential systems, including some of the developing world's most successful democracies like India, Botswana, Trinidad and Tobago and Papua New Guinea. Conversely, all the new presidential democracies from this period suffered some form of democratic breakdown. Overall, parliamentary systems have a rate of survival over three times that of presidential systems.

Disadvantages

The major disadvantages of parliamentary systems include:

Tendency towards ponderous or immobile decision-making. The inclusiveness that typifies grand coalitions can easily turn into executive deadlocks caused by the inability of the various parties to agree on a coherent position on issues of disagreement. This was typified by the "immobilism" that affected Fourth Republic France and that was partly responsible for General de Gaulle's assumption of presidential power. Decision-making deadlock was in part responsible for the breakdown of power sharing under Cyprus's 1960 constitution. The latter period of the National Party's participation in South Africa's government of national unity in 1996 is a more recent example of the potential for such arrangements to result in deadlock and to then have the potential to undermine the very unity that they were intended to stimulate.

4.3 Executive Type: Presidentialism versus Parliamentarism

Lack of accountability and discipline. Critics also argue that parliamentary systems are inherently less accountable than presidential ones, as responsibility for decisions is taken by the collective cabinet rather than a single figure. This is especially problematic when diverse coalitions form the executive, as it becomes increasingly difficult for electors to establish who is responsible for a particular decision and make a retrospective judgement as to the performance of the government.

Propensity towards weak or fragmented government. Some parliamentary systems are typified by shifting coalitions of different forces, rather than by disciplined parties. Under such circumstances, governments are often weak and unstable, leading to a lack of continuity and direction in public policy.

Survival of new parliamentary democracies may be attributable to other factors. Finally, the successful record of survival of parliamentary democracies cited above is mitigated by the fact that almost all the successful cases are former British colonies, with the majority being small island nations in the Caribbean and the South Pacific – a concentration which suggests that other factors apart from parliamentarism may be responsible for their democratic success.

An alternative critique of parliamentarism sees it as being as or more conducive to unadulterated majority-rule than even the purest forms of presidentialism. In reality, many parliamentary governments, particularly in new democracies, are *not* comprised of inclusive multi-party coalitions but rather by disciplined single parties. In divided societies, such parties can represent predominantly or exclusively one ethnic group. When placed in a parliamentary system, a 51 per cent majority of the seats in such cases can result in 100 per cent of the political power, as there are few or no ameliorating devices to restrain the power of the executive – hence the term "elective dictatorship" associated with some cases of single-party parliamentary rule. Moreover, and in direct contrast to the separation of powers that occurs under presidentialism, many parliaments *in practice* provide a very weak legislative check on governments because of the degree of party discipline – which means that a slim parliamentary majority can win every vote on every issue in the parliament. In such cases, parliamentary government can lead to almost complete winner-take-all results.

4.3.2 Presidentialism

Presidentialism has been a popular choice amongst many new democracies in the last decade. In fact, almost all the new demo-

cracies in Asia, Eastern Europe and Latin America in this period
have chosen presidential systems as the basis of their new democracy. While the influence of the United States, the world's
best known presidential system, is probably partly responsible
for this trend, recent experience has also highlighted a number
of advantages of presidentialism.

Advantages

**A directly elected president is identifiable and accountable to
voters to a high degree.** The office of the president can be held
directly accountable for decisions taken because, in contrast to
parliamentary systems, the chief executive is directly chosen by
popular vote. It is thus easier for the electorate to reward or
retrospectively punish a president (by voting him or her out of
office) than is the case with parliamentary systems.

**Ability of a president to act as a unifying national figure, stan-
ding above the fray of sectarian disputes.** A president enjoying
broad public support can represent the nation to itself, becoming a symbol of moderation of the "middle ground" between
rival political groupings. To play this role, however, it is essential
that the rules used to elect the president are tailored so as to
achieve this type of broad support, rather than enabling one
ethnic or regional group to dominate (see section 4.4 on
"Electoral Systems for Divided Societies" for further details).

Higher degree of choice. The fact that presidential systems typically give voters a dual choice – one vote for the president and
one vote for the legislature – means that voters are usually presented with a considerably higher degree of choice under presidential systems.

Stability of the office and continuity in terms of public policy.
Unlike parliamentary governments, which can shift and change
completely without recourse to the electorate, the president and
his or her administration normally remains relatively constant.
In many presidential systems, the terms of office are rigidly
fixed, which can give greater stability in office and predictability
in policy-making than some parliamentary alternatives. This
leads, in theory at least, to more efficient and decisive governance,
making it attractive for those cases where governments change
frequently because of weak parties or shifting parliamentary
coalitions, or where hard political decisions, such as contentious
economic reforms, need to be taken.

Disadvantages

Presidency captured by one political or ethnic group. The
major disadvantage of presidentialism for divided societies is the

4.3 Executive Type: Presidentialism versus Parliamentarism

propensity of the office to be captured by one political or ethnic group. This can create particular difficulties for multi-ethnic societies. In such situations – which are common in societies attempting to make a transition to democracy from a period of deep-rooted conflict – the office of the president can become a highly majoritarian device, ensuring almost complete political power with often a limited plurality of the total vote. This is particularly the case where there are two or three main groups all struggling for power. In such a case, the president can easily be perceived as the representative of one group only, and consequently has limited incentive to appeal to the needs and votes of these other groups. Under such a scenario, the office of the president can become a symbol of ethnic domination or subjugation: exactly the type of in-group/out-group symbolism that deeply divided societies need to avoid at all costs.

No real checks on the executive. This becomes even more true when there is a direct concordance between the president's party and the majority party in parliament. In this case (typified for many years by Mexico) the parliament has almost no real checks on the executive and can become more of a glorified debating chamber than a legitimate house of review. This problem can be exacerbated by the fact that a president, unlike a parliamentary prime minister, can become virtually inviolable during his or her term of office, with no mechanism for dismissing unpopular incumbents. Salvador Allende's election as president of Chile in 1970, for example, gave him control of the executive with only 36 per cent of the vote, and in opposition to the centre and right-dominated legislature. Some analysts have argued that Chile's 1973 military coup can be traced back to the system that placed an unpopular president in a position of considerable long-term power. While impeachment of the president by the legislature is a device built into many presidential systems, it remains the case that the presidency is a much less flexible office than the major alternatives.

Empirically associated with democratic failure. In marked contrast to the relative success of parliamentary democracies established between 1945 and 1979, *none* of the presidential or semi-presidential systems established during this period were continuously democratic. Presidential democracies were also twice as likely as pure parliamentary democracies to experience a military coup: in the period 1973–1989, five parliamentary democracies experienced a military coup compared to 10 presidencies. At the time of writing, there are only four presidential democracies that have enjoyed 30 years of continuous democracy: the United States, Costa Rica, Colombia and Venezuela. The shining example of the US apart, this is not an encouraging record of democratic stability.

4.3.3 Semi-presidentialism

A final executive type is what we call "semi-presidentialism"; that is, a situation in which a parliamentary system and prime minister, with some executive powers, is combined with a president who also has executive powers. The ministry is drawn from and subject to the confidence of the legislature. This is a relatively unusual model – found today in France, Portugal, Finland, Sri Lanka and one or two other countries – but has nonetheless been cited by some experts as being the most desirable executive formulation for fragile nascent democracies.

Advantages

Can combine advantages of presidentialism and parliamentarism. The appeal of the semi-presidential model is its ability to combine the benefits of a directly elected president with a prime minister who must command an absolute majority in the legislature. A move to semi-presidentialism has been recommended as a good "half way house" for some countries that want to combine the benefits of both models.

Mutual consensus requirement. Proponents of semi-presidentialism focus on the capacity of semi-presidentialism to increase the accountability and "identifiability" of the executive, while also building in a system of mutual checks and balances and the need for consensus between the two executive wings of government. This mutual consensus requirement can be a particular advantage for highly divided societies, as it requires a president to come to an agreement with the legislature on important issues, and thus to be a force for the "middle ground" rather than the extremes.

Disadvantages

Propensity for deadlock between and within the executive arms of government. Because a government's powers are effectively divided between the prime minister and the president – for example, foreign affairs powers being the preserve of the president while the prime minister and the cabinet decide domestic policy – a structural tension exists within the government as a whole. This can lead to deadlock and immobilism, particularly if, as has occurred in several semi-presidential systems, the prime minister and the president come from opposing political parties. The benefits of compromise and moderation can degenerate into a stand-off. This is especially the case when the division of responsibility between the two offices is not always clear (e.g., foreign policy in the French system), and where the timing and sequencing of elections between the houses differs.

4.3.4 Conclusion

The competing claims concerning the benefits of parliamentary and presidential systems of government are confusing and sometimes even contradictory. However, it is possible to glean several trends and tendencies.

Compromise, moderation and inclusion are keys to democratic stability. Firstly, both sides of the debate argue that their preferred model is, under particular circumstances, the best option for inducing compromise, moderation and inclusion. It is clear, therefore, that these characteristics are seen as being the key to democratic stability in deeply divided societies.

Size and distribution of competing groups are important factors in deciding on executive type. Two variables would appear to be of particular importance when choosing an executive structure: the *size* and *distribution* of the competing groups within society. Presidencies may have difficulty being perceived as unifying offices where there are three or four roughly equally sized groups, but likewise parliaments themselves have sometimes been an instrument of majority domination in divided societies where one group forms an absolute majority of the population. When Sri Lanka changed from a parliamentary to a presidential system of government in 1978, it did so partly because there was seen to be a need for a unifying national figure who could represent both the dominant (80 per cent of total) Sinhalese population, but also the minority Tamils. They did this by designing the electoral system so that Tamils could still influence the choice of president. In Kenya, by contrast, President Daniel arap Moi is typically perceived as representing his own Kalinjini tribe against the majority Kikuyu tribe, despite a distribution requirement which prescribes that to be elected president, a candidate has to receive at least 25 per cent of the vote in at least five out of the eight provinces.

Much depends upon the way in which the various offices are elected. As with all of the mechanisms described in this chapter, the competing benefits of parliamentary and presidential models cannot be viewed in isolation. For example, the nature of the electoral system is key, as are the different checks and balances that can be put in place to address specific fears and concerns. Many of the power-sharing virtues advocated by proponents of parliamentarism are premised on the assumption that minorities as well as majorities will be represented in the legislature, and that coalition governments rather than single-party rule will be the norm. For many countries, this means that a proportional electoral system is crucial to the success of parliamentary democracy as an agent of conflict management.

Similarly, a president's ability to encourage inter-ethnic moderation and compromise is often dependent upon electoral arrangements that offer clear incentives for compromise. Some scholars of ethnic conflict have argued that electoral arrangements which require some geographic distribution of the vote, or in which the second and third choices of voters are taken into account, offer the best models for investigation, as they encourage the elected president to become a pan-ethnic figure. By contrast, presidential or parliamentary elections held under a first-past-the-post system are more likely to produce outcomes in which the victor's support comes primarily from one geographic and/or ethnic region.

There is considerable room for flexibility and opportunity for innovation to maximize the advantages and disadvantages of each. It is worth remembering that all three classifications – parliamentarism, presidentialism and semi-presidentialism – are more ideal types than definitive models. There is considerable room for flexibility and opportunity for innovation to maximize the advantages and disadvantages of each. Some parliamentary countries such as South Africa, for example, call their prime minister a "President", thus maximizing the symbolic powers of the office while maintaining the structural advantages of a parliamentary system. Israel recently introduced a hybrid system in which the people nonetheless directly elect the parliamentary prime minister. Finland's semi-presidential system allows the president to share power with the prime minister on a nearly equal basis, but with specific responsibility for certain areas such as foreign policy. Creative constitutional engineering thus provides opportunities for maximizing desired characteristics while minimizing perceived disadvantages.

CONSTITUTING AN EXECUTIVE GOVERNMENT

Parliamentary system: The legislature is the principal arena for both lawmaking and (via majority decisions) for executive power.

Presidential system: The executive and legislative branches are separated, with executive authority residing outside the legislature with the president and his or her cabinet.

Semi-Presidential: Combines a parliamentary system featuring a prime minister who has some executive powers, with a president who also has executive powers.

	Parliamentary systems	Presidential systems	Semi-Presidential systems
Advantages	■ inclusiveness (can include all groups within the executive) ■ flexibility (parliamentary coalitions can change without recourse to elections) ■ checks and balances (executive is dependent on the confidence of the legislature) ■ empirically associated with democratic persistence	■ can be a unifying national figure ■ highly identifiable and accountable to voters ■ greater degree of choice for voters ■ stability and continuity of policy-making	■ can combine advantages of both presidentialism and parliamentarism ■ "mutual consensus" requirement
Disadvantages	■ possibility of executive deadlocks, stalemates and immobilism ■ problems of accountability as decisions are taken by the collective cabinet ■ lack of governing stability	■ centralization of authority in one person ■ inherently majoritarian and exclusive ■ empirically associated with democratic failure	■ dangers of deadlock between president and parliament ■ division of governing powers can be unclear

A MENU OF OPTIONS 3 [P. 189]

REFERENCES AND FURTHER READING

Lijphart, Arend. ed. 1992. *Parliamentary versus Presidential Government.* Oxford: Oxford University Press.

Linz, Juan. 1990. "The Perils of Presidentialism", *Journal of Democracy*, no. 1 (Winter 1990). pp. 51–69.

Mainwaring, Scott. 1993. "Presidentialism, Multipartism, and Democracy: The Difficult Combination", *Comparative Political Studies*, vol. 26, no. 2. pp. 198–228.

Shugart, Matthew S. and Carey, John. 1992. *Presidents and Assemblies: Constitutional Design and Electoral Dynamics.* Cambridge: Cambridge University Press.

Stepan, Alfred and Cindy Skach, 1993. "Constitutional Frameworks and Democratic Consolidation: Parliamentarism versus Presidentialism", *World Politics*, vol. 46, no. 1. pp. 1–22.

4.4 Electoral Systems for Divided Societies

Ben Reilly and
Andrew Reynolds

4.4 Electoral Systems for Divided Societies

The collective evidence from elections held in divided societies to date suggests that an appropriately crafted electoral system can help to nurture accommodative tendencies, but that the implementation of an inappropriate system can severely harm the process of conflict resolution and democratization in a plural state. In this section, we identify a number of instances where the electoral system itself appears to have encouraged accommodation, and those cases where it played a part in exaggerating the incentives for ethnic polarization.

4.4.1 *Introduction*
4.4.2 *Electoral systems and conflict management*
4.4.3 *Needs of transitional versus consolidated democracies*

Box 8	Electoral Systems Around the World (pp. 193–196)
Box 9	Ideal Qualities of Electoral Institutions for Transitional and Consolidated Democracies (p. 202)
A Menu of Options 4	Electoral System Choices for Divided Societies (p. 203)

4.4.1 Introduction

An electoral system is one of the most important mechanisms for shaping political competition, because it is, to quote Giovanni Sartori, "the most specific manipulable instrument of politics" – that is, it can be purposely designed to achieve particular outcomes. It can reward particular types of behaviour and place constraints on others.

In translating the votes in a general election into seats in the legislature, the choice of electoral system can effectively determine who is elected and which party gains power. Even with exactly the same number of votes for parties, one system might lead to a coalition government and another to a single party assuming majority control. An electoral system also has a major influence on the type of party system that develops: the *number* and *relative sizes* of political parties in parliament, and the internal cohesion and discipline of parties. For example, some systems may encourage factionalism where different wings of one party are constantly at odds with each other, while others might force parties to speak with one voice and suppress dissent. Different electoral systems may encourage or retard cross-party alliances. They can provide incentives for groups to be accommodatory or for parties to base themselves on hostile appeals to ethnicity or kinship ties. The choice of electoral system is therefore one of the most crucial institutional decisions for any post-conflict society.

An electoral system is designed to do three main jobs. First, it acts as the conduit through which the people can hold their elected representatives accountable. Second, it will translate the votes cast into seats won in a legislative chamber. The system may give more weight to proportionality between votes cast and seats won, or it may funnel the votes (however fragmented among parties) into a parliament which contains two large parties representing polarized views. Third, different electoral systems structure the boundaries of "acceptable" political discourse in different ways, and give incentives for those competing for power to couch their appeals to the electorate in distinct ways. In deeply divided societies, for example, particular electoral systems can reward candidates and parties who act in a co-operative, accommodatory manner to rival groups; or they can instead reward those who appeal only to their own ethnic group. However, the "spin" which an electoral system places on a wider political system depends on the specific divisions within any given society.

4.4.2 Electoral systems and conflict management

The comparative experience suggests that four specific systems are particularly suitable for divided societies. These are usually recommended as part of overall constitutional engineering packages, in which the electoral system is one element. Some constitutional engineering packages emphasize inclusiveness and proportionality; others emphasize moderation and accommodation. The four major choices in this regard are (a) list proportional representation, (b) the alternative vote, (c) the single transferable vote, and (d) strategies which explicitly recognize the presence of communal groups.

4.4 Electoral Systems for Divided Societies

Box 8

ELECTORAL SYSTEMS AROUND THE WORLD

There are countless electoral system variations, but essentially they can be split into nine main systems which fall into three broad families. The most common way to look at electoral systems is to group them by how closely they translate national votes won into parliamentary seats won; that is, how proportional they are. Most electoral system choices involve a trade-off: maximizing proportionality and inclusiveness of all opinions, or maximizing government efficiency via single-party governments and accountability. Figure One encapsulates the three main electoral system families of Plurality-Majority systems, Semi-Proportional systems and Proportional Representation systems.

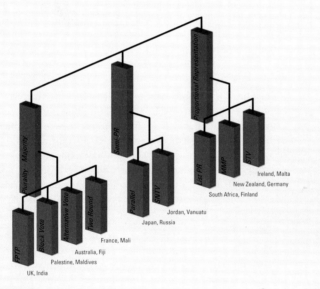

© International IDEA

Plurality-Majority Systems

These comprise two plurality systems, First Past the Post and the Block Vote, and two majority systems, the Alternative Vote and the Two-Round System.

1. **First Past the Post (FPTP)** is the world's most commonly used system. Contests are held in single-member districts, and the winner is the candidate with the most votes, but not necessarily an absolute majority of the votes. FPTP is supported primarily on the grounds of simplicity, and its tendency to produce representatives

beholden to defined geographic areas. Countries that use this system include the United Kingdom, the United States, India, Canada, and most countries that were once part of the British Empire.

2. The **Block Vote (BV)** is the application of FPTP in multi- rather than single-member districts. Voters have as many votes as there are seats to be filled, and the highest-polling candidates fill the positions regardless of the percentage of the vote they actually achieve. This system is used in some parts of Asia and the Middle East. A variation is the "Party Block", as used in Singapore and Mauritius: voters choose between parties rather than candidates, and the highest-polling party wins all seats in the district.

3. In the **Alternative Vote (AV)** system, electors rank the candidates in order of choice, marking a "1" for their favourite candidate, "2" for their second choice, "3" for their third choice, and so on. The system thus enables voters to express their preferences between candidates, rather than simply their first choice. If no candidate has over 50 per cent of first-preferences, lower order preference votes are transferred until a majority winner emerges. This system is used in Australia and some other South Pacific countries.

4. The **Two-Round System (TRS)** has two rounds of voting, often a week or a fortnight apart. The first round is the same as a normal FPTP election. If a candidate receives an absolute majority of the vote, then he or she is elected outright, with no need for a second ballot. If, however, no candidate has received an absolute majority, then a second round of voting is conducted, and the winner of this round is declared elected. This system is widely used in France, former French colonies, and some parts of the former Soviet Union.

Semi-Proportional Systems

Semi-PR systems translate votes cast into seats won in a way that falls somewhere in between the proportionality of PR systems and the majoritarianism of plurality-majority systems. The two Semi-PR systems are the Single Non-Transferable Vote (SNTV), and Parallel (or mixed) systems.

5. In **SNTV** systems, each elector has one vote but there are several seats in the district to be filled, and the candidates with the highest number of votes fill these positions. This means that in a four-member district, for example, one would on average need only just over 20 per cent of the vote to be elected. This system is used today only in Jordan and Vanuatu, but is most often associated with Japan, which used SNTV until 1993.

6. **Parallel systems** use both PR lists and single-member districts running side-by-side (hence the term parallel). Part of the parlia-

ment is elected by proportional representation, part by some type of plurality or majority method. Parallel systems have been widely adopted by new democracies in the 1990s, perhaps because, on the face of it, they appear to combine the benefits of PR lists with single-member district representation. However, depending upon the design of the system, Parallel systems can produce results as disproportional as plurality-majority ones.

Proportional Representation Systems

All Proportional Representation (PR) systems aim to reduce the disparity between a party's share of national votes and its share of parliamentary seats. For example, if a major party wins 40 per cent of the votes, it should also win around 40 per cent of the seats, and a minor party with 10 per cent of the votes should similarly gain 10 per cent of the seats. For many new democracies, particularly those that face deep divisions, the inclusion of all significant groups in the parliament can be an important condition for democratic consolidation. Outcomes based on consensus-building and power-sharing usually include a PR system.

Criticisms of PR are two-fold: that it gives rise to coalition governments, with disadvantages such as party system fragmentation and government instability; and that PR produces a weak linkage between a representative and her or his geographical electorate. And since voters are expected to vote for parties rather than individuals or groups of individuals, it is a difficult system to operate in societies that have embryonic or loose party structures.

7. **List PR systems** are the most common type of PR. Most forms of list PR are held in large, multi-member districts that maximize proportionality. List PR requires each party to present a list of candidates to the electorate. Electors vote for a party rather than a candidate; and parties receive seats in proportion to their overall share of the national vote. Winning candidates are taken from the lists in order of their respective position. This system is widely used in continental Europe, Latin America and southern Africa.

8. **Mixed Member Proportional** (MMP) systems, as used in Germany, New Zealand, Bolivia, Italy, Mexico, Venezuela, and Hungary, attempt to combine the positive attributes of both majoritarian and PR electoral systems. A proportion of the parliament (roughly half in the cases of Germany, New Zealand, Bolivia, and Venezuela) is elected by plurality-majority methods, usually from single-member districts, while the remainder is constituted by PR lists. The PR seats are used to compensate for any disproportionality produced by the district seat results. Single-member districts also ensure that voters have some geographical representation.

9. The **Single Transferable Vote (STV)** uses multi-member districts, where voters rank candidates in order of preference on the ballot paper in the same manner as Alternative Vote. After the total number of first-preference votes are tallied, a "quota" of votes is established, which a candidate must achieve to be elected. Any candidate who has more first preferences than the quota is immediately elected. If no-one has achieved the quota, the candidate with the lowest number of first preferences is eliminated, and their second preferences are redistributed among remaining candidates. And the surplus votes of elected candidates (i.e., those votes above the quota) are redistributed according to the second preferences on the ballot papers until all seats for the constituency are filled. This system is well established in Ireland and Malta.

List PR

List PR is an essential component of the constitutional engineering package known as *consociationalism*. Consociationalism entails a power-sharing agreement within government, brokered between clearly defined segments of society divided by ethnicity, religion and language. Consociational societies include Belgium, the Netherlands, Austria and Switzerland. The idea has four basic elements: (i) *grand coalition* (executive power sharing among the representatives of all significant groups); (ii) *segmental autonomy* (a high degree of internal autonomy for groups that wish to have it); (iii) *proportionality* (proportional representation and proportional allocation of civil service positions and public funds); and (iv) *mutual veto* (a minority veto on the most vital issues). These four basic elements ensure that government becomes an inclusive multi-ethnic coalition, unlike the adversarial nature of a Westminster winner-take-all democracy.

Proponents of consociationalism favour list PR because it: 1) delivers highly proportional election results; 2) is relatively invulnerable to gerrymandering; and 3) is simpler than many alternative systems for both voters and electoral officials and thus will be less open to suspicion. The successful use of list PR at South Africa's transitional 1994 elections is often cited as a good example of these qualities, and of the way list PR enables parties to place women or ethnic minorities in winnable places on their party list.

But there are also disadvantages. Because list PR relies on large, multi-member electoral districts, it breaks the geographical link between voters and their elected member. Geographically large multi-ethnic societies which have used list PR success-

4.4 Electoral Systems for Divided Societies

fully, such as South Africa and Indonesia, are now considering alternatives which would build in some geographic accountability via single-member electorates. Secondly, the wider argument for consociationalism rests on assumptions that may not always be viable in divided societies, such as the expectation that ethnic leaders will be more moderate than their supporters. Consociational structures may merely entrench ethnic politics, rather than work to encourage inter-ethnic alliances. So consociationalism may be a good strategy for deeply divided societies in *transition*, but less appropriate for promoting subsequent democratic *consolidation*.

The experience of list PR in post-Dayton Bosnia is a good example of how proportionality alone will not encourage accommodation. In Bosnia, groups are represented in parliament in proportion to their numbers in the community as a whole, but because parties can rely exclusively on the votes of members of their own community for their electoral success, there is little incentive for them to behave accommodatively on ethnic issues. In fact, the incentives work in the other direction. As it is easy to mobilize support by playing the "ethnic card", major parties in Bosnia have every incentive to emphasize ethnic issues and sectarian appeals. Bosnia's 1996 elections were effectively an ethnic census, with electors voting along ethnic lines and each of the major nationalist parties gaining support almost exclusively from their own ethnic group.

The Alternative Vote (AV)

An alternative approach to electoral system design is to choose a system which places less emphasis on proportional results but more emphasis on the need to force different groups to work together. The core of this approach is to offer electoral incentives to politicians to look for votes among other groups rather than just relying on supporters from their own group. The Alternative Vote (AV) enables voters to declare not only their first choice of candidate on a ballot, but also their second, third and subsequent choices amongst all candidates standing. This feature presents candidates with a strong incentive to try and attract the second preferences of voters from other groups (assuming that the voters' first preference will usually be a candidate from their own group), as winners need to gain an absolute majority of the vote under AV rules. Candidates who successfully "pool" their own first preferences and the second preferences of others will be more successful than those who fail to attract any second-order support. To succeed, candidates need to move to the centre on policy issues to attract floating voters, or to successfully accommodate "fringe" issues into their broader policy. There is a long history of both types of behaviour in Australian elections, the only established democracy to use AV, and in the ethnically fragmented state of Papua New Guinea, which has also used AV.

The more groups competing in a constituency, the more likely it is that meaningful "preference swapping" will take place. In many ethnically divided countries, however, members of the same ethnic group tend to cluster together, which means that the relatively small, single-member districts which are a feature of AV would, in these cases, result in constituencies which are ethnically uniform. Where a candidate is confident of achieving an absolute majority of first preferences due to the domination of his or her own ethnic group in an area, they need look no further to win the seat. This means that the "vote-pooling" between different ethnic groups which is a precondition for the accommodative influences of AV would not, in fact, occur. So AV works best either in cases of extreme ethnic fragmentation or, more commonly, where a few large ethnic groups are widely dispersed and intermixed. The use of AV-like systems for presidential elections in Sri Lanka and as part of the constitutional settlement in ethnically intermixed Fiji are both examples of this.

The Single Transferable Vote (STV)

STV stands as something of a mid-point between the use of list PR, which maximizes proportionality, and AV, which maximizes incentives for accommodation. Some scholars argue that under STV, the twin benefits of proportionality and accommodation can both be emphasized. As a PR system, STV produces largely proportional results, while its preferential ballot provides some incentives towards the vote-pooling approach outlined above, thus encouraging party appeals beyond defined ethnic boundaries. Segments of opinion can be represented proportionately in the legislature, but there is also an incentive for political elites to appeal to the members of other segments, given that second preferences are of prime importance.

STV has attracted many admirers, but its use for national parliamentary elections has been limited to a few cases – Ireland (since 1921), Malta (since 1947), the Australian Senate (since 1949), and at "one-off" elections in Estonia and Northern Ireland. As a mechanism for choosing representatives, STV is perhaps the most sophisticated of all electoral systems, allowing for

4.4 Electoral Systems for Divided Societies

choice between parties and between candidates within parties. The final results also retain a fair degree of proportionality, and since the multi-member districts are usually relatively small, the geographical link between voter and representative is retained. However, the system is often criticized because preference voting is unfamiliar in many societies, and demands a minimal degree of literacy and numeracy. STV counts are also quite complex, which can be a drawback. STV also carries the disadvantages of all parliaments elected by PR methods, such as under certain circumstances exaggerating the power of small minority parties.

The use of STV in divided societies to date has been somewhat limited and inconclusive. Two ethnically divided states have utilized STV in "one-off" national elections: Northern Ireland in 1973 and 1982, and Estonia in 1990. In both cases, little vote-pooling or accommodation on ethnic issues took place, and the elected parliaments exhibited little in the way of inter-ethnic accommodation. In contrast, however, STV has been used successfully in the Republic of Ireland and in Malta, maximizing both proportionality and, by using small multi-member electoral districts, an element of geographic accountability. STV was recently re-introduced to Northern Ireland as part of the Irish peace settlement (see Case Study), where it formed part of a wider prescription for power sharing between the Catholic and Protestant populations, and was successfully used there for the first post-settlement elections in 1998. Significant numbers of Catholics and Protestants used their preferences to transfer votes across group lines for the first time.

Explicit recognition of communal groups

A different approach to elections and conflict management is to explicitly recognize the overwhelming importance of group identity in the political process, and to mandate this in the electoral law so that ethnic representation, and the ratio of different ethnic groups in the parliament, is fixed. Four distinct approaches reflect this thinking:

Communal electoral rolls. The most straightforward way of explicitly recognizing the importance of ethnicity is a system of *communal representation*. Seats are not only divided on a communal basis, but the entire system of parliamentary representation is similarly based on communal considerations. This usually means that each defined "community" has its own electoral roll, and elects only members of its "own group" to parliament. Today, only Fiji (see Case Study) continues to use this system, and it remains as an optional choice for Maori voters in New

Zealand. Elsewhere communal systems were abandoned because communal electorates, while guaranteeing group representation, often had the perverse effect of undermining accommodation, as there were no incentives for political intermixing between communities. The issue of how to define a member of a particular group, and how to distribute electorates fairly between them, was also strewn with pitfalls.

Reserved seats for ethnic, linguistic or other minorities. An alternative approach is to *reserve* some parliamentary seats for identifiable ethnic or religious minorities. Many countries reserve a few seats for such groups: e.g., Jordan (Christians and Circassians), India (scheduled tribes and castes), Pakistan (non-Muslim minorities), Colombia ("black communities"), Croatia (Hungarian, Italian, Czech, Slovak, Ruthenian, Ukrainian, German and Austrian minorities), Slovenia (Hungarians and Italians), Taiwan (Aboriginal community), Western Samoa (non-indigenous minorities), Niger (Taurag), and the Palestinian Authority (Christians and Samaritans). But it is often argued that a better strategy is to design structures that nurture a representative parliament naturally, rather than to impose members who may be viewed as "token" parliamentarians with representation but no genuine influence. Quota seats can also breed resentment among the majority population and increase mistrust between minority groups.

Ethnically mandated lists under a block vote system. A third approach is to use *pre-determined ethnic lists* with the party block vote. Party block works like the standard block vote described earlier, except that electors vote for a party list of candidates rather than individuals. The party that wins most votes takes *all* the seats in the district, and its entire list of candidates is duly elected. Some countries use this system to ensure balanced ethnic representation, as it enables parties to present ethnically diverse lists of candidates for election. In Lebanon, for example, each party list must comprise a mix of candidates from different ethnic groups. Electors thus choose on the basis of criteria other than ethnicity. Singapore uses a similar system to increase the representation of its minority Malay and Indian community. But a critical flaw of the party block is the possibility of "super-majoritarian" results, where one party can win almost all of the seats with a simple majority of the votes. In the Singaporean elections of 1991, for example, a 61 per cent vote for the ruling People's Action Party gave it 95 per cent of all seats in parliament, while in 1982 and 1995 the Mauritian elections saw a parliament with no opposition at all. To counter this possibility, the

4.4 Electoral Systems for Divided Societies

Lebanese constitution pre-determines the ethnic composition of the entire parliament, and of key positions such as the president and the prime minister as well.

"Best loser" seats to balance ethnic representation in the legislature. A final mechanism sometimes used in conjunction with the party block vote is to assign seats to the "best loser" from a specified community. In Mauritius, for example, four "best loser" seats are allocated to the highest polling candidates of under-represented ethnic groups in order to balance ethnic representation. Recently, however, there has been a strong movement in favour of the abolition of such seats, which are seen as representing the last vestiges of communalism in Mauritian politics.

4.4.3 Needs of transitional and consolidated democracies

There is no perfect electoral system, and no "right" way to approach its design. But for all societies, not just divided ones, the major design criteria are sometimes in conflict with each other or even mutually exclusive. For example, increasing the number of seats in each district to increase proportionality will reduce geographic accountability between the electorate and the parliament. The electoral system designer must therefore go through a careful preliminary process of prioritizing which criteria are most important to their particular political context. For example, an ethnically divided state in Central Africa might want above all to avoid excluding minority ethnic groups from representation, in order to promote the legitimacy of the electoral process and avoid the perception that the electoral system was unfair. In contrast, while these issues would remain important, a fledgling democracy in a multi-ethnic state in Eastern Europe might have different priorities – e.g., to ensure that a government could efficiently enact legislation without fear of gridlock and that voters were able to remove discredited leaders if they so wished. Prioritizing among such competing criteria is the task of the domestic actors involved in the constitutional design process.

The respective needs of transitional versus consolidated democracies are often quite different. Put simply, the most important electoral requirement for democratic *transition* is usually a system that maximizes inclusiveness, is clearly fair to all parties, and presents minimal areas for potential pre-election conflicts (such as the drawing of electoral boundaries). These goals are best achieved by some form of regional or national list PR, which ideally leads to the election of a "grand" or "over-sized" coalition government. By contrast, democratic *consolidation* is more concerned with crafting a system which is responsive to the needs of voters, is accountable in both geographic and policy terms, and which typically leads to a coalition or single-party government that the voters can "throw out" if they do not perform. Such goals are achieved by a system based, at least to some extent, upon geographically small electoral districts. Thus South Africa, which successfully conducted its transitional 1994 election using a national list PR system, may change to some form of constituency-based system after its next elections in 1999. The differences between the needs of transitional and consolidated democracies are represented below.

In divided societies, some or even all of these ideals may have to be considered secondary to the overriding need to encourage moderate, accommodative politics. There is a tension between systems that put a premium on *representation* of minority groups (list PR and ethnically defined lists) and those that try to emphasize minority *influence* (AV and STV). The best option, of course, is to have both: representation of all significant groups, but in such a way as to maximize their influence and involvement in the policy-making process. This is best achieved by building into the system devices to achieve proportionality and incentives for inter-ethnic accommodation. But these goals are not always

---

Box 9   **IDEAL QUALITIES OF ELECTORAL INSTITUTIONS FOR TRANSITIONAL AND CONSOLIDATED DEMOCRACIES**

Transitional Democracy
- inclusive;
- simple for voters to understand;
- fairness in results (proportionality);
- minimize areas of conflict;
- simple to run;
- transparent;
- "grand" or "oversized" coalition governments.

Consolidated Democracy
- accountable;
- enables voters to express more sophisticated range of choice;
- ability to "throw the rascals out";
- responsive to electorate;
- promote sense of "ownership" of political process amongst voters;
- "minimal winning" coalitions or single-party governments.

ELECTORAL SYSTEM CHOICES FOR DIVIDED SOCIETIES

Electoral systems have been recognized as one of the most important institutional mechanisms for shaping the nature of political competition. Of the nine types of systems discussed, four are particularly suitable for divided societies. These four major choices are outlined below.

Type	List Proportional Representation (PR)	Alternative Vote (AV)	Single Transferable Vote (STV)	Communal rolls, Party Block vote
Description	Proportional representation elections that lead to an inclusive legislature which includes all significant groups. Under a full consociational package, each group is represented in cabinet in proportion to their electoral support, and minority interests are protected through segmental autonomy and mutual vetoes.	Majority system with in-built incentives for inter-ethnic party appeals. To maximize electoral prospects, parties need to cultivate the second preference votes from groups other than their own. There is a centripetal spin to the system where elites are encouraged to gravitate to the moderate multi ethnic centre. In ethnically mixed districts, majority threshold leads to strong incentives to gain support from other groups.	The electoral system delivers proportional results but also encourages politicians to appeal to the votes of members from other groups via secondary preferences. This can result in inclusive power sharing between all significant political forces, but also in incentives for politicians to reach out to other groups for preference support.	System explicitly recognizes communal groups to give them (relatively fixed) institutional representation. Competition for power between ethnic groups is defused because the ratio of ethnic groups is fixed in advance. Electors must therefore make their voting choice on the basis of criteria other than ethnicity.
Examples	Switzerland, the Netherlands, South Africa 1994	Papua New Guinea 1964–1975, Fiji 1997	Estonia 1990, Northern Ireland 1998	Lebanon, Singapore, Mauritius

mutually compatible. A second level of tension exists between those systems which rely on elite accommodation (especially list PR) and those which rely on the electorate at large for moderation (AV and, to a lesser extent, STV). Where elites are likely to be more moderate than the electorate, then list PR enables the major parties to include candidates from various groups on their ticket. Where the electorate is the major engine of moderation, then AV and other systems which encourage vote-pooling will result in the election of more moderate leaders and more accommodative policies. However, when neither group are likely to display moderation, then approaches which explicitly recognize the sources of conflict – such as reserved seats or ethnically mandated lists – may need to be considered, as this provides the best way of "defusing" ethnicity as an electoral issue.

REFERENCES AND FURTHER READING

de Silva, K. M. 1994. *Ethnic Diversity and Public Policies: Electoral Systems*, Geneva: UNRISD.

Horowitz, Donald L. 1991. *A Democratic South Africa? Constitutional Engineering in a Divided Society*. Berkeley, CA: University of California Press.

Inter-Parliamentary Union. 1993. *Electoral Systems: A World-wide Comparative Study*. Geneva: Inter-Parliamentary Union.

Jenkins, Laura D. 1994. *Ethnic Accommodation Through Electoral Systems*. Geneva: UNRISD.

Lijphart, Arend, and Bernard Grofman. eds. 1984. *Choosing an Electoral System: Issues and Alternatives*. New York: Praeger.

Reilly, Ben and Andrew Reynolds. Forthcoming. *Electoral Systems and Conflict in Divided Societies*. Washington, DC: National Research Council.

Reynolds, Andrew and Ben Reilly. 1997. *The International IDEA Handbook of Electoral System Design*. Stockholm: International Institute for Democracy and Electoral Assistance.

Sartori, G. 1968. "Political Development and Political Engineering", *Public Policy*, no. 17. pp. 261-298.

Taagepera, Rein and Matthew S. Shugart. 1989. *Seats and Votes: The Effects and Determinants of Electoral Systems*. New Haven, CT: Yale University Press.

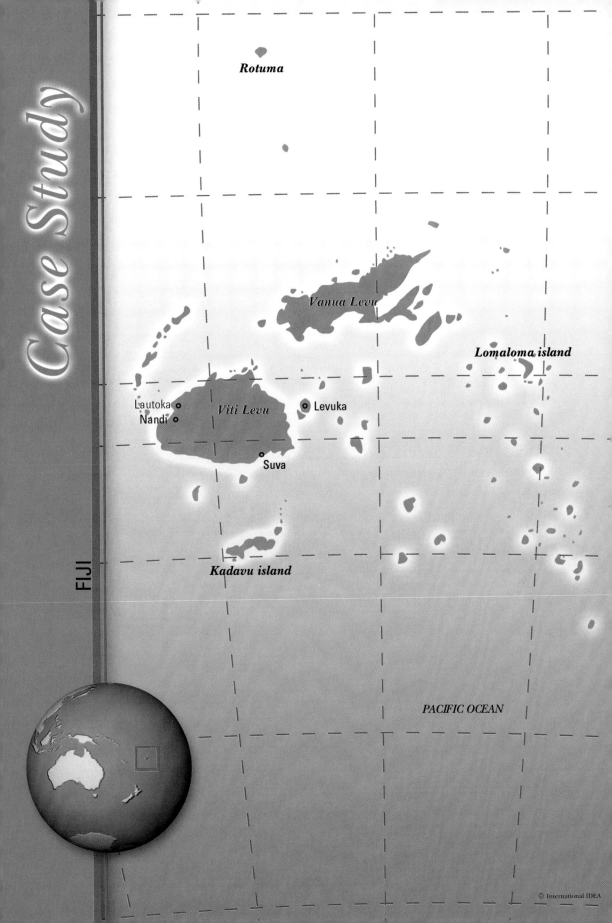

Case Study

FIJI

Rotuma

Vanua Levu

Lomaloma island

Lautoka
Nandi
Viti Levu
Levuka

Suva

Kadavu island

PACIFIC OCEAN

© International IDEA

Ben Reilly

Case   Study: Fiji

FIJI

Fiji, a South Pacific island with a population of approximately 750,000, has been the site of one of the most comprehensive recent attempts at "constitutional engineering": inducing particular political outcomes by the design and structure of political institutions. Parliaments, executives, courts etc., can be purposely designed and structured to achieve particular outcomes. Electoral systems, for example, can enable minorities to be represented in parliament, or they can ensure domination by a single ethnic majority. And different types of incentives to gain votes can induce politicians to build support across all groups, or can encourage a narrow sectarian focus on one group alone. The story of the constitution review exercise conducted as part of Fiji's return to democracy represents a good example of this process in action.

The primary source of conflict in Fiji concerns relations between Fiji's indigenous population (a mixture of the Melanesian and Polynesian groups found throughout the South Pacific islands) and the Indian Fijian community (mostly the descendants of indentured labourers who came from India to Fiji to work on sugar plantations in the 19th century under British colonialism). While other groups such as Chinese and Europeans are also present, Fiji's primary ethnic cleavage runs between "Indo-Fijian" (i.e., Indian) and indigenous (i.e., Melanesian and Polynesian) communities. The two communities maintain a high degree of separation in all spheres of public and private life. They speak different languages, practice different religions, work in different occupations, join different social groups, play different sports, and have very little day-to-day contact. Inter-marriage between the two groups, one of the best indicators of communal relations, is almost unheard of. Fiji is thus a classic plural society where, in the words of Joseph Furnivall, "different sections of the same community ... mix but do not combine".

Fijian society and politics have long been characterized by an uneasy coexistence between these two communities, with Indo-Fijians predominating in certain key areas of the economy (particularly the sugar-cane industry) and indigenous Fijians owning 90 per cent of the land but holding limited economic power. While the population ratios of the two groups are fairly similar (50 per cent indigenous Fijian, 44 per cent Indian on latest figures), there is very limited informal social or economic interaction between the two communities. Each group is also internally divided. The mostly Hindu Indian community has a sizeable (15 per cent) Muslim minority and a number of sub-identities, often based on their family roots in India. The indigenous Fijian population have retained significant and sometimes divisive elements from both original Melanesian and Polynesian social structures.

Following independence from Britain in 1970, Fiji appeared to make a relatively successful attempt at consolidating a new multi-ethnic democracy. But after the election of a government seen by the indigenous Fijian-dominated military as being overly close to the Indo-Fijian community, Fiji experienced two ethnically motivated military coups in the late 1980s. The coup leader, Major-General Sitiveni Rabuka, later justified the coups as necessary to prevent the bloodshed that would have resulted from outraged expressions of Fijian nationalism had the elected government continued in office. In 1990 a new, ethnically biased constitution enshrined a racial weighting in favour of the indigenous Fijian population, both in terms of civil rights and political representation. Through a new electoral system based completely on communal representation of ethnic groups (i.e., a separate electoral roll for Fijians, Indians and "general electors"), political competition between the groups was kept entirely distinct. These arrangements had their origin in the pre-coup electoral system, which was also based on communalism but where there was an additional proportion of "national" seats featuring open competition on a non-racial basis. Under the 1990 constitution the racial weighting under-represented the Indo-Fijian community, and reserved certain offices such as the prime ministership for indigenous Fijians. This, combined with the separate electoral roll for Fijian, Indian and other groups rendered true inter-ethnic political competition virtually impossible. Indigenous Fijians were guaranteed a majority in parliament, which thus turned into a classic in-group and out-group legislature: ethnic Fijians formed the government, while Indians and others formed the opposition.

In 1994, following economic difficulties, international condemnation (including expulsion from the Commonwealth of Nations) and high levels of emigration by the Indian community, the government established a Constitution Review Commission (CRC) to examine the constitution and recommend a more appropriate form of representation. The Commission's 1996 report, *The Fiji Islands: Towards a United Future*, recommended an entirely new non-racial constitution. It would combine strong constitutional guarantees of human rights (such as a Bill of Rights and a Human Rights Commission) with an innovative package of electoral arrangements designed to encourage the development of multi-ethnic politics in Fiji. The Commission recommended that Fiji move "gradually but decisively" away from communal representation in the direction of an open and non-racial electoral system.

The Commission thus viewed the electoral system as the most powerful tool for influencing the nature of Fijian politics. Political parties in many ethnically divided societies tend to be based around particular ethnic groups, and the Commission's stated objective was "to find ways of encouraging all, or a sufficient number, of them to come together for the purpose of governing the country in a way that gives all communities an opportunity to take part". The Commission carefully assessed and evaluated each of the major electoral systems against a set of specified criteria: the capacity to encourage multi-ethnic government; a recognition of the importance of political parties; the incentives presented for moderation and co-operation across ethnic lines; and effective representation of constituents.

Fiji

Case Study: Fiji

To maximize these requirements, the CRC recommended an Alternative Vote system. By making politicians from one group reliant on votes from the other group, the Alternative Vote could, the CRC argued, encourage a degree of "preference swapping" between the two, which could help to encourage accommodation between (and within) the deeply divided communities. Candidates who adopted moderate positions on ethnic issues and attempted to represent the "middle ground" would, under this logic, be more electorally successful than extremists, moving Fijian politics towards a more centralist, multi-racial competition for power. The CRC also argued that list Proportional Representation (list PR) would give too much power to party bosses and, because of the need for large national or regional districts, would fail to provide the necessary links between a voter and his or her member of parliament. Under PR systems, they argued, ethnic parties could expect to be represented in the legislature in proportion to their numbers in the community irrespective of whether they were inclined towards moderation or not. Hence PR, when combined with communal seats, offered "few incentives to parties to become more multi-ethnic in their composition or more willing to take account of the interests of all communities".

The ultimate success or failure of these measures in Fiji, however, is heavily dependent on the demographic distribution of ethnic groups and the way in which electoral boundaries are drawn. Rural Fiji has high territorial segregation, and the outer islands are almost entirely indigenous Fijian, so vote-pooling there will have to take place on issues other than ethnic ones, if it takes place at all. The situation on the main island and in urban centres is more mixed. The smallness of the island and the highly inter-mixed nature of many urban areas mean that electoral boundaries can be drawn so as to create districts which have reasonably mixed populations. If the makeup of these electorates are sufficiently diverse to enable genuine trading of preferences between groups, then the new system could well promote meaningful accommodation across cleavages, "the object being to force political parties to appeal for votes for their candidates from communities other than the one in which they are based". The issue of constituency boundaries and the demographic make-up of electorates are thus likely to be major points of contention as the electoral reforms are implemented.

But the 1997 constitution, as enacted, rejected some of the CRC's recommendations. Most importantly, the parliament did not make the recommended move away from communalism, and two thirds of all seats in the new 70-seat parliament will continue to be elected on a communal basis, leaving only one third of seats in which genuinely inter-ethnic competition will take place. The proportions of communal seats are set at 23 for indigenous Fijians, 19 for Indo-Fijians, one for Rotumans (a separate indigenous group from the outlying island of Rotuma) and three for "others". The remaining 25 seats will be allocated from an open electoral roll. A concern to make the system workable resulted in a choice of electoral system

Fiji

based on small single-member electoral districts, rather than the recommended larger multi-member districts. This meant that to achieve the type of "preference swapping" between different communities envisaged by the Commission, these small districts will have to be ethnically mixed – a difficult proposition. Finally, the new constitution adds mandated power sharing to the "integrative" electoral arrangements by providing that all parties who achieve at least 10 per cent of the vote must be represented in the cabinet in proportion to their vote share.

If the electoral system works as intended it should result in the election of a pool of moderate candidates dependent on the support of both political communities for their electoral survival, and thus a degree of accommodation between supporters of rival groups "on the ground" at the local level. But even if this does not occur, the mandated grand coalition cabinet provided by the constitution should ensure that both communities have to work together at the elite level at least. This double-dose of accommodation-inducing mechanisms means that there are a number of safety measures built into the new dispensation: if one should fail, backup measures are there to ensure at least a modicum of power sharing at another level.

Another aspect of the Constitution Review Commission, which may serve as a model for others, is the way in which the review process was actually conducted. The three-member Commission comprised representatives of both the Fijian and Indian communities, but was headed by a non-Fijian, former New Zealand governor-general Sir Paul Reeves, himself a highly respected representative of New Zealand's own indigenous (Maori) community. The Commission was thus structured to encourage both communities to have faith in its ability to arrive at a judicious outcome. The Commission also toured Fiji extensively, holding meetings and public hearings across the country. And they held extensive consultations internationally, holding public discussions with experts in Australia, Malaysia, Mauritius, South Africa, Great Britain and the United States. With the assistance of the UN Electoral Assistance Division, they commissioned papers from scholars on different aspects of democracy in divided societies, and met most of the major academic figures in the field. The Commission's inquiries were thus amongst the most comprehensive and well-planned of any recent exercise in constitutional engineering. The significance of process is thus a key lesson from the Fijian experience. By taking evidence as widely as possible and examining at first hand the experience of other multi-ethnic societies (e.g., Mauritius), the review process ensured that the final report could legitimately claim to be a comprehensive document.

The CRC report was widely seen as balanced and innovative. Moreover, the Commission was structured in such a way as to encourage acceptance of its outcome amongst the majority of both communities. It appealed to the middle ground. This was reflected in the response of parliament, which accepted most of the report *in toto* (bar the exceptions above) and tried to translate the recommendations into a new constitution. Opposition to the report's recommendations came from the more

Fiji

extreme elements of both communities. Nonetheless, the leadership and members of the major parties from both communities supported the new constitution. In late 1997, following the passage of the new constitution, the major parties formed a power-sharing government of national unity, with the leader of the 1987 coup, Sitiveni Rabuka, as Prime Minister and erstwhile leader of the Opposition, Jai Ram Reddy, invited to become Deputy Prime Minister. This itself represented a major breakthrough, which was as much a reaction to the co-operative spirit engendered by the constitution-making exercise, as it was to the provisions of the document itself.

REFERENCES AND FURTHER READING

Constitution (Amendment) Act 1997 of the Republic of the Fiji Islands, 25 July 1997.

Constitution Review Commission. 1996. *The Fiji Islands: Towards a United Future.* Parliamentary paper No. 34 of 1996. Parliament of Fiji, Suva.

Furnivall, J. S. 1948. *Colonial Policy and Practice: A Comparative Study of Burma and Netherlands India*, Cambridge: Cambridge University Press.

Lawson, Stephanie. 1991. *The Failure of Democratic Politics in Fiji.* Oxford: Clarendon Press.

Reilly, Ben. 1997. "Constitutional Engineering and the Alternative Vote in Fiji: An Assessment". In Brij V. Lal and Peter Larmour. eds. *Electoral Systems in Divided Societies: the Fiji Constitution Review.* Canberra: National Centre for Development Studies.

Fiji

4.5 Legislatures for Post-Conflict Societies

In a democratic political system, the legislature is the authoritative institution for the expression and resolution of policy conflict. Its authority is derived from its representative function in the state and its constitutional status as the supreme law-enacting body, and expressed not only through its constitutional status, but also via its composition and internal procedures and organization. In this section, we consider those features of legislatures that affect post-conflict societies.

4.5.1 *Introduction*

4.5.2 *Elections and members*

4.5.3 *Internal features: committees, floor, procedures, leadership, staff and facilities*

4.5.4 *Sources of power*

4.5.5 *One or two chambers?*

4.5.6 *Conclusion*

4.5.1 Introduction

In addition to its lawmaking function, the legislature acts as the main representative body of the state, reflecting society's divergent opinions at the political level. Legislatures are thus capable of expressing and resolving a wide variety of conflicts within society. The structure and procedural rules of a legislature, as well as the electoral basis of its membership, reward the ability to both express and resolve conflict. Legislatures create the conditions for the emergence of co-operative antagonists. Though they disagree on public policy, they must agree on structure and rules to provide the basis for the expression of their conflicts. Those same rules and structures make it possible to find compromise solutions to their problems, and thus develop the necessary skills to find solutions to other, more weighty, conflicts.

The means by which conflicts are expressed within a legislature are also the means by which conflicts are resolved. Most leg-

4.5 Legislatures for Post-Conflict Societies

islatures are comprised of members of political parties representing particular electoral districts or geographic areas; yet few areas or electoral districts are homogeneous on all types of issues, and neither are political parties. Each forces a degree of compromise among its supporters on a wide range of issues. Each also becomes the means by which compromises are forged on those issues which divide them. The search for agreement and compromise is thus a defining feature of legislatures, both in terms of their composition and in their internal structure and procedures.

The terms "legislature" and "parliament" may be used interchangeably. About half of the world's parliaments are *unicameral* (having just one chamber); about half are *bicameral* (having two chambers), though usually one is more active and important than the other. Bicameral systems have a main chamber (House of Commons, House of Representatives, Chamber of Deputies, etc.,) and a secondary chamber (the "upper" chamber, Senate, and so on). In almost all cases the "lower" chamber is more important than the "upper" one.

The term "parliament" originated in Britain, where a "parliamentary system of government" means that the chief executive (prime minister) is selected and removed by parliament. Bodies that follow the British practice are sometimes termed "Westminster" model parliaments. The European continental parliaments, though selecting chief executives in the same manner, have developed distinctive internal practices and structures. The US Congress, both in its separateness from the president and in its internal characteristics, is a distinct type by itself. Many new nations, and newly democratized ones, incorporate selected features from these existing models into their new constitutions and legislatures.

In newly independent and in older authoritarian countries, one of the pervasive conflicts is often between the executive and the legislature. The executive, often drawn from powerful families or with military support, can dominate the political system, leaving political parties fragile and legislatures ineffective.

As countries become less authoritarian, or as new democratic systems are instituted, the legislatures have become more free to act, but are often handicapped by inadequate human and material resources as well as by the practices of the past. This "opportunities-resources gap" has been noted in many post-communist democracies, as well as in such Asian countries as the Philippi-

The search for agreement and compromise is a defining feature of legislatures, both in terms of their composition and in their internal structure and procedures.

nes and South Korea, and in African nations including Ghana and now South Africa.

4.5.2 Elections and members

Democratic legislatures are directly selected through competitive elections held at intervals, usually not exceeding five years.

The most direct means of expression of social conflict in legislatures is through the elected membership. In most cases, the members tend to reflect population attributes of ethnicity, religion, social status and economic function. In traditional societies, members of legislatures often come from elite families with large land holdings. New types of members, as societies change, tend to be educated persons from urban industrial and commercial occupations.

One measure of the social success of minority groups is their ability to run for and be elected to legislative membership. It took many years in Europe for deputies from religious minorities to be admitted to parliaments, for example. In contemporary society, the number of women members in parliament is often viewed as a similar indicator of inclusiveness.

In some societies, there can be some difficulty in finding parliamentary members with sufficient educational and professional skills to be capable legislators. This problem is doubly critical for representatives of minority population groups or groups newly incorporated in to the political system. In post-communist democracies, and in countries in transition in Africa, there has been a shortage of skilled and experienced members for their newly energized parliaments.

Members of parliament have many options in their attitudes toward their representational responsibilities. While some may consider themselves as direct spokespeople for an issue or a population group, others may consider the whole district, or the whole nation, as more their proper responsibility as elected representatives. As political parties nominate candidates or as individuals propose themselves for parliamentary elections, one immediate question concerns the socio-economic attributes of the candidates. Does each candidate match an essential element of the electorate as measured by ethnicity, religion, gender, occupation, place of residence, and also age?

4.5.3 Internal features

The procedures through which debate is conducted and legislation passed are essential elements of the legislative process.

4.5 Legislatures for Post-Conflict Societies

The most formal location of decisions is in plenary session, "on the floor". Legislative committees, however, are also an important forum within which policy conflict is both expressed and managed.

Committees

The mechanism of committees is a major method by which legislatures consider issues. The number of committees usually ranges from 10 to 25 in any one legislature.

Proposed legislation is considered in committee before final voting on the floor. Typically, many topics considered by committees are ultimately resolved through compromises among many, if not all, parties. Any original proposal, even if offered by the government, is subject to amendment within the committees.

Generally, committees are formed to address specific topical subjects, and to parallel the structure of the government's ministries. In Westminster systems, however, many committees are formed temporarily for the consideration of a single bill, although in recent decades permanent committees have become a more established feature of such parliaments (e.g., Australia). South Africa has similarly modified its Westminster model to now include 27 "portfolio" committees to parallel the ministries. Committees have also been revised and strengthened recently in South Korea and Mongolia. In the latter parliament, the number of committees was increased, and public hearings have been held.

Committees not only consider proposed legislation, they also can review the budget and examine the conduct of ministers. These opportunities for review of policy-related action, in addition to law enactment, permit members to raise issues that concern specific constituencies, issue orientations, and population subgroups. The small size of a committee and the absence of news reporting permit members to reach compromises across party lines more often than is expressed in floor debate. The structure and composition of committees is therefore crucial to parties and to governments, for committees can become one of the main organizational locations in which government and opposition parties negotiate compromises.

Committees are additional means of representation beyond the party system. Topical committees can attract members whose constituencies are particularly affected by the committee's subject matter. For example, deputies from rural districts tend to become members of the legislature's committee on agriculture. Deputies may also express their training and personal interests through committee membership; for example, foreign policy committees tend to attract members who have a personal aptitude for international affairs, while committees on education and on justice tend to attract members with a background in teaching or the law, respectively. Not all members, however, are familiar with or even interested in the topics of their committees. In such cases, attendance may become a problem; in both Poland and South Korea, for example, committee absenteeism has been noted. A related problem is that parties can change their members on a committee, depending upon the specific topic at the moment.

The majority party or government coalition may be reluctant to share power in the committees with other and smaller parties. In most parliaments, committee chairs are distributed among all parties. In others, committee leadership is controlled exclusively by the majority, as for example in Romania, where the government parties hold the bulk of memberships of important committees.

Many different types of working groups can be developed within and across the formal and main committees. Some legislatures, such as Poland, form an ad hoc working group for each separate bill, which may include members from several different committees. Special problems are sometimes examined through the formation of a special purpose committee, the temporary character of which might extend from one week to several years.

Floor

When the whole legislature is assembled in plenary session, "on the floor", it is in its most authoritative but also most partisan form. The legislature makes decisions as a whole body through various forms of voting.

The arrangement of seats on the floor is usually in one of two patterns. In the Westminster model, two banks of seats face each other, typifying the adversarial arrangement of government and opposition. In the European continental model, the chamber is arranged as a semi-circle, symbolizing gradations of difference among many parties.

Although the dramatic moments of legislative conflict usually occur on the floor, and although the mass media usually concentrate on conflictual floor debate and votes, members will of-

4.5 Legislatures for Post-Conflict Societies

ten spend more time, and make more substantive progress, in committees.

Procedures

Rules define both the structure of committees and the procedures by which legislation is proposed and decided. The definition of committee jurisdiction, the right to offer amendments, and the sequence of floor debate, are all decided through rules of procedure.

Rules are very important: they prescribe and define the relationship between a majority and a minority. Rules permit the majority to act within defined procedures and thus within defined limits. Rules permit the minority to attempt to thwart or change action, but also within defined procedures and limits.

Rules typically are stated in general and inclusive terms, so that all types of motions and all types of controversies can be handled in similar ways. The great advantage of stable rules of procedure is that all members can know and work within the same framework of action. Rule stability brings predictability to proceedings, permitting members to negotiate across the issues and identities that divide them.

Many legislatures have experimented with rules to encourage the formation of consensus prior to the adoption of crucial legislation. Legislation to change the constitution, for example, frequently requires either extra-large majorities, or lengthened procedures, or both, prior to final adoption. These special procedures attempt to develop a broad consensus before final decisions are accepted.

Both structure and rules evolve over time. Within a competitive political party system, the likelihood increases that the party(ies) currently in the majority will become the minority in the next election, and vice versa. As each party experiences the circumstances of both government and opposition – majority and minority status – over a series of elections, they can learn through experience the value of stable and fair rules, and of efficient working structures within legislatures.

Leadership

A single presiding officer (the "Speaker", "President", "Talman", "Marshall", etc.) typically heads a legislature and oversees the rules and procedures. One or more central governing bodies will assist the presiding officer in creating the committee structure, in assigning bills to committees, in setting the legislative schedule, and in resolving disputes over both schedules and procedures. The composition of the legislature's officials and governing bodies has implications for representation. They are usually composed of party leaders. In addition, population groups and issue orientations within society would also seek to have sympathetic members on these governing committees. They can do so, however, only through political parties within the legislature.

Staff and Facilities

A parliament requires full time professional support staff to function with both efficiency and expertise. A staff is required for the clerical functions of recording debates and votes on the floor. Committees and parties require staff to arrange their working papers.

In addition to the clerical functions, a professional staff is required by active legislatures that seek to know enough about policy problems and government actions to make effective decisions. Such staff can be allocated to individual members, to committees, to parties, or can be organized and managed centrally. For example, the US Congress mainly allocates staff to individual members and to committees, while the Westminster model has developed a centrally managed staff, and the continental European parliaments also provide staff to their parliamentary parties.

The development of a trained and politically neutral staff depends upon, among other things, the willingness of dominant political parties and even executives to retain the same legislative staff each time power shifts among the parties or executive coalitions. In Nicaragua, for example, the shift in power in 1993 led to the dismissal of and also job changes for many of the legislative staff members. Staff remaining from prior authoritarian political regimes presents a related problem.

Though parliamentary chambers are often constructed for ornate display and ceremonial functions, the whole legislative building is a work site. The chamber itself requires adequate seating, lighting, ventilation, sound systems, and secretarial facilities. Each committee needs its own meeting room, and adjacent office space for its specialized clerical and professional staff. Eating facilities and informal space are essential for members who may meet long into the night following a full working day. Because members often travel long distances from home to parliament, some parliaments provide hotels. Most parliaments also have a library which itself can become a large complex set of

4.5 Legislatures for Post-Conflict Societies

rooms and facilities. Office buildings are needed, and must be located within easy walking distance of the main chamber.

As publicly visible institutions, legislatures are sometimes criticized for their cost. Whether or not a building is itself ornate, however, the more important consideration is that an efficient workplace is costly, and a competent policy analysis staff is also expensive. One essential element in the development of an active legislature is the provision of in-service training for people – both as members and as staff. Beyond financial cost, however, lies a broader issue. Post-dictatorship legislatures sometimes retain the secretive practices of the past, so that information about the legislature is made available to neither the public nor to the legislative members themselves. If some countries have "high information" parliaments, such as Britain, Sweden and Lithuania, others have "low information" parliaments, of which Moldova is but one example.

4.5.4 Sources of power: executives and political parties

Executives

Legislative autonomy varies with the parliament's relationship to the chief executive. Directly elected presidents can be a source of external constraint upon parliaments in a presidential system. In theory, a parliamentary system permits direct parliamentary selection and removal of the chief executive (prime minister, premier). In practice, however, disciplined political parties in many countries have curtailed this doctrine of "parliamentary supremacy". A majority party as in Britain, or majority coalition as in Germany, can expect parliament to adopt government legislation and to not raise embarrassing topics for investigation and complaint. The "rule of 80" applies in many parliaments: 80 per cent of all bills are from the government, and 80 per cent of government bills are adopted. Nonetheless, increasing fragmentation of the party system, in countries like India, Papua New Guinea and other well established democracies in the developing world, has seen parliaments re-assert their authority in recent years.

Typically, executives define the agenda of legislatures. More opposition to executive proposals may be expressed and acted upon in committee than on the floor. Cross-party alliances more easily develop in committee, while partisan views, both for and against the government, tend to be directly expressed on the floor.

The actual relationship between executive and legislature varies greatly. In authoritarian systems, executives dominate the legislature. In many others, the dominant party in the legislature is the agent of the executive. At the other extreme, illustrated by Scandinavian countries, the government is often a minority within its own parliament, and yet it governs effectively through issue-oriented temporary majorities and the striking of strategic alliances.

In between the British model of government ministers remaining as parliamentary members, and the American model of separation of powers, the European continental parliaments require ministers to resign their parliamentary seats, but also provide that they may attend and participate in parliamentary debates. Special seating arrangements both provide for and symbolize their distinctive office apart from, but intimate connection to, the parliament.

Political parties

Political parties are vital to legislatures in at least three respects: 1) organization and conduct of elections; 2) connection of executive to the legislature; and 3) internal management of the legislature. Through all three activities, parties and their leaders occupy a dual role: on the one hand, they define and express conflicts, while on the other, they seek ways to build majority consent to resolve those conflicts.

The leadership offices and committees of a legislature are filled through party negotiation. It is the parties and their leaders who decide the allocation of committee seats, and each party selects its own members to fill those seats. Parliamentary party leaders tend to treat each other as formal equals, with the result that small parties can participate in the collective structure and practices of decisions affecting the legislature as a whole body. The smaller the party, however, the less strength it possesses in a body in which the vote is the instrument by which decisions are made and power is allocated. Small parties may also suffer a shortage of members who have the time and expertise to sit on all committees and to monitor all proposed legislation.

4.5.5 One or two chambers?

Party dominance of legislatures often leads a country to create a second chamber with the intention of providing supplementary perspectives on public policy. Some are ineffective, e.g., the Canadian Senate, while others are very powerful, such as the

4.5 Legislatures for Post-Conflict Societies

Australian, American and Romanian upper chambers. Some are limited to a temporary veto function (e.g., the British House of Lords and the Polish Senate) where the upper chamber's rejection of a bill can be reversed by a second vote in the lower chamber. A few upper chambers are functional in composition, such as the Slovenian second chamber based on occupations, while some provide for special population subgroup membership – such as traditional chiefs in Fiji. Although federations all have a separate chamber of parliament formed by state or provincial electorates, their actual importance varies greatly, as illustrated by the varying powers of the Canadian and Australian Senates.

Because the lower chamber is directly elected, it is almost always the more active and politically powerful body in comparison to the other or second chamber. When joined with federalism, a second chamber presents regional majorities with the opportunity for direct representation in a country-wide parliament, even though they are themselves part of a national minority. Nigeria, as a federation during its Second Republic, is an example. So appropriate design of second chambers, like the choice of electoral system, can diversify opportunities for representation and sharing of power. Yet the results are not always predictable. In post-communist democracies such as Poland, for example, the Senate has a very different district and electoral system than the more active chamber, and yet the result in party shares of seats is about the same. In Romania, with similar district and election systems, the party results are similar, and yet the make-up of the two chambers is very different.

Two separate legislative chambers can create difficulties in basic organizational and procedural matters, as illustrated by both Chile and Argentina as new post-military democracies. The two chambers, when controlled by different party majorities, also hold very different views about the organization and functions of their separate professional staff offices. Resulting delays and mutual recriminations may lessen the sense of legitimacy of the whole institution.

Most of the extra features obtained through a second chamber can also be structured into a single chamber through the electoral and district system. In the single chamber of Hungary, for example, members are elected from three different sets of overlapping constituencies. The German Bundestag, likewise, has two sets of members elected from very different types of districts and using two different election systems. The main consideration in designing two separate chambers is that the two sets of districts and election systems be calibrated to compliment one another. Nevertheless, neither the party nor policy consequences are clearly predictable in advance of application and experimentation in practice.

4.5.6 Conclusion

Legislatures as instruments of representation and conflict resolution present two major dilemmas, each of which is a combination of opportunity and challenge. First, a legislature's structure as a bicameral or unicameral institution features a dynamic tension between the electoral system for, and the powers of, the chamber(s). Second, legislatures face the daunting task of defining neutral rules of procedure and decision-making, and then of applying those rules evenly among all parties over a series of elections and terms during which the composition of majorities and minorities often change.

No one design for a legislature will work under all circumstances. In a democracy, the legislature, the executive, and the party system act as interdependent parts of the larger political system. The actions and characteristics of the others condition what each can do. The essential condition is that each element fit in some working relationship with the others.

There are examples of countries falling apart, such as Czechoslovakia, or turning to military rule, such as Nigeria, when the legislatures are unable to fulfil their tasks or are overwhelmed by outside events. In some instances, the lack of a stable majority in parliament has directly led to either military government or the institution of a strong executive, of which the current French Fifth Republic is an example. There are also many examples of legislatures that have instituted major reforms in their societies and also in themselves. The formerly aristocratic parliaments of Europe gradually introduced democracy. The formerly all-male legislatures of Europe and the United States adopted female suffrage. Parliaments elected under conditions of religious or ethnic exclusion gradually introduced religious toleration and abolished racial segregation. These reforms, unlike many of the failures noted above, have occurred slowly. The most dramatic examples of major shifts of political power in the 1990s include the former communist states, South Africa, and Mexico. In each case, bargaining replaced domination as the relationship among parties and between government and parliament, while the legislature itself was revitalized and reorganized.

The greatest restraint upon the propensity for a majority to exercise its power arbitrarily is the prospect of becoming a minority in the next election. The greatest restraint upon the propensity of the minority to unilaterally obstruct legislative action is the hope of becoming the majority in the next election. Some prospect of alternation in power is thus a basic precondition for the evolution and institutionalization of a functioning legislature.

REFERENCES AND FURTHER READING

Agh, Attila. 1995. "The Experience of the First Democratic Parliaments in East Central Europe", *Communist and Post-Communist Studies*, vol. 28, no. 2. pp. 203–214.

Bradshaw, Kenneth and David Pring. 1981. *Parliament and Congress*. 2nd ed. London: Quartet Books.

Copeland, Gary W. and Samuel C. Patterson. eds. 1994. *Parliaments in the Modern World*. Ann Arbor, MI: University of Michigan.

Doering, Herbert. 1995. "Time as a Scarce Resource: Government Control of the Agenda". In Herbert Doering. ed. *Parliaments and Majority Rule in Western Europe*. New York, NY: St. Martins Press.

Lees, John D. and Malcolm Shaw. eds. 1979. *Committees in Legislatures: A Comparative Analysis*. Durham, NC: Duke University Press.

Liebert, Ulrike and Maurizio Cotta. eds. 1990. *Parliament and Democratic Consolidation in Southern Europe*. London: Pinter.

Mezey, Michael L. 1979. *Comparative Legislatures*. Durham, NC: Duke University Press.

Olson, David M. 1994. *Democratic Legislative Institutions*. Armonk, NY: M.E. Sharpe.

Olson, David M. 1997. "Paradoxes of Institutional Development: The New Democratic Parliaments of Central Europe", *International Political Science Review*, vol. 18, no. 4. pp. 407–416.

Olson, David M. and Philip Norton. eds. 1996. *The New Parliaments of Central and Eastern Europe*. London: Frank Cass.

Olson, David M. 1995. "Parliament by Design", *East European Constitutional Review*, vol. 4, no. 2. pp. 56–90.

Tsebelis, George and Jeannette Money. 1997. *Bicameralism.* Cambridge: Cambridge University Press.

World Encyclopedia of Parliaments and Legislatures. 1997. Washington, DC: Congressional Quarterly.

Case Study

SRI LANKA

INDIA

Tamil Nadu
Pudukkottai
Nagappattinam

Karaikkudi

Palk Strait

Point Pedro
Jaffna

Rammad
Palk Bay

Gulf of
Mannar

Mannar
Mankulam

Northern

Mullaittivu

Trincomalee

Anurodhapura

North Central

Puttalam
Galoya

Maho

North Western
Batticaloa

Kurunegala
Eastern

Matale
Kalmunai

Negombo
Kandy

Central

Colombo
Badulla

Moratuwa
Pottuvil

Opanake

Southern

Hambantota

Galle
Matara

INDIAN OCEAN

© International IDEA

K. M. de Silva

Case Study: Sri Lanka

SRI LANKA

Sri Lanka was often referred to as a "model" colony in the early years after independence from Britain (1948 to the mid-1950s), since the national political leadership opted for a negotiated transfer of power, in contrast to the agitation in India. Indeed, the leadership deliberately chose to follow the constitutional evolution of the "settlement" colonies of Canada, Australia and New Zealand into independent statehood.

A decade of peaceful consolidation of power by the United National Party (UNP) governments of 1947 to 1956 was followed by several decades of conflict. Sri Lanka's descent to political instability came in three stages, beginning with the period mid-1955 to 1961 when two sets of communal riots broke out against the background of a unilateral change in language policy. After a period of quiescence in the mid- and late 1960s there was a second phase of confrontation and violence, culminating in the riots of 1977. Six years of relative quiet followed until the outbreak of anti-Tamil riots in 1983. Thereafter, ethnic violence has been a regular feature.

The conflicts in Sri Lanka illustrate the operation of some of the most combustible factors in ethnic relations: language, religion, long historical memories of tensions and conflict, and a prolonged separatist agitation. Sri Lanka's recent political experience also provides a case study in the internationalization of ethnic conflict. Internationalization of Sri Lanka's ethnic conflict has two aspects: Indian intervention, and the growth of a Tamil *diaspora* community – the direct consequence of the current ethnic conflict. In addition, the Sri Lankan experience illustrates the important point that minorities seeking redress of grievances, and guarantees of protection of their identities, are not always agents of democratic change or liberalism.

The current conflict is much more complex than a straightforward confrontation between a once well-entrenched minority – the Sri Lanka Tamils – and a now powerful but still insecure majority – the Sinhalese. These two groups constitute the principal, but not the only, players. They have two conflicting perceptions. Most Sinhalese believe that the Tamil minority has enjoyed a privileged position and that the balance must shift in favour of the Sinhalese majority. The Tamils for their part claim that they are now a harassed minority, victims of frequent acts of communal violence and calculated acts and policies of discrimination. Most Tamil fears and insecurity stem from the belief that they have lost the advantageous position they enjoyed under British rule in many sectors of public life in the country; in brief, a classic case of a sense of relative deprivation.

Major Issues and Efforts at Management

Despite the tensions and violence that have been a feature of life in post-independence Sri Lanka, there also has been an irrepressible strand of pragmatism,

Sri Lanka

227

which eventually helped in moderating the outcome of many of the contentious issues. For instance, religious strife between Buddhists and Christians (especially Roman Catholics), one of the most divisive factors in Sri Lankan public life for 80 years, has ceased to be a contentious issue in politics since the early 1970s. Indeed, religious tensions are only of very limited significance in the current conflict.

Another example is the settlement reached on the status of immigrant Indian Tamils. The problem of the political status and voting rights of immigrant Indian communities overseas came to the fore, first in Sri Lanka, and as early as 1928–1931. Accommodation reached between 1964 and 1974 – on the number of Indians to whom Sri Lankan citizenship would be granted – and further elaboration of this policy between 1977 and 1988, constituted a major political accomplishment considering the passions and fears that this question had aroused since the late 1920s.

The accommodation reached after the violence associated with the introduction of language policy reform in 1956 is even more significant. Initiatives between 1958 and 1978 all but conceded parity of status to the Tamil language with Sinhala. Explicit parity of status of the two languages came in 1987–1988 as part of a political settlement brokered by the Indian Government. The political benefits, however, have proved elusive.

Employment

The bitterness underlying the controversies on employment is explained in part by the conflict between Tamils' traditional anxiety to maintain the employment levels in the state services they had grown accustomed to under British rule, and the attempts of Sinhalese to insist on what they regard as their legitimate share. The economic resources of the Northern Province, the principal area of Tamil settlement in the island, are severely limited. In the late 19th century it was evident that the increasing population of the region could not be accommodated in the traditional land-based occupations. The Tamils turned to the state's bureaucracy and the professions for employment. By the early 1900s, Tamils had become singularly dependent on government service; precisely because they had no deep roots in the island's plantation economy or trade, they sought to defend their dominant position in the public service all the more zealously – a reflection of the limited opportunities for employment available to them on the Jaffna peninsula. This made them exceptionally vulnerable and sensitive to changes in language policy, to educational reform before independence, and to changes in the mechanisms for admission to tertiary education in the 1970s.

After independence, competition for posts in the public service increased, especially with the rapid expansion of educational opportunities in Sinhalese areas. This greatly reduced traditional Tamil prospects of government employment. Over the next 25 years the Sinhalese would overtake them in almost every sector of state employment and in the professions. For a while they retained their advantageous

Sri Lanka

Case Study: Sri Lanka

position in some professions – medicine, law and engineering – but lost this by the early 1980s. This represented the intellectual capital of the past – carefully gathered, protected and augmented – but, in their eyes, not expanding rapidly enough to overcome what they saw as the disadvantages of the new policy changes; policies which would adversely affect the next generation of Tamils. Today the number of Tamils in *all* grades of state employment has declined to 10 per cent or less, a third or fourth of what it was in the early 1940s.

Education

Changes in university admissions policy have contributed substantially to the sharp deterioration of ethnic relations in Sri Lanka in the last two decades, and to radicalizing the politics of Tamil areas in the north and east. The crux of the problem was that the Tamils, who constitute about an eighth of the total population, had for years a dominant position in the science-based university faculties. In 1970, the United Front coalition introduced a system of standardization of marks by language for the university entrance examination. This placed Tamil students at a disadvantage in that they had to obtain higher aggregate marks to enter the university, in the medical, science and engineering faculties, than the Sinhalese. Thereafter, a district quota system was also introduced which gave an advantage to students in rural areas and underdeveloped communities. All this represented a departure from the traditional practice of selecting students on the basis of an open competitive examination. The Tamils saw this policy as deliberately discriminatory.

In the late 1970s and early 1980s the newly elected UNP Government changed this policy, and moved towards a more equitable admissions system, as well as affirmative action policies for rural areas (for Sinhalese, Tamil and Muslim alike). Nevertheless, memories of the unilateral and discriminatory change in university policy of the early 1970s remain fresh in the minds of Tamils, despite the substantial expansion of university places in medicine and engineering since 1979 for students from all sections of the population. The Tamils' share of places in the engineering and medical faculties has varied from 35 per cent to 25 per cent since 1978–1979, to around 15 per cent in more recent years.

This system has now developed powerful vested interests, which resist all attempts to return to a merit-based system. The most vocal supporters of the system are the Muslims and the Indian Tamils, with the Tamils of the Eastern Province and from parts of the Northern Province (outside the Jaffna peninsula) being joined by Sinhalese from more rural parts of the country. The most recent (1994–1995) development is that Tamils from the Jaffna peninsula, hitherto the most vocal critics of the system, joined in asking for the status of a disadvantaged district for Jaffna itself. They succeeded in securing this advantage.

Land distribution

Next, there is the accommodation reached on one of the Tamil's long-standing grievances, the distribution of state-owned land among landless peasants. Tamil

Sri Lanka

politicians have generally claimed that the Sri Lankan state has used state-owned land as a means of changing the demographic pattern in what they call the "Traditional Homelands of the Tamils", primarily state-owned land in the Eastern Province. A formula for the distribution of state land was devised in 1984, after long negotiation between representatives of the Sri Lankan government and Tamil politicians led by the Tamil United Liberation Front (TULF): state-owned land on major irrigation schemes would be distributed on a quota system which reflected accurately the population profile of the island, with the Sinhalese getting 74 per cent and the Tamils, Muslims and Indians 12 per cent, six to seven per cent and five per cent respectively. The Tamils were permitted to use their island-wide quota in any area they chose, and naturally it was assumed that they would concentrate their quota in the Eastern and Northern Provinces. On minor irrigation schemes, the distribution of state land would reflect the demographic pattern of the district or province in which the scheme was based.

The wide support this formula received from almost all parties to the dispute, including the TULF, reflected a recognition, implicit more than explicit, that inevitably the Sinhalese, more than others, would benefit because they are the largest number of landless peasants.

The Politics of Devolution

Finally, we turn to the most intractable problem of all – devolution. Differences of opinion over devolution have proved to be more difficult to resolve than any other issue; this, despite the great deal that has been achieved between 1980 and 1987 in establishing a second tier of government (a major political achievement given the failure of previous attempts in 1957–1958 and 1965–1968). Politicians are caught between the Sinhalese electorate's deep-rooted suspicions about the political consequences of devolving more power to the provinces, and the Tamils' insistence on transferring greater power to the provinces or regions at the expense of the central government. Tamil demands range from the creation of a large Tamil-dominated North-Eastern Province, to the establishment of a federal political structure with a weak centre and more powerful provinces or regions. This is quite apart from the Liberation Tigers of Tamil Eelam's (LTTE) insistence on a separate state as a non-negotiable demand.

Devolution has proved to be an insuperable obstacle to practical political management because it touches on some of the most durable fears, suspicions and prejudices that divide the country. The resistance to transferring greater power to the provinces in Sri Lanka springs from such fears. The proximity of the Jaffna region in northern Sri Lanka to Tamil Nadu in southern India, formerly a reservoir of Tamil separatist sentiment in India (and a region that has encouraged, nurtured and protected Tamil separatist groups from Sri Lanka) presents one major concern. Devolution of power to provincial councils is suspect, even when it has been intro-

Sri Lanka

Case Study: Sri Lanka

duced, because of fears that it could spur separatist pressures in the north and east of the island. Large sections of the Sinhalese view the Tamils' pressure for devolution of power as the first step in an inevitable progression to separation of the Tamil majority areas of the country from the Sri Lankan polity. Historical memories contribute greatly to the disquiet and apprehensions the Sinhalese feel about South India, especially the perception of South India as the single most powerful and persistent threat confronting Sri Lanka and the Sinhalese.

Those in the forefront of the Tamils' agitation for devolution of power have always been vague, deliberately or unconsciously, in the terminology used in their arguments. The close links that were established in more recent times between Tamil political groups ranging from the TULF to various separatist groups, with the government and opposition in the southern Indian state of Tamil Nadu, have naturally aggravated the situation; the establishment of training camps in Tamil Nadu for separatist activists making forays into the northern and eastern coastal regions of Sri Lanka has further exacerbated this. The result is that decentralization which was, and should be, a purely Sri Lankan matter has taken on a cross-national dimension; India's role as mediator in the political negotiations between the Sri Lanka Government and representatives of Tamil opinion in the 1980s is the most conspicuous feature of this dynamic.

Pressure for decentralization of administration is limited to the Tamils, and largely to the Tamils living in the north and east of the island, where they are either a majority or form a substantial minority. There is no pressure from other ethnic groups; indeed, there is strong opposition to it. The demographic profile of the Eastern Province, where the Tamils are a minority (40 per cent of the population) remains a critical stumbling block in the long drawn out negotiations on the creation of a province or region amalgamating the Northern Province with parts or the whole of the Eastern Province. The LTTE will accept nothing short of a separate Tamil state. The deadlock over this issue continues to the present day. A section of Muslims, led by the Sri Lanka Muslim Congress, has reacted to this by urging the creation of a separate administrative unit in the Eastern Province in which the Muslims would constitute a majority. A more elaborate version of this demand calls for a Muslim province with its main base in the Eastern Province, but with enclaves or sub-units elsewhere such as in the Mannar district of the Northern Province.

One of the unfortunate consequences of concentrating attention on district and provincial units, and on supra-provincial units, has been the neglect of one of the less controversial and more viable forms of decentralization – local government institutions at the municipal and urban council levels and village council levels. The three principal municipalities, Colombo, Kandy and Galle, were established in 1865–1866, while the origins of smaller urban and town councils and village councils date back to the early 20th century. The last comprehensive examination of local

Sri Lanka

government institutions and its problems took place as early as 1954–1955. Thereafter, largely because of the agitation of Tamil parties for the creation of district and provincial councils, the focus has been almost exclusively on the second tier of government.

The decision of the 1980 Presidential Commission on development councils to abolish village councils and transfer their functions to local level units of the District Development Councils and to informal (i.e., theoretically non-political) village organizations, did not yield any of the anticipated benefits. That decision was based on a mixture of political considerations and a misplaced idealism. The TULF, who argued in favour, hoped to strengthen the district councils, and to bring all other local government institutions under the supervision of district councils. Others argued that the administrative costs of running these village councils had increased to the point where little money was left for development programmes. In addition there was the belief that informal but popular village bodies could cut across party alignments and bring people of the village together for common development projects; in other words, that they would serve as means of de-politicizing the village between national and district council elections. It soon became clear that the mechanisms and informal institutions substituted for village councils did not provide either the administrative efficiency or the anticipated responsiveness to local needs. Village councils were re-established in 1988–1989 and the first elections were held in 1991. Nevertheless there has been no systematic attempt to examine the financial viability of village and urban councils, or the power, functions and resources of municipalities. While Sri Lanka has avoided the worst features of South Asian urbanization so far, its continued ability to do so will depend very much on the effective functioning of its local government institutions, especially its municipalities.

The External Factor

India has had three roles in Sri Lanka's ethnic conflict. The first, which was intensified with Indira Gandhi's return to power in 1980, was that of a covert supporter of Sri Lankan Tamil political activists operating in India. This covert support continued until 1987. Second, the Tamil Nadu factor forms an important facet of India's complex role in Sri Lankan affairs. Seldom has a constituent unit (a province or a state) of one country influenced the relationship between it and a neighbouring country with such intensity. The India-Tamil Nadu-Sri Lanka relationship is thus unique in international affairs. Admittedly India's own role is more complex than merely reacting to the pressures of domestic policies in Tamil Nadu. Nevertheless, concerns about the latter have been an important consideration. Tamil Nadu governments have provided Sri Lankan Tamil separatist activists with sanctuaries, training and bases. The Indian central Government was involved in this, and also tolerated the provision of training facilities and the existence of camps and bases in other parts of the country. These actions started with Indira Gandhi in the early 1980s, well before the riots of July 1983 in Sri Lanka.

Sri Lanka

Case Study: Sri Lanka

India's third role – that of mediator – began under Mrs Gandhi as a calculated political response to the anti-Tamil riots of July 1983 in Sri Lanka; the policy was continued under Rajiv Gandhi. India's policy shifted from mediator to active participant in late 1987 and continued until the mid-1990s. That too is almost unique in the history of mediation in ethnic conflict: never before, or very rarely indeed, has a mediator taken on the role of combatant, and waged a war against sections of a minority, for which it was a presumed guardian, and in a neighbouring state at that.

Indian intervention began with giving aid to one or other of the Tamil separatist groups. This assistance was given, in part, to sustain the struggle to the point of compelling or persuading the Sri Lanka Government to alter its strategy, and to negotiate a settlement under Indian auspices. Second, in 1987 the Indian Government sought to resolve the conflict itself, by acting as a mediator, applying sanctions to one, some or all parties to the conflict, and underwriting a settlement. In the process the Indians became a common enemy to all or some of the warring factions. The Indian intervention reveals how the consequences of the internationalization of an ethnic conflict are not necessarily those that the affected parties generally anticipate; indeed, the intervention was not advantageous to the presumed beneficiaries. On the contrary, internationalization actually prolonged the conflict and made many of the parties to the conflict more intractable. Again, when large regional or global powers enter a domestic ethnic dispute playing the role of sponsors and suppliers, the interests of the external contenders may supersede the original issues in the conflict.

The hard lesson that emerges from India's mediation and interventionist role in Sri Lanka's ethnic conflict is that most outside powers have less to offer by way of example from their own political system and political experience than they think they do. To be drawn into an ethnic conflict in a neighbouring state is the worst mistake that a regional power can make, as Israel and Syria have learned in Lebanon. The reluctance of the Sri Lankan Government to consider, much less accept, another episode of external mediation stems from the pronounced failure of Indian mediation, and the heavy political costs it inflicted on Sri Lanka's democratic system.

Sri Lanka

4.6 Human Rights Instruments

Democratic procedures and values provide the means to deal sensibly and fairly with civil conflicts. But for democracy to serve as the framework for the peaceful coexistence of communities, it has to be defined in both procedural and substantive terms. Herein lies the importance of legal and constitutional norms, elaborated in recent years for the purpose of defining and protecting rights.

4.6.1 Introduction

Many of today's most pressing issues – human rights, self-determination, nationalism, international security and co-operation – are all connected with identity and ethnicity. In trying to formulate policies to deal with such issues, one particular difficulty is that religious or ethnic claims and identities are not always negative. Indeed, concession to some of these claims may help to allay minority fears and give them a sense of security. Furthermore, religious and ethnic affiliations may be important to the psychic and moral well-being of communities, which it would be wrong to deny. Thus a balance needs to be struck between the problems that ethnic, religious and national loyalties can cause and the difficulties that can result from their obstruction. Striking this balance presents one of the fundamental challenges of our time: the reconceptualization of the state to accommodate a diversity of cultures, religion, languages and groups.

Sometimes the difficulty in agreeing on a policy arises from a disagreement on values. Tensions frequently exist between those

4.6 Human Rights Instruments

who espouse individual claims and preferences, and those who support religious and ethnic principles. For example, the acceptance of group rights, which frequently helps to resolve some claims, is problematic with respect to individual rights. In several Commonwealth countries, such problems have arisen in an acute form. The position women occupy under group (customary) law is often subordinate to that of men: they suffer discrimination with respect to the care and custody of children, marriage laws, division of labour, or entitlement to property or inheritance (as in India, South Africa, Canada, and many other states that recognize personal or customary law). Difficulties can also arise in the relations between members and non-members of groups that are given special treatment (as in Quebec). Even when a clear and effective policy can be discerned, a small dissident group intent on preventing or upsetting a settlement may frustrate implementation. A prime illustration is the persistent opposition to, or frustration of, a settlement in Sri Lanka by extremist groups within the Tamils and Sinhalese communities.

The relationship of such conflicts to democracy is often complex. Democratic ideas of self-determination have promoted quests by various communities within a state to emphasize their differences from other groups in order to establish their claim as a separate "people". Crude claims of majoritarianism have led to the oppression of minorities, leading to the suppression of their rights and their alienation from the state. There is no doubt, however, that democratic procedures and values also provide the means to deal sensibly and fairly with conflicts. But democracy can only provide a useful framework for the negotiation and settlement of conflict if it is defined in both procedural and substantive terms. This is why legal and constitutional norms that define and protect rights are so important. Based on principles of fairness, social justice and good practice, they provide a substantive framework for the operation of democracy and place a limit on the power of the majority.

The entitlement to democracy itself is now a principle that underlies norms that provide the framework for addressing ethnic and other conflicts. The principle of self-determination, recognized in the UN Charter as the basis of decolonization, was extended to "all peoples" in two covenants in 1966 – the *International Covenant on Civil and Political Rights* (hereafter ICCPR) and the *International Covenant on Economic, Social and Cultural Rights*. Together with the *Universal Declaration of Human Rights* these form the International Bill of Rights.

Legal and constitutional norms that define and protect rights provide a substantive framework for the operation of democracy and place a limit on the power of the majority.

> *The will of the people shall be the basis of the authority of government; this will be expressed in periodic and genuine elections which shall be by universal and equal suffrage and shall be held by secret vote or by equivalent free voting procedures.*
>
> *Everyone has a right to take part in the government of his country, directly or through freely chosen representatives.*
>
> Universal Declaration of Human Rights, Article 21

International norms have developed through both the elaboration of these general human rights norms as well as the enunciation of specific instruments dealing with minorities, groups or anti-discrimination. Below we outline some of the major instruments that have been formulated to define and protect human rights.

4.6.2 Instruments dealing with religious and ethnic persecution

The first major instrument to deal with religious and ethnic bigotry and persecution was the *Convention on the Prevention and Punishment of the Crime of Genocide* (1948), which intended to "liberate mankind from such an odious scourge". It declared genocide a crime under international law (Art. I). Genocide may be punished in the courts of the state where the offence was committed or by an international penal tribunal.

> *Genocide: acts committed with a view to "destroy, in whole or in part, a national, ethnical, racial or religious group as such: (a) killing members of a group; (b) causing serious bodily or mental harm to members of the group; (c) deliberately inflicting on the group conditions of life calculated to bring about its physical destruction in whole or in part; (d) imposing measures intended to prevent birth within that group; or (e) forcibly transferring children of the group to another group".*
>
> Article II

Another instrument that penalizes, under international law, conduct directed against an ethnic group is the *International Convention on the Suppression and Punishment of the Crime of Apartheid* (1973).

> *Apartheid: the establishment and maintaining of "domination by one racial group of persons over any other racial group of persons and systematically oppressing them" by: (a) denial to*

4.6 Human Rights Instruments

> *members of the second group right to life and liberty of person (including murder or other forms of inhuman treatment); (b) deliberate imposition on a racial group of living conditions calculated to cause their physical destruction; (c) deny to the group rights to participate in the political, social, economic and cultural life of the country, and restrictions on work, trade union activities, movement, freedom of expression, etc; (d) the division of the population along racial lines, including the prohibition of mixed marriages; (e) exploitation of the labour of one group, in particular through forced labour; and persecution of groups and individuals who oppose apartheid.*

Article II

Such offences may be tried by the courts of any signatory state that may acquire jurisdiction over the accused or by an international penal tribunal (Art. V).

These two conventions are supplemented by the more general concept of crimes against humanity as part of customary international law (which constitute, among other things, the jurisdiction of the Yugoslavia and Rwanda war crimes tribunals). These instruments and rules essentially aim at prohibiting extreme forms of persecution, but they have not been particularly successful. Furthermore, they do not provide any positive rights to minorities. Indeed, the development of international law has been marked by significant ambivalence regarding the positive obligations of states with respect to persons or communities belonging to minority language, religious or ethnic groups. There has been reluctance, on the one hand, to recognize these communities as such, preferring to refer to the rights of *persons* belonging to such communities (which may not be sufficient to accommodate all the needs of the community). On the other hand, there has been a reluctance to impose any positive obligations on the state to protect the interests of these communities; rather it is considered sufficient that there should be a general prohibition of discrimination against them, an attitude typified by Article 27 of the ICCPR:

> *In those States in which ethnic, religious or linguistic minorities exist, persons belonging to such minorities should not be denied the right, in community with the other members of their group, to enjoy their own culture, to profess and practice their own religion, or to use their own language.*

ICCPR, Article 27

4.6.3 Specific instruments to protect minorities

All UN and regional instruments on rights proclaim the equality of all persons, regardless, *inter alia*, of race or religion; prohibit discrimination in the enjoyment of rights and freedoms; and guarantee the freedom of religion and conscience. The horrendous persecution on the basis of religion or ethnicity has changed perspectives somewhat, as has a growing concern, particularly in the west, with identity politics.

This change in perspective is reflected in several developments. First, the UN Committee on Human Rights has begun to give a more "positive" orientation to Article 27 of the ICCPR. It now holds the view that, in some instances, the state must take positive steps to ensure the effective enjoyment of rights guaranteed in the article. Also, it is prepared to hold, that, in some cases at least, the identity of a community can only be preserved by the recognition of what may be called the collective rights of the community (see its General Comment on Article 27 (1994)).

Second, realizing that negative obligations on the state to protect minorities were not sufficient in all instances, the international community formulated specific instruments for minorities. One of the earliest of these was the *International Convention on the Elimination of All Forms of Racial Discrimination* (1965), which condemns racial discrimination of any kind which has the purpose or effect of nullifying or impairing the recognition, enjoyment or exercise, on an equal footing, of human rights and fundamental freedoms in the political, economic, social, cultural or any other field of public life (Art. 1). Signatory states condemn all propaganda and all organizations that are based on ideas or theories of superiority of one race or group of persons of one colour or ethnic origin, or which attempt to justify or promote racial hatred and discrimination in any form. States have to take "immediate and positive steps" to eradicate all incitement to, or acts of, such discrimination (Art. 4). The state not only has to ensure that its own laws and practices comply with this obligation, but also that it does not sponsor, defend or support racial discrimination by any persons or organizations (Art. 2 (a) and (b)). It includes the positive duty on states to encourage, where appropriate, integrationist multi-racial organizations and movements and other means of eliminating barriers between races, and to discourage anything which tends to strengthen racial division (Art. 2(e)).

In 1981, the General Assembly adopted the *Declaration on the Elimination of All Forms of Intolerance and of Discrimination Based on Religion or Belief.*

> *Religion or belief, for any one who professes either, is one of the fundamental elements in his conception of life and that freedom of religion should be fully respected and guaranteed.*
>
> Preamble

The expression "freedom of religion or conscience" is given a broad meaning to encompass worship and the right to assemble for purpose of worship; to establish and maintain appropriate charitable or humanitarian institutions; publications; instructions in belief; and to establish contact with individuals and institutions in matters of religion or belief at the national and international levels (Art. 6). The Declaration prohibits discrimination on the grounds of religion, any infringement of the right to religion or conscience, or coercion, which would impair a person's freedom to have a religion or belief (Art. 1). It requires that parents bring up children "in a spirit of understanding, tolerance, friendship among peoples, peace and universal brotherhood, respect for freedom of belief and belief of others, and in full consciousness that his energy and talents should be devoted to the service of his fellow men" (Art. 5(3)). The Declaration makes clear that the duty of the state is not merely the negative one to prevent discrimination, but that the state also has a positive obligation to ensure conditions in which tolerance can flourish.

The UNESCO *Convention against Discrimination in Education* (1960) not only prohibits discrimination in access to education on grounds of *inter alia* race or religion, but also requires signatory states to direct education to the full development of the human personality and to the strengthening of respect for human rights and fundamental freedoms; and to the promotion of understanding, tolerance and friendship among all nations, racial or religious groups (Art. 5(1)(a)). It also requires states to permit members of minorities to have their own schools and, under certain circumstances, education in their own language (Art. 5 (1)(c)).

4.6.4 Protecting women's rights

An instrument of particular significance is the *Convention on the Elimination of All Forms of Discrimination Against Women* (CEDAW, 1979). Although not directly concerned with discrimination or persecution on religious or racial grounds, its norms establish standards for the treatment of women (particularly, but not only, in equality with men) which have profound effects on religious dogma and practice. Women are guaranteed equal rights with men:

> *The "recognition, enjoyment or exercise by women, irrespective of
> their marital status, on a basis of equality of men and women,
> of human rights and fundamental freedoms in the political,
> economic, social, cultural, civil or any other field."*
>
> Article 1

States have undertaken, *inter alia*, to refrain from engaging in
any act or practice of discrimination against women and to ensure that all public authorities and institutions act in conformity
with this obligation (Art. 2(d)). States have to take all appropriate measures to modify the social and cultural patterns of conduct of men and women, with a view to achieving the elimination of prejudices and customary and other practices which are
based on the idea of the inferiority or the superiority of either
of the sexes or on the stereotyped roles for men and women
(Art. 5(a)). Women must be guaranteed the same legal capacity
as men (Art. 15). Women must also be granted the right freely
to choose a spouse and to enter into marriage only with their
free and full consent, and equal rights in marriage (Art. 16).

4.6.5 Recent initiatives

Attempts have been made in recent years to give some over-
arching unity or coherence to these developments for the protection of minorities, of which two are noteworthy. The more general of the two is the *Declaration on the Rights of Persons Belonging
to National or Ethnic, Religious and Linguistic Minorities,* adopted by
the UN General Assembly in 1992. In the Preamble, the General
Assembly states that the "promotion and protection of persons
belonging to national or ethnic, religious and linguistic minorities contribute to the political and social stability of states in
which they live". The Declaration requires that minorities be allowed full participation in public affairs. There is a special emphasis on the rights of minorities to practice and develop their
culture. For example, states are required to take "measures in
the field of education, in order to encourage knowledge of the
history, traditions, language and culture of minorities" (Art. 4).

> *States shall "protect the existence and the national or ethnic,
> cultural and religious identity of minorities within their
> respective territories, and shall encourage conditions for the
> promotion of that identity".*
>
> Article 1

4.6 Human Rights Instruments

> *States are required to "take appropriate measures so that, whenever possible, persons belonging to minorities have adequate opportunities to learn their mother tongue or to have instruction in their mother tongue".*
>
> Article 3

The other major initiative is the protection of the rights of indigenous peoples. A convention for the protection of indigenous peoples was adopted as early as 1959 under the auspices of the ILO. However, with the growing consciousness and cultural pride among indigenous peoples, the 1959 convention began to be resented for its patronizing and assimilationalist approach. Consequently a new ILO instrument, the *Convention Concerning Indigenous and Tribal Peoples in Independent Countries* was adopted in 1991. The principal objective is to ensure equal rights for indigenous peoples with the rest of the population of the country. However this equality is to be achieved "in a manner compatible with their aspirations and way of life" (Art. 2). Throughout there is an emphasis on the preservation and integrity of their culture and way of life. The participation of indigenous peoples in decisions that affect them is another principal theme. These objectives flow from recognition of the distinctive contributions of indigenous and tribal peoples to the cultural diversity and social and ecological harmony of humankind.

Of regional instruments, the most significant is the *Framework Convention for the Protection of National Minorities of the Council of Europe* (1994). It is based on assumptions that: (a) "upheavals of European history have shown that the protection of national minorities is essential to stability, democratic security and peace"; (b) "a pluralistic and genuinely democratic society should not only respect the ethnic, linguistic and religious identity of each person belonging to a national minority, but also create appropriate conditions enabling them to express, preserve and develop this identity"; (c) "the creation of a climate of tolerance and dialogue is necessary to enable cultural diversity to be a source and a factor, not of division, but of enrichment of each society"; and (d) protection of minorities forms an integral part of the international protection of human rights, and thus of international co-operation.

Its substantive provisions emphasize the guarantee of individual rights as well as collective rights; equality, including special measures if necessary; culture and identity, prohibiting forcible assimilation; promotion of cultural understandings and tolerance, particularly in education, media and culture; civil and political rights, including rights to establish institutions and associations; media for freedom of expression; the right to use minority languages; education about minority cultures; and the right of minorities to establish contacts with kin groups in other states. Also, it provides for the regional supervision of these provisions in member states.

4.6.6 Conclusion

These developments toward the recognition of group rights and the rights of the community are to be welcomed. They provide both a framework for negotiations to end conflicts as well as some solutions for such conflicts. They also suggest ways in which the state could be restructured. But as easy solutions can be sought in the recognition of group rights, especially when there is international mediation, it is equally important to realize that most of these instruments place a primary value on human rights. Human rights emphasize our commonality and our solidarity. Solutions that are based excessively on groups and their own sense of propriety tend to fragment people. They also tend to place in danger the rights of certain sections of persons within the group itself (such as women and children), as well as the rights of persons outside the group. Such denials of rights can be a further cause of conflict. The balance between human/individual rights and group rights needs to be established with great care and with full regard to human dignity and solidarity.

REFERENCES AND FURTHER READING

Cassesse, Antonio. 1995. *Self-Determination of Peoples: A Legal Appraisal.* Cambridge: Cambridge University Press.

Packer, J. and K. Myntt. eds. 1993. *Protection of Ethnic and Linguistic Minorities in Europe.* Abo: Abo Academy University.

Thornberry, Patrick. 1991. *International Law and Rights of Minorities.* Oxford: Clarendon Press.

United Nations. 1989. *A Compilation of Human Rights Instruments.* Geneva: United Nations.

4.7 Language Policy for Multi-Ethnic Societies

4.7 Language Policy for Multi-Ethnic Societies

The 20th century has been marked by innumerable ethnic conflicts based on the quest for native language rights. As with other issues of ethnicity, language diversity cannot simply be ignored. Indeed, demands for pluralist language policy are likely to accelerate in the future, and policy-makers will need to be prepared to accommodate language diversity while still promoting overall integration.

Most states in the contemporary world are multi-ethnic and multilingual. Consequently, policy-makers have to decide how to accommodate language diversity in a way that promotes rather than hinders overall integration. But what is the best and most democratic language policy? Is it one that promotes cultural assimilation or is it language pluralism? What are the political consequences of pursuing one or the other policy?

Some answers can be found, first, by looking at the comparative experience of multilingual states and second, by analysing the specific history and context of each particular case. As a rule, ethnic harmony is promoted if new states adopt a policy of *cultural pluralism* that recognizes the language rights of minorities while at the same timing to form a common civic and cultural identity. Yet circumstances and ethnic groups differ. Immigrant groups, for example, are far more accepting of language assimilation than are indigenous minorities or regional sub-nations. In addition, the rights of the latter are protected more thoroughly by international covenants and by international precedents. For this discussion, most of the propositions made relate to indigenous minorities or sub-nations of the state in question.

4.7.1 Why does language policy matter?

If a state's population consists of two or more language groups, policy-makers unavoidably have to make choices, whether they acknowledge this fact or not. In a multilingual state, language use is not just a private matter, since a particular language is used in any public communication. The central issue is which language or languages are used officially in the public sphere, i.e., in public education, state administration, the army, the courts and so on. Is one language designated as the state language, or are other languages given some space (either regionally, or in certain spheres such as education)? The state must decide on these issues, and its decisions will affect the power and identity of linguistic groups; this is the "politics of language". But why does language matter so much?

First, there is the psychological role that language plays: it ties into the self-esteem and pride of groups and individuals. This is especially true for smaller nationalities. Experts on the politics of multilingualism note that the status of the indigenous language is seen by emerging nations as a symbol of a new-found group dignity. The fate of a language has consequences for entire cultures, which may become endangered if that language is not used. In order for a language to survive, it must be used in many domains, including schools, the media and public interaction. Yet, while it is important to avoid raising cultural anxiety, it is also important to realize that the status of cultures reflects overall political power. Ethnic groups, and especially larger nationalities or sub-nations, want to exercise some degree of self-rule and avoid subordination. Native speakers of a dominant language gain certain social and career benefits; minorities, too, want equal opportunities.

Although language often is seen as having primarily a cultural significance, it also has a more practical value in a modern state. Language policy affects social and political access to careers and public goods. Which language is used when a citizen encounters public servants, and which language is used in tax forms or other papers produced by the state bureaucracy? Which language is used if one needs to call an ambulance or a fire fighter or seek assistance from police or social services? In modern states the sphere of interaction between citizens and the state is getting broader rather than narrower, and thus the scope of language use is expanding as well. The language that is used on electoral ballots, in parliamentary debates, or when the state publishes laws and regulations is also important, as it

The central issue is which language or languages are used officially in the public sphere, i.e., in public education, state administration, the army, the courts and so on.

4.7 Language Policy for Multi-Ethnic Societies

impacts on a citizen's ability to participate in his or her community. In other words, if a citizen has to use a non-native language in interactions with the state, this will influence the extent of his or her attachment to or alienation from the state.

Other language issues, regulated by the state and tied to identity, include the naming of streets or public buildings, and the use of personal names. The latter seems like an innocuous issue, but it can be a very sensitive topic. For example, the forced "Bulgarization" of Turkic and Muslim names by the communist government of Bulgaria in the 1970s incited ethnic conflict that culminated in the exodus of a large part of the Turkic minority. A less dramatic case involved the bureaucratic "Russianization" of personal names in the Soviet Union by requiring non-Russian minorities to adhere to the Russian tradition of using a patronymic (a name derived from one's father). Italy's outlawing of the German spelling of personal names in South Tyrol encouraged terrorism. Interestingly, the same policy applied in the Alsace region of France was relatively uncontroversial. This illustrates that the same policy can trigger different reactions in different contexts and that it is essential to examine the local context when analysing the importance of a particular issue in a specific state. In sum, there are a number of political, economic, and psychological factors that must be taken into account in forming language policy. In addition, it should be noted that official policy can do little to influence what happens when languages are used informally, in personal interactions.

4.7.2 Assimilation or pluralism

Language pluralism is the most democratic approach for multilingual societies; but there are alternative policies as well. Many states that have engaged in nation building in modern times have had either an explicit or implicit policy of *language assimilation*. The US, for example, presents a case where language assimilation for the sake of civic integration has been an explicit policy; France, on the other hand, has had an implicit policy. Since the French Revolution, becoming a French citizen has meant that French was the only language used in schools, administration, the army, and public life in general. While the dominance of the French language in France appears "natural" today, it is in fact the result of deliberate ethnic engineering. Despite some minority protest, it has been a successful policy of assimilation. Similar examples of assimilationist success can be found in other parts of the world, but one also can find just as many examples of assimilationist failure. Assimilation is most likely to fail if it is involuntary and if it involves territorially based minorities. Assimilation is no panacea, as it involves the loss of one identity for the sake of another.

Language pluralism, by contrast, begins with the assumption that assimilation is likely to lead to a backlash. It assumes that every group – as a group – wants to retain its identity, has the right to do so, and will fight to do so. To avoid the latter, and to create civic consensus, pluralists argue that, parallel with creating a joint identity, policy-makers need to grant convincing guarantees for the retention of sub-cultures. Pluralists safeguard the parallel use of two or more languages by saying "let us each retain our own language in certain spheres, such as schools, but let us also have a common language for joint activities, especially in civic life".

Language is a core issue in the politics of ethnicity. Fortunately, it is an easier issue to deal with than some other ethnic issues because language allows for multiple identities. Language knowledge is not an exclusive or immutable ethnic "given" similar to religion or race. People can speak several languages, and several languages can coexist. Specific arrangements differ from case to case, but all involve a two-track policy whereby one track gives space and guarantees for minority languages, and the other track promotes the learning of one or several state languages to allow communication and enhance mutual understanding.

Language conflicts can be managed by providing some spheres where minority languages are freely used and by giving incentives to learn other languages, especially a state language. People have a remarkable ability to learn languages when it is to their advantage to do so. It is commonplace in Europe and other parts of the world for people to speak more than one language. This can be promoted by an appropriate social reward structure, for example by making language facility a criterion for professional qualification and promotion.

4.7.3 Advantages of language pluralism

The advantage of a pluralist language policy is that, by granting minorities space within a society's culture, it represents both a policy of practical and symbolic inclusion. When two or more languages are accommodated in public schools or in other public domains, a state is demonstrating that there are "win-win" situations in ethnic politics. In this way, language pluralism has the

4.7 Language Policy for Multi-Ethnic Societies

potential of preventing the ethnic polarization of the population. In addition, by demonstrating a constructive solution to ethnic issues in one sphere, it can have a spillover effect to other spheres of ethnic relations.

Switzerland is a classic example of how culturally diverse groups can coexist amicably and how the accommodation of diversity can be a source of political consensus. Rather than trying to melt ethnic groups into a new cultural whole, the Swiss have used the affirmation of distinctiveness to bind them into a political unity. Citizens need to have a shared sense of belonging; in fact, this is the classic definition of a nation. A sense of belonging, however, does not mean that a nation needs to be culturally homogenous.

4.7.4 Potential drawbacks

Pluralist language policies need to be developed carefully to avoid any negative consequences. One potential problem is that language differentiation can be perceived as negative discrimination. The politics of plurality must make sure that separate ethnic institutions, such as minority schools or separate administrative offices, preserve rather than undermine the rights of minorities. Ethnic accord is most likely to be enhanced if such arrangements are voluntary and if ethnic groups are autonomous in deciding on specific programmes and approaches.

Another possible limitation of language pluralism is that it can turn into language separatism, i.e., the undermining of a common language. This has been a danger in post-Soviet Latvia and Estonia where a segment of the Russian settlers refuse to learn the local languages. The citizenry needs a common language, both literally and figuratively, to promote mutual understanding and to form and nurture one civic nation. Pluralist language policies require a careful balancing of state support for both the distinct languages of minorities and the common state language.

4.7.5 Language boards

When a new policy is being explored or implemented a special state language board needs to be created. Institutional variants of such boards have been instrumental in working out new language policies in Quebec, Catalonia, and the Baltic States, for example. Such boards include experts who analyse the sociolingual situation, draft policy proposals, and organize language learning programmes. The latter are especially important if a new language policy includes language requirements for civil service jobs, licensing or naturalization. Once a state policy openly acknowledges that a certain language facility is required for access to public goods, it has a duty to assist and monitor its acquisition.

In the early stages of mapping out a new language policy, research needs to examine patterns of language behaviour, attitudes within language groups and interactions between groups. Social scientists should be consulted about the role that language plays in the identity of a particular group and how powerful the symbolic meaning of language is for that community. The importance of language differs from group to group: in some cases a nationality defines itself primarily by its distinct language; in other cases language is less significant than other ethnic markers such as religion or territorial homelands. The specific political context of language policy also needs to be taken into account. If there have been recent cases of language repression, such as is the case in the non-Russian areas of the former Soviet Union, public debates should be encouraged to deal with this legacy and to decide what sort of remedial action to take. Major shifts in language policy need broad public support.

The creation of a state language board with a permanent staff as well as expert commissions requires significant resources, as do language learning programmes. In addition, language pluralism has a cost in terms of parallel publication of state documents in more than one language.

4.7.6 Comparative lessons

In cases where language groups are territorially rooted, language pluralism tends to be linked with territorial autonomy. The dignity of language groups can be enhanced by symbolic recognition of their distinctiveness, for example through the constitution, as is the case in Belgium, and as has been ardently pursued by the Quebecois. In the case of the Baltic States, special language laws passed at the time of the restoration of independence served as reassurance to the indigenous Baltic nations that their native languages would be protected in the future. Such formal legal reassurance is politically significant even when it is clear that much more needs to be done to assure language equity in practice.

When new states are constituted there may be unique opportunities to resolve ethnic conflicts by negotiating an agreement that involves trade-offs for various groups. For example, it may be possible to negotiate more language autonomy in return for

4.7 Language Policy for
Multi-Ethnic Societies

less territorial self-rule. Newly independent Malaysia illustrated a successfully negotiated *quid pro quo* according to which the Chinese settlers accepted the public dominance of the Malay language in return for a liberal naturalization policy. In this case it was also significant that the Chinese diaspora has had alternative ways to safeguard the survival of their language, through contacts with Chinese communities abroad, importing of books, and sending Chinese students to universities abroad.

The collapse of the Soviet Union and the death of Franco provide two recent examples of how democratization has led to more rights for minority languages. The two previously dominant languages, Russian and Spanish respectively, had to accommodate indigenous regional languages such as Latvian and Catalan. These cases also illustrate that language changes take time since subgroups of the population have to learn new languages.

Since 1991, as Latvia has been restoring its independent statehood, it has faced several major issues with respect to language policy. Most importantly, it has needed to reintroduce Latvian as the language of state and public affairs, without undermining the rights of Russophones. Also, it has needed to reintroduce language rights for smaller minorities. In 1988, Russian was the dominant language and Latvian was rarely used in official state and public activities. In order to redress this situation Latvian was made the formal state language in 1989 and was gradually reintroduced in practice as well. A massive state-sponsored language programme was begun to teach Latvian to Russian residents who in the past had relied on Russian as their only language; another major language programme was launched in the mid-1990s with the support of UNDP and several foreign aid programmes. The rationale for encouraging Russian bilingualism was that the Russian settlers needed to acquire Latvian in order to be able to fully function in Latvia and also to prevent a continuation of a situation where mostly bilingual Latvians had to accommodate monolingual Russians. Subsequently, the role and prestige of Latvian as the language of the land was slowly increased by what can be seen as a kind of linguistic "affirmative action". Since the first language laws were adopted in 1988, significant change has occurred; but it has been the result of great effort by the State Language Board, the Ministry of Education, and various minority cultural associations.

The logic of a democratic language policy is to protect the weaker languages and the languages of minorities. In the case of Latvia this meant that Latvian had to be promoted to reassert the language rights of the indigenous nation, and the languages of smaller minorities had to be recognized in schools and cultural life. Latvia's language policy since 1988 also included the tenet that one minority group – the Russians – cannot assimilate other minority groups within Latvia, as they had been doing until then. Smaller minorities such as Poles, Jews, and Ukrainians, were provided with native language schooling. Russians on their part have been able to continue schooling in Russian-language public schools.

Any shift in the hierarchy of languages takes time and has to be undertaken with sensitivity. The case of Latvia illustrates a two-track policy whereby one policy track aims at enhancing the use of an official language as a tool of state-building and formation of a civic nation, and the other track maintains minority language space, in this case primarily in the schools. This policy is based on the assumption that trying to engineer total linguistic homogeneity is impossible and politically dangerous. A *pax linguistica* is possible only if all groups feel that their languages are safeguarded. This is especially true in cases where one deals with a territory that represents the only place where a certain language is used; groups using a language that is used in kin-states tend to be culturally less anxious.

Recent findings of social scientists emphasize the impact of politics on the formation of ethnic identity and on the management of ethnic conflict. Policy-makers typically aim for integration, but how is this vague term understood? Before policies are chosen, the people making the decisions need to reflect on their assumptions. All too often they implicitly assume that integration means assimilation. Comparative analysis shows that while the integration of a state requires some commonality of language, this can very well mean the accommodation of several parallel languages.

REFERENCES AND FURTHER READING

Druviete, Ina. 1997. "Linguistic Human Rights in the Baltic States", *International Journal of the Sociology of Language*, 127. pp. 161–185.

Esman, Milton J. 1992. "The State and Language Policy", *International Political Science Review*, vol. 13, no. 4. pp. 381–396.

Horowitz, Donald L. 1985. *Ethnic Groups in Conflict*. Berkeley, CA: University of California Press.

4.7 Language Policy for Multi-Ethnic Societies

Fishman, Joshua A. 1989. *Language and Ethnicity in Minority Sociolinguistic Perspective*. Clevedon, Avon: Multilingual Matters.

Karklins, Rasma. 1994. *Ethnopolitics and Transition to Democracy: The Collapse of the USSR and Latvia*. Washington, DC: Johns Hopkins University Press.

Lijphart, Arend. 1977. *Democracy in Plural Societies*. New Haven, CT: Yale University Press.

Safran, William. 1992. "Language, Ideology, and State-Building: A Comparison of Policies in France, Israel, and the Soviet Union", *International Political Science Review*, vol. 13, no. 4. pp. 397–414.

Van Dyke, Vernon. 1985. *Human Rights, Ethnicity, and Discrimination*. Westport, CT: Greenwood Press.

4.8 National Conferences

National conferences and constituent assemblies have been a widely used mechanism for bringing together political groups to discuss and plan key aspects of a country's future development. They are a particularly useful means for reaching consensus on the political and institutional shape of a post-colonial or post-conflict state. In this section we consider the objectives of a national conference, how a national conference can be organized and implemented, and its advantages and weaknesses. In the case study that follows we look at how national conferences have impacted on the political development of five Francophone African countries.

4.8.1 Introduction

Constituent assemblies were a common mechanism during the post-World War Two "decolonization decades" to bring politicians and constitutional experts together to write a new constitution for an independent nation. India's independence Constitution, for example, was the result of three years of discussion and debate at a constituent assembly comprising eminent jurists, lawyers, academics and politicians. In other cases, such as Papua New Guinea, the elected parliament from the colonial era reconvened itself as a constituent assembly in 1975 to debate and then formally adopt a constitution. Other attempts have been less successful, such as the use of constituent assemblies to reach consensus on key political conflicts in Sri Lanka (1972) or to prepare an independence Constitution in Pakistan (1947–1954).

4.8 National Conferences

During the 1990s, however, there has been a new trend towards utilizing large national conferences, not as a means of decolonization but as a mechanism for political transition to democracy. The distinctive features of such national assemblies are that they typically include wide representation from civil society; are able to act with considerable autonomy from governments; and have proved particularly useful in forging an internal consensus on democratization and transition from conflict. This type of national assembly was widely used in Francophone Africa in the early 1990s as a means of harnessing pro-democracy forces. It has proven to be a key mechanism in promoting democratic transition and in effecting substantive political change (see Case Study National Conferences in Francophone Africa).

4.8.2 What is a national conference?

A national conference (or national debate, as it is referred to in some countries) is a public forum, held over an extended period, at which representatives from key political and civic groups are invited to discuss and develop a plan for the country's political future, preferably on a consensus basis. By convening a national conference, the central government allows other political groups to participate in a decision-making process, while still maintaining its own authority and control. In agreeing to hold and participate in a national conference the central government is not guaranteeing political freedom or the sharing of power with other political factions; rather it is agreeing to conduct a nationwide political dialogue and ideally, to jointly plan steps toward increased political representation and liberalization.

National conferences are designed typically to fulfil two goals: first, to address the demands for political liberalization, by being inclusive and highly visible, especially to the international community; and second, to achieve gradual, "managed" transition, often with the incumbent leadership believing that it can maintain control over the process. In many African countries, for example, national conferences opened up previously one-party systems by bringing together different actors to address the country's political problems, formulated new constitutional rules, and established electoral timetables. Some national conferences even achieved peaceful alternations in power. In this way they can be seen as an indigenously generated African contribution to political institution building and regime transition.

National conferences in Africa were usually "one-off" assemblies representing a wide range of individuals and corporate in-

National conferences are designed typically to fulfil two goals: first, to address the demands for political liberalization, by being inclusive and highly visible, especially to the international community; and second, to achieve gradual, "managed" transition, often with the incumbent leadership believing that it can maintain control over the process.

terests. They lasted from a few days to several months; contained several hundred to several thousand delegates (i.e., 500 in Benin, 1,200 in Congo, 4,000 in Zaire); and were often chaired by a nominally neutral church leader. Occurring in 12 African countries between 1990 and 1993, national conferences were largely a Francophone phenomenon (Benin, Chad, Comoros, Congo, Gabon, Mali, Niger, Togo and Zaire) although similar bodies were also convened in Ethiopia in July 1991, in South Africa in December 1991, and in Guinea-Bissau in 1992. Some attempts were also made in Burkina Faso, Cameroon, Central African Republic, and Guinea. In Côte d'Ivoire and Senegal the national conference idea hardly took root, and multi-party elections only confirmed the old regimes in power. In the late 1990s, there has been a resurgence of calls for national conferences to build consensus on reforming state structures, initiating transitions to democracy and resolving deep-rooted conflicts, such as in Kenya in 1997 and in Nigeria after the death of Abacha in June 1998. The case study that follows elaborates on the use and results of national conferences in five Francophone countries.

4.8.3 Objectives of a national conference

Prevent conflict. Initially, the objective of a national conference may be simply to prevent conflict by motivating political opposition groups to postpone violence while testing the government's actual commitment to peaceful political change.

Build national consensus on a country's political future. A fundamental objective of a national conference is to provide an opportunity for representatives of all sides to discuss, plan, and reach a maximum level of consensus on a country's political future, hence addressing potential and actual political crises. National conferences can be seen as democratic conflict management tools designed to negotiate democratic transitions by establishing new rules and institutions. A national conference or national debate also may be interpreted as a preliminary move toward limited democracy, in that it lays the foundation for crafting more inclusive institutions and democratic mechanisms, legalizing multipartism, drafting a new constitution and electoral system, achieving peaceful alternation of power, and setting a timetable for democratic transition.

Bolster citizen's support for state institutions. A government may initiate or agree to participate in a national conference to bolster its own legitimacy and popular support by creating a

4.8 National Conferences

more inclusive political climate, thereby reducing internal desta-bilizing factors. As a result of a national conference, the govern-ment may direct state institutions to be more representative and inclusive, in the hope that an increased perception of inclusive-ness will in turn bolster citizens' support for state institutions. Non-government political groups participate in a national conference in the hope of increasing the government's account-ability and expanding popular participation in the government.

"Level the playing-field". In certain instances, a national con-ference may be agreed to by parties in conflict when there is a clear recognition or acknowledgement that the government in power is no longer in a position to maintain the status quo; and because of a demand by the opposition parties that the govern-ment alone cannot deliver a solution to the conflict. In such a case, an all-party national conference is often the first step on the road to substantive negotiations. This process may be dis-empowering for the government, as a common precondition for such a conference is that all parties are regarded as equal in sta-tus. The key objective is to "level the playing-field" between the parties during the negotiations, with the ultimate aim being to forge a national consensus.

Governments often show resistance to a national conference because of this "equal status" dilemma, as it often has the effect of lowering their own status and according real status to parties that previously they may have regarded as enemies and "terror-ists". One way to address this obstacle is to structure the confer-ence so that "nothing is agreed until everything is agreed". This can mean that the government does not feel that it loses its power when the process begins, but only if an ultimate agree-ment is reached which is acceptable to it. In many ways, it is crit-ical that the negotiations simply commence, as that, in itself, may be the start of the process of dealing with perceptions and focusing on the real issues, both important objectives.

4.8.4 Implementation

Prerequisites. Prior to a national conference, *multipartism*, es-pecially the legalization of opposition parties, must be allowed. *Freedom of association, speech and assembly* must be guaranteed. In addition, the *media* must be involved to monitor and report on the events.

Organizers. While *governments* generally take the initiative in convening a national conference, internal and external pressures often have a significant influence. A foreign third party and/or domestic political pressure may play a role in convincing the government to hold a conference. A national conference can be organized by a committee consisting of members of various political groups, including opposition groups, as well as government members and the international community.

Participants. Without the participation of members of the *existing central government*, a national conference would have little significance. To maximize the impact of the conference, participants must include representatives of the key *social, religious, professional, and political interest groups* who wish to participate in the process. All possible participants should be invited to endorse the results of the conference, within limits of reason.

The presence of *international observers* may be helpful in assuring the process and results of the conference. Other participants may include academics, local government personnel, representatives from non-governmental organizations, human rights organizations, women's associations, trade unions and religious authorities, peasant groups and students, and aid donors.

Activities. Organizers of a national conference must agree on and draft an *agenda*, clarify the issues to be discussed, and convey the goals of the conference to all the participants. Depending on the outcome of the conference, it may be necessary for parties to agree on additional issues as well as on the implementation of the conference agreement, if any is reached. In such a situation, a *follow-up or "implementation group"* consisting of key parties, and perhaps members of the international community, should be formed and given the appropriate responsibility to ensure that progress made at the conference is consolidated and translated into action.

Cost considerations. Costs, such as preparation, transportation, and accommodation for the conference participants, may be prohibitive. The primary cost of the conference should always, if possible, be borne by the country itself. However, *foreign financial assistance* may often be necessary to organize a national conference and to help support its follow-up functions. Conference requirements include technical assistance and logistical support.

Set-up time. *Several months* are generally needed to plan and organize a conference. National conferences can be held over a long period (several months) or a short duration (from several days to a few weeks). The comparative experience ranges widely:

4.8 National Conferences

Benin (convened in February 1990 and lasted nine days), Congo (February 1991, three months), Togo (July 1991, one month), Mali (July 1991, 15 days), Niger (July 1991, 40 days), Zaire (August 1991, over a year, with interruptions), South Africa (December 1991, two years with interruptions), and Chad (January 1993, 11 weeks).

Timeframe. A national conference's ability to design sustainable institutional structures and mechanisms for conflict management is key. The impact of a national conference may be sustained if the conference is successfully used to develop a broad consensus on the country's "rules of the game" and political future, and if genuine follow-on actions are initiated. Adherence to the rules and mechanisms agreed upon largely depend on the political commitment of the parties and the underlying balance of power.

Limitations on government. Another consideration is the limitations placed on the powers of the government during the course of the conference. This may involve transitional arrangements aimed at ensuring that no action is undertaken that may affect the position of the parties or of the country. For example, the army may be confined to barracks, there may be a cease-fire agreement, or there may be a commitment to address key national issues such as education or economic policy jointly.

4.8.5 Impact

A national conference can have a different impact depending on the situation it seeks to redress: by *initiating political dialogue*, it can ease mounting tensions; as a *conflict resolution mechanism*, it can provide a framework for agreeing on the country's political institutions and rules through a negotiated democratic transition; and as a *conflict prevention forum*, it can create the rules and institutions for a stable democratic regime.

An announcement to organize a national conference can have a short-term effect on preventing conflict by groups previously involved in or planning political violence. These groups may adopt a wait-and-see attitude, and divert their efforts toward preparation for the conference. However, if no actual, substantive political changes result, such groups may return to violence with even greater zeal and additional disillusioned groups may choose to join them.

National conferences resulted in changes in government in Benin, Congo and Niger; and exerted significant political pressure on incumbent rulers in Zaire and Togo. In many instances, national conferences laid the ground work for competitive founding elections (Benin, Congo, Gabon, Mali, Niger and South Africa). The comparative experience suggests the following lessons:

- A national conference can be a useful *democratic conflict management tool*, as it is both inclusive and participatory, and initiates political dialogue to ease political crises;

- National conferences can have a significant impact on *governance*, on the political system, and even on forming a new political culture based on negotiation and compromise, by persuading groups to participate more actively in the political decision-making process;

- As a conflict resolution mechanism, a national conference can have a decisive influence on *negotiating democratic transitions* from authoritarian rule to democratic pluralism. It can provide a framework for achieving a peaceful alternation in power, drafting a new constitution, designing a new electoral system and setting a democratic timetable;

- A national conference can have a significant impact on *promoting democracy.* However, to sustain the political results of national conferences, the public must continue to pressure the government to continue with democratic political development;

- Through a national conference, political groups and representatives from various sectors can negotiate a plan for the country's political future;

- A national conference may help state authorities *gain greater popular support and legitimacy,* and instil greater public confidence in the government. A national conference may lay the groundwork for establishing a transitional government and relatively open elections. An incumbent government may also gain greater legitimacy by actively participating in discussions on economic development, power-sharing arrangements, human rights, country management, etc;

- Conference participants, representing a country's diverse political groups, can set *guidelines for formulating new political institutions,* such as a legislature and an electoral system, that could contribute to easing tensions among various groups in the country. The result of a national conference may be government agreement to direct state institutions

4.8 National Conferences

to be more representative and inclusive. Such agreements may be made in the hope that the increased perception of inclusiveness would in turn bolster citizens' support for state institutions;

– A national conference can help establish stable civilian governance and control and, at least in the short term, reduce the attraction of resorting to armed opposition for achieving political change.

ORGANIZING A NATIONAL CONFERENCE

National Conference: *A national conference is a public forum at which representatives from key political and civic groups are invited to discuss and develop a plan for the country's political future, preferably on a consensus basis. National conferences are designed typically to fulfil two goals: first, to address the demands for political liberalization; and second, to achieve gradual, "pacted" or "managed" transition, often with the incumbent leadership believing that it can maintain control over the process.*

IMPLEMENTATION

Sequence of Events:
■ Conferees acquire some degree of law-making authority;

■ Existing constitutions are revised, legislatures suspended or reformed, and transitional governments established (in other words, a form of regime transition by peaceful means);

■ Incumbent presidents are required to work with transitional governments or to surrender significant powers;

■ Conference participants draft a new constitution, or establish an independent commission to do so, and submit it to a referendum;

■ Free elections are held.

Prerequisites:
■ Multipartism, especially legalization of opposition parties;

■ Freedom of association, speech and assembly;

■ Media involvement to monitor and report on events.

Organizers:
■ Governments usually, often influenced by foreign third party and/or domestic political pressure;

■ A committee, consisting of representatives of government, other political groups and the international community can organize national conferences.

Participants:
■ Members of existing central government;

■ Representatives of key social, religious, professional, and political interest groups;

■ Other participants can include academics, local government personnel, NGOs, human rights organizations, women's organizations, trade unions, students, and aid donors;

■ International observers.

Activities:

- Draft an agenda; clarify issues to be discussed; convey conference goals to all participants;
- Depending on outcome, organize "implementation group" to ensure follow-up.

Cost Considerations:

- Primary cost of conference organization (preparation, transportation, accommodation, etc.) should be borne by the country itself, if possible;
- Additional foreign financial assistance may be needed for organization and follow-up.

Set-Up Time:

- Usually several months are needed to organize;
- Conference can last between several days and several months (Benin lasted nine days; Congo, three months; South Africa, two years with interruptions).

ADVANTAGES OF A NATIONAL CONFERENCE

Initiates new political dialogue:

- Initiates political dialogue that is both inclusive and participatory, to ease crises;
- Can help develop a *new political culture* by persuading groups to participate more actively in the political decision-making process and by emphasizing compromise and negotiation.

Conflict management mechanism:

- Can negotiate democratic transitions from authoritarian rule to democratic pluralism;
- Can provide a framework for achieving a peaceful alternation in power by drafting a new constitution, designing a new electoral system, and establishing a democratic timetable.

Conflict prevention forum:

- Can help state authorities *gain greater popular support and legitimacy*, and instil greater public confidence in the government.
- Conference participants, representing a country's diverse political groups, can set *guidelines for formulating new political institutions*, such as a legislature and an electoral system, that could contribute to easing tensions among various groups in the country.

REFERENCES AND FURTHER READING

Baker, Bruce. 1998. "The Class of 1990: How Have the Autocratic Leaders of Sub-Saharan Africa Fared under Democratisation?", *Third World Quarterly*, vol. 19, no. 1. pp. 115–127.

Boulaga, Eboussi. 1993. *Les Conférences Nationales en Afrique Noire*. Paris: Editions Karthala.

Bratton, Michael and Nicolas van de Walle. 1997. *Democratic Experiment in Africa. Regime Transitions in Comparative Perspective*. Cambridge: Cambridge University Press.

Clark, John F. 1994. "The National Conference as an Instrument of Democratization in Francophone Africa", *Journal of Third World Studies*, vol. XI, no. 1. pp. 304–335.

Monga, Célestin. 1994. "National Conferences in Francophone Africa: An Assessment". Paper presented to the Annual Conference of the School of Advanced International Studies, SAIS, African Studies Programme, Washington DC, 15 April 1994.

Robinson, Pearl. 1994. "The National Conference Phenomenon in Francophone Africa", *Comparative Studies in Society and History*, no. 36. pp. 575–610.

Wiseman, John. 1996. *The New Struggle for Democracy in Africa*. Aldershot: Avebury.

Gibraltar

Algiers

Tunis

Mediterranean Sea

Casablanca

Tripoli

Alexandria

Cairo

In Salah

Red Sea

MALI

NIGER

CHAD

Port Sudan

Tombouctou

Bamako

Niamey

Ndjamena

Addis Ababa

BENIN

ETHIOPIA

TOGO

NIGERIA

GHANA

Porto Novo

Monrovia

Lagos

Port Harcourt

Bangui

UGANDA

Accra

Lomé

Kampala

Gulf of Guinea

Libreville

Mbandaka

Kisangani

GABON

DEMOCRATIC

RWANDA

CONGO

REPUBLIC OF CONGO

BURUNDI

Brazzavile

(formerly Zaire)

Kinshasa

TANZANIA

Kananga

Dar es Salaam

Luanda

Likasi

ANGOLA

ZAMBIA

Lusaka

ATLANTIC OCEAN

BOTSWANA

Gaborone

Johannesburg

SOUTH AFRICA

© International IDEA

Carlos Santiso

NATIONAL CONFERENCES IN FRANCOPHONE AFRICA

In the late 1980s and early 1990s, sub-Saharan African countries were faced with simultaneous pressures from within and from outside to liberalize their political systems. The economic crisis and the social unrest it created increased the demands on the political elite to liberalize the political system. The international environment also changed dramatically, as the Cold War and its system of "protectorates" in the developing world gave way to a greater emphasis on democracy and democratization, especially by donor governments and the international community.

Confronted with strong resistance, increasing protest, and economic crises, authoritarian rulers in many countries recognized the need to renew legitimacy by opening up the political system and beginning a dialogue with opposition forces on democratic reform. Citizens began to pressure single-party regimes to expose themselves to multi-party elections. One mechanism that helped facilitate this process was the use of national conferences. These conferences opened up space for political dialogue and consensus by including opposition political parties and civil society organizations.

As we have discussed, a national conference can provide a forum for opposing groups to discuss and negotiate political issues in a peaceful, structured environment, before a violent conflict erupts. In terms of conflict management, national conferences can provide a structured institutional framework for negotiation and consensus building and can be used to try to resolve growing political demands and opposition to the current regime without resorting to repression and force.

In this section we look at the impact of national conferences in five Francophone countries.

Benin

By 1989, Benin was in a state of crisis. The economic and social unrest that broke out in 1989 became a mass movement for democratic renewal. When government repression failed to curb protest, the military-installed President Mathieu Kérékou, who had been in power for 17 years, began to make political concessions, first by appointing a prominent human rights activist and legal reformer to the government, and second by announcing a broad amnesty for political opponents. However, the demands for greater political liberalization were not assuaged. Attempting to re-capture the political initiative, Kérékou announced in December 1989 that the People's Revolutionary Party of Benin (PRPB) would abandon its Marxist ideology and its monopoly on power by permitting the legal formation of opposition parties, and by convening a national conference to discuss changes to the Constitution.

National Conferences in Francophone Africa

A commission was created to prepare a "national reconciliation conference" that would include broad elements of political society to discuss the country's future. Participants would include the government, political parties (both from the nascent opposition and the majority), trade unions, religious associations, army representatives and women's groups. Initially, the conference was to have no more than an advisory role and was regarded by some in the opposition as a diversionary tactic. In a strict legal sense, the conference had no constitutional standing at the outset. Furthermore, none of the participants to the conference could claim a popular electoral mandate because the membership of the conference was appointed rather than elected. However, the appointment of the Archbishop of Cotonou as chairman of the conference gave it a moral legitimacy.

By the time the national conference was convened in February 1990, Kérékou had lost control of political events. He hoped that the national conference would provide an opportunity for him to retain power and enlarge his power base by opening up the political system and by making certain concessions. However, the 488 delegates soon declared themselves sovereign. Kérékou's immediate response was to describe this decision as a "*civilian coup d'état*". In the end, however, he accepted the decision given his weak position, the popular support enjoyed by the democratic opposition, and the uncertain support of the army. The conference agreed to allow Kérékou to retain the presidency, pending democratic presidential elections and provided that he accepted the decision of the conference; it also decided that Kérékou would not be prosecuted for any "crimes" he had committed while in office.

Subsequently, the conference suspended the constitution, dissolved the National Assembly, created the post of prime minister and appointed Nicéphore Soglo, a former World Bank official, as prime minister. A new constitution was drafted, which allowed presidential term limits and multi-party elections. The Constitution was approved by referendum in December 1990 by 96 per cent of the population. Competitive parliamentary elections were held in February 1991 and presidential elections were held in March 1991. Twenty-four political parties and 13 candidates, including Kérékou and Soglo, contested the parliamentary elections. Soglo's coalition, the Union for the Triumph of Democratic Renewal, won the largest share of parliamentary seats and Soglo became President.

Following this decisive electoral defeat, Kérékou asked for forgiveness for abusing power during his tenure in office. The interim Government agreed not to prosecute the outgoing dictator and Kérékou responded by pledging loyalty to the new government. Ultimately, Kérékou regained power through democratic elections in 1996.

What had begun as an assembly with no clearly defined agenda and somewhat arbitrary membership found itself within the space of a few days dismantling the long established, albeit precarious, authoritarian regime and creating the institutional framework for the democratization of the political system of Benin.

Congo (Brazzaville)

Before democratization, the Congolese political system exhibited many similarities to that of Benin. The state was ruled by a militarized single party with strong Marxist-Leninist tendencies, the Congolese Labour Party (PCT) led by Col. Denis Sassou-Nguesso.

Deterioration of the economy and mounting social unrest led to the gradual erosion of the PCT's political monopoly, and by 1990, some liberalization of the political system was already underway. In July 1990, the principle of a transition to multipartism was accepted, political prisoners were released, and by the end of the year, Marxism-Leninism was abandoned. In January 1991, in the hope of controlling and neutralizing the process of political liberalization, Sassou-Nguesso took the initiative to legalize the formation of political parties. In early 1991, he convened an all-party national conference to chart the country's political future. The national conference comprised 30 political parties and 141 associations and was convened for a three-month period starting February 1991. However, almost immediately, the conference was suspended for one month because of a dispute between the PCT and the opposition concerning the balance of representation. In March, when the conference was reconvened, the various opposition groups gained an absolute majority of both conference delegates (700 out of the 1100) and seats on the conference governing body (seven of the 11 seats). As in Benin, a Roman Catholic bishop was elected as chairman of the conference.

Although Sassou-Nguesso had insisted that the conference should be consultative, he was forced to agree to opposition demands that the conference be declared a sovereign body that did not require government approval for its decisions. Having established its authority, the conference then proceeded to dismantle the existing authoritarian political structure before the conference itself was dissolved in June 1991. Sassou-Nguesso was allowed to retain the presidency for an interim period but lost most of his powers, including control of the army, which were transferred to the prime minister who became the head of the government. The conference established a new legislature, the High Council of the Republic, which drafted a new constitution to be submitted to a referendum. It also chose a new prime minister, André Milongo, a non-party political technocrat and World Bank official.

By December 1991, the interim legislature had produced a draft constitution but, in January 1992, the transition process was threatened by a mutiny by sections of the army. Popular protests and Sassou-Nguesso's unwillingness to support the coup foiled the attempt and the new constitution was approved by referendum in March 1992, after a five-month delay.

National Conferences in Francophone Africa

Multi-party elections took place in July–August 1992. Although Sassou-Nguesso and the PCT contested the presidential and parliamentary elections, they were defeated in both by the new opposition party, Pascal Lissouba's Pan-African Union for Social Democracy (UPDAS). The democratic experiment in Congo, however, collapsed in 1997–1998 when Sassou-Nguesso returned to power by force.

Mali

In contrast to Benin and Congo (Brazzaville), the national conference in Mali had a more limited role in the transition process and served more as a consensus-building mechanism after the overthrow of Moussa Traoré's dictatorship.

Widespread opposition to harsh conditions under Traoré's 22-year dictatorship, and mounting demands for a multi-party system, erupted in rioting in the streets of the capital Bamako and other towns during the first months of 1991. On 26 March 1991, Traoré was ousted by a military coup under the reform-minded leadership of Amadou Toumani Touré. A Transitional Committee for the Salvation of the People (CTSP), composed of 10 military and 15 anti-Traoré civilians and headed by Touré, was formed. The CTSP appointed Soumana Sacko, a highly respected senior UNDP official, as Prime Minister and a technocratic government was formed. On 5 April 1991, the CTSP authorized the formation of political parties and declared its intention to rule for a nine-month period ending with a constitutional referendum and multi-party elections. From the outset it was decided that the CTSP was to act as a transitional authority pending the establishment of democratic institutions. As part of this process, the CTSP established a national conference in July and August 1991.

The conference was composed of 1,800 delegates, 42 political parties and 100 associations. These groups discussed the precise details of the transition to democracy and the drafting of a new constitution. The principle of the transition itself had already been decided upon before the conference opened. Thus, in contrast to the two previous examples, the conference did not feel the need to assert its sovereignty and it was accepted that Touré and the CTSP would remain in power until democratic elections could be held. Unlike Kérékou and Sassou-Nguesso, Touré made it clear that he had no intention of taking part in the elections.

The national conference in Mali was not primarily an arena for managing conflict between an incumbent regime and a competing opposition. The main task of the conference was to detail the way forward from the legacy of the past regime and to draw up a new constitution that could then be approved through referendum. The new constitution for what was designated as the Third Republic confirmed the existence of a multi-party system, together with the independence of the judiciary, freedom of association, speech and assembly, and the right to strike. The constitution was approved by referendum in January 1992 with elections taking place soon after, won by Alpha Oumar Konaré of the Adema party.

Togo

For more than a quarter of a century, the Togolese political system has been dominated by the daunting figure of Etienne Eyadéma, who came to power in a coup in 1967. Since 1969, Togo had officially been a single-party state with the Rally of Togolese People (RPT) as the ruling party. In reality, the RPT was a military-backed front for the highly personalized rule of Eyadéma and his Northern Kabre ethnic tribe.

Encouraged by events elsewhere in the region, popular pressure for democratization built up from early 1990. In March 1991, Eyadéma agreed to the establishment of a multi-party system but refused to concede opposition demands for a national conference. It was clear that both the enthusiasm of the opposition for a conference and the reluctance of Eyadéma were influenced by the way both sides perceived events in Benin: whilst the opposition was eager to replicate the Benin experience, Eyadéma was determined to avoid it.

In June 1991 a new coalition of opposition forces formed the Democratic Opposition Front (FOD), which included political parties and trade unions, and launched an indefinite general strike. In the short term, this pressure paid off and Eyadéma agreed to a national conference, which opened in July 1991 with 1,000 delegates and with the bishop of Atakpame as chairman. The conference soon proclaimed itself sovereign. Government representatives rejected such a proclamation and walked out of the conference. Although they returned one week later, they refused to accept the conference's self-proclaimed sovereignty: Eyadéma argued that sovereignty could only be based on universal suffrage, which the conference lacked. Although government forces were represented at and participated in the conference, they made it clear that they would not be bound by any decision taken.

In retrospect, it is clear that the Togolese national conference significantly overestimated its own real power and underestimated that of the incumbent regime. As in Benin, the conference decided to strip Eyadéma of most of his powers, establish a new interim legislature and government, dissolve the RPT and choose a human rights lawyer as interim prime minister. On August 26, Eyadéma suspended the conference and surrounded it with troops. Although he subsequently allowed the conference to proceed to its ceremonial ending on August 28, it was clear that real power remained in Eyadéma's hands. After the conference, Eyadéma used the army to harass his political opponents and maintain a firm grip on power. Although presidential elections were held in 1993, they can hardly be considered "free and fair".

Democratic Republic of Congo (formerly Zaire)

Zaire (now the Democratic Republic of Congo) also had a national conference, but former President Mobutu Sesi Seko managed to control and neutralize the process, frustrating all attempts by the national conference to accomplish any genuine and substantial regime change through multi-party elections. Until 1990, when Mobutu agreed to allow a multi-party system, Zaire was in theory a single-party state

National Conferences in Francophone Africa

with the Popular Movement of the Revolution (MPR) the only legal party to which every citizen automatically belonged. In practice, the MPR was simply a vehicle for the one-man rule of Mobutu, resting on his control of the army and especially the Presidential Guard.

In 1990, following mass pro-democracy demonstrations, anti-government strikes and pressure from external patrons, Mobutu agreed to allow the existence of opposition parties; 130 were formed, which meant that the opposition was highly fragmented. In April 1991, he announced that a national conference would be convened. Mobutu, following widespread anti-government protest, suspended the conference even before it convened. A fragile coalition known as the Sacred Union was ultimately formed and the Zairian national conference eventually opened in August 1991. Although it remained in formal existence until December 1992 (far longer than the other West African national conferences), it was frequently suspended and clashes between government and opposition forces occurred regularly. The conference produced a draft constitution, but Mobutu remained in control, and the country became chronically unstable.

Zaire's National Sovereign Conference in 1991–1992, and the follow-up High Council of the Republic in 1993–1994, while not succeeding as an instrument of democratic transition from Mobutu's authoritarian, have contributed to the opening of political space. These forums allowed opposition forces to wield some influence, to the point where at times there were competing claims of governmental authority from the High Council and the decaying Mobutuist regime. Prominent opposition figures such as Etienne Tshisekedi emerged to challenge the regime and even to briefly share power as the democratization experiment was launched, but before it lagged. Furthermore, the process led to extensive planning for elections slated for 1997 – elections that did not take place, after civil war broke out in the country and the rebel forces of current President Laurent Kabila defeated Mobutu's military. Nevertheless, many Congolese politicians, especially opposition figures, continue to refer to the work of the national conference, and particularly its constitutional vision of a federal democracy with a high degree of devolution. This vision of a federal state could set the stage for renewed efforts to democratize the Democratic Republic of Congo under the Kabila Government.

Lessons Learned

The national conferences in Benin, Congo and Mali were relatively successful in providing an institutional mechanism for the transition to a more democratic political system. However, it would be misleading to view a national conference as some sort of institutional magic wand that can be used to produce a democratic transition. The Togolese and Zairian experience failed to produce a democratic transition, even though this was the hope of the opposition in both cases. In the case of Togo, Eyadéma succeeded in controlling and neutralizing the process, sometimes with the use of force and intimidation, while in Zaire the entire process was a farce designed to regain some international legitimacy.

National Conferences in Francophone Africa

Strengths

Forum for all sides to express view. A national conference provides a vehicle for all sides, from the national level to the grass-roots level, to express its views, interests and political objectives. This inclusive dialogue process facilitates the building of a national consensus on fundamental rights and interests with the intention of developing a stable and democratic social order. Arriving at a national consensus is critical especially during those times when government legitimacy is fading and political institution building is required. It is interesting to note that, without exception, all 11 countries that convened national conferences recorded advances in political liberalization up to 1992.

Weaknesses and lessons

Can be neutralized and manipulated by incumbent. It is very difficult to anticipate which issues will be addressed at a national conference and how participants will manage a conference. A national conference can begin with chaotic disagreement over conference membership and participation, as the government and the opposition struggle for control over conference management. Although structural factors are important, the degree of control over the process of democratic transition by autocrats and their ability to impose conditions on the process should not be ignored. The national conference process can be neutralized and manipulated by incumbent rulers.

Indeed, the Francophone African experience demonstrates that, as conferences were convened one after the other, incumbent rulers tried to control the process and gradually learned how to neutralize it. Mobutu's Zaire illustrates a case of a neutralized and manipulated national conference used more as a tactical tool than a genuine forum for negotiated political reform. Some leaders refused to countenance a national conference at all (like Biya in Cameroon or Kolingba in the Central African Republic). Others tried to twist the process to their advantage: Bongo, in Gabon, caught the opposition off-guard when he convened a national conference without warning and manipulated the proceedings. Others remonstrated and dissembled: Eyadéma withdrew his government delegation from the Togo conference after it declared itself sovereign and suspended it altogether when the conferees attempted to remove his powers over the armed forces. In South Africa, the opposition ANC walked out of CODESA in June 1992, interrupting proceedings for several months and using their participation as a bargaining tool (see South Africa Case Study). Sassou-Nguesso's experience was a sharp lesson for presidents on the importance of controlling the transition personally. Seibou, in Niger, having been stripped of all but his honorific powers within a month by the national conference, took the decision to stand down from the presidential nomination rather than face humiliation. In some instances, heads of state used the military to intimidate, incarcerate or even eliminate opponents. In Traoré's case it was counterpro-

National Conferences in Francophone Africa

ductive, since the Malian army refused to be tools of oppression. By contrast, Eyadéma in Togo successfully used the army to direct the "democratization process" from 1990 until his re-election in 1993.

Timing. Although the different national conferences reflect different socio-economic contexts, they also were shaped by the different timing strategies used by the incumbent regimes: specifically a *fast/slow approach.* The fast approach by incumbents involved the establishment of the national conference at an early stage in order both to keep the initiative and not to give enough time to the opposition to organize; the slow approach consisted in delaying the speed of the subsequent process in order to buy time to construct support and deny that support to the opposition by, for instance, trying to split the opposition or co-opting it into the majority.

Instability. National conferences (with the exception of South Africa and Kenya) were predominantly a Francophone African phenomenon occurring in one-party regimes (10 out of the 11 countries) and in political systems resembling the French "semi-presidential" structure. This system can eventually lead to dual conflicting forces at the top if the parliamentary majority – and the government – is not congruent with the presidential majority (see section 4.3 on "Executive Type" in this handbook). This situation, when it occurred, tended to increase the instability of the political system.

High expectations. In some cases, national conferences raised exaggerated expectations regarding the efficacy of such a mechanism for democratic transition, irrespective of other circumstances – as the Benin experience reveals. Nevertheless, such a vehicle or mechanism may still present an opportunity to bring about genuine political change.

Balance of power. Comparison of the success and failure of the national conference in providing a genuine transition to a more democratic form of rule suggests that in many cases the outcome was largely determined by the resources of real power, especially economic and military power, which opposing sides in the conflict were able to employ against each other. These varied domestic power equations counted more than the procedural similarities or dissimilarities of the various conferences.

Luc Huyse

4.9 Transitional Justice

> ### 4.9 Transitional Justice
>
> *Strategies for coping with the past have ranged from massive criminal prosecution of the supporters of the previous order to unconditionally closing the book. In this section we review some of these strategies and examine the pros and cons of prosecution and punishment. In the next section, we examine two mechanisms in greater detail – truth commissions and war crime tribunals.*
>
> **4.9.1** *Policies for coping with the past*
> **4.9.2** *The case for and against prosecution and/or lustration*
> **4.9.3** *The case against punishment*
> **4.9.4** *Constraints*
> **4.9.5** *Conclusion*
>
> | Box 10 | Policies for Coping with the Past (p. 274) |

4.9.1 *Policies for coping with the past*

Coping with the past during the transition from a repressive regime to a democracy has taken a wide variety of forms. All policy choices involve answers to two key questions: whether to remember or forget the abuses, and whether to impose sanctions on the individuals who are responsible for these abuses. Some of these policies are offender-oriented (amnesty, prosecution and lustration), others are victim-oriented (compensation and symbolic measures). Truth commissions are directed towards both offenders and victims.

Amnesty. The granting of absolute amnesty is at one end of the spectrum. In some cases the unrestricted pardon is the result of the self-amnesty that the outgoing elite unilaterally award themselves before the transition gets underway. In other instances impunity is the outcome of negotiations between old and new leaders. In Uruguay, for instance, the government that succeeded the military dictatorship enacted, under pressure from the military, an amnesty law in 1986. A third route toward impunity is when democratic forces agree to confer immunity to individuals who committed crimes defending or opposing the previous regime, as was the case in post-Franco Spain.

Truth commissions. Forgiving but not forgetting is the substance of a second major policy choice. Its usual format is the national or international truth commission (see following section). The first goal of such a commission is to investigate the fate of individuals, and of the nation as a whole, under the preceding regime. Its aim is not to prosecute and punish. Examples of truth commissions include the Chilean National Commission on Truth and Reconciliation (1990), the South African Truth and Reconciliation Commission (1995–1998) and the UN-sponsored Truth Commission in El Salvador (1991).

Policy choices involve answers to two key questions: whether to remember or forget the abuses and whether to impose sanctions on the individuals who are responsible for these abuses.

Lustration. Disqualification of agents of the secret police and their informers, of judges and teachers, of civil servants and military personnel is a third way to address the question of reckoning for past wrongs. It sometimes includes the loss of political and civil rights. In some of the post-communist countries of eastern and central Europe, the screening of officials has been the only policy step.

Box 10

POLICIES FOR COPING WITH THE PAST

1. **Amnesty.** Absolute amnesty can be granted through self-amnesty that the outgoing elite unilaterally award themselves, through negotiations between old and new leaders, or through agreement by the new democratic forces.

2. **Truth Commissions.** The main goal is to investigate the fate of individuals and of the nation as a whole, not to prosecute and punish.

3. **Lustration.** Disqualification of the agents of the secret police and their informers, of judges and teachers, of civil servants and military personnel.

4. **Criminal Prosecution.** This can be done by an international body (e.g., International Criminal Tribunal for the Former Yugoslavia), or by national courts.

5. **Compensation.** Compensation by the state (monetary reparation, free medical and psychological treatment, reduced interest on loans for education and home building) and the establishment of permanent reminders of the legacy of the past (monuments, museums, public holidays, etc.)

4.9 Transitional Justice

Criminal prosecution. The most radical interpretation of acknowledgement and accountability is outright *criminal prosecution* of the perpetrators. This task can be taken up by an international body, as in the case of the International Criminal Tribunal for the Former Yugoslavia. National courts also perform this function. A recent example is Ethiopia where some 5,000 officials of the fallen Mengistu regime have been named for trial. By contrast, as a strategy for dealing with the past, criminal prosecution has encountered almost no support in post-1989 Eastern and Central Europe and in the post-authoritarian regimes of Latin America.

Compensation. Prosecution and/or general knowledge of the truth might be seen as an incomplete dealing with the crimes of the previous regime. Additional steps may include *compensation* by the state (monetary reparation, free medical and psychological treatment, reduced interest on loans for education and home building) and the establishment of *permanent reminders of the legacy of the past*, such as monuments, museums, public holidays and ceremonies. In South Africa, such measures are seen to provide channels for the non-violent expression of pain and anger.

4.9.2 The case for prosecution and/or lustration

In the ongoing public debate over post-transition justice, political leaders, academics and other analysts are divided on numerous points. The most divisive question, by far, is how to balance the demands of justice against the many, mainly political, factors that make prosecution a major risk to the new regime. Those who emphasize the beneficial effects of prosecution bring forward two crucial reasons. First, punishing the perpetrators of the old regime advances the cause of building or reconstructing a morally just order. The second reason has to do with establishing and upholding the young democracy that succeeds the authoritarian system.

Reconstruct a morally just order. Proponents of prosecution argue that "justice must be done" in order to rebuild the moral order that has been broken. They believe that the successor government owes it, first of all, as a moral obligation to the victims of the repressive system. Post-authoritarian justice serves to heal the wounds and to repair the private and public damage that the antecedent regime provoked. By serving as a sort of ritual cleansing process, it also paves the way for a moral and political renaissance. Asked by Adam Michnik, a prominent leader of the Polish opposition to communist rule, what he thought of such cleansing, the German writer Jurgen Fuchs answered:

"If we do not solve this problem in a definite way, it will haunt us as Nazism did. We did not denazify ourselves, and this weighed on us for years."

Strengthens fragile democracies. Many believe that in the first months after a transition, the survival of the successor regime depends on swift and firm action against pro-authoritarian officials and their followers. Such action is seen as a necessary protection against sabotage "from within". Moreover, if the prosecution issue remains untouched other forms of social and political disturbance may be triggered, with perhaps a risk of vigilante justice with summary executions, or unbridled screening of political personnel, journalists and judges may be instigated, as was the case in post-communist Poland.

Legitimacy. What a new or reinstated democracy needs most, however, is legitimacy. Failure to prosecute and lustrate may generate feelings of cynicism and distrust towards the political system. This is precisely what has happened in some Latin American countries.

Long-term democratic consolidation. Some analysts believe that prosecutions also advance long-term democratic consolidation. They argue that amnesty endangers the inculcation of codes of conduct based on the rule of law. They claim that a discriminatory application of the criminal law, privileging certain defendants (such as military leaders), will breed cynicism toward the rule of law.

Deter future human rights abuses. Prosecutions, finally, are seen as the most potent deterrence against future abuses of human rights.

4.9.3 The case against punishment

Some analysts argue that prosecuting those alleged to bear responsibility for the crimes of the past is both risky and ambivalent. There is no guarantee, they say, that its effect will be beneficial for democracy. They argue that partisan justice always lurks behind the scenes and that prosecutions can have highly destabilizing effects on an immature democracy. Raoul Alfonsin, Argentina's first elected president after the collapse of the military regime wrote:

"In the final analysis, punishment is one instrument, but not the sole or even the most important one, for forming the collective moral conscience."

4.9 Transitional Justice

May violate rule of law and thus weaken new regime's legitimacy. Young democracies place a high value upon the rule of law and human rights, but post-transition justice involves a number of decisions that may trespass on these legal principles. It may force the successor elite to violate rule of law principles today while judging the undemocratic behaviour of yesterday, which can weaken considerably the legitimacy of the new regime.

For example, the principles of the separation of powers and of judicial impartiality are at stake when dealing with the question of who will act as the judges of the authoritarian regime. Political pressure, time constraints and the unavailability of sufficient judicial personnel may lead the post-transition elite to create special tribunals in which lay-judges play a prominent role. This, the opponents of prosecutions argue, makes lapses from important legal norms almost unavoidable. Such special courts can, indeed, become instruments of partisan vengeance since non-professional judges are easier targets for pressure by the executive, the media and public opinion. This is what happened in post-war Belgium and France some 50 years ago.

Justice after transition must take place within a timeframe. This frame consists of answers to two questions: do we accept *ex post facto* criminal legislation? And will the existing statute of limitation be lifted or upheld? The first question deals with the *nullum crimen sine lege, nulla poena sine lege* principle. This principle means that no conduct may be held punishable unless it is precisely described in a penal law, and no penal sanction may be imposed except in pursuance of a law that describes it prior to the commission of the offence. The second question, dealing with the lifting of the existing statute of limitation is particularly acute in post-communist countries. Atrocities against life and property took place mostly in the late 1940s and during the 1950s. In most cases, as in Hungary where a 30-year statute of limitations, exists, criminal proceedings for the most reprehensible human rights abuses are precluded by reason of lapse of time. Those who disapprove of prosecutions assert that post-transition trials ultimately will result in changing the rules of the game after the fact, either by applying retroactive legislation or by recommencing the statute of limitation once it has run out.

Post-transition justice tends to be emergency justice. This is particularly true if it comes in the early phases of the transition. The climate is then seldom well suited for a scrupulous sorting out of all the gradations in responsibility for the abuses of the past.

Survival of democratic process. A new or reinstated democracy is a frail construct. For that reason impunity or, at least, tolerance in the handling of past abuses might be a prerequisite for the survival of the democratic process. There is, first, the risk of a destabilizing backlash. Military leaders who feel threatened by projected prosecution may try to reverse the course of events by a coup or a rebellion. This problem especially haunts the young democracies of Latin America.

Creation of sub-cultures and networks hostile to democracy. A prolonged physical and social expulsion of certain sections of the population, based on criminal court decisions, may obstruct democratic consolidation by driving the supporters of the previous regime into social and political isolation. This in turn could result in the creation of sub-cultures and networks, which in the long run will become hostile to democracy.

Precludes reconciliation. Criminal prosecutions may also preclude the reconciliation required for a democracy to function. The need for closing the ranks is one of the main arguments of advocates of amnesty laws. See Uruguayan President Sanguinetti's justification of an amnesty law pardoning abuses of a previous military regime: "The 12 years of dictatorship have left scars which will need a long time to heal and it is good to begin to do so."

Administrative and managerial personnel. The viability of a young democracy depends too on its efficacy. A far-reaching purge of administrative and managerial personnel can be counterproductive as it endangers the badly needed political and economic development of the country. Prudent considerations of the problematic consequences of dismissals from civil service and high industrial jobs have been heard regularly in post-communist eastern and central Europe.

Dealing with the past is an inescapable task for new democratic regimes. Successor elites may be put off by the many delicate and explosive aspects of such assignment. But there is no way out. Choices must be made. One of Samuel Huntington's guidelines to democratizers reads:

"Recognize that on the issue of 'prosecute and punish vs. forgive and forget', each alternative presents grave problems, and that the least unsatisfactory course may well be: do not prosecute, do not punish, do not forgive, and, above all, do not forget."

4.9 Transitional Justice

A major problem is that some of the arguments in the debate on pardon versus punish are quite contradictory. Most political leaders, journalists and academics seem to agree that the crucial challenge is to strike a balance between the demands of justice and political prudence or, in other words, to reconcile ethical imperatives and political constraints. This is no easy enterprise. It entails a difficult and, on occasion, tortuous cost-benefit analysis. All costs and gains, political and moral, of pardoning and punishing must be balanced against each other.

4.9.4 Constraints

In their confrontation with the many questions and dilemmas which dealing with the past poses, political and judicial elites have limited freedom of action. Several factors restrict the number of accessible politico-legal strategies: earlier experiences with post-transitional justice; the international context at the time of the regime change; the presence or absence of organizational resources; and the state of the judiciary.

But the determining factor in how a state is able to deal with its past depends on the balance of power between the forces of the old and the new order during and shortly after the transition. There are three scenarios: (1) a clear victory of the new forces over the old order, as in a violent overthrow or the collapse of the repressive regime (e.g., Ethiopia); (2) reformers inside the forces of the past initiate democracy (e.g., Soviet Union); (3) joint action by a negotiated settlement between governing and opposition groups (e.g., South Africa).

The most important consequence of the mode of transition is the density of political constraints it generates. The widest scope for prosecutions and punishment arises in the case of an overthrow. Almost no political limits exist. Full priority can be given to the thirst for justice and retribution. A totally different situation comes up if the transition is based on reform or compromise. In that case the forces of the previous order have not lost all power and control. They are to a certain degree able to dictate the terms of the transition. The new elite have only limited options. They may be forced to grant the outgoing authorities a safe passage in return for their total or partial abdication. The need to avoid confrontation becomes the rationale for exchanging criminal prosecution and severe lustration for a policy of forgiveness.

4.9.5 Conclusion

Many of the policy suggestions mentioned above are based on the premise that post-authoritarian elites can actually make choices. However, the first lesson of the study of past examples is that the actions of such elites are a function of the circumstances of the journey to democracy. The second conclusion is that there are no miracle solutions to the question of how to deal with a repressive past. In almost all cases the passage of time has not fully exorcised the ghosts of this past. Too much forgiveness undermines respect for the law, induces the anger of those who suffered, is an impediment to an authentic reconciliation and an invitation to recidivism. That is why most analysts argue that if the balance of forces at the time of the transition makes a negotiated mildness inevitable, a truth-telling operation with full exposure of the crimes of the former regime is the least unsatisfactory solution. Memory, it is said, is the ultimate form of justice. The truth is both retribution and deterrence, and undermines the mental foundation of future human rights abuses.

REFERENCES AND FURTHER READING

Huntington, Samuel P. 1991. *The Third Wave: Democratization in the Late Twentieth Century.* Norman and London: University of Oklahoma Press.

Jongman, A.J. ed. 1996. *Contemporary Genocides: Causes, Cases, Consequences.* Leiden: PIOOM.

Kritz, Neil J. ed. 1995. *Transitional Justice. How Emerging Democracies Reckon With Former Regimes.* Volume I: General Considerations, Volume II: Country Studies, Volume III: Laws, Rulings, Reports. Washington, DC: United States Institute of Peace.

"Law and Lustration: Righting the Wrongs of the Past". 1995. Special issue of *Law and Social Inquiry,* Journal of the American Bar Foundation, vol. 20, no. 1.

"Accountability for International Crimes and Serious Violations of Fundamental Human Rights". 1996. Special issue of *Law and Contemporary Problems.* Durham, NC: Duke University Press. vol. 59, no. 4.

O'Donnell, Guillermo and Phillipe Schmitter. eds. 1986. *Transitions from Authoritarian Rule: Prospects for Democracy.* Baltimore, MD: Johns Hopkins University Press.

Michael Lund

4.10 Reckoning for Past Wrongs: Truth Commissions and War Crimes Tribunals

*As discussed in the previous section, when communities have
been victimized by the government or by another group during
a conflict, underlying feelings of resentment and the desire for
revenge cannot be alleviated unless the group is allowed to
mourn the tragedy and senses that wrongs have been
acknowledged, if not entirely vindicated. In an environment
where there is no acknowledgement of or accountability for past
violent events, tensions among former disputants persist.
Hence, confronting and reckoning with the past is vital to the
transition from conflict to democracy. This section addresses
two mechanisms to achieve this accounting: truth commissions
and war-crime tribunals.*

During protracted periods of authoritarian rule and violent
conflict, support for democratic mechanisms and the rule of law
can atrophy. It is important to rebuild confidence in democratic government and eliminate such practices as political killings
and ethnic cleansing in order to facilitate the transition to a civil
society. The transformation can also be hindered by lingering
feelings of injustice and mistrust on the part of the population
against the government and other ethnic groups. In addition,
the prospects for sustaining the peace process after a settlement

may be prejudiced if perpetrators of atrocities remain in positions of power or are seen to be continuing to act with impunity in the country or in their own communities.

Truth Commissions

4.10.1 Description

A truth commission is a body established to investigate human rights violations committed by military, government, or other armed forces under the previous regime or during a civil war. Truth commissions are not courts of law. Their primary purpose is to provide an accurate record of who was responsible for extra-judicial killings, such as assassinations and "disappearances", massacres, and grievous human rights abuses in a country's past, so that the truth can be made part of a nation's common history and the process of national reconciliation can be facilitated.

Truth commissions are not courts of law. Their primary purpose is to provide an accurate record of who was responsible for extra-judicial killings in a country's past, so that the truth can be made part of a nation's common history and the process of national reconciliation can be facilitated.

Truth commissions also address the demand for justice by victims and their families by providing a forum for victims to relate their stories as well as an official public record. By acknowledging the truth and assigning responsibility for violations to certain individuals, both the violators and the victims can come to terms with the past. Truth commissions do not focus on a specific event, but look at violations committed over a broad period of time. Truth commissions are usually established immediately after a peace settlement has been reached, since at this point the new regime is generally strong in relation to the military and other segments of society. A commission usually exists temporarily; its mandate usually ceases with the submission of a report of its findings. It is not intended as a prosecutorial body, but its findings may be used in separate judicial proceedings.

The legacy of brutal internal conflict or authoritarianism is often a lingering sense of injustice and mistrust of the government on the part of the citizens and thus a lack of confidence in new democratic mechanisms. A truth commission can enhance the process of national reconciliation by reducing the population's fear and mistrust of the government and demonstrating the new regime's commitment to democratic ideals, thus facilitating change in the public's perception of the government. Accepting responsibility for past violations displays respect for the rights of individuals and rule of law, which enhances the legitimacy of the new regime. Truth commissions can also be especially beneficial in "buying time" during the period of transition from the temporary political arrangements established by a peace process to the establishment of permanent judicial institutions.

4.10 Reckoning for Past Wrongs: Truth Commissions and War Crimes Tribunals

Box 11

EXAMPLES OF TRUTH COMMISSIONS

Truth commissions have become a widely used tool in the transition from conflict or oppression to democracy, especially in Central and South America and Africa.

— **Chile's National Commission for Truth and Reconciliation.** In 1990, at the urging of non-governmental organizations, the president of Chile established a "National Commission for Truth and Reconciliation" to investigate violations committed over the previous 17 years of military rule. This commission worked for nine months, with a staff of over 60 people, and was able to thoroughly investigate each of the 3,400 cases submitted. Most notable in the Chilean example is that, following the commission's suggestion, the government created a mechanism for the implementation of the commission's recommendations.

— **Commission on the Truth for El Salvador.** In the case of El Salvador, the creation of the "Commission on the Truth for El Salvador" was written into the peace settlement ending the 12-year civil war in that country. Given the fragile foundation of the El Salvador settlement and the highly polarized nature of the country, the truth commission did not include any Salvadorans. Instead, the UN appointed three highly respected international figures to the commission. The mandate granted the commission six months to complete its investigation and submit a report, although it was later granted a two-month extension.

— **The South African Truth and Reconciliation Commission.** In South Africa, three commissions have been created. In 1992, Nelson Mandela created a "Commission of Enquiry" to investigate treatment of prisoners at African National Congress (ANC) detention camps. This is a rare example of a political party organization establishing a commission to investigate its own abuses. The findings of this commission were criticized for being biased and Mandela named a new commission consisting of three commissioners, from South Africa, Zimbabwe and the US. In December 1995 the Government set up a two-year "Truth and Reconciliation Commission" composed of 17 members and chaired by Archbishop Desmond Tutu. The commission's task included investigation of crimes committed by both the Government and the opposition during the struggle against apartheid, as well as consideration of amnesty for perpetrators and reparations to victims.

4.10.2 Tasks and activities

Truth commissions have performed the following functions:

- Investigation of past human rights violations committed over a given period of time by the government, military or other armed forces.

- Reporting of the commission's findings to government. Such reports can publicly identify individual perpetrators of human rights violations and recommend action to be taken by the government against these individuals. They can also include recommendations covering military and police reform, judicial reform, and ways of strengthening democratic institutions. In some cases, such as in South Africa, the report can also include recommendations on how to apportion reparations among victims.

- As part of their investigations, commissions can gather information on victims, locate victims' remains for their families, and search for persons who still may be alive.

- Examination of the context under which abuses occurred and analysis of what made such events possible, in order to lessen the likelihood of their recurrence.

- Education of the public on human rights through media reports and publications of the commission's findings.

- Granting of amnesty to those perpetrators who have fully confessed their crimes. This was the case in the South African Truth and Reconciliation Commission, where an amnesty committee, staffed primarily by judges, heard applications for amnesty.

4.10.3 Strengths and limitations

Truth commissions are often the result of a negotiated compromise between parties in conflict. As a result, they can be handicapped from the beginning depending on the political climate in which they take place. For example, they may place more emphasis on truth and pardon and less on justice, thus potentially leading to disappointment in the long term. In evaluating the efficacy of a commission at a later stage, therefore, it is important to remember that at the time the commission was negotiated, parties' options may have been limited and that the mere formation of a truth commission may, in itself, have played a valuable role in the transition process.

Can maintain peace during transition. Truth commissions can play an integral part in the maintenance of the peace process during the early stages of transition from conflict to a permanent legitimate government by representing one of the first visible manifestations of the transition to the new democratic order. Truth commissions provide an impartial mechanism by which the current regime can display respect for individual rights, which helps to enhance their legitimacy. This in turn can help build confidence in democratic mechanisms.

Truth commissions are limited in implementing recommendations. The mandate of truth commissions usually prevents them from playing an active role in the implementation of their recommendations. If there is no real commitment on the part of the government to reform, many of the commissions' recommendations can go unheeded.

They are not a substitute for criminal justice. Truth commissions are separated from the formal judicial process and, though it can lead to such a process, actual prosecution of individuals responsible for abuses has been rare.

They cannot investigate the current situation. As the purpose of a truth commission is to bring a nation to terms with its past, it cannot investigate the current situation. Therefore, abuses by the new regime are often overlooked. An example of this can be seen in El Salvador, where death squads continued to operate after the peace settlement was in place. If there is no group monitoring the current regime, victims are often hesitant to testify for fear of reprisal. A truth commission does not take the place of a permanent human rights monitoring body.

4.10.4 Organization

Establishment, personnel and structures

The executive branch, parliament or international organizations such as the UN have created truth commissions. Once the commission has been created, the establishing body then appoints individuals to serve as commissioners. The number of commissioners can vary, ranging anywhere from three to 30. The commissioners should comprise well-respected individuals representing a cross-section of society, such as politicians, lawyers, judges, and human rights personnel. In some cases where the country is extremely polarized, as in El Salvador, the commissions may be made up entirely of foreign citizens.

An executive secretary or chairperson, often appointed by the establishing body, heads the commissions. Personnel should include administrative and technical support staff.

Resources needed

The main resources needed for an effective commission include: financing, appropriate information, a venue, modes of transportation, and skilled staff. In most cases, funding for the commissions has come from the government. In some instances, funding has come from international foundations, NGOs, foreign governments, or, as in El Salvador, from the United Nations.

Access to files of human rights cases from the country's courts or from human rights organizations is especially beneficial. Commissions also need the physical infrastructure necessary to conduct their investigations. This includes access to transportation in order to address complaints throughout the country as well as adequate office space, where victims and witnesses can come to give testimony. Among the staff required may be human rights specialists, social workers and forensics experts.

Links to other mechanisms

Truth commissions work quite effectively in conjunction with war crimes tribunals. A tribunal is endowed with the actual judicial and prosecutorial powers lacked by truth commissions. Yet tribunals often cannot be established until later in the peace process, after judicial reforms have taken place. Truth commission investigations can begin immediately and serve to fill in this time gap, thereby allowing time for establishment of a tribunal.

Also, as mentioned above, as truth commissions are not mandated to investigate current human rights abuses, a permanent human rights monitoring body should also be established.

DESIGNING A TRUTH COMMISSION

Truth Commission: *A body established to investigate human rights violations committed by military, government, or other armed forces under the previous regime or during a civil war. Truth commissions are not courts of law. Their primary purpose is to provide an accurate record of who was responsible for extra-judicial killings such as assassinations, "disappearances" and other human rights abuses.*

DESIGN FACTORS

Impartial and transparent. The appointment and composition of the commission must be both impartial and transparent; its members must be capable of acting independently and professionally.

Sufficient authority. The commission must be vested with sufficient authority to collect information and to maximize the impact of its recommendations. The commission established in Chad was authorized by presidential decree to collect documentation, take testimony, and confiscate material as necessary. The commission in South Africa was highly successful in its investigations due to its powers of subpoena, and search and seizure.

Flexible mandate. The commission must be given a flexible mandate to decide what types of abuses to investigate.

Realistic timeframe. The commission should have a mandate of limited duration, but one that provides a realistic timeframe or includes mechanisms for extension.

IMPLEMENTATION FACTORS

Sufficient funding and staff. The most successful commissions have had a large support staff. The "National Commission for Truth and Reconciliation" in Chile had over 60 staff members and was therefore able to investigate each case brought before it. In the Philippines, however, the commission did not have staffing levels to investigate the overwhelming volume of complaints received.

Perceived impartiality of the commissioners. The South African Government selected commissioners by committee rather than governmental appointment.

Confidential investigations. Confidential investigations can overcome witnesses' fear of granting testimony. Investigations may be conducted privately if fairness can be guaranteed and the findings are made public. In El Salvador, information was kept confidential until publication of the commission's report.

CONTEXTUAL REQUIREMENTS

Real commitment on the part of the government to respect individual rights and democratic mechanisms.

Strong civilian government in relation to the military. It is difficult for a truth commission to recommend action against members of the military, if the government cannot enforce it.

Impartial media. The existence of impartial media to broadcast commission's findings.

CHALLENGES AND PITFALLS

Threats to commission personnel and/or potential witnesses. Some commissions have reported an unwillingness by victims to testify for fear of reprisals.

Too short or too long a timeframe for the commission's operation. Most truth commissions have been granted a six- to nine-month mandate, but this short a timeframe may limit a commission attempting to investigate and document thousands of cases. Yet setting no deadline for completion of the commission's work is even more problematic. The truth commission in Uganda has been operating for nine years and has lost the confidence of much of the population.

Politicization. Commissions are often used as a political tool to enhance a regime's popularity without a true commitment to reform. The government's claimed commitment is often belied by its tendency to grant amnesty to the perpetrators of violations.

Limited mandate. A truth commission's mandate should be broad enough to allow for the investigation of all forms of abuse. If the commission's mandate is limited in scope, the full truth is not made public and the feelings of injustice and mistrust among the population remain.

Claims of denial of due process. Although truth commissions do not have prosecutorial powers, their allegations against those who have committed human rights violations are often perceived as a guilty verdict. For this reason, commissions have been criticized for denying due process to those accused. The argument over due process versus exposing the truth has arisen in debates over whether or not to identify perpetrators of abuses or victims in commission reports. To address this issue, many commissions have established processes by which those accused have the opportunity to present evidence in their defence.

War Crimes Tribunals

4.10.5 Description

A war crimes tribunal is a judicial body created to investigate and prosecute individuals accused of violations of human rights or humanitarian law in the wake of violent conflict. Such violations include crimes against humanity and other crimes outlined in the Fourth Hague Convention and the Geneva Conventions. By placing the responsibility for human rights violations on specific individuals, rather than a social or ethnic group, a war crimes tribunal can help to defuse ethnic tensions. Actual prosecution of these individuals fulfils the victims' needs for justice, which is necessary for the process of reconciliation. Finally, setting a precedent of accountability for human rights violations ends the notion of impunity and works to deter future perpetrators.

Box 12

EXAMPLES OF WAR CRIMES TRIBUNALS

A tribunal is generally an international body, although national courts can carry out similar functions. Although war crimes tribunals have not been widely used since the Nuremberg trials of Nazi officials after World War II, two prominent recent cases can serve as examples.

- **International Criminal Tribunal for the Former Yugoslavia (ICTY).** In 1993 the United Nations Security Council Resolution 827 created the International Criminal Tribunal for the Former Yugoslavia (ICTY). The ICTY was mandated to prosecute individuals allegedly responsible for violations of international humanitarian law during armed conflict in the territory of the former Yugoslavia from 1 January 1991 until a date to be determined after the restoration of peace.

- **International Criminal Tribunal for Rwanda (ICTR).** In 1994 the United Nations Security Council adopted Resolution 955, which established the International Criminal Tribunal for Rwanda (ICTR). Similar to the ICTY, the tribunal in Rwanda was tasked with prosecuting individuals responsible for genocide and crimes against humanity committed in Rwanda between 1 January, and 31 December, 1994. The ICTR also has jurisdiction for prosecuting Rwandan citizens who committed such violations in neighbouring states.

The purpose of war crimes tribunals is to restore peace and deter future violations by enforcing the norms they uphold. The key difference between a truth commission (as discussed above) and a war crimes tribunal is that a tribunal has the ability to prosecute those persons accused of human rights violations. A tribunal provides the accused with a fair trial and opportunity to defend oneself.

4.10.6 Tasks and activities

War crimes tribunals undertake the following tasks:

– Investigate, prosecute and sentence persons allegedly responsible for violations of international humanitarian law and human rights abuses.

– Provide victims the opportunity to testify in public or have their testimony recorded.

– Educate the public on humanitarian norms and human rights.

4.10.7 Strengths and limitatitions

The key difference between a truth commission and a war crimes tribunal is that a tribunal has the ability to prosecute those persons accused of human rights violations.

A war crimes tribunal holds the potential for taking strong, concrete steps toward building a society based on the rule of law through a process that is seen to be fair and law-based. The criticism of the post-World War Two Nuremberg trials – that they imposed retroactive norms and victors' justice on the accused – no longer applies. In the intervening years, the notion of individual responsibility for war crimes has become internationally accepted. Additionally, as with Rwanda and Yugoslavia, an international tribunal under the UN need not be controlled by "victors" and therefore cannot be accused of seeking revenge. The effectiveness of a war crimes tribunal is hampered, however, by four main factors.

No consensus on penalties. Although individual accountability for war crimes has become an accepted norm in the international arena, there is no corresponding consensus on the penalties to be imposed for those crimes. The international community highlighted this situation in the Rwanda case where the punishment under Rwandan national law for some crimes differs greatly from the penalties endorsed. If different judicial bodies mete out different punishments for the same crimes, it can undermine the sense of justice that the tribunal is meant to instil.

**4.10 Reckoning for Past Wrongs: Truth
Commissions and War Crimes Tribunals**

Lack of an enforcement mechanism. Tribunals have the power to issue arrest warrants for war criminals, but do not have the police authority to apprehend those who have been indicted. In this effort, tribunals are reliant upon the co-operation of the local government and of other relevant international bodies in tracking down and capturing war criminals. Yet, as seen with NATO in Yugoslavia, these bodies may resist performing this portion of their mandate because it may place peace-keepers at risk of retaliation. But lack of enforcement may severely hinder the effectiveness of tribunals, thereby eroding public confidence in their usefulness.

Cannot stop a conflict in progress. Although tribunals may begin their work before hostilities completely cease (as in Yugoslavia), they cannot themselves stop a conflict that is in progress. In fact, it is possible that the naming of particular individuals who still have the ability to carry on the conflict may harden their resistance to ending it and provide further motivation to continue the struggle. This problem can be alleviated to the extent that tribunals are established before a war arises, such as would be the case were there to be, as some have advocated, a permanent international criminal court. This kind of established tribunal could have a deterrent effect on future violations.

Scope of prosecution depends on whether the conflict is internal or international. Under the Geneva Conventions, if a conflict is internal, a perpetrator can only be prosecuted for genocide or crimes against humanity, but not for grave breaches of the Geneva Conventions on humanitarian law or other war crimes. Genocide and crimes against humanity have stricter definitions and are more difficult to prove than war crimes. The war in Yugoslavia was deemed an international conflict, therefore the ICTY has the ability to prosecute war crimes and grave breaches of the Geneva Convention, as well as genocide and crimes against humanity. As the conflict in Rwanda is an internal matter, the ICTR's jurisdiction only covers the latter. Thus, when used to adjudicate internal conflict, the jurisdiction of a tribunal is limited.

4.10.8 Organization

Establishment, personnel, and structures

The United Nations Security Council created the ICTY and the ICTR. In both cases the UN adopted a series of resolutions calling first for the establishment of a commission to investigate violations of humanitarian law and then, upon recommendation of the commission, the establishment of a tribunal to prosecute those guilty of violations. The timeframe and territory covered by each tribunal was established upon their creation.

In the case of Rwanda, the question arose as to whether to create an international or national mechanism for prosecution. An international tribunal was preferred on the basis that it would be less biased, have a wider jurisdiction, and have more resources at its disposal. However, it was argued that a national tribunal would serve to enhance the legitimacy of the new regime and would be more sensitive to the local community's needs. In Ethiopia, a war crimes court conducted proceedings regarding the acts of officials of the Dergue ruling group under the dominance of President Haile Mariam Mengistu. Currently, the ICTR is based in Tanzania, and it is working in conjunction with Rwandan national courts to prosecute war criminals, although the Tribunal has primacy over national courts.

Both tribunals have the same three-section structure. The three arms are the Judges' Chambers, the Offices of the Prosecutor, and the Registry. The judges are divided into two trial courts of three judges each and a five-judge appeals chamber. The judges are responsible for issuing indictments and hearing and deciding cases. The UN General Assembly elects the judges serving on the tribunals. The Office of the Prosecutor has the responsibility for investigating alleged crimes, framing indictments, and prosecuting cases. The chief prosecutor is appointed by the UN Security Council and is assisted by a deputy prosecutor and other staff. The Registry is the administrative division of the tribunal and performs a wide array of functions including recommending protective measures for witnesses, providing counselling for victims, and handling appointment of defence counsel. Although the ICTY and the ICTR are separate entities, they do share some of the same personnel, such as the five appellate judges and the chief prosecutor.

Resources

An international tribunal needs substantial financial, personnel and infrastructure resources.

The ICTY has sought $US 70,000,000 from the United Nations to cover operating costs for 1998. Funding for the tribunals has come primarily from the United Nations, although some funding is received from voluntary contributions. A large staff is necessary for conducting investigations and administering the tribunal. Approximately 400 people staff the ICTY. A tribunal should have access to computer and storage facilities for court records, testimony and evidence.

Another important resource is legal and investigatory expertise. In order to maintain credibility, a tribunal must conduct thorough and fair investigation and trials. To this end, evidence must be carefully gathered, documented, and preserved, and prosecution and defence attorneys must be highly competent. Many non-governmental organizations have contributed volunteers and conducted training programs for tribunal staff.

Links to other mechanisms

As discussed above, the work of war crimes tribunals is closely related to that of truth commissions. Both fulfil investigatory functions to seek the truth and hold individuals accountable for violations of human rights. War crimes tribunals can utilize information gathered by commissions, which have investigated human rights abuses. Also, as seen in the Rwanda case, international tribunals can work in conjunction with national courts by dividing the workload.

4.10.9 Conclusion

Transitional justice remains one of the most widely debated aspects of post-conflict reconciliation and democracy building. The type of transitional mechanisms discussed in this section are attracting increasing attention in many different jurisdictions. Two prominent but still uncertain cases of democratic transition – Bosnia and Indonesia – have both been accompanied by calls for the establishment of local truth and reconciliation commissions, for example. Despite the very different circumstances in which these two countries find themselves – post-war reconstruction under the auspices of the international community in Bosnia, and an uncertain transition from authoritarian rule in Indonesia – the attraction of some mechanism to address wrongs committed in the past remains strong. This illustrates the potential perceived utility of such mechanisms for delivering justice, even under very different circumstances.

The possible establishment of a permanent international criminal court to prosecute war criminals and perpetrators of genocide is another illustration of the emerging international consensus on the issue of transitional justice. Such a court would effectively supplant the temporary mechanisms used since World War Two to prosecute crimes against humanity, such as the Nuremberg and Tokyo war crimes tribunals and the ad hoc United Nations tribunals for Rwanda and the former Yugoslavia. The court may have jurisdiction over the most serious crimes of concern to the international community, such as genocide, crimes against humanity and war crimes. It would not supersede national courts but rather play a complementary role. The court would particularly play a role when national institutions are unable to act – such as where existing institutions have collapsed due to internal conflict, or where a state is unwilling to act to try its own nationals. In sum, it appears that post-conflict societies may well soon have a permanent international forum from which to seek justice.

DESIGNING A WAR CRIMES TRIBUNAL

War Crimes Tribunal: *A judicial body created to investigate and prosecute individuals accused of violations of human rights or humanitarian law in the wake of violent conflict. The purpose of a war crimes tribunal is to restore peace and deter future violations by enforcing the norms it upholds. The key difference between it and a truth commission is that a war crimes tribunal has the ability to prosecute persons accused of human rights violations.*

DESIGN FACTORS

Staff. Ample staff with appropriate expertise.

Placement. Situated in a location where it will have the most public impact on the society affected, as a visible image of justice.

IMPLEMENTATION FACTORS

Credibility. Maintenance of credibility by investigating and prosecuting all sides of a conflict equally and precluding in absentia trials.

Use of accepted rules of procedure and standards of evidence. The ICTY and the ICTR utilize the same set of rules in order to avoid questions of fairness.

Number of defendants. Reduction of the number of defendants to a manageable range by focusing prosecutorial efforts on the central core of individuals who planned and organized the systematic violations of humanitarian law, as opposed to everyone who may have committed abuses.

CONTEXTUAL REQUIREMENTS

- Co-operation from relevant international bodies in the apprehension and enforcement of indictments.
- Support of local government and its participation in the proceedings.

FACTSHEET 4 [P. 295]

CHALLENGES AND PITFALLS

Lack of evidence. It can be difficult to gather enough evidence to support convictions. In the case of senior officers it can be especially difficult to link the perpetrator with the crime. These difficulties can be enhanced when a tribunal can only prosecute crimes against humanity or genocide. Under these conditions, the tribunal must prove a systematic attempt to destroy an ethnic group.

Compliance. States are often reluctant to co-operate in the apprehension of indicted war criminals. States can actively inhibit apprehension by granting immunity to the alleged criminals. Kenya and Zaire have both harboured individuals indicted by the ICTR.

Timing. Tribunals cannot begin operation immediately, as they first must have a trained staff and infrastructure in place. These delays can lead to frustration and a lack of support on the part of the population. This can hamper a tribunal's effectiveness in achieving its goals of building confidence in democracy and the rule of law.

Security concerns. As with truth commissions, potential witnesses may fear reprisals and therefore may be deterred from testifying.

Lack of resources. Shortage of funding and/or trained personnel can erode the effectiveness of a tribunal.

4.10 Reckoning for Past Wrongs: Truth Commissions and War Crimes Tribunals

REFERENCES AND FURTHER READING

Truth Commissions

Buergenthal, Thomas. 1995. "The United Nations Truth Commission for El Salvador". In Neil J. Kritz. ed. *Transitional Justice*. Washington, DC: United States Institute of Peace Press.

Carnegie Corporation of New York. July 1997. "A House No Longer Divided: Progress and Prospects for Democratic Peace in South Africa". Report to the Carnegie Commission on Preventing Deadly Conflict.

Cassel, Jr., Douglass W. 1995. "International Truth Commissions and Justice". In Neil J. Kritz. ed. *Transitional Justice*. Washington, DC: United States Institute of Peace Press.

Cullen, Robert. August 1993. "Cleansing Ethnic Hatred", *The Atlantic*, vol. 272, no. 2.

Hayner, Priscilla B. 1995. "Fifteen Truth Commissions – 1974 to 1994: A Comparative Study". In Neil J. Kritz. ed. *Transitional Justice*. Washington, DC: United States Institute of Peace Press.

Kritz, Neil J. "War Crimes and Truth Commissions: Some Thoughts on Accountability Mechanisms for Mass Violations of Human Rights". Report for AID Conference: Promoting Democracy, Human Rights and Reintegration in Post-Conflict Societies, 30–31 October, 1997.

Montville, Joseph V. 1993 "The Healing Function in Political Conflict Resolution". In Dennis Sandole and Hugo van der Merwe. eds. *Conflict Resolution Theory and Practice*. Manchester: Manchester University Press.

Neier, Aryeh. 1995. "What should be Done About the Guilty?". In Neil J. Kritz. ed. *Transitional Justice*. Washington, DC: United States Institute of Peace Press.

Popkin, Margaret and Naomi Roht-Arriaza. 1995. "Truth as Justice: Investigating Commissions in Latin America". In Neil J. Kritz. ed. *Transitional Justice*. Washington, DC: United States Institute of Peace Press.

War Crimes Tribunals

"Rwanda: Accountability for War Crimes and Genocide". Special Report on a United States Institute of Peace Conference. 1995.

Meron, Theodor. 1993. "The Case for War Crimes Trials in Yugoslavia", *Foreign Affairs*, vol. 72.

Ndahiro, Tom. 1996. "Failing to Prevent, Failing to Punish", *Tribunal*. Institute for War and Peace Reporting.

"Fact Sheet on The International Criminal Tribunal for the Former Yugoslavia", Coalition for International Justice. 20 November, 1997.

"Fact Sheet on The International Criminal Tribunal for Rwanda". Coalition for International Justice. 25 November, 1997.

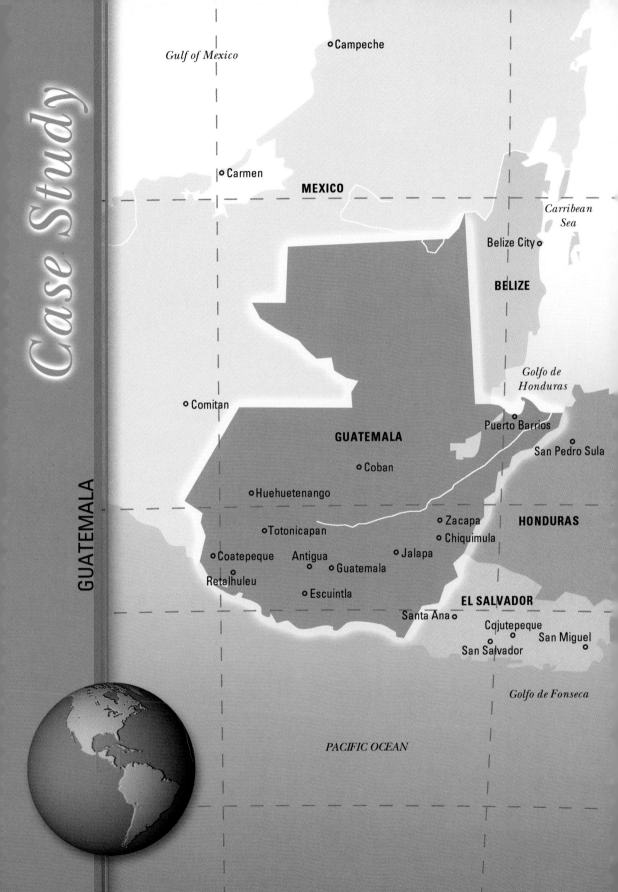

Case Study

GUATEMALA

Gulf of Mexico

Campeche

Carmen

MEXICO

Carribean Sea

Belize City

BELIZE

Golfo de Honduras

Comitan

Puerto Barrios

San Pedro Sula

GUATEMALA

Coban

Huehuetenango

Zacapa

HONDURAS

Totonicapan

Chiquimula

Coatepeque

Antigua

Jalapa

Retalhuleu

Guatemala

Escuintla

EL SALVADOR

Santa Ana

Cojutepeque

San Miguel

San Salvador

Golfo de Fonseca

PACIFIC OCEAN

© International IDEA

Michael Lund

GUATEMALA

Overview

The December 1996 signing of a final peace agreement between the Government of Guatemala and the Guatemalan National Revolutionary Unity officially ended a 36-year civil war and was the culmination of a series of 14 previous accords. The Guatemalan peace process was noteworthy in several important respects:

- the accords covered a wide range of democratization, human rights, and socio-economic issues, the resolution of which would radically change Guatemala's governing processes and social relations; but agreement on these issues preceded, rather than followed, a formal cease-fire;

- rather than the settlements leading to elections and creating a new democracy, the peace process was fostered to some extent by electoral and democratic processes that preceded the war by several years (but these processes became more vigorous and significant as they were brought into the peace process);

- the negotiations deliberately solicited and incorporated views expressed by the business community and other elements of civil society; and

- implementation of certain accords was handed over to special national commissions and forums devised and run primarily by Guatemalans, rather than to organs and representatives of the UN and the international community.

But despite the inclusiveness of the peace process and the breadth of the settlement, a significant gap still persists between the main protagonists in the negotiations and the interests of ordinary Guatemalans. Thus, if the various implementation mechanisms prove unable to overcome the influence of entrenched corporate and military interests, many of which are represented in the Congress, they will fail to alter relations between various interests, which is needed to progressively attain the accords' far-reaching goals.

The Conflict

Reacting to a history of diplomatic and military intervention in Central America by the United States and Britain on behalf of foreign commercial interests, a nationalist movement emerged in the 1940s which elected two reformist presidents who were determined to modernize Guatemala economically, expand its social services, and bring about land reform. But this "Guatemala Revolution" was thwarted in 1954 by the US Central Intelligence Agency. An invasion force was launched, providing the pretext for a *coup d'état* in the capital: a more authoritarian government was installed, which repealed agrarian reform policies and clamped down on political opposition.

Until the mid-1980s, Guatemala was ruled by military-dominated governments that were repressive and variously corrupt. They suspended democratic institutions

Guatemala

and the rule of law, banned political parties and trade unions, and engaged in illegal repression through "disappearances", extra-judicial killings, torture, and other human rights violations. The communist party organized a Marxist-Leninist resistance movement that received support from the Cuban Government and adopted the guerrilla tactics of the day. Its nucleus was former military personnel opposed to Guatemala being used as a base for the April 1961 Bay of Pigs invasion in Cuba. The first phase of the conflict ended, however, when the army essentially defeated these forces by the end of the 1960s.

The second phase began with the emergence of two new resistance organizations in the mid-1970s, operating primarily out of the indigenous areas of the country. The Government continued to ban and persecute all leftist organizations, to perpetrate torture and extra-judicial killings, and to conduct rural scorched-earth campaigns. Thus, the armed conflict constituted a struggle between, on the one hand, a rural-based insurgency and populist urban democratic opposition movement, and on the other hand, a corporate and military-controlled government. With competing Cold War ideologies also at stake, both sides had external suppliers of money and weaponry. The indigenous Indian populations were especially hard-hit by the war. *Campesinos* were recruited to fight as guerrillas or in government-led "civil patrols", and the Government in particular targeted thousands of innocent indigenous Indian communities in rural areas suspected of harbouring guerrillas. Thirty years of war left 100,000 to 150,000 civilians dead or "disappeared", over one million displaced persons and refugees, and over 400 villages completely destroyed. Overall, the Government and paramilitary forces were estimated to have been responsible for 80 per cent of the non-combatant deaths and for 50,000 disappearances, giving Guatemala the reputation as Central America's worst human rights violator.

In 1982, an alliance of guerrilla forces and leftist and populist forces formed the Guatemalan National Revolutionary Unity (URNG). By the mid-1980s, the URNG had garnered wide support in Guatemalan society, including many Catholic priests, as well as foreign sympathy; a degree of military stalemate had set in. For its part, the military saw the need by 1985 to begin to return to democracy. Multi-party democracy was formally restored, and since then elections have been regularly held.

However, participation in the elections remained low, coup attempts remained a threat, and the Government did little to address economic issues or social inequalities. Military-influenced governments continued to take advantage of a weak judicial system and corrupt police force to maintain power. Criminal violence and drug trafficking flourished.

Ultimately, the military and the main business interests supporting it realized they could not achieve economic growth through foreign investment and aid unless peace was restored. In addition, the labour unions and other opposition groups, who had reorganized themselves into the Union and Popular Action Movement

Case Study: Guatemala

(UASP) in 1988, began to advocate pragmatic social and economic reforms that could make headway in negotiations. By the early 1990s, the Guatemalan conflict had shifted to a primarily political struggle over issues of representation and public policies. Widening support for meaningful democracy was evident.

The Negotiation Process

As the Cold War drew to a close and several other Central American governments held democratic elections, two regional peace efforts also provided the impetus for specific negotiations. The Contadora group, composed of Colombia, Venezuela, and Panama and led by Mexico, came close to mediating an agreement in 1985. In 1986, Guatemalan President Cerezo convened a summit meeting of the five Central American presidents in Guatemala, where they committed themselves to negotiations to achieve peaceful settlements of the three ongoing wars, to further democratization and development, and notably, to the role of the United Nations rather than the Organization of American States as facilitator and mediator. In Guatemala, a National Commission on Reconciliation was created with Bishop Toruno of Zacapa as chair.

Toruno initiated informal consultations among representatives of different sectors of civil society: the legal political parties, business people, priests and lay church leaders, unions, and academics. The result was agreement on the need for constitutional reform, more popular participation in government, respect for human rights, and improved social welfare.

Toruno then facilitated direct negotiations between the Government and the URNG in 1991. This produced an agreement on democratization principles, international verification, an agenda and procedures for further discussion, and the role of a UN mediator, but made little progress regarding civil rights. Further talks in 1993 produced a framework agreement that then led to four accords on human rights, refugees, a truth commission and indigenous rights.

Five further accords were signed in 1996 regarding socio-economic and agrarian issues, civilian power and the military, a cease-fire, constitutional reform, and re-integration and reconciliation of former combatants. By late 1996, no less than 15 accords, including the final peace agreement in December 1996, had been negotiated over five years between the URNG and three successive governments.

Although these accords were fostered and mediated by regional leaders, domestic leaders, and particularly the UN, the progress of the peace process in Guatemala can be attributed more to the changes occurring in Guatemalan politics than to the tutelage of the UN and the international community. A confluence of pressures came from several directions: a populist-oriented armed insurgency; modernizing rightwing governments; a strengthening of civilian politicians vis-à-vis the military; the rising influence of civil society (initially the economic interests of the emerging Guatemalan business class but increasingly labour and other mass-based groups); and the influence of reformism within the military itself.

Guatemala

The Settlements

The human rights accord of March 1994 pledged the Government to end impunity for human rights violations and illegal security structures, and foresaw the creation of professional security forces, the protection of human rights workers, and the immediate establishment of MINIGUA, a UN verification body. MINIGUA's tasks were to investigate and publicize human rights violations, ensure follow-up in addressing them, and assist others in promoting protection against human rights violations and in creating a culture of respect for human rights. The resettlement accord of June 1994 called for improving local conditions and services to allow the return of uprooted people, expediting the processing of their return, and for legal changes to encourage return of land to original owners or their compensation. Another June accord created a three-member commission to document past human rights violations since the beginning of the conflict. This truth commission has the power to determine institutional responsibility for violations of human rights, but not to name names or bring cases for prosecution.

The indigenous population, composed of Mayan, Xinca, and Garifuna peoples, was not represented in any peace negotiations. But the need to address their interests was clearly recognized. Thus, the rights of the indigenous population were explicitly addressed in a sweeping agreement in 1995. This accord affirmed the Government's intention to address discrimination against the majority indigenous population, by reforming the municipal code, decentralizing the educational system, promoting media rights for indigenous peoples, and recognizing the need for communal ownership of land. All 22 linguistic groups in Guatemala were accorded official status, and the Government committed itself to support the use of their languages. But the details were left to the implementation process, through the work of the designated commissions.

A definitive cease-fire was agreed between the Government and the URNG in May 1996, along with a socio-economic accord that included agrarian issues. The accord addressed taxes, expenditures on health, housing and education; citizen participation in decision-making; a land bank, and access to land for *campesinos*. But it did not require tax reform and said little about land reform. The peace process culminated in the September 1996 accord, which required reforms in the legislative, judicial and executive branches. The role of the military was redefined, and its size reduced by a third. The existing police force would be transformed into a professional civilian body, the civil defense patrols that had fought guerrillas in the highlands were abolished, and internal security was given to a civilian intelligence agency. Subsequent accords addressed the details of the cease-fire, created an electoral commission, and reincorporated the URNG into the normal legal life of the country.

Guatemala

Case Study: Guatemala

Implementation

The accords pointed toward a major restructuring and transformation of Guatemalan society. But the accords did not themselves require structural changes; their specific meaning was left to be settled by new implementation mechanisms that were created or envisioned by the accords. These mechanisms can be divided into international and domestic mechanisms for carrying out various agreements, and the actual changes in the ways of government itself, some of which resulted from the accords and some of which occurred apart from the formal negotiations process.

MINIGUA implemented the human rights provisions of the March 1994 accord by setting up offices throughout the country to take complaints on violations and promote local capacity for human rights. This deterred violations and thus enabled the 1995 elections to proceed peacefully.

National-level institutional innovations involved representatives of domestic interests in the complex issues and responsibilities of effecting a durable peace. These included commissions on the identity and rights of indigenous peoples, judicial reform and modernization, the displaced, civil-military relations, incorporation of the URNG, etc.

One of the most unusual processes was the Assembly of Civil Society (ASC), mandated by the January 1994 accord with Bishop Toruno in the chair. For eight months in 1994, a broad array of social, labour, women's, and religious groups, along with major political parties, met and developed consensus positions on all aspects of the peace process agenda. All sectors except the business community were involved. Their recommendations were then forwarded to the UN moderator of the talks. Subsequent agreements between the Government and the URNG were then to be submitted to the ASC for ratification, thus giving them the character of national commitments. The ASC gave opposition groups an opportunity to work together in developing concrete policy proposals.

Other changes occurred completely apart from any specific accord, but were obviously spurred by it. To show good intentions toward the peace process as well as to obtain international legitimacy, the military abolished forced conscription in mid-1994 and the system of military commissioners in 1995, and it demobilized the civil defense patrols in 1996, even before the peace accord required it.

Prospects

There is little immediate likelihood of a renewed war in Guatemala, because the URNG and Government have come to control their militant flanks. But violence and intimidation continue and re-escalation remains possible. The military continues to play a role in public security, and thus behind the scenes in politics as well, in part because of increased crime, kidnappings, and drug trafficking and because the dismantling of the civil defense patrols has left a security vacuum in the coun-

Guatemala

tryside where disputes over land are arising. But the military itself has yet to be held to a significant accounting of past human right abuses because of its continued political influence and the weakness of the judiciary system. A Public Prosecutor's Office has been established and the new code on criminal procedure is in effect, but justices still have difficulty rendering decisions independently. The police force, moreover, is insufficiently staffed and continues to have links to some of the militarized groups. The truth commission has only operated since 1997, and its limited powers make it unclear whether it will strike a balance that adequately alleviates the deep grievances felt by the many victims of past offenses.

The least advanced aspect of the accords is the removal of discrimination against indigenous peoples and the transformation of rural society and local decision-making. It is being assumed that more equitable social policies and higher social spending will be possible when efficiency is gained from economic reforms, economic growth stabilizes, and state revenues increase. And yet the Congress continues to be dominated by groups that represent more established and better-off national interests, who seem committed to fighting against implementation of the accords.

The Guatemalan parties have gone to the international community to pay for over half of the $US 2.6 billion needed to implement the accords from 1997 to 2001. But it is the broad-gauged and intersecting processes that have been set in motion in Guatemala that will mainly determine whether, over the long term, the country will leave the traditional patterns of governance clearly behind. Although large business interests predominate, Guatemala's politics overall are fragmented, and the channels for the participation of hitherto excluded groups of citizens are only beginning to have influence.

In spite of its implementation problems, the Guatemalan peace process has demonstrated the value of giving detailed attention to issues of process and consultation, even though it may be argued that there has been insufficient progress on core issues such as social inequalities. Questions of how truly participative the process has been in terms of including affected groups from outside the major parties (such as indigenous communities, trade unions, etc.) have also been raised. The initial credibility and legitimacy of the democratization experiment may not last long without attention to these issues, and meaningful progress on the widespread social changes envisaged in the peace settlement.

REFERENCES AND FURTHER READING

Byrne, Hugh. December 1996. "The Guatemala Peace Accords: Assessment and Implications for the Future". Washington Office on Latin America (WOLA).

Holiday, David. February 1997. "Guatemala's Long Road to Peace", *Current History*. pp. 68–74.

Kovaleski, Serge. "Guatemala Mourns Crusading Bishop". *Washington Post*, 29 April, 1998. p. A23.

Guatemala

McCleary, Rachel. February 1996. "Guatemala: Expectations for Peace", *Current History*. pp. 88–92.

Padilla, Luis Alberto. June 1997. "Peacemaking and Conflict Transformation in Guatemala", Working Paper of the Conflict Early Warning Systems Project (CEWS), University of Southern California, Department of Political Science.

Prado, Tania Palencia and David Holiday. February 1996. *Towards a New Role for Civil Society in the Democratization of Guatemala*. Montreal, Canada: International Centre for Human Rights and Democratic Development.

Guatemala

4.11 Building an Electoral Administration

A country emerging from a conflict may need to build or restructure the processes by which it conducts elections. In this section, we identify some of the major issues that need to be considered in developing the form and structure of a country's electoral administration.

4.11.1 *The nature of the electoral process*

4.11.2 *Critical factors in election administration*

4.11.3 *Functions of an electoral administration*

4.11.4 *Location of the electoral body*

4.11.5 *Fears and concerns*

4.11.6 *Conclusion*

| Box 13 | Electoral Administration: International Trends (pp. 315–316) |

One of the central issues that a country emerging from a protracted conflict must consider is the nature and suitability of its electoral administration system. The previous electoral administration may have been damaged or destroyed or perhaps, as is more often the case, may lack credibility and legitimacy through its association with the previous government. Or it may be simply necessary to alter certain aspects of the existing administration to address particular concerns. These decisions will have significant consequences for a country's democratic development.

But before any legislative provision is made, the principles and procedures of a free and fair electoral process must be made absolutely clear. In addition, the most appropriate institution to manage this process, as well as its level of autonomy and location, must be decided. Depending on these decisions, specific provisions relating to an electoral administration should be enshrined in the appropriate legislation.

This section examines the three essential questions that need to be addressed in structuring an electoral administration system:

4.11 Building an Electoral Administration

- Who or what body should be charged with the responsibility of supervising and organizing an election?
- What form should that body take?
- Where should that body be located?

4.11.1 The nature of the electoral process

There are certain features about the electoral process, both practical and political, which must be kept in mind when considering the type and location of an electoral body:

- Elections are *national* and *local* events. They require a centralized effort that is able to extend into all areas of the country.
- Elections should be *accessible*. Administrators must understand and fulfil this objective.
- Elections are *high-pressure* events. Once an election date is set, election administration involves meeting a series of deadlines; the political penalty for missed deadlines is high, both for election administrators and for the government.
- Elections involve *high stakes*. The credibility of elections is tied to national stability, and the winning and losing of elections is tied to political party power. In many post-conflict situations, elections themselves can precipitate a return to violence.
- Elections are *expensive*. The administration of elections requires the capacity to spend money economically, efficiently and without fraud.
- Elections are *periodic* events. National elections usually take place at widely spaced intervals. At the time of elections, an enormous short-term staff is required, which then needs to be down-scaled between elections.
- Election administration is much more *publicly orientated* than many other government functions.
- Election administration is *specialized*. There is no other government function quite like preparing for elections (except perhaps preparing for war). It requires the mobilization of tens of thousands of people on an extremely precise timetable. It also requires moving a myriad of forms, supplies and equipment to thousands of locations throughout the country. Boundary demarcation, voter registration and many other technical duties of the election authorities, are

Those in charge of election administration must ensure that the organization and conduct of an election is right the first time; failure to fulfil even a simple election task or activity may not only adversely affect the quality of the services delivered, but may jeopardize public perception of the competence and impartiality of the election administrators.

also specialized tasks.

- Election administrators must be able to balance the demands of the *public at large* with the rights of *individuals*, especially the marginalized and the disadvantaged.

- Elections must exhibit an overriding concern for the greater *public good*, as opposed to the good of special interests.

- The electoral process should be *predictable*, ruled by law commonly understood and universally applied.

- Elections must ultimately be a *nation building* exercise, rather than a divisive one.

4.11.2 Critical factors in election administration

The primary objective of an electoral administration body is to deliver free and fair election services to the electorate. In doing this, it must undertake its functions in an impartial and efficient manner. It must ensure that the integrity of each election process is adequately safeguarded from incompetent election officials and fraudulent manipulators. Those in charge of the administration must ensure that the organization and conduct of an election is right the first time; failure to fulfil even a simple election task or activity may not only adversely affect the quality of the services delivered, but may jeopardize public perception of the competence and impartiality of the election administrators.

The most important attributes of any free and fair election, and of the body vested with running an election, include:

- independence and impartiality;
- efficiency;
- professionalism;
- impartial and speedy adjudication of disputes;
- stability; and
- transparency.

Independence and impartiality. The functioning of an electoral body should not be subject to the direction of any other person, authority or political party; it must function without political favour or bias. The body in charge of administering or supervising an election must be able to operate free of interference simply because any allegation of manipulation, perception of bias, or alleged interference, will have a direct impact not only on the credibility of the body in charge, but on the entire process. There are many instances in which the perceived influ-

4.11 Building an Electoral Administration

ence of a political party or parties over the electoral machinery has severely detracted from the validity of the election result. In established democracies which have a long history of relatively free and fair elections there may be, and often are, instances where allegations of abuse or bias are raised against an electoral administration; these allegations are then adjudicated upon, and do not necessarily detract from the credibility of the overall process. However, for developing and emerging democracies, there is a much greater degree of vulnerability to allegations of undue influence and bias, thereby making the entire process more susceptible to credibility judgements, which then inevitably result in a limited acceptance of election results and of the process as a whole.

Efficiency. This is an integral component of the overall credibility of the electoral process. In the face of repeated allegations and instances of incompetence, it is difficult for an electoral body to maintain its credibility. Efficiency is critical to an electoral process in that technical breakdowns and problems can, and do, lead to chaos and a breakdown of law and order. A variety of factors impact on efficiency, such as competency of staff, professionalism, resources, and most importantly, sufficient time to organize the election.

Professionalism. Elections are so important for the functioning of a democracy that a specialized group of experts, steeped in the knowledge of election procedures and the philosophy of free and fair elections, is warranted to conduct and manage the process. The advantages of having permanent, highly trained and committed experts as employees to manage and facilitate the electoral process are obvious; the benefits can be seen in countries with permanent and professional electoral administrations, such as Elections Canada and the Australian Electoral Commission, whose electoral expertise has been drawn upon by a variety of developing countries in Asia, the Pacific, Africa, Latin America and the former Soviet states. Many permanent commissions are able to organize an election on extremely short notice and on instruction from the government of the day; they are, in effect, in a permanent state of readiness.

It should be noted that even in many European countries (e.g., the Scandinavian countries and France) in which elections are organized by government ministries, there is a permanent body within that ministry which is tasked with the full-time management and conduct of elections.

Impartial and speedy adjudication. Provisions should be made for a special mechanism to process and adjudicate electoral complaints, as allegations of abuse and disputes between parties or in relation to the election management body are inevitable. Political parties, and civil society in general, are entitled to have their complaints heard in a speedy and efficient manner and by a judiciary or a body in which they have faith.

In societies in which confidence in the judiciary is low, political participants have insisted that a separate adjudicatory process be set up for electoral issues. The electoral administration's credibility will depend, in large part, on its ability to handle election-related complaints. Given the fears and suspicions that often exist during transitional periods, the electoral body should be given the resources and jurisdictional ambit to meet the expectations of the population in ensuring free and fair elections. In South Africa's first democratic elections in 1994, one of the mechanisms employed by the parties was to establish a division within the Independent Electoral Commission to monitor the entire administration and conduct of the electoral process and to ensure that it was free and fair in all its aspects.

Transparency. The overall credibility of an electoral process is substantially dependent on all relevant groups, from government and civil society, participating in the formation and functioning of the electoral structure and processes. In this respect, the value of constant consultation, communication and co-operation between the electoral administration, the political parties and the institutions of society cannot be over emphasized. In the formulation of the legislative framework of an electoral administration, this aspect should receive particular attention.

4.11.3 The functions of an electoral administration

The functions of an election administration body vary from country to country. In some countries, for example, the electoral body handles the adjudication of electoral disputes while in others they are handled by a completely separate structure. Many countries have separate "demarcation committees" that determine the boundaries of constituencies. The division of responsibilities can also vary. For example, the electoral administration body can have the overall supervisory or monitoring role for elections, while a government ministry or department can undertake the administrative functions. There are at least eight areas around which functional divisions must be established within an electoral commission:

- a *personnel division* to recruit and train officials throughout the country;

- a *financial division* to manage the budget;

- a *legal division* for drafting regulations, developing procedures and evaluating complaints;

- an *investigative division* to review complaints;

- a *logistical and administrative division* responsible for administration of the process, communications, and distribution of election materials;

- a *data processing* or *information technology* division for processing election results and statistics;

- an *information and publicity* division to develop education programmes and to disseminate decisions taken by the commission; and

- a *liaison division* with the task of interacting with government and independent agencies.

4.11.4 The location of an electoral body

Once the functions and features of an electoral body have been considered, it is then necessary to determine where that body should be situated. To put it in its simplest form, there are two competing options: inside the government, or outside the government in an electoral commission. However, there are substantial variations on these two options, based on a variety of facts and circumstances, four of which are discussed below.

Government approach. The first model is that the electoral body is located within a government ministry and is charged with the responsibility of conducting and managing elections and utilizing all the resources of that ministry and the civil service to achieve the task. This system works well in cases where the civil service is respected as being professional and politically neutral. This is used in many western European nations.

Supervisory or judicial approach. A variation on the above is that a government ministry is tasked with the conduct of the electoral process, but is supervised by an independent electoral commission consisting of selected judges (i.e., the case in Pakistan and Romania). The task of the commission is to oversee and monitor the conduct of the electoral process by the relevant government ministry.

Independent approach. The third model is that an independent electoral commission is established that is directly accountable to a minister, a parliamentary committee or to parliament. Some electoral commissions utilize government resources from provincial administrations and local authorities (e.g., India). In other cases, the commission may establish its own infrastructure at a national, regional and local level (e.g., Australia). In either case, independent electoral commissions need to have a substantial degree of financial and administrative independence from the executive government. But while they may be financially and politically independent, they remain subject to stringent financial controls determined by parliament.

The selection process for appointing electoral commissioners should be transparent and impartial. Ideally, the selection should be based on a consensus of the political parties contesting the elections and be individuals with the relevant experience and expertise and who also have a reputation for independence and integrity. The precise number of commissioners may vary from one, with a number of deputies, to any reasonable number. However, the number of commissioners should not be such as to make the operation of the commission unwieldy and cumbersome.

Multi-party approach. A fourth model is to have all registered political parties designate representatives to the national election commission. This ensures that various interests are represented on the commission and that each party can exercise some form of oversight concerning the operation of the commission. The problem associated with this is that in transitional situations, the number of parties often proliferates, thereby resulting in an unwieldy and ineffective commission. Secondly, the commission may be comprised of individuals who lack the requisite skills and/or experience to ensure effective operation of the commission.

4.11.5 Fears and concerns

In every electoral process, and particularly in countries in transition, there are often genuine fears and concerns relating to both technical or administrative areas of potential abuse or incompetence, and which reflect the critical interests of a particular party or constituency. It is essential, without compromising the integrity of the process, to address the specific interest or concern before it affects the legitimacy of the entire process. Typical fears or concerns can include:

– Concern that electoral officials are from or linked to a community rather than imposed from outside;

4.11 Building an Electoral Administration

Box 13

ELECTORAL ADMINISTRATION: INTERNATIONAL TRENDS

In established democracies, national and local government officials often handle electoral administration; while ordinary courts settle disputes, as they have a tradition of fairness and neutrality and generally enjoy the confidence of the electorate.

In emerging democracies, on the other hand, there is an increasing trend to establish an independent electoral commission. This is seen as an important step in building traditions of independence and impartiality, as well as in building the confidence of the electorate and parties in the electoral process. Most new democracies in recent years have adopted independent electoral commissions. Their positive contribution in difficult or transitional situations can be seen, for example, during the 1991 parliamentary elections in Bangladesh and the 1992 presidential election in Ghana, as well as during the first democratic elections in Namibia, South Africa and Mozambique.

Africa. The trend in Africa, particularly Southern Africa, is towards establishing independent electoral commissions, which have varying degrees of autonomy in terms of their relationship with the government of the day (e.g., South Africa, Namibia, Ghana, Malawi, Mauritius and Mozambique).

Asia. Independent electoral commissions are a long-standing feature of a number of Asian democracies, including India and Sri Lanka. Emerging Asian democracies, such as Thailand and the Philippines, have also followed the route of establishing an independent electoral commission.

Commonwealth countries. Commonwealth countries, such as Australia, Canada and India as well as a number of African Commonwealth states tend to favour the adoption of an independent electoral commission as the vehicle for the administration of their electoral processes.

Eastern Europe. Hungary, Slovenia, Romania, Poland, Czechoslovakia and Bulgaria, all established central commissions for their crucial transitional elections in 1989 and 1990. Russia can also be added to this list.

Latin America. In Latin American countries there is a long history of electoral administration which pre-dates similar reforms in Spain. As a consequence, the influence of the colonizing states on election administration practice, generally, has been limited and has led to the development of a wide variety of approaches. Furthermore, the liberalization of political systems in the last decade has led to substantial changes in the electoral system and major electoral reforms. Specific examples include Nicaragua and Costa Rica where the national electoral authorities have status as a "fourth branch" of government.

In Argentina, Brazil, Chile and Uruguay, legislation defines the
electoral authority as an independent institution, but operating
within the judiciary. In Panama, the electoral tribunal has
complete autonomy to manage its own budget once funds have
been allocated for this purpose by the executive and approved by
the legislative assembly. The budgets of most of the electoral
authorities are prepared to cover ongoing operating costs, often
related to the permanent register and for the conduct of periodic
elections. The budgetary authority generally requires the approval
of the executive. In Mexico, a permanent electoral council, the
Federal Election Institute (IFE) was established to organize the
national electoral process; a second body, the Federal Electoral
Tribunal, adjudicates electoral complaints. In addition, an
independent special prosecutor to prosecute electoral crimes
(ranging from excess campaign expenditures to intimidation or
vote buying) was also created.

Western Europe. Most West European countries locate the
electoral administration within a government ministry, usually the
Ministry of Interior; a permanent department within the ministry
is established to manage elections. In the majority of these
countries the organization and the resources of the established
political parties allow them to conduct sophisticated and detailed
monitoring exercises to ensure an impartial administration of the
election process.

The most effective model depends upon the relative maturity
of the national political system. In cases where election
administration previously was in government hands with a one-
party or other authoritarian system with no opposition, voter
confidence is only likely to be inspired if opposition party
representatives or nominees are co-opted into election
administration, or if the commission is seen to be independent
from government and political influence. The process of
appointment of commissioners is important and should be as
inclusive and participatory as possible.

Also, the adoption of a type of electoral administration that
meets international principles is not, in itself, sufficient to ensure a
free and fair process. Provisions must be made to ensure it is
credibly implemented and administered. Achieving this objective
requires that election officials are impartial and/or independent
and that the electoral contestants and the public perceive them as
such. Where impartiality is in doubt, election commissions and
review bodies comprising representatives from diverse political
interests may provide a remedy by achieving balanced composition.
Administration, a system of checks and balances, whereby the electoral commission is subject to review by independent legislative,
judicial and monitoring bodies, enhances the credibility of the
process.

4.11 Building an Electoral Administration

- That electoral officials and structures should be permanent and not transient entities that change according to varying circumstances;

- Lack of training and discipline of electoral officials in relation to electoral processes;

- Need for a speedy, efficient and impartial adjudication system in relation to electoral complaints;

- Need to keep costs to a minimum and avoid waste and fraud;

- Concern that one party may dominate the process;

- Concern that there may not be complete independence and impartiality;

- Need for co-ordination between the provincial and national elections as well as their relations with the local government elections;

- Concern that the incumbent party may abuse and manipulate government resources to its advantage.

It is important that each of these concerns is considered. In this regard, the value of constant consultation, communication and co-operation between the political parties and the institutions of society needs to be re-emphasized. Only after giving each of these concerns due consideration can a decision regarding the appropriate type and location of an electoral body be reached. If a particular fear or concern cannot be met or allayed in relation to the form, structure and location of the electoral administration, then an appropriate safeguard or checking mechanism should be installed to ensure that parties do not become disaffected and alienated from the process. Safeguards can include:

- Appointing an independent adjudicatory mechanism for complaints;

- Appointing a special "demarcations committee" accountable to parliament;

- Having an independent broadcasting authority for regulating the quality, time and access provisions for broadcast media;

- Having the department of census or a "census committee" for population counts as the basis for demarcating constituencies;

- Having particular aspects such, as finances and budget, made accountable to a parliamentary committee or body;

- The entire electoral administration can be made accountable to parliament, or to a multy-party committee, if necessary.

4.11.6 Conclusion

The crucial factors to be taken into account in any evaluation of appropriate electoral administration systems include:

– the recent history of a country, particularly in relation to the nature and extent of its recent conflict and the type of interaction between the parties;

– the relative maturity of the national political system;

– the resources of the country (financial and material);

– the potential credibility of the intended electoral body;

– the potential competence of the intended electoral body;

– the exigencies of the electoral process such as speed and flexibility;

– the danger of interference by an individual, organization or government with the electoral process;

– the necessity to ensure an equitable distribution of capability and resources in terms of election administration throughout the country, thereby eliminating the risk and perception of elections being competently run in certain areas and not in others;

– the necessity for the adoption of a long-term view in choosing an electoral administration, bearing in mind the dynamic nature of society and politics.

It is the electoral administration, or body charged with the management and conduct of the election, that sets the tone and direction of the electoral process. This is particularly true in post-conflict situations, where neutrality and fairness in democratic elections is a key to building long-lasting social peace.

It is the responsibility of election administrators to lay a sound foundation for the delivery of free and fair election services. They will be judged by the public on the basis of their efficiency and impartiality. In this regard, an electoral administration's independent or neutral status, ability to identify and appoint competent and impartial staff, and its success in delivering what the country sees as a free and fair election will ultimately be the test of its success.

A final critical factor is the issue of the cost and sustainability of the structures and procedures established. Each and every decision concerning the location and form of an electoral adminis-

4.11 Building an Electoral Administration

tration will have cost implications. Unless the structure decided on is affordable and can be maintained by the country, it will not be sustainable in the long term.

REFERENCES[1] AND FURTHER READING

Dundas, Carl W. 1993. *Organising Free and Fair Elections at Cost Effective Levels.* London: Commonwealth Secretariat.

Paper presented by Larry Garber (USAID) at the African Election Administrators Colloquim in Victoria Falls, Zimbabwe, November, 1994.

Goodwin-Gill, Guy S. 1994. *Free and Fair Elections in International Law.* Geneva: Inter-Parliamentary Union.

[1] Thanks to Pat Keefer of the National Democratic Institute (USA) and Keith Klein of the International Foundation for Election Systems (USA), on whose advice to the South African Constituent Assembly in 1995 I have drawn for this section.

4.12 National Machinery for Gender Equality

Transitions from deep-rooted conflicts offer a unique opportunity to lay the foundation of a democratic and equal society. Central to any transition process is the need to examine closely the gendered aspects of nation building and to institute concrete mechanisms to ensure that all people – women and men, girls and boys – can enjoy freedoms and participate equally in society. In this section we examine how national machinery for gender equality can be institutionalized by looking at how three countries, Uganda, Australia and South Africa, have addressed this issue. In the case study that follows we discuss the implementation of one mechanism in greater detail, South Africa's Commission for Gender Equality.

Women have played a major strategic role, both on the battle-front and in critical support areas, in a number of conflicts over the last two decades. Moreover, women have been especially vulnerable in recent warfare. They have made substantial sacrifices and borne tremendous burdens in order to advance freedom

4.12 National Machinery for Gender Equality

and democracy. Despite their important contributions, and in spite of the fact that commitments and tributes have been made regarding the attainment of an equal society, often in practice this has not occurred. A post-conflict settlement offers the opportunity to develop and implement structures in government and in society, at an early stage, to ensure that the promises made are kept, and to make sure that the issue of gender equality is not marginalized.

During the past decade, there has been an unprecedented emphasis on ensuring that transition processes include concrete and holistic mechanisms to address gender inequality as part of the nation-building process. In fact, mechanisms to address gender issues have shifted from small and often under-resourced bodies to more comprehensive and powerful machineries. The international debate on gender equality and women's emancipation has moved away from viewing equality as an issue that concerns only women, to an understanding of the implications of unequal power relations on society as a whole. Feminist activists and experts have argued that gender equality issues should not be treated as separate "women's issues", but as structural questions that confront society in general.

Feminist activists and experts have argued that gender equality issues should not be treated as separate "women's issues", but as structural questions that confront society in general.

The current debate on gender equality examines the unequal division of labour and access to and over resources, and the ways in which women and men are affected by programmes and policies that are supposed to benefit society at large. This analysis encourages an understanding that broad socio-cultural processes and socialization influence the roles that women and men play. In order to address gender-differentiated responsibilities and differentiated access to and over resources and decision-making, a comprehensive and systematic strategy is needed.

4.12.1 Constitutional mechanisms

The constitution, as the supreme law of the land, is a starting point for addressing gender equality and in setting precedents for the entire society. Many bills of rights include clauses that explicitly address gender equality. In countries like Namibia, Canada and South Africa, these clauses are seen as crucial for advancing women's rights and equality. South Africa, for example, is hailed internationally for not only institutionalizing equality for women in its constitution, but for providing a strong framework to address other forms of inequality such as discrimination on the grounds of sexual orientation. In many countries, gender-neutral language is used throughout the constitution to ensure that women are not excluded. Again South Africa's constitution goes one step further in that it specifically uses gender-sensitive language, spelling out issues and their implications.

Since constitutions are interpreted by courts, it is important that the method of constitutional and judicial review also enhances gender equality. In addition to the role of high courts in judicial review, general systems of legal administration have serious implications for women in terms of access to legal recourse and redress against administrative actions that perpetuate sexual discrimination. In South Africa, for example, the Constitutional Court, although not established for gender equality issues *per se*, is seen as an important institution for ensuring that interpretation of the law and the constitution is in keeping with principles of equality.

**Box 14 GENDER EQUALITY IN THE CONSTITUTION:
THREE EXAMPLES**

— **South Africa.** *The state may not unfairly discriminate directly or indirectly against anyone on one or more grounds, including race, gender, sex, pregnancy, marital status, ethnic or social origin, colour, sexual orientation, age, disability, religion, conscience, belief, culture, language and birth.*

Chapter 2, Bill of Rights

— **Namibia.** *No persons may be discriminated against on the grounds of sex, race, colour, ethnic origin, religion, creed or social or economic status.*

Article 10

— **Canada.** *Every individual is equal before the and under the law and has the right to the equal protection and equal benefit of the law without discrimination based on race, national or ethnic origin, colour, religion, sex, age, or mental or physical disability.*

Bill of Rights

4.12.2 Executive and administrative structures

But formal equality, as provided for in a constitution and related laws, does not guarantee substantive equality; provisions in the constitution for substantive equality must support formal equality provisions. The concept of substantive equality involves creating access to legal and constitutional remedies for inequalities that stem from particular disadvantages.

4.12 National Machinery for Gender Equality

During the 1970s and 1980s, debates on these issues emphasized the need for an overarching body that could address the concerns of women. In 1976, the United Nations launched the Decade for Women, recommending that member states ratify the Convention on the Elimination of All Forms of Discrimination Against Women (CEDAW) and implement "national machinery" for the improvement of the status of women. In response to this call, many countries established special women's ministries and programmes to promote the advancement of women. National machinery refers to a variety of structures and legal frameworks inside and outside government to build and promote gender equality in all spheres of life. These can include:

– Ministries for women's affairs/gender and development

– Departments of women's affairs

– Offices on the status of women

– Gender desks in line ministries

– Commissions for gender equality

The definition of "national machinery" is extended in many countries to include institutions that monitor human rights and related issues; in this way gender equality issues are seen also as human rights issues. In Canada, for example, the Human Rights Commission may take up gender issues. Similarly, in South Africa, the Human Rights Commission, the Constitutional Court and the Office of the Public Protector (Ombudsperson) are seen as crucial structures, amongst many others, for gender equality issues. In Namibia, the Office of the Ombudsperson is specifically briefed to include gender equality issues in its scope of investigation.

4.12.3 Ministries for women's affairs

The "traditional" ministry for women's affairs is part of the administrative bureaucracy of the state and receives its own budget. Its functions may include, among others, drafting policy on women's issues; drafting legislation for tabling in parliament; representing the interests of women in the cabinet or to the head of state; and conducting development programmes for women. Most women's ministries do not enjoy status in the cabinet. They fall under the president or prime minister's office, which means they have less autonomy and power to influence policy. In France, however, the women's ministry can veto legislation.

A major criticism of women's ministries is that they can become ghettoized "dumping grounds" for all issues that deal with gender equality and women's issues. They are allocated smaller budgets as a result of the low priority and importance assigned to them. As a result, ministers outside the women's ministry can fail to address gender equality issues in their jurisdiction. Women's ministries are often linked with other portfolios concerning children, disabled people, youth and development, as is the case in Uganda.

4.12.4 Ministry for Gender and Community Development: the case of Uganda

The Ministry for Gender and Community Development in Uganda was established in 1988, at the end of the long and horrific Ugandan civil war. Then called the Ministry for Women in Development, Youth and Culture, the ministry has existed under a variety of names. Its current name reflects the shift in thinking, especially by Ugandan women who wield influence, that a women's ministry cannot do it alone and that real attempts must be made to integrate gender issues in the work of other ministries.

In the early 1990s, the head of the Ministry for Gender and Community Development was appointed vice president of Uganda; a move seen by many as a real boost for the ministry. Currently, the ministry is strengthened by the presence of two ministers of state, one responsible for gender issues and the other for community development issues. The ministers of state are similar to deputy ministers in other countries, with the added advantage that they sit in the cabinet.

Despite many people's reservations with such ministries, Ugandan women feel that this structure, which has served them for nearly 10 years, works well for their situation. They view the ministry as a declaration of their government's commitment to address women's concerns and gender equality issues.

Nevertheless, Ugandan women are also quick to point out the problems that the ministry faces. The most significant problem is lack of funding. From the start, the ministry did not get sufficient funds allocated for its work. Uganda is a poor country and the civil war that ravaged the country has created shortfalls in many areas. The lack of funding created not only a problem for the ministry's operations but also reflected lack of national priority for these issues. Despite being headed by the vice president, the work of the ministry, in fact, is not considered a priority issue. There are also concerns about the extent to which the ministry is independent and able to challenge government policy.

In addition to the women's ministry, Uganda and other countries such as Australia and South Africa have gender desks in line ministries and other independent bodies (discussed below).

4.12.5 The Office of the Status of Women: the case of Australia and South Africa

A second mechanism, the Office of the Status of Women (OSW), evolved out of the recognition that women's machinery should be located in a central co-ordinating department and not exist as a separate marginal entity. The OSW is located in the highest decision-making offices. The major objectives of the OSW are:

– To shape government policy to ensure that gender equality issues are integrated into the overall policies and programmes of government;

– To help develop a gender policy framework for government and develop mechanisms to monitor and evaluate progress;

– To provide government with all information necessary to implement programmes for gender equality;

– To monitor government progress or lack thereof in implementing government policy, international covenants and charters;

– To develop systems for disaggregation of gender in all government information;

– To co-ordinate gender desks or women's units in line ministries.

In Australia, executive responsibility for the status of women in the federal government is located in the prime minister's office, while policy advice and administration is provided by an Office of the Status of Women, based in the Department of the Prime Minister and Cabinet and managed by a senior civil servant.

The Office on the Status of Women in South Africa, similar to its Australian counterpart, is based in the presidency, currently in the deputy president's office. It is headed by a deputy minister responsible for gender equality and youth development, but its ultimate head is the deputy president. The OSW is represented in the cabinet through submissions and presentations made by the deputy president's office.

Like its Australian counterpart, the OSW's major objective is to influence and shape government policy in order to ensure that gender equality issues are integrated into the overall policies and programmes of government. The South African OSW is also charged with developing a gender policy framework for government and developing mechanisms for monitoring and evaluating progress or lack thereof. Currently, the OSW is developing mechanisms for gender disaggregation of all government information and statistics. This is seen as a crucial mechanism for monitoring progress. Countries like Sweden, which disaggregate their information on the basis of gender, report substantial achievement in terms of making visible the impact of policy, budget, laws and programmes on the lives of women.

Similar to the women's ministry in Uganda, the OSW co-ordinates with line ministries and monitors their performance. The Australian OSW has developed important mechanisms for evaluating government progress and for ensuring effective communication and consultation. Over the years, it has pioneered the "Women's Budget Statement" which is a commentary on the implications and impact of national expenditure on the lives of women and in advancing the status of women. South Africa has its "Women's Budget Initiative", produced by the Committee on the Quality of Life and Status of Women in conjunction with the Finance Portfolio Committee in parliament and other structures like the Commission for Gender Equality.

One of the major strengths of the OSW is its location inside the government machinery rather than as a separate entity. Both the Australian and the South African models are focused on policy co-ordination with government rather than on programme delivery. This model ensures that mechanisms that address gender equality are established in all departments, rather than the OSW becoming the "dumping ground".

4.12.6 Gender desks/focal points in line ministries

In addition to women's ministries, women's departments, gender commissions and other structures, many countries have "gender desks" or "gender focal points" in line ministries. As the debate shifted towards having more comprehensive machinery for women's issues, gender focal points were recognized as an important component of the national machinery. Gender desks or "women's units" as they are called in Australia (or "cells" in India) are small offices in line ministries. They are responsible for monitoring progress on women's issues and on advising on gender policy. The advantage of gender focal points is that they are integrated into the departments and are part of the departmental machinery. They have access to discussions in line ministries and have the potential to affect policy and budgetary provisions.

The disadvantage of gender focal points is that they do not have direct access to the cabinet, and consequently are not involved in decision-making at the cabinet level. Departments themselves determine their priorities, making it difficult to prioritize gender equality issues. Similarly, it is often left to departments to determine the scope of influence and priority given to gender focal points. Often, the desks do not enjoy support staff. There is also danger of marginalizing gender focal points within line ministries or creating a departmental "dumping ground" for gender equality issues. In Uganda, women have warned emphatically against gender focal points, saying that often the officers appointed are not senior enough to wield any authority in the department.

4.12.7 National machinery in the legislature

The legislature is one of the most crucial institutions in the national machinery. While electing women to parliament is seen as one of the best mechanisms for promoting gender equality, in the past decade the debate has emphasized the need to develop strategies that seek to take women beyond numbers, to ensure that the equality agenda is entrenched in parliament. There are several options for promoting and mainstreaming the gender equality agenda into the legislative process. These include:

- Special committees or women/gender committees;
- Women's caucuses (multi-party);
- The requirement that a certain number of women representatives are present in the legislature before a bill is passed;
- Ensuring that on every parliamentary committee there is one person representing gender issues.

The major objective of these mechanisms is to ensure that any legislation passed takes into account women's experiences and equality issues. In the case of South Africa, for example, the Committee on the Quality of Life and Status of Women plays a major role in monitoring the implementation of CEDAW, the Beijing Platform of Action and the overall equality programmes. This committee, like the Australian OSW, has also initiated a women's budget initiative. Women's caucuses can also become a platform for women across the political spectrum to meet, set an agenda and lobby on women's issues.

These structures also provide viable mechanisms for women in NGOs and civil society in general to interact and work with women in parliament. However, it is often difficult to get a multi-party women's caucus established, especially in historically divided countries like South Africa. There, a Women's Parliamentary Group has taken a long time to get going but it is successful in keeping issues alive. Many of these structures can also be replicated at provincial and local government levels.

4.12.8 Successes and failures of the national machinery

From the experiences of the countries discussed above, certain features that have proven valuable in enhancing the effectiveness of national machinery for women include:

- effective independent advisory councils;
- power and authority to effect change;
- transparency and inclusivity;
- good links between national machinery and the women's movement as well as links with women at grass-roots level;
- methods in which machinery is established and implemented; in countries where the structures are a result of debates and discussions from the grass roots and constituency levels, rather than top-down structures, they appear to be more successful;
- in some cases, highly visible ministers and parliamentarians and public education mechanisms have helped boost these structures.

Among the common weaknesses include:

- the possibility of marginalization of these structures;
- lack of research and research capacity;
- gender insensitivity in the judiciary; and
- lack of funding.

4.12.9 Conclusion

All options have inherent strengths and weaknesses, and the success or failure of each is often influenced by issues beyond the power of the institutions themselves. Often, the arrival at a workable and effective option involves trial and error. There is no straight path to be walked and there are no formulas. The process involves a little bit of dancing, trying this step and that until a comfortable rhythm is found. It is also important to note that without democratic organs of civil society and women's organizations, national machinery cannot work effectively.

4.12 National Machinery for Gender Equality

There is a need for a dynamic and creative relationship between the "formal" structures of the national machinery and civil society. Whatever machinery is chosen, the over-arching principle remains the same – addressing women's issues is critical to the broader emphasis on inclusion stressed in this handbook.

We can all learn from each other's histories, successes and failures. Countries that are going through transition have the added advantage of creating something new. In creating a national machinery, imagination and political will are of fundamental importance. Without them, even the best mechanisms will fail.

REFERENCES AND FURTHER READING

Bazilli, Susan ed. 1992. *Putting Women on the Agenda*. Johannesburg: Ravan Press.

Bryce, Quentin. May 1993. "Developing Effective Government Machinery for Women: The Australian Case". Paper presented at the Conference on Ensuring Gender Equality in the New South Africa, Johannesburg.

Gasa, Nomboniso. 1995. "Strategies for Effective Intervention". Unpublished paper presented at the International Symposium for Gender Equality. Managua, Nicaragua.

Ginwala, Frene. 1992. "Women and the Elephant". In Bazilli, Susan. ed. *Putting Women on the Agenda*. Johannesburg: Ravan Press.

Karam, Azza. ed. 1998. *Women in Parliament: Beyond Numbers*. Stockholm: International IDEA.

Kazibwe, Speciosa Wandira. 1992. "A national scheme for the advancement of women in Uganda". Paper presented at the Workshop on Structural Mechanisms to Empower Women in a Democratic South Africa, University of Durban, Natal.

O'Neil, Maureen. May 1993. "Is the Canadian Experience Relevant?" Paper presented at the Conference on Ensuring Gender Equality in the New South Africa, Johannesburg.

Report of the Information and Evaluation Workshops, Commission for Gender Equality, Pretoria, June 1997.

Gender Equality Act, No 39 of 1996, Republic of South Africa.

The Constitution of the Republic of South Africa, 1996.

MECHANISMS FOR ENTRENCHING GENDER EQUALITY

National machinery must be institutionalized to ensure that gender equality issues are acknowledged, respected and implemented. Government, and society in general, must commit to gender equality at an early stage to make sure that these issues do not get marginalized. Below we list some of the mechanisms by which this can be achieved and implemented, and the advantages and disadvantages of each.

	Mechanism/ Objective	Implementation	Advantages	Disadvantages
I. Constitution and Bill of Rights	Constitutions delineate principles and reveal a country's political commitment to issues. Therefore, wherever possible, gender equality should be enshrined in constitution.	During negotiation processes, in societies emerging from conflict, during a constitutional review process, in established democracies; Negotiation process offers a tremendous opportunity to ensure that gender equality is integrated and entrenched in the building of a new nation.	Because of the prominence of the constitution and its legal standing, it is easier to influence society in which the law of the land declares a commitment to gender equality.	No disadvantages, except that constitutional provisions do not guarantee equality. Legislation and other mechanisms to ensure substantive equality must complement constitutional provisions; General agreements and statements of intent made at negotiating tables do not always translate into long-lasting commitment to equality.

	Mechanism/ Objective	Implementation	Advantages	Disadvantages
II. National Machinery in Government *Ministry for Women's Affairs*	Act as catalyst in building gender equality; Responsible for implementation of government gender policy; Represent women and gender equality issues in government; Monitor implementation of gender equality programmes by other ministers; Prepare government reports in relation to equality; Draft gender equality policies or frameworks.	Usually headed by minister or deputy minister; Allocated budget by central budgeting office; Senior political staff is usually appointed by the minister; Senior civil servants usually pulled from civil service or recruited from outside.	Access to decision-making processes and offices; Possibilities to influence government policies and programmes; Status in the cabinet (if headed by a minister); Equal status with other ministers, which minimizes possibility of being undermined.	Danger of marginalization in cabinet and in government in general; May become "dumping ground" or "ghetto" for women's issues; Since part of the government, ability to challenge government is limited; Often, if not always, underfunded with little support structure; May become isolated from women's movement; Resentment by other ministers for "interfering" with their departments; Appointment of minister by government can be inhibiting, particularly in relation to political independence.

	Mechanism/Objective	Implementation	Advantages	Disadvantages
II. National Machinery in Government *Office of the Status of Women*	Shape and influence government policy; Help develop gender framework for government; Help develop mechanisms to monitor and evaluate progress; Provide government with all relevant information necessary to implement programmes for gender equality; Co-ordinate gender equality work within government.	Can be provided for in the constitution as part of national machinery or established by act of parliament; Usually headed by a minister or deputy minister; Senior political staff appointed by minister; Senior civil servants recruited from civil service or from outside.	Located within government, often in president's or prime minister's office; Can easily integrate with work of departments as it is not a "separate" ministry; Can provide expertise for gender work in the government.	Usually has limited status in relation to the executive; May have limited influence on government policy; Its strength depends on the support of its political head (e.g., the president/prime minister); As with the ministry, fact that head is appointed by government may be inhibiting.
II. National Machinery in Government *Gender Desks*	Co-ordinate gender policy at departmental level; Part of implementing team at departmental level; Monitor progress or lack thereof.	Usually provided for in the country framework for national machinery (usually in the national strategy document).	Can be easily integrated in the department; Offers opportunity to integrate gender work in departmental programmes; Can be involved in actual implementation of gender equality policies in departments.	No direct access to cabinet; Often no support staff; Can become a departmental "dumping ground"; Officers often have little authority; Cannot work on its own.

	Mechanism/Objective	Implementation	Advantages	Disadvantages
III. Independent and Statutory Bodies *Commission for Gender Equality*	Review existing and new legislation; Investigate complaints or acts of discrimination on grounds of gender; Conduct public education on issues pertaining to gender equality; Conduct research; Monitor/review policies of public funded bodies in relation to implementation of gender equality; Recommend legislation.	Inddependent, statutory body; Accessible to the public; Open and public appointment process of members.	Platform for public debate of gender policies and education; Has significant power to effect implementation of policies and programmes by government and public institutions (e.g., universities, private companies); Independent statutory body, so not tied to government.	Needs adequate funds; Needs political support.

	Mechanism/Objective	Implementation	Advantages	Disadvantages
IV. National Machinery in the Legislature *The Committee on the Status and Quality of Life for Women*	Ensure that gender equality considerations are integrated in all legislation tabled before parliament; Monitor implementation of Beijing Platform of Action and CEDAW; To provide platform and point of influence for women's movement and NGOs.	According to parliamentary rules regulating establishment of portfolio and special committees.	Part of legislative process; Offers invaluable entry point for women's movement and other actors; Ability to influence legislation; Often can propose bill in parliament.	Often under-funded.
IV. National Machinery in the Legislature *Women's Caucuses/Groups*	Platforms for women parliamentarians to meet, share experiences and strategize on forwarding gender equality agenda in parliament; Provide space for women across party-political lines to lobby on various issues.	According to parliamentary rules.	Provide opportunities for women to interact; NGOs can lobby effectively through women's caucus.	Often difficult to establish; Some political parties do not like idea of women's caucuses; Process of arriving at working relationship is complex and exhaustive; Often women's causes do not

A MENU OF OPTIONS 5 [P. 334]

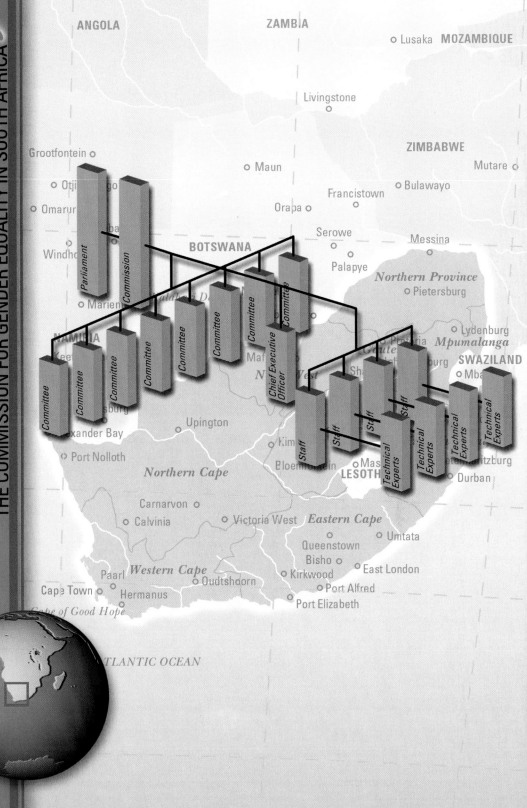

© International IDEA

Nomboniso Gasa

THE COMMISSION FOR GENDER EQUALITY IN SOUTH AFRICA

The struggle for gender equality in South Africa is a long and complex one. South African women struggled to ensure that during the transition to democracy, their experiences and their needs would be taken into account. During the negotiations for a democratic settlement in South Africa, it was apparent that both the principles of equality and non-sexism as well as the concrete mechanisms to achieve these goals must be enshrined in the constitution. The model that South Africa chose to ensure this is the product of years of vigorous debate, consultation and comparative analysis. While it draws on features from the international experiences of Australia, Canada and Uganda, the result is uniquely South African.

The South African national machinery has five main components:

– The Commission for Gender Equality;

– Structures in the legislature: special committees such as the Committee on the Quality of Life and the Status of Women, and the women's caucus;

– Structures in the administration: the Office on the Status of Women, and gender focal points in line ministries;

– Other bodies: Human Rights Commission, Office of the Public Protector and the Constitutional Court;

– Organs of civil society: e.g., NGOs and the women's movement.

In this section, we focus on the Commission for Gender Equality as one example of how national machinery for women's issues can be organized and implemented.

Objectives

The Commission for Gender Equality (CGE) is one of the six State Institutions Supporting Democracy enshrined in Section 119 of the South African Constitution. The commission's objective is to promote gender equality and work towards equal status between women and men. According to the Gender Equality Act of 1996, the CGE is an independent statutory body that should not be subject to any pressure from government or any other person.

The CGE is not an implementing body. It makes recommendations to parliament and government and monitors the effective implementation of programmes to effect equality. Specifically, it has the following powers and functions:

– To monitor and review policies and practices of all publicly funded bodies including the business sector;

– To review existing and new legislation to ensure that it promotes equality, and, where necessary, to recommend new legislation to parliament;

– To investigate complaints on any gender related issue; if need be it may refer to other structures such as the Human Rights Commission or the Constitutional Court;

The Commission for Gender Equality

- To monitor and report on compliance with international conventions such as the Convention on the Elimination of All Forms of Discrimination Against Women, or the Beijing Platform of Action and other South African documents like the South African Charter for Effective Equality;

- To conduct research or recommend that research be conducted to further the objectives of the commission;

- To investigate matters that are brought to its attention, the CGE may search any premises on which anything connected with investigation is or is suspected to be violating the constitutional provisions for gender equality; may call people or institutions to appear before it in order to pursue any investigations brought to the attention of the CGE and may hold public hearings on any issue relevant to its work.

Membership

- **Composition.** The CGE is composed of 12 members, women and men, who are broadly representative of provincial diversity in South Africa.

- **Appointment of members.** The state president, following an open and democratic nomination process, appoints the commissioners. The process of appointing members to the commission is crucial in ensuring that the body is independent and efficient. It is a public process to which a number of people and organizations contribute: the government publishes a notice in the government gazette and invites nominations; the notice is publicized in major newspapers and radio stations, including local stations; names are submitted to a multi-party ad hoc committee set up for this purpose in parliament; this committee shortlists and interviews candidates; interviews are open to the public; the final names are then put to the president after review by parliament; the president makes the final choice and appoints the commissioners and designates the chairperson. This process, although long and time-consuming, is very important in ensuring that the commission that emerges is one to which South Africans from different backgrounds can relate. It makes it easier for people to know the commissioners, to improve access to the commission, and to curb nepotism.

Structure and personnel

- **Provincial offices.** One of the critical aspects of the legacy of apartheid in South Africa is the uneven development of provinces and the marginalization of the rural provinces. The policy of the democratic government is to try and redress these imbalances. In keeping with these principles, and also understanding the critical need to be accessible to all South Africans, the CGE decided to have provincial offices. The provincial offices are headed by a commissioner and have the necessary administrative and research facilities.

- **Committees.** The CGE has a number of committees concerning matters such as legal issues, policy and research, public education, and so on. The committees are

The Commission for Gender Equality

headed by a commissioner and comprise experts and activists in the specific area.

– **Staff.** The CGE has an extensive backup staff, including researchers, legal experts and administrators. A Chief Executive Officer (CEO) heads the administrative staff.

© International IDEA

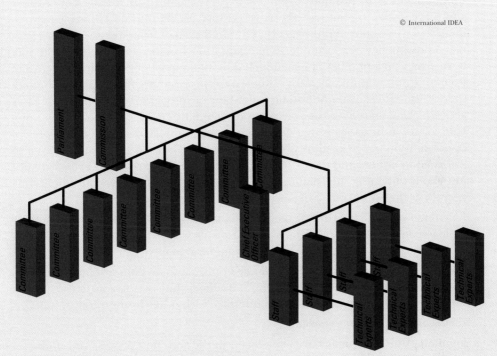

South African Commission for Gender Equality

* Handbook on National Machinery, Courtesy of the CGE

Strengths

– **Provides a forum for discussion, education and implementation.** The CGE can play a critical role in ensuring that constitutional provisions for gender equality are implemented. It provides a forum in which issues pertaining to gender equality are addressed. It is a useful instrument for educating the public about their rights and for raising national consciousness.

– **Power and authority.** The CGE has the power to effect the changes that are required. If its recommendations are ignored, or if key politicians or the private sector fail to address gender inequalities in their institutions, the CGE can

The Commission for Gender Equality

take these issues to the Constitutional Court.

– **Includes people with different expertise and experience, both experts and activists.** The strength of the CGE lies in the manner in which it approaches its work. It is comprised of people with different expertise and experience and includes a balance between experts and gender equality activists.

– **Commitment to accessibility.** Commissions of this nature are usually seen as aloof and inaccessible. In contrast, the most positive aspect of the CGE is its commitment to accessibility, and the fact that it values the contribution and experiences of its constituency. For example, in its 12-month existence, the CGE has held public hearings on a number of issues, including the impact of poverty on the lives of women. In these public hearings, women from previously marginalized communities define their own understanding of how poverty affects their lives and their access or lack thereof to the constitution's gender equality provisions. The rationale for these hearings is that gender oppression interfaces with other forms of oppression. In order to address inequalities on the basis of gender there is a critical need to understand these "other" oppressions. These public hearings are not just about obtaining information, but about bringing the issues onto the public agenda so the country can engage in discussion and debate.

– **Enabling factors.** The work of the commission is greatly facilitated by a number of factors including the provisions in the South African Constitution and the general political climate which is positive to gender equality.

– **Flexible and open mandate.** The commission's mandate does not limit the areas of investigation, research and litigation; it allows the commission to look at the variety of forms of inequality and its interface with other forms of oppression.

Limitations and resources needed

– **Funding.** Although pains have been taken in the selection process and in its creation to ensure that the CGE is independent, government nevertheless allocates its funding. There is a general agreement that funding for commissions of this nature, in the future, should be allocated in the national budget and not by individual government departments. This would help to ensure that the commissions are able to evaluate government policy and practices objectively and fairly. Funding is a crucial issue, since without funding and resources the extent to which these structures can work effectively is severely limited. It is important that the funding is seen to be without strings attached.

– **Marginalization.** Despite the powers and scope of the CGE and despite its dynamism, there is still a danger of marginalization. This danger can be eradicated depending on the work that the CGE is able to accomplish, since marginalization of gender equality is a result of lack of consciousness and/or political commitment.

The Commission for Gender Equality

**Case Study: The Commission for
Gender Equality in South Africa**

- **Resources needed.** The main resources needed by the CGE are financing, political support, information, access to key files and documents (government or otherwise), and skilled and experienced staff.

- **Political support.** Political support is important because it sends a message of how seriously the government of the day views these structures. This support and respect can help ensure that the commission has access to all key government documents.

Lessons learned

- **Accessibility and confidentiality.** Accessibility of the commission to ordinary people and the confidentiality with which issues are taken up is very important. Some of the people approaching the commission may feel the need to keep their identities secret and information confidential. It is important that this is respected.

- **Links with other mechanisms.** The CGE will be effective if it works in conjunction with other structures of the national machinery and other constitutional bodies such as the Human Rights Commission and the Truth and Reconciliation Commission. There should be an understanding that there is an overlap between its work and the work of these other bodies. This interaction is also important in ensuring that gender equality is not marginalized and that the different constitutional bodies integrate gender considerations into their work.

- **Power and authority to effect change.** Advisory and monitoring roles are important, but they work more effectively when commissions have the power to enforce the policies and constitutional provisions.

- **Adequate funding and skilled staff.** The need for adequate funds and skilled staff cannot be overemphasized. Unfortunately, the first budget for the CGE, allocated by the Department of Justice, was very low and thus made a mockery of the independence and authority of the commission. This was part of the international trend in which governments establish mechanisms for equality and then strangle them with lack of adequate finances. Running costs of structures like these are expensive, but it is important that governments invest in the national machinery as it is a crucial aspect of nation building.

- **Open and public appointment process.** It is also important that the appointment of commissioners be an open and public process. Perceived bias of the commissioners can seriously damage both the image and the work of the commission.

The South African Commission for Gender Equality is a positive landmark in that country's quest for accessible democracy and equality. It is an effective mechanism for promoting gender equality and increasing national awareness.

The Commission for Gender Equality

341

However, its success depends on a variety of factors, many of which are beyond the commission's control. Based on this understanding, South Africans opted for a "package" of mechanisms rather than one structure. Within this package the CGE is a crucial component.

Chapter 5

Sustaining the Democratic Settlement

For a peace agreement to endure, parties to the conflict must be motivated to avoid a return to bloodshed.

The overriding determinant of whether a peace agreement will endure is the extent to which the parties to the conflict continue to be motivated to avoid a return to bloodshed.

Once agreement has been reached, it must endure – and that is the focus of this chapter. First, this chapter highlights general principles that should underlie a settlement's implementation; next, it analyses the key issues which can either obstruct or advance the implementation and sustainability of a settlement; finally, it looks at the role of the international community in assisting with the settlement and its implementation process.

**Carlos Santiso,
Peter Harris and
David Bloomfield**

Sustaining the Democratic
Settlement

5.1 Introduction

I n order for a peace agreement to endure, the overriding
determinant is the extent to which the parties to the conflict continue to be motivated to avoid a return to bloodshed. If the parties are motivated to avoid this worst outcome,
the settlement is more likely to hold; if any one of them
thinks that violence will reap greater rewards than playing
the democratic game, the settlement will fail. Democracy
offers an alternative model for managing conflicts, but it is
not perfect. As discussed in Chapter 4, interim devices such
as power-sharing arrangements may be essential to keep the
conflicting parties committed to democracy during the crucial early months and years of a settlement, but it is no substitute for an ongoing commitment to democratic values in
the long term.

During the design of the settlement, the selection of
appropriate institutions or mechanisms will be essential for
that settlement to be both viable and sustainable in the long
term. This is an area that deserves focused attention: an agreement has little value if it cannot be properly implemented and
sustained. Indeed, more harm may be done to the process if
an agreement reached does not hold, than if it were never
reached in the first place. The consequent failure may result
in the breakdown of trust and the apportioning of blame
between the parties. This will jeopardize the entire process.
In Angola, the consequences of the breakdown of the Bicesse
Accords, when Jonas Savimbi refused to accept the result of
the first post-conflict election in 1992 and resumed the war in
an attempt to gain power by force, resulted in the subsequent death of approximately 300,000 people. In Rwanda in
1994, Hutu extremists rejected the Arusha peace accords; the
consequence was the genocide of an estimated 1,000,000
Rwandans. It is therefore imperative to ensure that the settlement persists and is sustained, particularly in the early transitional stage when the process is at its most vulnerable.

*If the parties are
motivated to avoid a
return to bloodshed,
the settlement is more
likely to hold; if any
one of them thinks
that violence will reap
greater rewards than
playing the
democratic game, the
settlement will fail.*

345

The purpose of this chapter is to examine the challenges and obstacles that may affect the sustainability of structures and of the broader process, once agreement has been reached and implementation of the transition phase has commenced. In some countries, even after agreement has been reached and the violent conflict ended, the manner of the implementation (or non-implementation) of the agreement has weakened the settlement. The Oslo Agreement and the Declaration of Principles signed in Washington DC in 1993 by the PLO and Israel, for example, detailed a framework for the implementation of specific phases that would address the concerns and interests of both parties. Unfortunately, that implementation, including the functioning of several key structures, has virtually ground to a halt since the election of the Likud Government in May 1996. Sustained efforts to revive the peace process continue. The validity and legitimacy of those peace agreements depended on the implementation of the parties' obligations, which is increasingly in doubt.

In certain cases, implementation may become mired in an administrative morass, be threatened by corrupt practices, or lead to an over-centralization or concentration of power. The role of properly constituted democratic institutions becomes central, not only to ensure the functioning of the government and the broader society, but also to act as a check on the power and influence of government. The liberation of Zimbabwe from white minority rule in 1980 as a result of the Lancaster House Agreement in London, for example, was hailed as the dawn of a new era. Eighteen years on, successive scandals involving corruption, nepotism and maladministration have increased the risks of possible civil conflict.

There is also a danger of too much attention being devoted to the *form* of the institutions detailed in the agreement at the expense of the *substance,* or underpinning democratic framework, that ensures these institutions work. For example, an agreement may include provisions for periodic democratic elections. However, elections themselves cannot ensure a democratic outcome. Unless other elements of competitive political process are in place to ensure a "level play-

5.1 Introduction

ing-field", the original agreement on elections may be of little consequence.

Similarly, an election that merely confirms previously existing inequalities of power and cements the status quo will not advance the democratic process. As one scholar noted of the wave of democratization in Africa:

> *the continent had over-emphasized multi-party elections ... and correspondingly neglected the basic tenets of liberal governance. [Thus,] formal compliance has been commonplace in the continent, but real changes, evidenced in the drastic and fundamental re-composition of structures, institutions, patterns and goals of politics have been very few and far between.*

The changing needs and interests of the parties also affect the sustainability of a settlement. The interests which a particular institution was originally structured to address may have altered or dissipated. For example, proportional representation may be necessary and appropriate for a first generation election in ensuring an inclusive legislature for the *transition* to democracy. But the subsequent need for democratic *consolidation* may require a greater degree of geographic representation or electoral accountability, and thus the possible adoption of a mixed or different system. The debate on the choice of a permanent electoral system in South Africa is a good example of the tension between such different needs. Similarly, several mechanisms described in this handbook, such as power-sharing arrangements, can be used temporarily at certain stages of the process and abandoned at others. Preferences and perceptions change over time, and the implementation must be responsive to this by building in an appropriate degree of flexibility.

The responsibility for ongoing assessment and support for an agreement lies firstly with the parties and the constituent sectors of society and, secondly, with the international community. A widespread belief that the international community is primarily responsible for this task has arisen from the frequent lack of internal capacity and resources of countries emerging from a deep-rooted conflict, and from the perceived impartiality of the international community. But such an abdication of domestic responsibility from the agreement is dangerous: it can lead to a disempowering of the parties, placing distance between them and the agreement, and resulting in neglect of key responsibilities. The international community can help at the initial stages, but it cannot guarantee settlements over the long term. In Haiti in 1995, for example, after the restoration of the Aristide Government to power, elections were planned as part of the normalization of society. The timing and processes leading to these elections caused concern among Haitians, with the result that when it came to the organization of the elections, a common view expressed was that if the international community was so keen on elections, then they should pay for them as well as organize them.

The ownership of and commitment to the democratic peace process by the parties involved is thus crucial in sustaining a settlement. This does not mean that international assistance should be curtailed, but merely that the country or parties involved should bear the onus, as much as their resources and capacity permit, for the implementation and sustenance of their own settlement. The international community tends to support peace settlements for a relatively limited time, quickly scaling down and ultimately ending its assistance as its priorities and interests change. Accordingly, in our examination of the task of sustaining an agreement, we will look at both the internal and external perspectives of building a sustainable settlement. Such a process should be seen as being distinct from sustaining or consolidating *democracy*, a far broader and more complex topic which this handbook, and particularly this chapter, will address only in part.

5.2 Basic Principles

New democracies are inherently fragile. Once a new system of government has been designed, agreed to and implemented, the priority is to consolidate it. Scholars assert that complete consolidation is reached when democratic structures have become so institutionalized in society that alternative types of regime have become unthinkable; in short, when democracy has become "the only game in town". In terms of *behaviour*, no significant group within society is actively attempting to create any alternative system or to secede from the established one. In terms of *attitude*, society at large has come to believe that whatever problems arise can be handled within the existing parameters of this democratic system. And *constitutionally*, the new sets of norms, laws and institutions for dealing with conflict have embedded themselves in the political structure.

But such an evolution takes time. How do we reach that point where the settlement and the consequent system become effectively self-sustaining? Part of the answer lies in protecting the structures that have been established, so that they have time to root themselves into the fabric of a new society. That protection comes initially from adherence to three guiding principles: *transparency, accountability* and *participation*. These principles are not completely new to us at this stage in the handbook; they are also important considerations during the phase of outcome design. But subsequent to a settlement, they become crucial benchmarks to evaluate the continuing health of a settlement.

One of the central aims of installing a democratic structure is to be better able to manage conflict and difference: monitoring its capacity to do so indicates clearly the chances for sustainability. This evaluation procedure is the basis for most of what follows in the next section. We look at the principles behind, and the concerns regarding, various methods of monitoring a new system's ability to handle tension and conflict. This includes not only predictable conflicts along previously existing identity-group lines, but also new, unexpected or unforeseen issues of dispute.

5.2.1 Transparency

Transparency refers to openness of the government system. The process of governing needs to be both visible and understandable to the population. As such, it will reassure them that it is trustworthy, and encourage their support and co-operation, rather than risking their alienation. This is especially important in the early stages of a new settlement. Although the democratic settlement may have been conducted and reached in secrecy, its implementation requires a change in behavior, by opening up the policy-making process and the government to public scrutiny. This change in attitudes is sometimes a major challenge for transitional governments, because it implies the acceptance of criticism and dissidence as a healthy "check and balance". Such scrutiny, however uncomfortable it may be, tends to improve the responsibility and accountability of government, and ultimately contributes to the sustainability of the consolidation process by making it more legitimate.

The degree of transparency, accountability and participation provide three crucial benchmarks to evaluate the continuing health of a settlement.

Transparency implies a two-way dialogue between the government and the governed. It provides feedback mechanisms to the government, which are essential to a government's capacity for self-reform. One of the great fears of the governed is corruption within government. Indeed, there may be good historical reasons for such suspicion. Transparency provides a defense against such assumptions. It also offers a defense against corruption itself, since open government makes corruption more difficult. Finally, transparency in government processes also increases accountability and offers safeguards against the usurping of power (see section 5.3.7 on usurpation).

5.2.2 Accountability

Accountability refers to the *answerability* of government to the law and to the people – an essential ingredient of a new democracy. As long as the government remains, in real terms, answerable to the population, a self-sustaining regulatory process is set in motion. Accountability obviously figures most clearly in elections: if the voters don't like a government's record, they can vote it out of office. But accountability works in at least two other ways as well.

First, in order to maximize accountability it is possible to put institutions in place which monitor a government's progress, and which can review, comment upon and criticize its performance. Such institutions (which will be dealt with in more detail under section 5.3.11; "Checks and Balances") need a substantial degree of independence in order to function as proper watchdogs, to truly make the government accountable and to offer, where necessary, criticisms which will be taken seriously.

Second, accountability is inherent in the separation of powers which characterizes most democratic systems. Most important in this separation is an independent judiciary, which retains both the right and the capacity not only to criticize a government but, where necessary, to place constraints upon it, block possible attempts to over-extend its sphere of influence, and to rule on the legality or otherwise of its behavior. In a democratic system, no one should be above the law, including members of the government. If the source of the rule of law is seen to be separate from the organs of government, even the notion of accountability can serve to constrain possibly retrogressive actions.

There is no shortage of examples of newly installed democracies where the government, either in the form of a president or a ruling party, gradually usurps power by enacting decrees which override elements of the constitution or parts of the new structures designed in the settlement process: Russia, Peru, Venezuela, Colombia and Argentina come immediately to mind. The simplest way of protecting against such abuse of power is to share out power beyond government. With a strongly defined judiciary and legal system, such abuses are rendered illegal, and there is a body independent of government that retains the power to call it to account for its actions.

5.2.3 Participation

When people feel a part of the system, they take a share of responsibility for it and play a role in making it work. At a basic level, the electoral process symbolizes such participation. Voting is a fundamental part of being involved in governance by having a real say in the choice of government. But participation must exist *between* elections too. The attraction of many of the power-sharing formulae, electoral system choices, national conferences and other mechanisms outlined in the previous chapter, for example, is precisely the way that they build confidence by ensuring inclusion of all significant stakeholders in the transition process.

A key agent of participation is what social scientists call civil society. Civil society refers to the conglomeration of organizations and associations which spring up in any society, independent of government and reflective of the interests of citizens. It includes advocacy groups, churches, human rights organizations, sports clubs, trade unions, NGOs, professional associations, industry interests, indeed almost any grouping that comes into existence voluntarily in autonomous form among people.

It is extremely difficult to consolidate a new democracy without a healthy civil society. Civil society operates as the intermediary between the basic units of a society – families and individuals – and the state as represented by the government. As such it can be a powerful means for people to participate in, comment upon, and if necessary criticize the government. Its great strength is its autonomy: it becomes simply what the individuals involved want it to become, and takes no direction from government. Civil society acts both as a channel for participation and to provide useful checks and balances on government action, ensuring accountability and transparency, especially in cases where political parties are weak and fail to provide an effective opposition. Ideally, the relationship between government and civil society will be mutually energizing: not only can civil society engender democratization, but in return democratic structures of government facilitate and encourage lively participation by civil society.

Political solutions are always more likely to succeed when they are owned by the people, rather than imposed upon them. The inclusion of minority groups who were excluded from the negotiation process is central for the sustainability of the agreement, in order to prevent their transformation into spoilers. For example, the December 1996 peace agreement in Guatemala was a two-party negotiation between the government and the URNG, excluding majority indigenous communities, other political parties, trade unions, and many others. These groups, if not included, could obstruct or even derail the process, particularly if (as in Guatemala) there is a perceived disjuncture between elite and popular "ownership" of the process.

The role of political parties, especially opposition parties, as censors on government action, is also a fundamental feature of democratic consolidation. Political parties are the means through which citizens aggregate their political preferences, participate in the government and voice their concerns. In a sense, they serve as the intermediary between government and civil society. The first steps taken towards democracy generally involve the end of the monopoly on power of the government party in single-party states and the legalization of political parties. There is widespread agreement amongst political scientists that broadly based, coherent political parties are among the single most important factors in promoting effective and sustainable democracy. Strong party systems, some contend, are both reflections of and indispensable prerequisites for good democratic performance.

5.3 Issues and Concerns

The implementation and sustaining of a peace settlement is fraught with difficulties and obstacles. There will always be developments, both political and social, that threaten a peace process. These may be difficult to foresee – such as, for example, the subsequent rise of nationalism from a minority group whose needs were not addressed by the settlement. In addition, the activities of "spoilers" are always hard to predict and plan for. Apart from the problems related to the building of trust and reconciliation, there may also be substantial difficulties associated with the construction and development of damaged or shattered economies and infrastructures. Depending on the objec-

5.3 Issues and Concerns

tives of the settlement, such aspects as the redistribution of assets and the transformation of government may well be beyond the resources and capacity of the parties.

There will also have been expectations raised by the settlement process itself, and by the parties in the course of mobilizing the support of their constituencies for the process. These expectations may be realistic or unrealistic, but in either case they place an onus on the parties and the process to deliver. If that does not take place, very soon trust is eroded, recriminations take place, relationships break down and the process stumbles. Particularly in transitions from dictatorships and authoritarian regimes, expectations are often unrealistically high. This results in disappointment, disaffection and loss of constituencies. In some countries, a disillusioned public has even voted leaders from previously undemocratic regimes back into power. The moderation of expectations to a realistic level, and the assessment of delivery in relation to those expectations, is an important part of identifying potential points of breakdown and conflict at this critical stage of the transition process.

To ensure that momentum is not lost, all possible steps need to be taken to remove any possibility, excuse or means for parties to attack the settlement and return to conflict. It is therefore imperative that potential difficulties which may negatively affect the process are identified and acted on at an early stage. We therefore list here some key issues and concerns that may affect the sustainability of a settlement. Some of the issues raised may appear to be relatively straightforward and simple, but it is precisely these issues which have, in practice, hindered or even derailed many nascent peace processes.

To ensure that momentum is not lost, all possible steps need to be taken to remove any possibility, excuse or means for parties to attack the settlement and return to conflict.

5.3.1 Monitoring and evaluation

All settlements require ongoing assessment to check progress and maintain focus. This can comprise keeping to agreed timeframes, ensuring that delivery meets expectations, and guarding against neglect, abuse or manipulation of the process or the institutions that comprise it. Monitoring and evaluation mechanisms should ideally be built into the settlement itself. This was the case in South Africa, where the UN monitored the implementation and maintenance of the 1991 National Peace Accord, which was aimed at ending the political violence that was tearing the country apart and threatening the entire transition. In El Salvador, monitoring of the 1991 Chapultepec Accords was built into the process through the establishment of an internal mechanism: the National Commission for the Consolidation of Peace had the task of drafting legislation on agreements and monitoring its implementation, while the United Nations was tasked with monitoring and verification of the peace agreement.

However, the key lies less in external monitoring or even enforcement, and more in maintaining the continued *internal* commitment of the parties by ensuring that the process meets realistic expectations. Optimally, the parties to the agreement, provided they have the resources and capacity, should conduct monitoring and evaluation. They should be supported in this endeavor by the relevant sectors in civil society such as business, trade unions, churches and other groupings. This in itself contributes to the process of building national consensus and the development of social compacts.

There is a major difference between short-term monitoring of key security issues and long-term monitoring of a peace settlement, and of the level of scrutiny required in each case. A particularly important element, such as the decommissioning of weapons, may require an independent evaluation exercise. One example of this was the work carried out by UN peace-keepers in Mozambique in 1994 and again, with much less success, in Angola in 1996 and 1997. One component may be so critical that its non-implementation will undermine the entire settlement. In such situations, effective monitoring and urgent remedial action is critical. Just as important is the evaluation of particular institutions or structures, such as the transformation of the armed forces, the administration of justice or the education system.

The effect of an evaluation will be greatly enhanced if it is seen to have been carried out by an impartial body. This may be a multi-party committee, preferably operating on the basis of consensus, or a body whose composition is agreed to by the key parties, or simply an independent international body such as the UN or some other intergovernmental agency with the necessary authority, independence, expertise and experience. There are also numerous watchdog organizations who have the experience and expertise to assess such specialized areas.

A related issue is the capacity to take action and make reforms in response to concerns expressed in the evaluation process. The obligation to address such concerns and take remedial action must be clear and unambiguous. At the same time, the parties, civil society and the international community need to react

5.3 Issues and Concerns

in a consistent and uniform manner if it appears that a settlement process is being manipulated or abused and is in danger of collapsing. Bearing in mind the limited ability of the international community to react on an urgent basis, it is always preferable to have clear obligations that are understood by all parties in the event of a breach or breakdown in implementation. ∎

5.3.2 *Waning commitment of actors*

The continued support of the parties for the settlement is crucial. The moment that important participants to the agreement start to criticize the settlement or distance themselves from it, the process is in jeopardy. The support of a party will generally be determined by the extent to which it feels that its interests are being met and the extent that it remains bound to the settlement.

One of the greatest risks to the implementation of a peace agreement originates from a recalcitrant party or individual who decides to manipulate or even destroy the settlement. Hun Sen's July 1997 intra-government coup against his coalition partners in Cambodia following the UN-sponsored election in 1993 is an example of how settlements can collapse from within. There are many mechanisms that can be employed to lock a party into an agreement and deal with recalcitrant groupings. They fall into three broad categories:

– The use of incentives, inducements or rewards to try to keep a spoiler in the process by addressing their problems and fears. The simple allocation of senior cabinet posts has satisfied many potential malcontents, in the past, as has the judicious distribution of privilege and status. Accommodatory behavior was applied by the UN and the US, without success, to Savimbi's UNITA in the Angolan conflict in 1992 and 1993.

– Establishing or re-affirming a binding framework to govern conduct by those involved, and designing mechanisms to deal with any breach. This can result in the legitimization or delegitimization of a party. The Khmer Rouge's exclusion from the 1993 Cambodian elections, due to its failure to decommission its weapons, was an example of this.

– The use of coercion, such as the use or threat of force, or threatened withdrawal of support for the new regime. This was used with differing degrees of success in Rwanda and Bosnia.

Other mechanisms include the use of binding agreements with consequent commitments and ongoing obligations; agreed codes of conduct from which a party cannot be seen to walk away; the application of pressure on a party from within its own constituency; and pressure from the international community, via a combination of "carrots and sticks", involving both incentives (investment, trade, credibility and status) and sanctions (political isolation, economic embargoes of strategic items such as oil, trade boycotts, and armed intervention).

However, the surest way of keeping a party in the settlement process is for that settlement to deliver: to meet interests, to satisfy concerns, and to allay fears. But it is not simply a question of the commitment of the leaders or the parties to the settlement: equally critical to success is the support of their constituencies and of the key sectors in civil society. These sectors must feel that the new regime is *their* regime, and that they have influence over it at both policy and practical levels.

5.3.3 Lack of resources and capacity

The issue of resources and capacities is one that arises at every phase of the process, from pre-negotiation to implementation. In many cases there is such a disparity of resources between the various parties that a crucial actor may be unable to participate fully, if at all. The major consideration to be borne in mind by both internal and external actors is that no party should be placed at a disadvantage in the process purely due to lack of resources.

When crafting the agreement, there needs to be a realistic assessment of resources and capacities to ensure proper implementation. This should include an evaluation of the resources and capacities of the parties themselves, and should be as detailed as possible, as inconsistencies between the political agreement reached and the financial resources available to implement it may undermine the settlement. For example, there is little point in agreeing on substantial mechanisms to address an issue like land redistribution if the incoming government lacks the finances to compensate landowners (if that was agreed), or the capacity to administer the land re-allocation.

New regimes are often in the difficult position of having to undertake dual reforms, political and economic, simultaneously. On the one hand, they may have to rebuild a shattered state and economy, which requires the mobilization of financial resources for short-term recovery, economic stabilization and reconstruction. On the other hand, they have to strengthen the state's capacity for public policy management, especially macro-economic policy, and long-term planning. If the internal skills and resources to carry out such reforms are lacking, then this needs to be acknowledged and addressed either by the country itself or by the international community.

The international community itself has a serious obligation to ensure that, in its willingness to assist, it does not allow itself to be an accomplice in the building of unrealistic expectations, or allow itself to bankroll processes that are ultimately beyond the means of the country concerned. In Nicaragua, the first election in 1990 was heavily funded by the international community, a pattern that was repeated in 1996. Now, the international community has stated that such levels of support are unsustainable and that the government of Nicaragua must investigate ways of substantially reducing costs, which places a further burden on a state that already has limited resources. In Mozambique, the cost of the first post-conflict election in 1994 was borne entirely by the international community and was so expensive that the Mozambican Government cannot hope to sustain a similar electoral process without substantial external support. While this is an area where the international community plays one of its most important roles – namely the provision of financial and material resources to sustain the settlement and transition process – it must be careful that it does not encourage the establishment of unsustainable institutions.

5.3.4 Deteriorating economy and development

Economic policy, and in particular a specific policy for economic development, is a central part of any settlement. And, as noted above, a population tends generally to harbour expectations of economic improvement under a new regime. The best and most carefully designed settlement can easily fail without a sound economic underpinning. An economy that fails to deliver either on underwriting the costs of a new dispensation or on the development and improvement of the population's circumstances will soon lead to trouble. This is, of course, very easy to say and very difficult to protect against. In particular, establishing the processes and institutions of a new administration is extremely expensive – the more so if, as is often the case, prolonged pre-settlement violence has resulted in economic and infrastructural devastation. Some vital developments may have to be delayed in a process of prioritization dictated by resources.

The deepening of economic reforms and the consolidation of democratic reforms require time. *First generation* reforms stabilize the economy and initiate its reconstruction. *Second generation* reforms then aim to reform the state and build institutions that will sustain reform and achieve development.

Additionally, if economic resources turn out to be unequally distributed between previously warring groups, this can swiftly feed into a renewed sense of grievance among the underprivileged and undermine the chances of successfully seeing the settlement through its transitional phase. Following Cambodia's 1993 elections, for example, the FUNCINPEC Finance Minister initiated major reforms to the economy, budget and processes for fiscal accountability, with considerable support from the international community. Both his own party and the opposition turned on him, however, accusing him of treason and eventually removing him from office and from party membership. Consequently public confidence plummeted, not only concerning the degree of corruption in government but also regarding the entire settlement implementation. Similarly, in Zimbabwe, Robert Mugabe's pre-election promise of a land redistribution programme – a core element of development policy – ran aground not because the land was unavailable but because the government did not find or make available the resources to buy it.

Peace building also entails strict budgetary planning, especially in fiscal policy. Tax collection is an essential element of any government's economic resources and an effective tax collection system also shows the commitment of the country to contribute financially to its own economic recovery. In Guatemala, the inability of the government to collect taxes at a sufficient level, following the December 1996 peace agreement, has given rise to problems in implementation and concerns within the international community.

The capacity to design, formulate, implement, assess and, if need be, change policies is crucial for economic policy-making and management. This requires the existence of effective parliamentary procedures to enact economic regulations; an efficient judicial system to enforce property or land rights; competent and accountable executives; the supremacy of the rule of law and the existence of an environment of legal security; public sector and public administration reform, especially in terms of human resources management; and transparency and accountability of policy-making and implementation in areas such as public procurement. Monitoring bodies are also necessary to

5.3 Issues and Concerns

measure such relevant economic issues as growth, distribution, and development. Often an economic research institute can play an informed role in monitoring and advising upon such issues.

The credibility and efficiency of state structures in turn affect the credibility and efficiency of economic policy, particularly in convincing economic agents of the coherence, stability and pre-dictability of the policies adopted and the stability of the policies implemented. Often, democratic transitions will themselves gen-erate instability and uncertainty. Here is a contradiction: while democracy is the "institutionalization of uncertainty" in the political realm, economic activity needs a certain degree of cer-tainty and predictability. Hence, basic rules and norms have to be consolidated. Moreover, political instability generated by, for example, fragile government coalitions, can weaken the ability of a government to implement coherent and consistent policies in the long term. However, the predictability of policies is rooted not so much in the stability of governments themselves, but in the consistent application of and respect for the basic norms and rules of good governance and democratic competition for power. The normative framework for democratic governance is thus a key factor in long-term economic development.

5.3.5 Implementation delays

During negotiations to design the settlement, a timetable will have been agreed for the implementation of the various ele-ments. This may involve the establishment or reform of a variety of institutions and events such as elections, parliamentary reform, new security organs, weapons hand-overs, prisoner release and so on. Implementing these core changes is vital to sustaining the momentum of the settlement. Beyond their own substantive value, the achievement of each of these changes acts to build mutual confidence and trust between previous political rivals and to institutionalize further co-operation.

Delays in this process can raise very serious problems, while also serving as warning signs of problems ahead. Some delays may be unavoidable. But others may well imply a reduction of commitment among some parties to the settlement or a reneg-ing on what was agreed. There is great value then, in regularly reviewing the progress of the timetable: How much has been ac-complished? How much of that has gone on schedule? Where are the delays developing? What or who to holding up progress, and why? Does the timetable need to be adjusted? Should there be more consultation with the population?

Despite an agreed timetable, delays in Israeli troop withdrawals rang early alarm bells for the progress of the Israeli-Palestinian peace process, including the Oslo Accord and subsequent agreements. The 1998 Northern Ireland agreement built in strict timetables and sanctions to punish delays in implementation of several of its elements, including standing mediation and arbitration mechanisms. Delays, whether for good or bad reasons, breed discontent. A monitoring and implementation team may be needed to assess progress on all the aspects of the agreement, whether formed as a cross-party group or as an international one. A formally appointed all-party agency which meets at agreed regular intervals can function to "take the pulse" of progress, to develop solutions to hold-ups, or to give transparent explanations for unavoidable delays.

5.3.6 Undermining fundamental rights and freedoms

Internationally recognized standards of human rights and fundamental freedoms should be explicitly promoted as part of a new agreement. Promotion of human rights is often the first area of focused support by the international community in the political arena. Efforts to strengthen the rule of law and respect for human rights place emphasis on the institutions that formulate and interpret law and social policy (legislatures and the courts) as well as on those which implement and enforce them (government departments, police forces and the military).

A democratic settlement to a deep-rooted conflict will normally include a mechanism for the protection and guarantee of fundamental human rights. Depending on the context, this may involve a very significant degree of change from the preceding regime. Failure to implement these changes, or continuing curtailment of some rights for some groups, can challenge the effectiveness and status of the new dispensation, threatening the very heart of the agreement.

Human rights watchdogs can be established – or sometimes brought in from outside – to address specific rights abuses. Are press freedoms being infringed? A media watchdog, independent of both government and media business interests, can assess the situation and report. Are prisoners being abused? An independent prison authority could carry out an assessment of grievances and remedies or, if resources preclude that, international NGOs such as the Red Cross or Amnesty International could assist. Official investigatory organs, commissions or tribunals can bring to light the degree of adherence to human rights standards. Training in these issues will also contribute to challenging the motivation and origins of rights-related abuses.

5.3.7 Usurpation

This term refers to a type of abuse of power. Specifically, it means that a governing group or individual comes to power on the basis of the agreed settlement but then begins to abrogate more power to itself than was identified in the constitutional basis of the agreement.

Arrangements for the distribution of political power are typically defined in a constitution. Generally, they will include one core protection against this kind of abuse: a formal separation of powers. Usurpation occurs when, subsequent to taking office, a president or ruling party subverts this delicate balance of power and claims for itself the right to, say, appoint the judiciary, declare war, suspend the constitution, or extend its permitted period in office, or begins to draw distributed power back to the centre by dismantling regional legislatures or cutting finance to such bodies.

Many examples of such behavior exist, particularly in relation to presidents who suspend constitutional processes and choose to rule by decree. Russian President Boris Yeltsin, for example, responded in 1993 to illegal acts by the Russian Parliament by suspending the constitutional court, dismantling local government structures, and so on, to effectively create what analyst Fareed Zakaria describes with some trepidation as "a Russian super-presidency". Presidents Fujimori in Peru, Lukaschenko in Belarus, Menem in Argentina, and many more have – for a variety of motives, not always completely negative ones – made similar usurpations. While not entirely dismantling the democratic structures of the state, they become, in the phrase, "democratic dictators", damaging at least the spirit and content if not the letter of the settlement. In many cases, democratic stability rests on the opposite process to usurpation: a devolution of power throughout society – to local governments, regional authorities, autonomous agencies, and so on.

Regular assessment, therefore, needs to be made of the distribution of power in the new administration. Changes need to be noted and challenged or consented to by all, particularly constitutional changes. By way of illustration, the extension of a president's term of office beyond the limit prescribed in the constitution may be a warning of things to come. A drift of power towards the centre is usually symptomatic of a weakening of the original terms of the negotiated agreement. A constitutional review process, officially installed and independently managed, may be one effective way to institutionalize the business of protecting the ground-rules of the administration. Sometimes, options are relatively limited: in Cambodia, following Hun Sen's "coup" of July 1997, the international community attempted to deal with the usurpation by isolating the government and pushing ahead with election plans, rather than attempting to redress the usurpation directly.

5.3.8 Corruption and nepotism

The holding of political power permits a wide range of nepotistic or possibly corrupt practices: partial policy decisions in return for favours, political appointments as rewards to favored individuals or groups, policy formation aimed at acquiring personal wealth or influence, and so on.

The outcome of such corrupt practices is two-fold. First, it produces a government that governs according to its own narrowly defined and partial interest at the expense of other interests in society. Second, it breeds deep popular cynicism that will inevitably obstruct the business of good government.

Mechanisms that instil public accountability and transparency can put the brakes on corrupt practices. After the South African elections, for the first time in that country, a code of conduct was introduced which set careful limits on behavior relating to the acceptance of gifts and favours, thus reducing the risk of corrupting influences. Similar codes of conduct for politicians, for appointment processes and for lobbying practices can curtail corruption, as can, in the longer term, the establishment of official regulatory mechanisms. In many countries, a parliamentary register exists where politicians must disclose any personal interests that may impinge on their ability to make impartial policy decisions. Such mechanisms do not explicitly prevent corrupt practices by politicians and public servants, but they establish boundaries beyond which behavior can be punished. It is, of course, vital not only that such regulatory processes exist, but that they are enforced in actionable ways.

The judicial system must guarantee and enforce transparency through real mechanisms of monitoring compliance and redressing violation of rights. The oversight function of the judiciary over both the executive and the legislature, and generally of the entire public administration, are important elements in democratic consolidation, especially in the fight against corruption. To

5.3 Issues and Concerns

be able to play this role, the judiciary itself must be fair and impartial, and perceived as such. Access to it must not be limited or curtailed.

5.3.9 Maladministration

While the effects of maladministration may appear similar to those of corrupt government, its cause is more likely to be inability or inexperience, unintentional rather than by design. Whatever the reason, however, incompetent governing will fundamentally undermine the settlement. Maladministration can produce paralysis in government, and can be swiftly taken advantage of by opponents of the peace process. Maladministration also makes the practice of corruption much easier due to confusion and lack of controls or regulating mechanisms.

The same political education programmes mentioned in Chapter 3 as an aid to preparing people for the negotiation process can be extended to the post-settlement situation. Since 1995, for example, the Khmer Institute of Democracy, a Cambodian NGO, has been training government officials in election processes. Additionally, interaction with counterparts from other countries, and with the international community in general, can bolster the confidence and skills of an incipient regime.

It is essential that the parties to the settlement, as well as the international community, carry out a practical and realistic needs assessment of the areas in government administration which require strengthening. Frequently, a new government may be reluctant to admit that it has limited expertise in a given area, and therefore may not ask for assistance. The consequences of this failure to acknowledge a deficiency and request assistance will ultimately have far greater effects on a government than mere embarrassment. Limitations acknowledged and acted on may be forgiven, but incompetence, delays and possible cover-ups all serve to undermine the consolidation of a new regime.

Several mechanisms exist to prevent or redress the consequences of maladministration. The system of the *Inspection Général de l'Etat* in Francophone countries provides an oversight mechanism within the public administration to address maladministration and corrupt practices. The Ombudperson system, originally developed in Sweden but now a common mechanism world-wide, provides an appeal mechanism for private citizens to redress apparent violation of their rights by the public administration.

5.3.10 Levels of safety and security

Security and justice systems are basic responsibilities of the state and are at the core of sovereignty. A predictable and reliable legal system facilitates the peaceful resolution of disputes and favours the emergence of an environment conducive to economic investment and activity. Security sector reform is also an essential dimension of peace building, via human rights training and respect for the basic principles of humanitarian law, as elaborated in international human rights instruments. Successful reform depends heavily on the existence of a justice system capable of investigating and punishing abuses and misconduct. Thus security and judicial systems are intimately linked.

Often, in the immediate post-settlement or transitional phase, the country may be emerging from a prolonged period in which violence was widespread and general perceptions of security and safety were minimal. For a community or society to rebuild its own self-confidence and develop confidence in its new regime, stability and security need to be recovered.

Part of the settlement agreement may have referred to disarmament and demobilization of opposing armed forces. The timetable for such processes is particularly important. Failure to disarm leaves the country with many weapons, which can all too quickly be turned to other purposes: crime, intimidation, and so on. Likewise, former armies or militias, if not disarmed and demobilized, may descend into banditry. Both of these developments can pose immediate threats to a new regime's ability to maintain law and order and to develop widespread respect for the rule of law.

In Haiti, when President Aristide entered office, no police force existed in any significant form, as the Ton-Ton Macoute and the police of the previous dictatorship, who had been the enforcers of law, had fled. The international community worked with the new government to select around 400 individuals for a law-and-order course in Toronto, Canada. For the first 18 months of the regime, the Haitian State was policed almost entirely by Canadian police officers, until the new Haitian personnel were ready to take control.

While careful monitoring of the timetable for action will alert one to delays or derailments in the decommissioning process, processes to deal with such problems also must be established. The establishment of the rule of law, respect for human and minority rights, civil security and inclusive democratic institutions and mechanisms help to encourage the successful return and reintegration of refugees, internally displaced populations and demobilized former combatants. Retraining and rehabilitation, downsizing and demobilizing, and legislation can all be considered effective in dealing with such forces. A disarmament commission can oversee the work, setting principles and procedures for the handing-over of weapons. Often, given the history of antagonism, only a third party will be trusted by all to fulfil the task fairly. UN peace-keepers have played such a role in several post-conflict situations: Mozambique, Angola, El Salvador, and so on. In these cases, they either accepted the hand-over of weapons directly from combatants (sometimes with cash or in-kind payments) or verified their destruction. In Northern Ireland an independent commission from Finland, Canada and the US examined the decommissioning problems, and produced a set of guidelines and principles as a basis for discussion.

On the other hand, the post-war phase may be characterized by a greatly enlarged and still extant national army of the previous administration. The potential for a disgruntled military to oust a democratic regime is well documented around the world. Civilian control of the military, and of the monopoly on the legitimate use of force, is an essential element. This closely relates to the legal status of police forces and the responsibility for maintaining internal security. The privatization of violence, in the form of organized crime (Russia) and paramilitary groups (Congo-Brazzaville, Somalia), can be immensely destabilizing. In many African countries, an unaccountable military is still a major source of political uncertainty and instability.

5.3.11 Checks and balances

In every political process, and particularly in countries in transition or emerging from a conflict, there are often genuine fears and concerns among important constituencies in the society. In general, it is these concerns that motivate positions and negotiation strategies. A party's fears may relate to a broad concern, such as the survival of a language, or to a fundamental freedom such as movement or association. These broad concerns will generally be dealt with in the substance of the main agreement and will reflect the key issues on the table.

There are, however, other smaller issues that may be of a more technical nature or relate to areas of potential administrative abuse and corruption. Where possible, these concerns should be dealt with as part of the negotiation process, and an extensive exercise should be undertaken by all of the parties involved to try to identify areas where the process could be abused or thwarted in the future. Appropriate mechanisms – "checks and balances" – need to be put in place to protect the transition process. They are usually specific in purpose and directed at a particular sector. Examples of checks and balances would include:

- Ombudsperson offices to redress violation of citizens' rights;
- Independent broadcasting authorities to address issues relating to the media;
- Judicial services commissions to address issues relating to the selection of judges;
- Civilian secretariats to control or alternatively supervise the transformation of police and defense forces;
- Joint economic policy units to oversee economic policy-making;
- Human rights commissions to address human rights concerns;
- Public protectors to address infringement by security forces;
- Amnesty provisions;
- Land commissions to address issues of allocation and redistribution of land;
- Independent electoral commissions;
- Consensus forums to manage transition processes in key sectors such as health, education, housing and economic policy.

Since credibility is crucial to success, the process by which these mechanisms are instituted is important, as is the selection of persons who will lead and staff them. If these bodies are seen as compliant mechanisms for the government, they will not address the real fears that they were intended to deal with. Any body intended to act as a "check" on the behavior of government or parties must also be invested with the necessary resources, power and authority to carry out its duties. Regulatory authorities have to be above suspicion and fully accountable.

"Check and balance" institutions may be permanent bodies, or they may have a limited life cycle applying only to a specific phase of the process. In South Africa, there was real concern that the Nationalist Government would, during the negotiation process but prior to the first democratic election, make decisions on crucial aspects such as economic policy, monetary loans and education that would endure for years. To safeguard against this, a transitional executive authority was established, as well as a number of consensus forums to manage critical areas of government until the time that a new government came into being after the April 1994 election.

There is also a need to have flexibility in the agreement in order to retain the capacity to address issues as they arise (which they inevitably will). In South Africa, it was not foreseen at the time of the national negotiations in 1993 that traditional leaders in the provinces would become a powerful lobby. As a result of sustained political and legal pressure, the Council of Traditional Leaders was established to provide them with political representation and to establish a vehicle to address their interests. A distinctive feature of the peace agreements in both South Africa and Northern Ireland was the proliferation of bargaining institutions created, which enabled issues to be separated out and dealt with in a more devolved and consensus-oriented manner than if all power remained concentrated at the centre.

In this area of checks and balances, Chapter 4 may prove useful, as it details many of the options and comparative experiences that have been utilized in different countries. While the fears and concerns may be real and present a substantial challenge, if there is focused attention devoted to finding a mechanism to address a particular fear, a start will have been made to alleviate it.

5.4 International Dimensions

This section examines the international community's approach to building sustainable democracy. It does not cover the various forms of practical on-the-ground assistance that is often rendered by the international community, but rather the context in which such assistance is deployed. First it examines the gradual emergence of a *democratic entitlement*, especially at the regional level: in various locations, regional organizations are increasingly important aid donors and thus setters of aid policies. Many of them now have overt democracy-related criteria for aid and development assistance. Then, it examines the international dimension of *democracy assistance:* the rise of overtly political aid policies and, specifically, of democratic conditionality in those policies.

5.4.1 The United Nations

The United Nations has been the single most influential democracy-promoting organization over the last 50 years. Although analysis of the role of the United Nations *per se* is beyond the scope of this handbook, several dimensions of its changing role in relation to democracy-promotion and conflict can be identified. There also exist a number of excelent recent studies and reports on the subject, such as Connie Peck's *Sustainable Peace: The Role of the United Nations and Regional Organizations in Preventing Conflict.*

The scope of the United Nations' democracy-promotion activities has expanded significantly since the late 1980s, especially in the fields of preventive diplomacy, peace-keeping and post-conflict peace building. In the June 1992 *An Agenda for Peace,* then UN Secretary-General Boutros Boutros-Ghali envisioned a comprehensive doctrine for promoting, sustaining and developing peace in the world along a policy continuum from conflict prevention to conflict resolution. This continuum includes: preventive diplomacy, peace-making, peace-keeping, and post-conflict peace building. The 1997 *Agenda for Democratization* tries to set a comprehensive approach to the promotion and consolidation of new or restored democracies.

The international and regional context dramatically affects the internal dynamics of a democratic peace process.

The UN's tools for the peaceful settlement of disputes are contained in article 33 of the UN Charter. In an effort to institutionalize conflict prevention structures, the UN Secretariat was restructured in the early 1990s and three departments were created to manage preventive diplomacy efforts: the Department of Political Affairs (DPA), including an "early warning" cell, the Department of Humanitarian Affairs (DHA), and the Department of Peacekeeping Operations. DPA was given the primary responsibility regarding conflict prevention and preventive diplomacy, and an Electoral Assistance Division was created specifically to assist in the running of transitional elections. Further reforms initiated in 1997 by Secretary-General Kofi Annan further streamlined the secretariat, consolidating the role of DPA as the focal point for dealing with post-conflict peace building, with DHA activities now handled by an emergency relief coordinator.

In terms of democracy advocacy, there exists a myriad of declarations, resolutions and conventions (detailed in section 4.6 on "Human Rights Instruments") around which member states congregate to reinforce their joint commitment to democracy and human rights. The universal membership of the United Nations, however, restricts its pro-active role in this field. Since 1988, the issue of democracy has appeared annually on the

5.4 International Dimensions

agenda of the General Assembly and generated a series of resolutions to promote democratization, and a series of international
conferences on "New and Restored Democracies" have been
held. The United Nations directly facilitated transitions to democracy in Namibia (1989), Nicaragua (1990), Cambodia
(1993), and El Salvador and Mozambique (1994) by assisting
contending forces to transform themselves into political parties,
and by supervising (and sometimes conducting) free and fair
elections. The UN has also played a substantial mediation role
in many deep-rooted conflicts around the world, such as in Afghanistan.

5.4.2 Democracy assistance and foreign aid

Since the late 1980s, the international community has introduced a normative and political dimension to its development
co-operation policy and introduced new criteria for aid and foreign policy, with *good governance* and *democracy* as core objectives.
Reform of the state, strengthening of democratic institutions
and the rule of law, respect for human rights and the creation of
an enabling environment for economic and political development have become core requirements for external development
aid, thus emphasizing the importance of the political context of
development. International security organizations, which used
to focus on traditional peace-keeping, have broadened their
areas of intervention to address conflict prevention and, particularly, post-conflict peace building. Development aid policy, too,
has broadened its scope to embrace conflict management and
peace building. Traditional conditionality – setting overt political conditions for economic assistance – has been progressively modified. These policies play out along three main
themes:

- *democracy assistance:* the promotion of democracy and democratization processes in recipient countries as a main
  objective of foreign aid;
- a *democratic requirement:* making aid conditional on a democratic political system in a recipient country, or on a commitment by the recipient country to democratic development;
- *democratic conditionality:* the reduction, suspension, or
  threat of withdrawal of foreign assistance in the event of interruptions to democratic development or reversals of democratic gains.

5.4.3 Regional perspectives

Regional frameworks for security dialogue and co-operation have been steadily evolving in recent decades. There has been increasing development of a new form of regionalism based on a shared commitment to democratization and the defense of democracy. The European Union (EU), the Organization of American States (OAS) and the Organization of African Unity (OAU), in particular, have demonstrated a renewed determination to try to deal with internal conflicts and democratic development.

These regional organizations provide a framework, as well as supporting structures and mechanisms, for strengthening democratization processes. They generate regional synergies, and provide member states with a platform to discuss common problems, craft joint solutions and take collective action. Many now include a *democratic clause* in their membership requirements: member states must abide by certain democratic norms and principles, whose breach may result in suspension of membership or punitive measures.

Most regional blocs – the EU, the OAS, the OAU, the Organization for Security and Co-operation in Europe (OSCE), and so on – have membership criteria which include various forms of commitment to, and evidence of, domestic democratic practices (see, for example, the section on Europe below). Some international organizations, in particular the United Nations, have a wealth of pro-democracy declarations, conventions, covenants and charters around which member states congregate to reinforce their joint commitment to maintaining human rights and so forth. One very powerful example is the OAS's Resolution 1080, which commits its members to communal and immediate action in the face of "any sudden or irregular interruption of the democratic political-institutional process or the legitimate exercise of power by the democratically elected government in any member state". So membership can be a very effective factor in underpinning the commitment to democratic structures, and of course joining the democratic club brings the significant and practical support of fellow-members. Furthermore, the available evidence suggests that the more a country engages in regional and international integration, the less likely it is to become embroiled in armed conflicts with another state. The following sections examine the growth of democracy-promotion policies, institutions and inducements at the regional level.

5.4 International Dimensions

Europe

Europe provides the most sophisticated web of interlinked and mutually reinforcing institutions and mechanisms for conflict prevention, management and resolution via norms of democracy. The range of such tools available to parties in conflict has significantly increased in the last decade. European regional organizations provide incentives for democratic development by requiring new members explicitly to adhere to democratic principles, including respect for human and minority rights, the rule of law and good governance.

The pro-democratic influence of such membership criteria is important both before and after a state actually joins the organization. Becoming a member is a long and complex process that requires prior agreements establishing a co-operative framework for strengthening and deepening reform. Once membership is attained, there is continued convergence towards common democratic policies in members' political systems.

European Union (EU). A western European economic organization, the EU has set stringent economic and political criteria for membership. Since the 1993 Copenhagen Summit, these include democracy, respect for human rights, supremacy of the rule of law, and observance of fundamental freedoms. The possibility of EU membership has strongly influenced the countries of eastern and central Europe to further consolidate their democratic gains and sustain momentum for political reform. In addition, the EU has been supporting democratization processes in eastern and central Europe since the early 1990s, providing "positive measures" of support to democratization.

An interesting case is Turkey, which has had a long-standing and comprehensive co-operation agreement with the EU, without so far actually meeting the threshold for membership. Arguably, the prospect of membership, and significant and sustained support from the EU, has helped Turkey to maintain the momentum of its political reform agenda and provided it with a strong incentive to democratize further.

An EU *suspension clause* was added in 1997 which provides for the suspension of some or all membership rights in the event of a violation of the Copenhagen principles. The principles are also at the core of EU foreign policy: democracy and democracy promotion has long been a central plank of its Common Foreign and Security Policy.

Council of Europe. A trans-European institution mandated to promote parliamentary democracy, the Council imposes political conditionality for membership: a member must be a democracy prior to entrance, or at least demonstrate commitment towards democratization and political reform. To qualify for admission, a country must meet tough standards in the realm of human rights, including minority rights, by ratifying the existing conventions. More importantly, the normative work of the Council of Europe (in terms of international conventions) as well as its human rights enforcement mechanisms (the European Court and Commission for Human Rights) has had a significant influence over member states, both in terms of international legal commitments and domestic law. Today, practically all the states of eastern and central Europe are full members, while the remaining countries (e.g., members of the Commonwealth of Independent States) have guest status and can still benefit from various co-operation programmes. Indeed, the transition to democracy in eastern and central Europe after the fall of the Berlin Wall has brought tremendous challenges to the Council of Europe: from 16 member states originally, its constituency has now grown to 40 (as of April 1998). Most of the new members are transitional, and hence fragile, democracies. In 1997, the Council established monitoring and verification mechanisms for assessing a state's compliance with its membership commitments and obligations.

North Atlantic Treaty Organization (NATO). A trans-Atlantic military organization, NATO has declared civilian control of the military a prerequisite for its membership. It refined its structures and mechanisms for conflict prevention and management, confidence building and reform support, by establishing the North Atlantic Co-operation Council (NACC) in 1991 and the *Partnership for Peace* in 1994. NATO membership has been a priority for eastern and central European countries' foreign policy since the break-up of the Warsaw Pact. The Madrid Summit in July 1997, which agreed in principle on the integration of four eastern and central European countries into NATO, and defined a framework for closer co-operation, has demonstrated the significant contribution that regional collective security institutions can have in the internal reform process.

Organization for Security and Co-operation in Europe (OSCE). A trans-Atlantic security organization, the OSCE has strengthened its confidence-building, conflict-prevention and fact-finding mechanisms for investigating threats to stability in

5.4 International Dimensions

Europe. While it has neither the structures nor the military capabilities for peace-enforcement and peace-keeping, it is a forum for pan-European discussion and co-operation, especially concerning human and minority rights issues, confidence building and conflict prevention. The OSCE has also facilitated negotiations in deep-rooted conflicts between Azerbaijan, Armenia and Armenian separatists in Karabakh.

Within the OSCE, the Office for Democratic Institutions and Human Rights (ODIHR) – originally known as the Office for Free Elections – is responsible for furthering human rights, democracy and the rule of law, including electoral assistance, observation and monitoring. The High Commissioner on National Minorities also plays a significant role via monitoring and fact-finding missions. The quiet, behind-the-scenes diplomacy by the High Commissioner has played a role in defusing tension and addressing the needs of minorities, particularly in eastern Europe. Other mechanisms include the European Pact on Stability in Europe of 1995, aimed at setting mechanisms for the peaceful resolution of border and minority disputes, and the Convention and Court on Conciliation and Arbitration (which entered into force in 1994), which can be a useful tool for minority conflict prevention (such as in the case of minorities in Hungary and Romania).

Latin America

Organization of American States (OAS). A pan-American security organization, the OAS has adopted a proactive stance in support of democracy. It recognizes that the solidarity of American states requires that each member be a "representative democracy" and that it needs to be proactive in its efforts to preserve democracy among its members. The fact that all OAS members in Latin America have become progressively more democratic in recent years has been a fundamental factor in its development over the last decade.

In 1991, OAS member states met in Santiago, Chile, to endorse a "Commitment to Democracy and the Renewal of the Inter-American System", which reaffirmed their "firm political commitment to the promotion and protection of human rights and representative democracy, as indispensable conditions for the stability, peace, and development of the region". This was followed by the adoption of Resolution 1080 in 1993. This enables the secretary-general of the OAS to "call for the immediate convocation of a meeting in the event of any ... sudden or irregular interruption of the democratic political and institutional process, or of the legitimate exercise of power by the democratically elected government of any of the Organization's member states".

These mechanisms have been invoked in Haiti in 1991, in Peru in 1992, in Guatemala in 1993 and in Paraguay in 1996. In Guatemala, for example, the OAS condemned the attempted "self-coup" by President Serrano, which led to the restoration of constitutional government. In Paraguay, the refusal of the army commander, General Oviedo, to step down led to a constitutional crisis. Swift reaction by the OAS, however, enabled President Wasmosy to regain control.

Resolution 1080 is clearly a valuable mechanism for bringing the regional and international community together for co-ordinated responses to threats to democracy anywhere in the hemisphere. Indeed, Oviedo himself recognized that its arrival may mean the end of the era of military coups in Latin America. A recent additional OAS Protocol allows for the suspension of a member whose democratically elected government is overthrown by force.

A *Unit for the Promotion of Democracy* was established in June 1990 to assist OAS member states in democratic institution building, and to encourage dialogue and consensus. It was mandated "to respond promptly and effectively to member states which, in full exercise of their sovereignty, request advice or assistance to preserve their political institutions and democratic procedures".

MERCOSUR. An interesting phenomenon has been the increasing political assertiveness of regional trading blocs in the defense of democracy. For instance, the decisive influence of MERCOSUR in the 1996 crisis in Paraguay deserves mention. Founded in 1991 by Argentina, Brazil, Paraguay and Uruguay to foster regional integration and trade, MERCOSUR's economic clout makes it influential in non-economic matters as well. In the run up to the May 1998 presidential elections in Paraguay, the possibility of preventive action taken by MERCOSUR members influenced that country's internal political dynamics and helped ensure that the scheduled elections were free, fair and held on time.

Africa

Organization of African Unity (OAU). Progress has been made towards enhanced African capacities for conflict prevention and peace-keeping by the OAU, a pan-African security organization.

Southern African Development Community (SADC). Sub-regional organizations have taken the lead in the promotion of democracy in the continent. In 1992, SADC endorsed democratic principles and committed its member states to democracy, respect for human rights and the supremacy of the rule of law.

Economic Commission of West African States (ECOWAS). A regional economic organization established in 1975, ECOWAS broadened its mandate in 1993 to include responsibility for preventing regional conflicts, such as in Liberia and Sierra Leone. Since 1990, it has taken an increasingly assertive role in conflict prevention and resolution: of instance, in 1997 it was designated to bring about the restoration of the constitutional government in Sierra Leone. ECOWAS subsequently authorized the intervention of a West African peace-keeping force, ECOMOG, to restore the democratically elected government to power in February 1998.

Asia-Pacific

Developments in the Asia-Pacific region have been more limited.

The **Asia-Pacific Economic Co-operation (APEC)** forum. A regional economic organization established in 1989, and the South Asian Association for Regional Co-operation, founded in 1985, provide regular platforms to broaden dialogue beyond economic matters, but have not as yet specifically addressed the issue of democracy.

The **Association of Southeast Asian Nations (ASEAN).** The most well established regional organization, ASEAN was originally created to promote economic co-operation, and has shied away from more explicit involvement in promoting democracy. However, ongoing democratization in the Philippines and Thailand, and the 1998 transition in Indonesia, ASEAN's largest and most powerful member, may signal the beginning of a more assertive role.

Other

Commonwealth of Nations. A 54-member community of countries most of which were once part of the British Empire, the Commonwealth provides its members with a useful platform for dialogue and collective action. It works to advance democracy within its member states through democracy assistance programmes. It can resort to suspension of membership for flagrant violations of democracy. In the past, the Commonwealth has adopted a proactive anti-apartheid stance and forced South Africa to withdraw its membership in 1961. It imposed sanctions on Rhodesia in 1965. In 1991, the Harare Declaration committed member states to democracy, good governance, human rights and the rule of law. A Commonwealth Ministerial Action Group (CMAG) was established in 1995 to address breaches of the declaration. In 1995, Nigeria's membership was suspended by the Commonwealth heads of government, and the CMAG engaged in discussions to re-establish democracy in Nigeria. In 1997, the Commonwealth withdrew recognition of the regime in Sierra Leone after the army overthrew the elected government. The same year, Fiji was re-admitted to the Commonwealth after passage of a new, non-racial constitution following a 10-year absence caused by the 1987 coups.

5.4.4 International assistance: democratic governance and development co-operation

The second dimension of international assistance to democracy and democratization is the increasingly strong political conditionality attached to international development co-operation policies by major bilateral and multilateral donors.

The 1990s have witnessed the expansion of *political aid*, especially democracy assistance and the promotion of participatory development and good governance. The debate within the international development community increasingly emphasizes the need to assist parties to resolve conflict and achieve sustainable peace. Although the policies of the different actors reflect sometimes diverging political agendas, there is a growing conviction that sustainable economic development goes hand-in-hand with the promotion of democracy. Support for democratic political development is seen as a fundamental value in itself, a means to achieve inclusive and participatory economic development, and a tool for conflict prevention, management and resolution.

Policy priorities of bilateral donors largely dictate the definition and channelling of international development assistance, and have a decisive impact on multilateral donors' policies and agendas. Provisions for democracy assistance have been more explicitly articulated in, and more effectively implemented by, the bilateral component of foreign aid, directly managed by the donor country's agencies and subject to its foreign policy agenda. Indeed, bilateral development agencies, which respond to a domestic constituency and divergent foreign policy agendas, have been at the forefront of the debate on political conditionality and democracy assistance. However, budgetary pressures in

5.4 International Dimensions

donor countries have both reduced and narrowed the scope of their interventions. Under tight budget scrutiny, international development assistance has to be effective, efficient and accountable. Simultaneous pressure on the aid budget and an increasing focus on democratization require that foreign aid itself be transparent, accountable and efficient. Democratic governance, by strengthening the enabling environment for optimal development co-operation, has thus become the focus of most technical co-operation.

The Development Assistance Committee of the Organization for Economic Co-operation and Development (OECD-DAC) has identified a range of approaches for working with developing country partners on participatory development and good governance, on the basis of a common commitment to broadly based economic development. Official DAC guidelines spell out the political dimension of foreign aid, in both *positive* measures (democratic conditionality) and *negative* measures (democratic sanctions). The DAC identifies four dimensions of good governance:

– the rule of law (a predictable legal environment and enforcement regime, with an objective, reliable, and independent judiciary);

– public sector reform (based on efficiency, transparency, accountability, responsiveness and accessibility of government and state institutions, especially public administration);

– improving public sector management (enhancing accounting, budgeting and civil service reform);

– controlling corruption, improving transparency and accountability of public policies and reducing excessive military expenditure.

Although the OECD-DAC draws a distinction between democracy, human rights and good governance (the latter conceived in terms of public sector performance as a sound economic management system), these different dimensions are mutually reinforcing. Sustainable development, according to the DAC, is fostered by enhancing participation, democratization, good governance, respect for human rights and prevalence of the rule of law.

Democratic Structural Stability

Aid and development can contribute vitally to conflict prevention and peace building, by promoting the emergence and progressive consolidation of *democratic structural stability*. An environment of structural stability, says the OECD-DAC, is one featuring "dynamic and representative social and political structures capable of managing and resolving disputes without resort to violence. Helping to strengthen the capacity of a society to manage tensions and disputes without violence is a vital part of development work". By providing incentives for consensus, stressing the inclusive and participatory nature of their interventions and making their financial support conditional on democratic development, development agencies can also be a catalyst for the broader inclusion of social groups in discussion and negotiation processes.

Democratic Conditionality

Many donors emphasize positive measures to support democratization and democratic governance, while maintaining some preparedness to take negative measures – up to and including suspension of aid. Political conditionality, defined as the reduction, suspension, or threat of withdrawal of assistance because of interruptions to democratic development or reversals of democratic gains, has many dimensions. Increasingly, political conditionality is conceived as a complement to economic conditionality, both being mutually reinforcing for the sustainability of economic reforms and the attainment of sound economic development. Evidence suggests that well-institutionalized democracies are more likely to produce efficient and sustainable economic and social policies, because they provide a stable, inclusive, consensual and participatory political-institutional framework.

One example of democratic conditionality was the French Government's announcement at the France-Africa Summit in 1990 that it would, in the future, tie economic aid to political development. This contributed to the downfall of President Kérékou in Benin, and to the subsequent spread of national conferences for democratic reform in most of Francophone Africa (see Case Study). Democratic transitions occurred in Mali, Niger and Madagascar and more equivocal political openings in Chad, Congo (Brazzaville)–since reversed in 1997–, Côte d'Ivoire, Cameroon and Gabon.

Aid Sanctions

The imposition or threat of sanctions can signify either a donor's opposition to a particular political regime (such as in Haiti, Kenya and Malawi), or a specific response to more negative political developments (such as in Guatemala, Zambia or Lesotho). In such circumstances, aid sanctions can induce change.

5.4 International Dimensions

Donors can "tip the balance" by working with internal opposition movements to induce a political transition (for example Kenya or Malawi), or demand specific reforms before aid is resumed (for example in Guatemala or Zambia). Aid sanctions had a significant impact in Malawi in 1992–1993 where the freezing of a $US 74 million aid package provided a clear signal that Hastings Banda's regime could not hold out indefinitely against both national and international pressure. Aid measures in Haiti were part of a broader sanctions package aimed at restoring President Aristide. In Thailand (1991–1992), Lesotho (1994), Sierra Leone (1996) and El Salvador (1990–1992), donors made a less tangible contribution, using aid or the threat of its withdrawal to influence political developments.

The power of international aid donors to induce democratic change or reverse democratic regression through aid conditionality is proportional to the dependence of the aid recipients upon them, and to the unity of the donor community. However, unco-ordinated or inconsistent conditionality policies may have disruptive effects and worsen an already fragile situation. Foreign aid can be used and abused by conflicting parties as a resource to prolong their conflict.

The "Concentration" of Foreign Aid: Democracy Assistance Programmes

While *political conditionality* by donor governments has the stated intention of exerting pressure to implement political reforms, *democracy assistance programmes* are specifically designed to support and strengthen democratic development. Despite their limitations, they may provide an effective stimulus for recipients to strengthen the underpinnings of peace building. For example, Canada has targeted its aid allocations to "favour countries which demonstrate respect for human rights" and consequently suspended, reduced or re-targeted aid to China, Haiti, Indonesia, Sri Lanka and the then Zaire (now the Democratic Republic of Congo).

Concentrating aid on a limited number of recipients committed to democratic reform is increasingly popular among bilateral donors. As budget stringency constrains donors' overseas development assistance (ODA) expenditure, most agencies are focusing it more sharply on countries most in need and demanding a commitment to sustainable economic development and democratization.

5.4.5 Bilateral development agencies

Within bilateral development agencies, the *"group of like-minded countries"* (the Netherlands, Norway, Sweden, Finland, Denmark and – at times – Canada) are extremely innovative. They exert considerable influence on the international development policy debate, and have been instrumental in mainstreaming democracy-oriented policies, both bilateral and multilateral, into aid programmes.

In 1990, the Norwegian Parliament allocated $US 10 million of its aid budget to the Norwegian Fund for Democracy. In the same year, Nordic ministers issued the "Molde Communiqué", which stressed the importance of democracy in sustaining economic development, and pledged active support for human rights and democratization. Since 1994 democratization and human rights have also occupied a prominent place in Danish aid policy. Democratic development was explicitly included in Swedish aid policy in 1978. The Swedish International Development Agency (Sida) includes a Department of Democracy and Social Development. In 1997, a special Division for Democratic Governance was created and a first draft of Sida's *Programme for Peace, Democracy and Human Rights* published. Sida also offers support to political parties in developing countries.

Peace and democracy are similarly core policy priorities for the USA. The US Agency for International Development (USAID) launched an historic reorientation of its mission and mandate with the announcement of the "Democracy Initiative" in December 1990. This established the promotion of democracy as a central aim with four components: to strengthen democratic institutions, to integrate democracy into the USAID programme, to reward progress in democratization by increasing country allocations, and to establish rapid-response mechanisms. By one estimate, USAID spent some $US 500 million in 1996 on democratic governance programmes. For Africa alone, this funding increased from $US 5.3 million in 1990 to $US 119 million in 1994.

Other major donors have increasingly followed suit. Canada's development aid priorities include increasing respect for human rights, promoting democracy and better governance, and strengthening civil society. In 1996, the Canadian Department of Foreign Affairs and International Trade established a "peace-building initiative", including a peace-building fund, demonstrating Canada's commitment to democratic development and hu-

5.4 International Dimensions

man rights. German criteria for the allocation of development aid includes respect for human and legal rights, participatory democracy, the rule of law, the liberalization of economic policy and the adoption of market-oriented economic systems, and development orientation of public policies. Japan, now the world's largest bilateral donor, proclaimed in its 1992 ODA Charter that more attention should be given to "the promotion of democratization, the introduction of a market-oriented economy and respect for human rights", explicitly linking economic development to political reform and the reduction of excessive military expenditures. There is also an emerging trend towards the establishment of specific governmental agencies to promote democracy, such as Canada's International Center for Human Rights and Democratic Development or Australia's Centre for Democratic Institutions.

The EU, which channels over 17 per cent of its member states' total ODA, mainly in grant form, places special emphasis on defending human rights and promoting democracy "to develop and consolidate democracy and the rule of law, and respect for human rights and fundamental freedoms". Incentive financing and positive measures in support of human rights and democracy in developing countries have totaled 526 million ECU since 1992. The Lomé Convention, which regulates preferential trading arrangements between the EU and 71 developing countries in Africa, the Caribbean and the Pacific, was revised in 1995 to make the privileged relationship conditional upon the recognition and application of democratic principles, the consolidation of the rule of law and good governance. In addition, an explicit "suspension clause" was included to address violations of "essential elements" of the convention, including democratic principles. Democratic governance became an "objective" of EU aid and a fund for "incentive allocations" was created to support institutional development, good governance, democratization and human rights.

Similarly, the United Nations Development Programme (UNDP) is placing the democratic governance agenda more centrally in its policies, both at the regional level, through regional departments responsible for programme implementation, and at the central strategic policy-planning level with the establishment of a Management Development and Governance Division. As of 1995, one third of UNDP resources are allocated to democratic governance endeavours ($US 1.3 billion).

5.4.6 Multilateral development banks

According to the standard World Bank definition, governance encompasses (i) the form of political regime; (ii) the process by which authority is exercised in the management of a country's economic and social resources for development; (iii) the capacity of governments to design, formulate and implement policies and discharge functions.

With the exception of the Inter-American Development Bank, which includes democracy in its approach towards governance, most development banks make a distinction between governance as "sound development management" and democracy as a "sound political system". They tend to resist interfering with or taking into account the form of the political regime of the recipient countries in their assessment for economic and financial assistance. Politics and economics are not totally separable, but each bank defines its own distinction between politics and economics in its operational framework according to its constituency and governing statutes. This distinction is often artificial: if economic development is to occur and be sustained, a sound political framework must exist. The political conditionality of *good governance* tries to affect policy-making, to promote effectiveness and efficiency in economic performance and policy.

The thinking behind *democratic governance* is based on a concern with the sustainability of programmes financed by multilateral and bilateral development institutions, especially the international financial institutions and regional development banks: sustainable development requires a predictable and transparent framework for policy design, and an enabling environment for citizens' participation and private initiative. Democracy offers a combination of institutions and processes for the efficient and effective conduct of public policy and participatory and inclusive politics.

The International Monetary Fund

In its balance-of-payments assistance, the International Monetary Fund (IMF) pays attention to the governance context, and reference to good governance is an increasingly important dimension of IMF policies. Given its membership and mandate, the IMF position on the political context in the recipient country is somewhat ambiguous. Nonetheless, the IMF has directly addressed the need for institutional reforms as part of its aid package to countries such as Indonesia during that country's financial and political crisis in 1998.

5.4 International Dimensions

Conditionality is often used to address corruption: "Financial assistance from the IMF in the context of completion of a review under a programme or approval of a new IMF arrangement could be suspended or delayed on account of poor governance". Corrective measures would then be a precondition for a resumption of financial assistance. In July 1997, the IMF suspended its assistance to Kenya, following civil unrest over constitutional and electoral reform, pending the outcome of elections.

The World Bank

The World Bank increasingly emphasizes the need for good, open and inclusive governance. Its first public document on governance in 1989, in the context of sub-Saharan Africa, stressed that the source of Africa's development problems was a "crisis of governance": corrupt, coercive, overcentralized and arbitrary rule could not sustain economic development. In 1993, 57 governance-related projects were approved. The World Bank's *1997 World Development Report* addresses this issue, and refers to democracy as a sound governance system. Given the interdependence of "economic governance" and "political governance", of economics and politics, the Bank has increasingly been engaged in capacity-building and institutional development activities, addressing corruption, and supporting civil society. Corruption is the main focus of the World Bank's governance policy. It has identified the following elements as essential criteria for good governance:

- transparency (open policy-making by the legislative arm of the government);
- accountability (accountability of the executive for its actions);
- predictability of policy (professional ethos in the bureaucracy);
- participation (strong civil society role in public affairs);
- rule of law (control of behavior in all public institutions).

The World Bank's Articles of Agreement inhibit intervention in the political arena, but its endorsement of *good governance* and its anti-corruption programmes indicate an increasing willingness to address institutional frameworks and national governance capacities. Recently, the Bank emphasized the need for open and inclusive governance for sustainable development, stressing the political dimension of its activities. In July 1997, the Bank established a Post-Conflict Unit aimed at increasing the coherence of the Bank's approach to post-conflict reconstruction, with a strong emphasis on the rebuilding of institutions, with the aim of designing and implementing transitional strategies and early reconstruction.

The Inter-American Development Bank

The Inter-American Development Bank (IDB) employs a broad concept of *democratic governability* in its lending policies. It explicitly endorses and actively supports democratic consolidation processes in Latin America. Among the multilateral development banks, the IDB is clearly the most politically assertive. Today, all 26 borrowing members of the IDB have democratically elected governments. Indeed, both the IDB and the OAS appear to be pushing the democratic agenda in the region more comprehensively than, say, the UN or the World Bank. In its 1996 strategic policy planning, the IDB identified four main areas for attention and support: the executive branch, the legislative branch and democratic institutions, the justice system, and civil society. As of April 1997, 27 projects had been approved in these areas, amounting to approximately $US 300 million, including support for dispute resolution systems in Nicaragua, for an Arbitration and Conciliation Centre in Uruguay, for the Bolivian National Programme of Governability, and for strengthening democratic institutions in Paraguay.

Other Regional Development Banks

The *Asian Development Bank* (ADB) follows World Bank parameters on good governance, and makes these criteria an explicit element of its development evaluations and activities. Its policy embraces "sound development management" including accountability, predictability and transparency.

The *European Bank for Reconstruction and Development* (EBRD) has, in its Charter, made economic assistance to eastern and central Europe conditional on a commitment to "multiparty democracy, pluralism and market economies".

5.5 Conclusion

The principles of transparency, accountability and particularly participation and inclusiveness are recurrent themes throughout this chapter. If properly adhered to, these principles will serve to protect and insulate a peace settlement from many of the obstacles and issues that have the potential to derail its implementation. The developing international consensus on the importance of the role of democratic institutions and struc-

5.5 Conclusion

tures is reflected in the growing normative emphasis placed on democracy by international and regional actors, lending further weight to these key principles.

The implications of "democratic conditionality" in regional membership and aid policies, and what some commentators have characterized as an "emerging right to democratic government", need to be considered with caution. Democracy cannot be imposed from the outside, however well-meaning or well-funded those outside interests may be. Sometimes, strict conditionality can actually undermine prospects for moderate reformers. We therefore emphasize in this chapter that the focus of structuring a peace settlement and building a sustainable democracy must place primary responsibility on the parties to the conflict themselves. The role of the international community is to assist and support rather than to prescribe and impose. The commitment has to come, first and foremost, from the domestic parties.

The formulation of a unified and consistent approach to democracy building by the international community is another aspect that requires attention. There are too many occasions when international bodies have pursued a narrow self-interest or been driven by a desire to improve their "market share", to the neglect of the overall transition process. This implies greater consultation and co-operation, both amongst each other and between the international community and the domestic parties, throughout the process to ensure that the appropriate assistance is given and also to ensure that problems are dealt with jointly. This means that effective evaluation mechanisms need to be built into a settlement in order to detect potential points of breakdown and enable a quick and effective response by all those concerned with its implementation.

There appears to be a growing recognition by the international community that conflict prevention must address the root causes of disputes and manage ongoing sources of conflict in a constructive and structured manner.

There does, however, appear to be a growing recognition by the international community that conflict prevention should not only be confined to preventive diplomacy or early warning systems, important as these may be, but must include settlements that address the root causes of the disputes and manage ongoing sources of conflict in a constructive and structured manner. The challenge for the international community is to translate this renewed awareness and commitment into concrete policy and actions at both an international and domestic level. The precise form that these new policies and actions will take is the primary issue that now confronts all organizations and governments seriously committed to sustainable peace building.

REFERENCES AND FURTHER READING

Boutros-Ghali, Boutros. 1994. *An Agenda for Development*. New York, NY: The United Nations.

Boutros-Ghali, Boutros. 1995. *An Agenda for Peace*. 2nd edition. New York, NY: The United Nations.

Boutros-Ghali, Boutros. 1997. *Agenda for Democratization*. New York, NY: The United Nations.

Carothers, Thomas. Autumn 1997. "Democracy Assistance: The Question of Strategy", *Democratization*, vol. 4, no. 3. pp. 109–132.

Crawford, Gordon. 1996. *Promoting Democracy, Human Rights and Good Governance through Development Aid: A Comparative Study of the Policies of Four Northern Donors*. Centre for Democratization Studies, Working Paper on Democratization.

Crawford, Gordon. 1997a. "Foreign Aid and Political Conditionality: Issues of Effectiveness and Consistency", *Democratization*, vol. 4, no. 3. pp. 69–108.

Crawford, Gordon. 1997b. *Promoting Political Reform Through Aid Sanctions: Instrumental and Normative Issues*. Centre for Democratization Studies, Working Paper on Democratization.

de Feyter, Koen, Kaat Landuyt, Luc Reyams, Filip Reyntjens, Stef Vandeginste, Han Verleyen. June 1995. *Development Cooperation: A Tool for the Promotion of Human Rights and Democratization*. Antwerp: University of Antwerp.

Diamond, Larry. 1995. *Promoting Democracy in the 1990s; Actors and Instruments, Issues and Imperatives*. New York, NY: Carnegie Corporation of New York.

Diamond, Larry, Marc F. Plattner, Yun-han Chu and Hung-mao Tien. eds. *Consolidating the Third Wave Democracies*. Baltimore, MD: Johns Hopkins University Press.

Farer, Tom. 1996. *Beyond Sovereignty; Collectively Defending Democracy in the Americas*. Baltimore, MD: Johns Hopkins University Press.

Gyimah-Boadi, Emmanuel. 1996. "Civil Society in Africa", *Journal of Democracy*, vol. 7, no. 2. pp. 118–132.

Halperin, Morton H. and Kristen Lomasney. 1993. "Toward a Global 'Guarantee Clause' ", *Journal of Democracy*, vol. 4, no. 3. pp. 60–69.

Halperin, Morton H. and Kristen Lomasney. 1998. "Guaranteeing Democracy: A Review of the Record", *Journal of Democracy*, vol. 9, no. 2. pp. 134–147.

Huntington, Samuel P. 1996. "Democracy for the Long Haul", *Journal of Democracy*, vol. 7, no. 2. pp. 3–13.

Sustaining the Democratic Settlement

Inter-American Development Bank. 1996. *Modernization of the State and Strengthening of Civil Society.* IDB Strategic Planning and Operational Policy Department. Washington, DC: IDB.

International Monetary Fund. 1997. *Governance: The IMF's Role.* Washington, DC: IMF.

Jeldres, Julio A. 1996. "Cambodia's Fading Hopes", *Journal of Democracy*, vol. 7, no. 1. pp. 148–157.

Linz, Juan J. and Alfred Stepan. 1996. "Towards Consolidated Democracies", *Journal of Democracy*, vol. 7, no. 2. pp. 14–33.

Luckham, Robin. 1996. "Faustian Bargains: Democratic Control Over Military and Security Establishments". In Robin Luckham and Gordon White. eds. *Democratisation in the South: the Jagged Wave.* Manchester: Manchester University Press.

Munck, Ronaldo. 1989. *Latin America: the Transition to Democracy.* London: Zed Books.

Naim, Moises. 1995. "Latin America: The Second Stage of Reform". In Larry Diamond and Marc F. Plattner. eds. *Economic Reform and Democracy.* Baltimore, MD: Johns Hopkins University Press.

Nelson, Joan M. and Stephanie Eglington. 1992. *Encouraging Democracy: What Role for Conditioned Aid?* Policy Essay 4. Washington, DC: Overseas Development Council.

Nelson, Joan M. and Stephanie Eglington. 1993. *Global Goals, Contentious Means: Issues of Multiple Conditionality.* Policy Essay 10. Washington, DC: Overseas Development Council.

O'Donnell, Guillermo. 1996. "Illusions About Consolidation", *Journal of Democracy*, vol. 7, no. 2. pp. 34–51.

OECD-DAC. 1994. *DAC Orientations on Participatory Development and Good Governance.* Paris: OECD.

OECD-DAC. 1995. *Participatory Development and Good Governance.* Paris: OECD.

OECD-DAC. 1997a. *Final Report of the Ad Hoc Working Group on Participatory Development and Good Governance.* Paris: OECD.

OECD-DAC. 1997b. *Guidelines on Conflict, Peace and Development Cooperation.* Paris: OECD.

OECD-DAC. 1997c. DAC Expert Group on Aid Evaluation. *Evaluation of Programs Promoting Participatory Development and Good Governance.* Synthesis Report. Paris: OECD.

Peck, Connie. 1998. *Sustainable Peace: The Role of the United Nations and Regional Organizations in Preventing Conflict.* Washington, DC: Carnegie Commission on Preventing Deadly Conflict.

Przeworski, Adam et al. 1995. *Sustainable Democracy.* Cambridge: Cambridge University Press.

Przeworski, Adam, Michael Alvarez, Jose Antonio Cheibub and Fernando Limongi. 1996. "What Makes Democracies Endure?", *Journal of Democracy*, vol. 7, no. 1. pp. 39–55.

Stedman, Stephen John. 1997. "Spoiler Problems in Peace Processes", International Security, vol. 22, no. 2. pp. 1–47.

Steering Committee of the Joint Evaluation of Emergency Assistance to Rwanda. March 1996. *The International Response to Conflict and Genocide: Lessons from the Rwanda Experience.*

The World Bank. 1992. *Governance and Development.* Washington, DC: The World Bank.

The World Bank. 1994. *Governance: The World Bank Experience.* Washington, DC: The World Bank.

The World Bank. 1997. *1997 World Development Report; The State in a Changing World.* Washington, DC: The World Bank.

The World Bank. 1998. *Post-Conflict Reconstruction; The Role of the World Bank.* Washington, DC: The World Bank.

United Nations Development Programme. 1997a. *Governance for Sustainable Human Development.* UNDP Policy Document. New York, NY: UNDP.

United Nations Development Programme. 1997b. *Gobernabilidad y desarrollo democrático en América latina y el Caribe.* New York, NY: UNDP.

United Nations Development Programme. 1997c. *The Shrinking State; Governance and Sustainable Human Development.* UNDP Regional Bureau for Europe and the CIS.

United Nations. 1992. *Handbook on the Peaceful Settlement of Disputes between States.* New York, NY: United Nations.

Whitehead, Laurence. ed. 1996. *The International Dimensions of Democratization; Europe and the Americas.* Oxford, England: Oxford University Press.

Williamson, Johns. 1993. "Democracy and the 'Washington Consensus' ", *World Development*, vol. 21, pp. 1329–1336.

Conclusion

Consolidating democracy is never easy. It requires skilled leadership, an active civil society, functioning political institutions, and – most importantly – a significant degree of *time*. These are scarce commodities in even the most benevolent transition to democracy. In a post-conflict scenario, however, the challenges are multiplied many times over. Deep-rooted conflicts impact negatively on almost every area of political and social relations. Civil society is often weak or highly partisanized or both; leaders and local elites are usually the very people who have until recently been engaged in the conflict itself; the economy will have been severely damaged; and the basic institutions of government have either ceased to function or face severe crises of legitimacy. Under such conditions, attempts to reconstruct a sustainable democracy face huge obstacles. It is not surprising, therefore, that the record of promoting democracy in such cases includes many failures and relatively few unambiguous successes.

The consolidation of democratic governance relates both to the existence of a conducive institutional framework, and the respect for and compliance with democratic procedures. It is therefore vital that any assessment of the progress made in implementing an agreement adopts a holistic view of the agreement and of its implementation. The various phases that this handbook focuses on, from pre-negotiation to implementation, should all be regarded as part of one continuous process that requires constant vigilance and evaluation.

What overall lessons do these successes and failures hold for would-be democracy builders? The first is that more attention needs to be paid to the *process* by which one reaches a peace settlement rather than simply concentrating on a scenario's *outcomes*. The distinction between process and outcome is one of the starkest lessons of post-settlement peace building in the 1990s. In 1998, two long-lasting and seemingly intractable conflicts – Northern Ireland and Bougainville – finally reached peace agreements. These two conflicts have many parallels: both have been long-running disputes over autonomy that had claimed several thousand lives; both involve complicated questions of territorial and cultural sovereignty; and both have been seemingly impervious to resolution, despite numerous previous attempts at a settlement. These underlying factors did not change in either case in the lead-up to their respective peace agreements. The substantive issues concerning questions of regional autonomy mechanisms had also been debated and discussed over a number of years: the mechanisms contained in the 1998 "Good Friday" agreement in Northern Ireland, for example, had been around for some time as part of earlier peace proposals. What did change in both cases, however, was a renewed focus on the *process* by which negotiations took place.

In Northern Ireland, this meant genuinely inclusive talks in which all elements – including extremists from both sides – were brought into the process as equal players, rather than being left to disrupt proceedings from outside. The presence of a skillful and committed chair who earned the respect of all sides, in the shape of former US Senator George Mitchell, and political leaders of the major moderate factions committed to seeing agreement reached, was also crucial. In Bougainville, New Zealand's intervention as a respected but impartial third party enabled talks to be held in a neutral environment that encouraged the building of mutual trust and commitment. There, the key to the peace settlement was not what the agreement said but what it failed to say: key issues concerning independence and future autonomy arrangements for Bougainville were left out of the agreement altogether, to be addressed at a later date. In both the Northern Ireland and Bougainville cases, then, the process by which negotiations were held was a key to their success. Peace talks were structured in such a way as to promote dialogue, trust and commitment – the keys to building a lasting peace.

Attempts to resolve similar conflicts elsewhere would benefit from more focused attention on this issue at an early stage in negotiations, rather than the rushed and often ill-thought through agreements that characterize so many failed settlements. Of course, many agreements are rushed precisely because of the urgency of the issues involved: in places like Bosnia, Rwanda and Burundi, the overriding importance of the agreements was to stop the killing. If they succeeded in this key aim but failed to establish sustainable democracy, this can hardly be a source of blame for the architects of those settlements. But it does illustrate that rushed agreements aimed primarily at stopping conflict may not be the best base on which to try to build a viable democratic state.

The international community and domestic actors alike need to see democracy as a long-term process of building trust from within, rather than a quick-fix solution that can be imposed from without. The international community's obsession in the early 1990s with elections as a form of conflict resolution is perhaps the most obvious manifestation of this "quick-fix" mentality. The world is littered with elections, often conducted at the behest of the international community, which only served to inflame and politicize the root causes of conflict. The 1993 elections in Burundi, for example, served as a catalyst for the devastating ethnic conflict that was to follow by bringing the Tutsi-Hutu rivalry into sharp relief. Similarly in Rwanda, pressures for multipartism and democracy were translated into mobilization of ethnic interests and intensified ethnic competition over control of the state. In certain other countries, internationally sponsored elections were imposed by the international community as a form of exit strategy for their involvement. But elections are the beginning of a democratic process, not the end-point, and any genuine strategy for the promotion of democracy following a deep-rooted conflict needs to view elections as only the first step in a long-term process.

Elsewhere, the failure was not one of the elections *per se*, but rather the lack of forethought that went into them. In both Algeria in 1991–1992 and Burundi in 1993, inappropriate electoral systems produced a winner-take-all outcome which encouraged the "loser" to turn to violence rather than accept the outcome. In Angola, the fact that the constitution centralized power in a one-person office – the presidency – meant that it offered few incentives for a loser to stay in the process. In Bosnia, the 1996 elections held after the signing of the Dayton Accord took place in an environment of fear that served to solidify rather than break down ethnic divisions. The choice of electoral system itself exacerbated this problem by replicating the deep divisions between ethnic groups in the legislature. In Cambodia, a free and fair electoral process that was technically faultless elected two main parties, each of whom had expected to control power alone. A clumsy post-election power-sharing arrangement that had no constitutional basis was hastily cobbled together and, unsurprisingly, fell apart within a few years.

With the benefit of hindsight, all of these cases would have benefited from more careful forethought as to exactly what the elections in question were supposed to achieve, how they would be likely to impact upon the political environment, and, most importantly, how they could be designed to achieve more sustainable outcomes. This could have included, for example, the diffusion of powers to a parliament in the Angolan case, electoral system design to encourage inter-ethnic accommodation in Bosnia and constitutionally mandated power-sharing arrangements in Cambodia. Elsewhere, the devolution of power to provinces or local areas, autonomy arrangements for particular regions, special recognition of group or indigenous rights, reparation and reconciliation commissions, gender equality mechanisms, peace committees and a host of other devices have been used to manage deep-rooted conflicts or stop existing ones from escalating.

The utility of these types of arrangements and many others, highlights the point that the distance between the success or failure of democracy is often not that large. Well-designed institutions which address real issues through creative structuring of incentives and constraints can achieve much; so can carefully structured peace talks aimed at bringing all interests "inside the tent". Conversely, democracy-promotion is often threatened by the imposition of institutions which work well in western countries but which aggravate problems in divided societies. Greater study of the way different democratic institutions work in different societies is thus crucial to democracy promotion in the next decade.

So too is the international community's continued support for democracy building as a long-term process rather than a short-term event. The key to democratic consolidation is time, and the successive repetition of periodic events such as elections, so that patterns of behaviour become regularized over the long term. It is virtually impossible to consolidate democracy without this *iterative* factor. This is also, however, the issue that is most consistently overlooked by domestic democracy builders and the international community alike.

More important than either institutional engineering or international support, however, is the key role of local, indigenous support for democracy. Democracy as a form of government is synonymous with questions of domestic sovereignty and domestic jurisdiction. It remains, for the time being at least, a form of government predominantly associated with states and their sub-regions, rather than international or regional groupings. This means that the importance of local actors in making democracy work is paramount.

Amongst local actors, no group is more important than political leaders. Virtually ever successful transition to democracy discussed in this manual depended primarily upon far-sighted, courageous and creative political leadership. Leaders who are prepared to make sacrifices, to make deals with their political foes, to negotiate, to move forward when others are afraid or unwilling, are essential to building a sustainable democracy. But leaders alone can only do so much. Without fundamental support for peace and democracy amongst a population, no amount of enlightened leadership can succeed. Fortunately, examination of deep-rooted conflicts around the world suggests that, in almost all cases, ordinary people, men and women, remain fundamentally committed to democracy. They are also inevitably the biggest losers when democracy breaks down. Building a sustainable peace requires the fundamental harnessing of ordinary people behind democratic values – values based, above all, on the people themselves being the ultimate arbiters of their political leadership and their country's destiny.

Contributors

Harris

Peter Harris
South African human rights lawyer. In 1993, he was a National Peace Accord regional director, and was Chief Director of the Monitoring Directorate of the Independent Electoral Commission for South Africa's transitional 1994 elections. He has been an operations consultant to the UN, and led the establishment of South Africa's National Commission for Conciliation, Mediation and Arbitration. Formerly Director of Programmes at International IDEA, he now heads a consultancy group in Johannesburg.

Reilly

Ben Reilly
Senior Programme Officer at International IDEA. An Australian national, he has previously served as an adviser in the Department of Prime Minister and Cabinet in Canberra. He has advised on issues of constitutional design in a number of divided societies around the world, including Bosnia, Fiji, Kyrgyzstan and Indonesia. He holds a PhD in Political Science from the Australian National University, and is co-author of *The International IDEA Handbook of Electoral System Design*.

Mark Anstey
Director of the Industrial Relations Unit,
University of Port Elizabeth, South Africa,
and author of *Practical Peacemaking: A Mediator's
Handbook* (Jutta and Co Ltd 1993).

Christopher Bennett
Director of International Crisis Group's Balkans
Project. He is author of *Yugoslavia's Bloody
Collapse* (Hurst, London, and New York
University Press, New York, 1995).

David Bloomfield
Born in Belfast, author of *Peacemaking Strategies
in Northern Ireland* (1997), and
Political Dialogue in Northern Ireland (1998).
He holds an MA in Peace Studies and a
PhD in Conflict Resolution. Now a consultant
trainer and writer, and Research Fellow at
the University of Ulster's Centre for the Study
of Conflict, he is completing a book on the
1996–1998 political negotiations in Ireland.

K. M. de Silva
Executive Director of the International
Centre for Ethnic Studies, Sri Lanka, and
author of *A History of Sri Lanka* (1981); *Regional
Powers and Small State Security: India and
Sri Lanka 1977–1990*; and *Reaping the
Whirlwind: Ethnic Conflict, Ethnic Politics in Sri
Lanka* (1998).

Nomboniso Gasa
South African feminist and political activist.
She has served on the South African
Commission for Gender Equality and several
other organizations. She is currently working
on her book on South African women in the
political struggle, *Reclaiming our Voices*.

Ghai

Yash Ghai
Sir YK Pao Professor of Public Law at the University of Hong Kong. He has taught in Tanzania, Britain, the US, Sweden, Singapore and Fiji. He has published extensively on comparative public law, human rights, ethnic relations, state-owned companies and the sociology of law. His most recent book is *Hong Kong's New Constitutional Order: The Resumption of Chinese Sovereignty and the Basic Law* (1997).

Huyse

Luc Huyse
Professor of Sociology and Sociology of Law at the University of Leuven Law School (Belgium). He has written widely on the role of the judiciary in transitions to democracy. He is currently studying the trials of the Mengistu officials in Ethiopia.

Karklins

Rasma Karklins
Professor of Political Science at the University of Illinois at Chicago. In addition to many articles, she has published *Ethnopolitics and Transition to Democracy: The Collapse of the USSR and Latvia* (Johns Hopkins, 1994) and *Ethnic Relations in the USSR: The Perspective from Below* (Allen & Unwin, 1986), which was awarded the 1987 Ralph J. Bunche award from the American Political Science Association.

Lund

Michael Lund
Senior Associate at the Center for Strategic and International Studies and Creative Associates International, Inc., both in Washington, DC. He is author *of Preventing Violent Conflicts: A Strategy for Preventive Diplomacy* (US Institute of Peace, 1996).

Charles Nupen
An independent consultant, and formerly the Director of the Commission for Conciliation, Arbitration and Mediation in South Africa.

David M. Olson
Professor of Political Science and Director of the Parliamentary Documents Center for Central Europe at the University of North Carolina at Greensboro, USA. Author of *Democratic Legislative Institutions: A Comparative View* (1994), he is a specialist in comparative legislative organization and functioning.

Anthony J. Regan
Australian lawyer who has advised on constitutional issues in Papua New Guinea and Uganda. He is currently a Senior Fellow in the Department of Political and Social Change, Research School of Pacific and Asian Studies, Australian National University, Canberra.

Andrew Reynolds
Assistant professor in the Department of Government and International Studies at the University of Notre Dame, USA. A British national, he is also a Fellow of the Hellen Kellogg Institute for International Studies and the Joan B. Kroc Institute for International Peace Studies. Reynolds is the author or editor of five books dealing with the politics of elections; his latest being *Electoral Systems and Democratization in Southern Africa* (Oxford University Press).

Santiso

Carlos Santiso
Senior Programme Officer at International
IDEA focusing on democracy assistance and
good governance. He graduated from the
Institut d'Etudes Politiques of Paris, France
(1993) and Columbia University, New York,
United States (1995). Before joining
International IDEA, Mr Santiso held different
positions within the Department of Political Af-
fairs of the United Nations, at the Delegation of
the Commission of the European Union to the
United Nations and at the Cabinet of the
French Prime Minister.

Sisk

Timothy D. Sisk
American political scientist and public policy
practitioner he teaches international conflict
resolution at the Graduate School of
International Studies of the University of
Denver in Colorado, and is Senior Associate of
the Fund for Peace in Washington, DC. He has
authored books and articles on the United
Nations, international intervention in ethnic
conflicts, democracy in developing countries,
and elections and electoral systems.

About International IDEA

International IDEA was founded by 14 states in February 1995, and started practical work in mid-1996. Today the Institute has 22 members, 17 governments: Australia, Barbados, Belgium, Botswana, Canada, Chile, Costa Rica, Denmark, Finland, India, Namibia, The Netherlands, Norway, Portugal, South Africa, Spain, Sweden; and five international non-governmental organizations: the Inter-American Institute of Human Rights (IIHR), the International Federation of Journalists (IFJ), the International Press Institute (IPI), Parliamentarians for Global Action (PGA) and Transparency International (TI). It also has co-operative agreements with the International Commission of Jurists (ICJ), the Inter-Parliamentary Union (IPU) and the United Nations Development Programme (UNDP). Switzerland also contributes to the work of the Institute. International IDEA's statutes allow for new members.

The Board of Directors

Sir Shridath Ramphal, *Chairman*
Former Secretary-General of the Commonwealth and Co-Chairman of the Commission on Global Governance.

Ambassador Thorvald Stoltenberg, *Vice-Chairman*
Ambassador of Norway to Denmark, former Foreign Minister and Minister of Defence of Norway, and UN Special Representative in the former Yugoslavia.

Hon. Henry de Boulay Forde
Lawyer and former Foreign Minister and Attorney General of Barbados.

Dr Adama Dieng
Secretary-General of the International Commission of Jurists.

Dr Frene Ginwala
Speaker of the National Assembly, South Africa.

Prof. Colin Hughes
Professor of Political Science, University of Queensland and former Electoral Commissioner of Australia.

Ms Mónica Jiménez de Barros
Executive Director of PARTICIPA and member of the Truth and Reconciliation Commission, Chile.

Mr Manmohan Malhoutra
Former Assistant Secretary-General of the Commonwealth and adviser to the former Prime Minister of India, Mrs Indira Gandhi.

Lord Steel of Aikwood
Former British MP, former leader of the British Liberal Party, founding member of the Liberal Democratic Party, and former President of Liberal International.

Ms Aung San Suu Kyi
General Secretary of the National League for Democracy in Burma and Nobel Peace Prize Laureate.

Ms Maureen O'Neil
President of the Canadian International Development Research Centre.

Dr Erling Heymann Olsen
Former Speaker of the Danish Parliament (Folketing) and Professor of Economics at the University of Roskilde.

———

The Institute's work is not the reflection of any specific national interest, but is based on the statutes on which the members have agreed.

Objectives of the Institute:

– To promote and advance sustainable democracy world-wide;
– To broaden the understanding and promote the implementation and dissemination of the norms, rules and guidelines that apply to multi-party pluralism and democratic processes;
– To strengthen and support national capacity to develop the full range of democratic instruments;
– To provide a meeting-place for exchanges between all those involved in electoral processes in the context of democratic institution-building;
– To increase knowledge and enhance learning about democratic electoral processes;

- To promote transparency and accountability, professionalism and efficiency in the electoral process in the context of democratic development.

International IDEA has the following advantageous characteristics which assist it in undertaking such tasks:

- It is global in ownership and scope;
- It is expressly devoted to advancing democracy as its main task;
- It brings together in its governing body, on an equal footing, governments and professional international organizations involved in the process of furthering democracy; and
- It regards democracy as an evolving process and is able to take on long-term projects.

Decisions about what work International IDEA undertakes is guided, in part, by the uniqueness of its members, which in turn reflect the diverse partners that are found in national democracies. The governments that founded International IDEA believed that the time had come for the creation of a dynamic institute that could creatively and practically assist in sustaining and developing a democratic process in a large number of countries.

Publications

Beyond Elections '96: A Two-Year Window of Opportunity for Democracy – Proposals for the Transition towards Peace and Democracy in Bosnia and Herzegovina

Evaluating Election Observation Missions: Lessons Learned from the Russian Elections of 1996

International Election Observation: Lessons Learned
(A round-table jointly organized by the United Nations Electoral Assistance Division and International IDEA, 10–12 October, 1995)

Evaluación del Impacto de la Asistencia Externa en el Proceso Electoral Nicaragüense
ISBN: 91-89098-18-8 (1998)

Report of the "Democracy Forum" in Stockholm, 12–14 June, 1996

Report of the 1997 International IDEA, Democracy Forum

Report of the Roundtable on National Capacity-Building for Democracy (12–14 February, 1996)

Voter Turnout from 1945 to 1997: A Global Report on Political Participation (*A comprehensive world-wide compilation of voter turnout statistics since 1945.*)
ISBN: 91-89098-04-8 (1997)

Code of Conduct Series (ISSN: 1402-6767)

Code of Conduct for the Ethical and Professional Discharge of Election Observation Activities (English, French, Spanish)
English ISBN: 91-89098-10-2 (1997)
French ISBN: 91-89098-14-5 (1998)
Spanish ISBN: 91-89098-16-1 (1998)

Code of Conduct for the Ethical and Professional Discharge of Election Administration Activities (English, French, Spanish)
English ISBN: 91-89098-11-0 (1997)
French ISBN: 91-89098-15-3 (1998)
Spanish ISBN: 91-89098-17-X (1998)

Capacity-Building Series (ISSN: 1402-6279)

1. Democracy in Romania: An Assessment Mission Report
ISBN: 91-89098-03-X (1997)

2. Consolidating Democracy in Nepal: An Assessment Mission Report
ISBN: 91-89098-02-1 (1997)

3. La Démocratie au Burkina Faso, Executive Summary/Rapport de Synthése
ISBN: 91-89098-08-0 (1997)

4. La Démocratie au Burkina Faso, Rapport de la Mission d'Analyse, La Cadence du Développement Démocratique au Burkina Faso
ISBN: 91-89098-07-2 (1998)

5. Democracy in Burkina Faso, Assessment Mission Report The Cadence of Democratic Development in Burkina Faso
ISBN: 91-89098-24-2 (1998)

6. Democracia en Guatemala, La misión de un pueblo entero
ISBN: 91-89098-23-4 (1998)

Handbook Series (ISSN: 1402-6759)

1. The International IDEA Handbook of Electoral System Design (*An easy-to-use guide describing what factors to consider when modifying or designing an electoral system.*)
ISBN: 91-89098-00-5 (1997)

2. Women in Parliament: Beyond Numbers
(A handbook examining the political impact women have made through parliaments.)
ISBN: 91-89098-19-6 (1998)

The International IDEA Technical Paper Series for Election Administrators (ISSN: 1403-3275)

The Internet and the Electoral Process
ISBN: 91-89098-21-8 (1998)

Publications about International IDEA

Newsletter (three times a year)

International IDEA's Statutes

International IDEA's Declaration

Work in Progress, January 1998

Information Brochure

Information Leaflet

For more information about International IDEA's publications, the languages in which they are available and cost, please contact the International IDEA Information Services. Many of International IDEA's publications are on our Website: www.idea.int

Address: Strömsborg, S-103 34 Stockholm, Sweden
Phone: +46 8 698 37 00, Fax: +46 8 20 24 22
E-mail: info@idea.int

Index

A

B

C

F

G